NEVER AGAIN

THE STORY OF BOB HARDISTY
ENGLAND'S GREATEST AMATEUR FOOTBALLER

NEVER AGAIN

THE STORY OF BOB HARDISTY
ENGLAND'S GREATEST AMATEUR FOOTBALLER

Alan Adamthwaite

The Jacqal Press

First published 2010 by
The Jacqal Press
'Kailua-Kona'
21 Coley Grove
Little Haywood
Stafford
ST18 0UW

British Library Cataloguing-in-Publication data
A British Library CIP record is available

ISBN 978-0-9565376-0-7

Front cover photograph reproduced by kind permission of *The Northern Echo*.
Back cover photographs reproduced by kind permission of Kemley House Newspapers.

Typeset in Garamond by BBR (www.bbr-online.com)

Printed and bound in Great Britain by T.J. International Ltd, Padstow

'My name is Ozymandias, king of kings:
Look on my works, ye Mighty, and despair!'
Ozymandias (Percy Bysshe Shelley)

This book is dedicated to my wonderful wife
Jacqueline and beautiful granddaughter Fuchsia.
Without your constant support and encouragement,
it would never have been completed. I love you both.

CONTENTS

Appendix

AUTHOR'S NOTE

Every effort has been made to establish copyright ownership of photographs and other relevant material within this book. Unfortunately, because of the many company closures and mergers within the photographic and newspaper industries that have taken place over the last sixty years or so, it has proved impossible to trace the copyright in some cases. Where copyright has been ascertained, an appropriate acknowledgement has been posted.

The development of the World Wide Web and the Internet in recent years has resulted in many institutions updating records and formatting databases, a consequence being that much unwanted material and information—text as well as photographic—has been destroyed.

If anyone believes that their copyright has been infringed, then the author will be pleased to rectify the matter at the earliest opportunity and in any further editions of this book.

Special thanks to: *The Northern Echo* newspaper, *The Newcastle Chronicle* and *Journal* newspapers, *The Middlesbrough Evening Gazette*, The Football Association, Manchester United Football Club and, of course, Bishop Auckland Football Club.

For purposes of continuity, a small number of passages and quotations that originally appeared in my previous book *Glory Days* have been repeated in this work.

PREFACE

During my lifetime I have been fortunate to witness many exciting games of football and during those years have witnessed displays from many good players. Notice I use the word good, not great. Great is reserved for those of a different character and quality altogether. Great is the most over-used word in the English language, certainly in football reports and commentaries. Listen to any football match on the radio or watch on the television and just count the times that the word 'great' is used. It is so overused that it has become almost meaningless.

The north-east of England has produced many good players and I have been privileged to witness four of whom I believe to be deserving of the 'great' epithet; these are, Jackie Milburn, Sir Bobby Charlton, Sir Bobby Robson—and Bob Hardisty. The exploits of the first three have been covered in many football manuals and biographies over the years, totalling hundreds of thousands of words. However, Bob Hardisty's achievements have received little in the way of literary recognition. This is an attempt—perhaps a clumsy one—to rectify that omission.

Bob Hardisty was a household name in the 1950s and his quest to obtain an Amateur Cup winners' medal at Wembley, playing for his beloved Bishop Auckland, made him the housewife's favourite whenever they happened to make it to that famous stadium. His participation in three Olympic Games Tournaments made sure that his name was kept in the limelight. A friend of Matt Busby, it was Bob Hardisty who helped out the Scotsman in his hour of need, following the Munich Air Disaster in 1958.

Within the following pages I have endeavoured to tell the true story of Bob Hardisty's life—not an easy task as many papers and documents of that era have been lost or destroyed and many of his contemporaries are no longer with us.

Bishop Auckland Football Club, for whom Bob played from 1939 until 1958, have no records at all other than a few black-and-white team photographs prior to the 1970s. Thanks to Robert Hardisty (Bob's son) and 'Beth (his daughter), I have received untold help from the Hardisty family who have provided me with private letters and photographs. I can only hope that I have done the family and the great man himself, the justice that they deserve. It is for you, the reader, to decide if I have failed or accomplished the task in hand.

Sources for material have included interviews with Bob Hardisty's family, surviving contemporaries and team mates, newspaper reports, biographies, articles and official documents. Where I have received anecdotal narrative I have tried to obtain documentation proof but this has not always been possible and in such instances I have relied upon corroborative evidence.

Many people have helped me in my research for this work and I thank them all. Some have helped more often than others but I am loathe to single out any one person for particular praise as every fragment of information that has been related and passed on to me has been important. I thank each and every one of you for your time and efforts; such details have been gratefully received and treated like gold dust.

I cannot help but make a reference to my previous book about Bishop Auckland Football Club, *Glory Days*, that was well received when it was published in 2005. To all of you that obtained a copy I say, 'Thank you'. There is, however, one change of format that I have swayed from in this book and that is the use of the apostrophe when it comes to the spelling of St James's Park. As many of you are aware, Newcastle United Football Club proclaims on the wall of their stadium and on all correspondence that their ground is St James' Park. This was a spelling that I was forced to adopt for *Glory Days* yet I believe it to be incorrect. I have, therefore, in this work, adopted what I believe to be the precise form and throughout have used St James's Park. I would point out that this was the format used on all of the newspaper football reports until about the 1970s when the current incorrect version was widely adopted and accepted.

As for the contents of the following pages, I ask the reader to accept that I have attempted to write an accurate, honest and, hopefully, entertaining assessment of the footballing life of Bob Hardisty. Should any reader have any further information or wish to contact me to discuss any subject within these pages then please write to me at: 'Kailua-Kona', 21, Coley Grove, Little Haywood, Stafford ST18 0UW: Telephone 07933786724.

Alan Adamthwaite

FOREWORD

by John Barnwell

Agentleman of the game … that is how I remember Bob Hardisty.
I joined the best amateur football club in the country—Bishop Auckland—when I was a young lad of sixteen. The team was full of amateur internationals, all of whom were capable of playing at professional level.

Bob Hardisty may not have been the club's captain but he was certainly the main man. He was a leader of men, full of quiet confidence backed up by his footballing skills. And it was to him that others turned, if things were not going quite right. Rarely did anyone question his authority on or off the field.

I was always grateful that during my formative years of the game, Bob took me under his care to guide me through the minefield of a career in football.

Being born in the north-east of England, naturally I am as mad about football as anyone can be. I was brought up in an era when the game, professional as well as amateur, was as popular as ever. Newcastle United, Sunderland and Middlesbrough were the main providers of professional First Division football but the amateur game thrived too in this little corner of the world, aided not least by the deeds of Bishop Auckland Football Club. During the heydays of the 1950s, theirs was the stuff of fairy tales, with their almost annual ventures to Wembley in pursuit of amateur football's Holy Grail—the FA Amateur Cup.

Bob became a national celebrity as he sought to gain a winners' medal on Wembley's hallowed surface. No amateur player, before or since, has ever captured the imagination and support of the general public as this bald-headed football hero did. Capped by his country and selected to captain the Great

Britain football team at three Olympic Games, he could have been forgiven for hanging up his boots at the age of thirty-three, having suffered the agony of a third Wembley Cup Final defeat. He did not retire. He carried on. Did he achieve his goal? The answer is vividly described within the following pages, as are the unfortunate circumstances that caused me to leave the club—with Bob playing a major part!

Although he achieved fame through his football exploits, Bob Hardisty was a very private person and Alan Adamthwaite has done well to unearth such a degree of unknown material that should keep any lover of football, entertained.

INTRODUCTION

by Derek Lewin

There was a loud yell from inside the Wembley changing room. A naked figure appeared, running towards the plunge pool and jumped in. More yells continued as he thrashed about in the freezing cold water. He was too late for a warm bath but that did not seem to matter. He was celebrating his first Amateur Cup winners' medal.

JRE Hardisty, the greatest name in amateur football, but for the war years, would have been nationally known long before. Regrettably, like so many of that age, his best years had been lost to conflict. However, he made the most of it and in Bishop Auckland, that little market town in the south-west corner of County Durham, his name is revered. There is even a road named after him. You have to understand the football mentality of those northerners. I was already an international when I signed for Bishop Auckland. Jack Sowerby, the trainer, took me to one side before my debut and said; 'If people here saw John the Baptist walking in the town, they would first ask him what position he played.'

A football-mad town loved their home-grown Bob Hardisty, and deservedly so. He was a genius on the field, passing the ball forty or fifty yards with precise accuracy to within the stride of one of his team mates. This tall, balding figure controlled the game from the centre of the field with a footballing mind, seeing opportunities that others probably would not have even noticed.

I knew Bob very well over several years and often we played snooker on the Friday evening before a game in the Gentlemen's Club just off Kingsway. I also played cricket and golf with him and even went on a Coaching Course for a week, which he was taking in Durham. Despite this, I knew nothing of his personal life, a subject that he never discussed. He was an intensely private person yet so much a team man.

PART ONE

'The good die first'
The Excursion (William Wordsworth)

Chapter One

ROSEBUD

Weather conditions would soon turn from bad to treacherous.

The Elizabethan twin-engine jet taxied to the end of the runway for the third time in an hour. Snow was falling heavier now—slush and water were beginning to lie on the runway. Two previous attempts to take off had been aborted due to a lack of power in the aircraft's engines, causing it to slew on both occasions, much to the consternation of the crew and passengers. The pilot and co-pilot had deliberated whether to abandon any further attempts for that afternoon and wait for better weather, but if they did that, they and their passengers ran the risk of being snowbound for days. An experienced engineer was brought in to inspect the controls and find the cause of the fault but he had found nothing significant that should prevent the plane from lifting off the ground. Having discussed the situation at some length, the three concluded that the flight would be safe to proceed provided that they follow the engineer's advice—he had emphasised the need for full throttle to be applied later and more slowly on take-off than on the two previous attempts, as this would compensate for the seasonal low air pressure, giving extra thrust underneath the aeroplane's wings to enable take-off.

'One day, they'll make planes that don't have to make these stops for refuelling,' the captain had commented to the engineer.

The engines roared into a high-pitched whine as the rotor blades spun at a speed barely visible to the naked eye. The captain of *Zulu Uniform* communicated with the control tower and received confirmation that he was clear for take-off. For the third and, hopefully, last time, his co-pilot finalized the cockpit checking procedure as the radio officer sat at his controls, immediately behind them.

Flight 609 began its thunderous sprint down the snow covered tarmac.

In the main section of the aircraft, three cabin crew helped put thirty-seven anxious passengers and a young crying baby, at ease. Harry was sat by a window and looked out of the tiny port-hole, scowling at the falling snow. Some of the other passengers had not bothered to take off their overcoats due to the freezing conditions outside and were dressed in complete contrast to the flight attendants who looked resplendent in their pale blue/grey uniforms.

As the plane accelerated he tried to make out the metre markers … 300 … 400 … 500. 'This is a bloody long runway,' he thought. 'Come on plane, get up, third time lucky.' He tried to remember what it was that one of his fellow passengers had said earlier about 'the point of no return'—that critical point at which the pilot must decide from which there would be no stopping and the plane would have to continue on its take-off run, no matter what. 'Have we reached that yet?' he thought.

800 … 900 … 'Surely we should be up by now,' he reasoned anxiously.

The whine of the twin engines dropped in pitch and the plane began to slew to the left, as previously but more rapidly. Unlike the two times before, when he had been able to brace himself in anticipation of the plane coming to a sudden halt, this time he was too late to take evasive action. The plane careered onward, crashing through the airfield's perimeter fence and crossing a main road that was, thankfully, devoid of traffic because of the poor weather. There was a crashing of glass, metal and brickwork somewhere to his left as the left wing was ripped from the fuselage, demolishing a lone house in the process. Bricks and masonry cascaded into the cabin as the metal was ripped apart and windows were blown out. The screeching of tyres was followed by thud after sickening thud. Seats were unhinged from their anchorage bolts and suitcases, briefcases and all sorts of other items were hurtled through the maelstrom. He heard screaming voices but was unable to comprehend what was being said. An explosion close to the right wing signalled that the aircraft was hitting a fuel storage depot that sent a wicked flaming burst of orange into the dark afternoon sky. His head lurched forward and then whip-lashed back with alarming force, almost decapitating him.

Blackness followed.

After what seemed an eternity, senses slowly began to return to his body. He had no idea of how long he had been unconscious.

Opening his eyes, he sucked in a sharp intake of breath only to receive a dagger-like stab to the lungs and a mouthful of blood from the cuts to his face. The pain subsided but returned again without warning, almost immediately. A few seconds later it subsided once more. He sat there, motionless. The air was acrid and he could smell fumes. Groaning voices were around him yet seemed distant as the monotonous whine of an engine mingled in the air with that of crashing metal. He tried to move his head but struggled. The thought went through his mind, 'What if it comes off? What if my bloody head comes off?'

'Don't be stupid you daft bugger! If it comes off you'll be bloody dead and nothing will matter. But you're not dead so move yourself and get out of this carnage,' he answered, in reply to his own question.

With numbed hands, he unstrapped the seat-belt that had saved his life and slowly moved his legs, struggling inch by inch to get out of the broken fuselage and edging towards a gaping hole caused by the crash. Crawling and staggering over tangled framework, he managed to make it to the opening and dropped down onto the snow-covered ground, realizing that he was standing in a field and not on a runway. All around him was chaos and devastation. He gazed, mortified at bodies that had been thrown from their seats and now lay in a tangled mess, oblivious to his own cuts and bruises and bloodstained suit and shirt. To his immense surprise, there were others that had survived the crash.

'Is that you, Harry?' he heard a voice say.

'Bloody hell, Bill, what in God's name has happened? Just look at this. Those are our mates lying there, dead.'

An explosion from the rear end of the plane brought their brief conversation to an end.

All around was desolation—Armageddon had arrived. A deformed propeller blade looked back at him as he tried to take in the enormity of what had just taken place in a maddening few seconds. Amidst all of this, another noise was added to the cacophony as a baby's plaintive cry was heard coming from the cabin that he had just vacated. Without any thought of the danger that may have lain in wait for him, Harry scrambled back with typical Irish bravado, inside the broken shell of what remained of the broken aircraft. Struggling through the wreckage, he managed to avoid the licking flames and slowly made his way to where the cries were coming from. Crouching down he discovered the baby, still wrapped in a blanket that her mother had used to keep her warm. He picked her up and cradled her to his chest and once more braved the gauntlet of flames before reaching the relative safety of the freezing cold outside. He looked around and saw a grief-stricken woman, whimpering. Without saying a word, he knelt down and passed the tiny bundle into a pair of embracing arms. The face that was black and covered in tears said, 'Thank you', without speaking. This blood-spattered man had saved her most precious possession.

Sirens wailed as the crews of ambulances, police cars and fire engines arrived and prepared for the steady exodus that would take the injured survivors to hospital. A more sombre resting place awaited the dead.

In the fading light, darkened by the charcoal smoke from the wreckage, Harry looked out at the distant neon light that greeted all passengers a mile away—'Munchen Flughafen' … Munich Airport.

The pink Vauxhall Wyvern made its interminably slow progress through the rush-hour traffic in Durham town centre. The driver should have known better. He could have by-passed the Roman city if only he had given his homeward journey more thought. He knew the city like the back of his hand and knew all of its roads and side streets inside out but at this time of day such knowledge was of little use as buses and lorries helped to slow any sort of progress to a minimum. It occurred to him that Durham was one of those ancient cities that had never come to terms with the automobile. It held city status due to its magnificent Norman Cathedral and could be considered rather small when compared with other cities but a combination of narrow streets and a barely adequate one-way system lay in wait for the motorist. Even those who knew the city were in despair at the thought of having to negotiate such narrow cobbled avenues. Traffic was further encumbered with the somewhat archaic—but necessary—system of the stop-go traffic system over Framwelgate Bridge, whereby vehicle access was controlled by a policeman from a booth in the market square next to the imposing statue of Charles William Vane Stewart, the third Marquess of Londonderry on horseback, well out of sight of the River Wear crossing.[†]

He tried to be patient, rhythmically drumming the steering wheel whilst Nat King Cole played *Smile* in his head. He had had a painfully slow day at the Education establishment where he had attended in his capacity as Area

---

[†] Some fifty years later, despite major road improvements, traffic movement in and around this ancient city has hardly improved.

Physical Training Organizer. His mood had not improved when he had been commissioned to attend a last-minute meeting just as he was about to leave. If only he hadn't spent more time with a couple of junior athletes that afternoon he would have missed the summons and be home by now with his feet up in front of the fire before he went out again to oversee more football training in the evening. Instead, he had wanted to encourage the keen youngsters who both excelled in running and did not want to appear disinterested in their ability.

As a result, he had been delayed and although the impromptu meeting had been a relatively short one—relating to some new financial proposals that the authority wanted to implement—it annoyed him to think that the meeting had not really been necessary at all, especially so late in the day. The matter could just as easily have been discussed tomorrow when everyone was fresh, instead of this afternoon when attendees had been checking their wristwatches anxious to get away to beat the forecast snowfall.

Now, here he was, annoyed with himself for not taking the turn-off for the Spennymoor road and, to further his irritation, here he was stuck behind a United bus on its trundling journey to Crook, some twelve miles away, with little chance of overtaking until well past Meadowfield. Thank God it would be Friday tomorrow with the weekend to look forward to but before that there was tonight's training session, bringing the reserves and youngsters along—one or two would be ready for the first team next season, he mused, proud that his coaching had played a part in their progress and development. They had better all turn up or they'll be for it, he thought.

Dark clouds filled the February sky and as the light snow began to get heavier a shiver ran through him. He moved his long, lean, left hand and absentmindedly searched for the heater switch—the car's one and only luxury—to turn it on. It didn't. 'Bloody hell, Rosebud, not now,' he thought. 'First I get stalled by that Finance Officer, then I forget to take the A167, then stuck in traffic behind a bloody big bus for God knows how long and now I'm going to freeze to death. What else can go wrong today? The sooner I get home the better.'

He continued to swear to himself. By now, Nat King Cole had been turned off in his mind as he had to constantly wipe the windscreen free of the misting that formed due to the warmth of his breath—the only other alternative would have been to drive with the car window down but in such cold weather that was not an option he wished to consider.

Fortunately, an opportunity to overtake presented itself just as the flow of traffic pulled out of Neville's Cross and a relieved smile crossed the driver's face. His mind filled up with thoughts of football and the ensuing weekend and gradually his mood brightened. As the adjacent fields began to accept a layering of fresh snow, he made the decision to take the turning off the A690 just before Willington and finish his drive home by way of Straker's Bank, thereby avoiding further traffic hold-up at Willington level-crossing. This time his decision was proved correct and, other than being delayed by a coal lorry delivering its load at Binchester, he was able to complete his homeward bound journey in comparative safety, if not in the best of temper.

He pulled up outside his house and gave the cold vehicle an equally icy scowl. He had taken to the model immediately he had seen photographs of it in the brochure and his employers agreed to obtain one for him. He would have preferred one with a less eye-catching colour but that would have meant waiting and he was impatient for its delivery, being prepared to take whatever was on offer immediately. It wasn't really pink but it could hardly have been classed as a red or a brown. Notwithstanding the exactitude of the colouration, this four-wheeled delight had been given the name *Rosebud*. At this moment in time, the owner reflected, it should have been *Ice Cube*!

He entered the four bedroom semi-detached house and greeted his wife with a peck on the cheek.

'Had a good day, pet?'

'Had better,' was the curt reply, spoken with more good humour than malice. He smiled at his young son and playfully tousled his fair hair. 'You all right, bonny lad?'

'Yes dad,' replied the six year old as he continued with his game.

His wife said, 'Sit yourself down and I'll bring you a cup of tea before we sit down to eat. I'll put the radio on so that you can catch the news, unless you'd prefer the television.'

She leaned over and turned on the Ekco, adjusting the Bakelite dial to the BBC Light Programme news and disappeared into the kitchen to prepare her husband's drink. The regular evening bulletin would be on in a few minutes at five o'clock, no doubt beginning with the usual political headlines regarding Prime Minister Harold Macmillan and his Conservative government.

The radio crackled into life but instead of the musical programme that should have been coming to an end, it was the sombre tone of the newsreader whose voice filled the room. The husband sat there in a daze, unable to take in all that was being said.

'… BEA Flight 609 … Munich.'

'… Feared dead … Roger Byrne … David Pegg …'

'… Journalists … critically injured.'

'… Matt Busby.'

'Oh, my God,' he muttered. 'Oh, my God.' He was finding it impossible to take in all that was being said and kept repeating 'Oh, my God' over and over again.

His wife heard him as she entered the room carrying a tray with a china teapot and two cups and saucers on it.

'What on earth has happened?'

For a few moments he just sat there as the radio announcer continued with his message, repeating what he had already said, as if to add further verification to an appalling tragedy for the benefit of his wife.

'Let's have the television on, Betty,' he murmured.

The tubes warmed up and the cathode ray began to show, in harrowing black and white, the disaster that had taken place just three hours earlier that afternoon on a German airfield near Munich. Much of the television pictures were shadowy and poor quality but the enormity of the aircraft disaster was clear. The spine of a new generation of football stars had been taken away in a few short seconds.

The husband and wife sat staring at the television, tears forming in their eyes and moistening their cheeks. Time stood still and yet inexorably moved on. All over the country and the continent, similar emotions were being displayed by everyone witnessing the same horrendous pictures. Eventually, he pulled himself up from his armchair and telephoned some of his friends to tell those who may not have known already, the terrible news.

Two cold cups of tea remained on the tray.

Newspapers and television stations filled the public with details as they emerged, drip by drip, and the full scale of the horror that all of the crew and passengers had gone through, became clearer. Harry Gregg, Irish international goalkeeper, had survived the crash and been able to walk clear of the wreckage only to return and save a young baby, it was reported. Commanding centre-half, Bill Foulkes, had also been one of the lucky ones to escape and had helped comfort the injured, as the safety crews, fire-fighters and ambulance personnel had gathered around him and the other survivors to take them to the hospital.

Just a few days after the accident, blame was being levelled at the aeroplane captain for attempting the take-off. It would be another seventeen years, after many enquiries, that it would be proven that he was not responsible and was able, therefore, to clear his name. At the same time, a bitter dispute was smouldering between the German Airport authorities and British European Airways (BEA) regarding the crash and its consequences.

Every hour, every day, the BBC and fledgling ITV tried to keep a nation hungry for news, informed of the injuries and fights for life that survivors of the crash endured. As television screens showed the fight for survival from the likes of Duncan Edwards, John Berry, Bobby Charlton and Matt Busby, the horror of the event became apparent to a stunned nation.

Bulletins were eagerly awaited from doctors and spokesmen at The Rechts der Isar Hospital in Munich and every degree of improvement in a patient's condition was grasped like the straws that they were. Duncan Edwards would lose his fight after fifteen days of intensive care, as would Captain Ken Rayment, co-pilot of the stricken Elizabethan jet, who died seven days after Edwards. But it was news of Matt Busby that this viewer wished to hear. Television pictures of his friend showed him surviving with the aid of an oxygen tent—he had suffered a collapsed lung due to every rib to his right side being broken and had a broken foot in addition to numerous cuts and bruises. He was horrified at the television pictures and wondered just how Matt would survive. But he knew that his old army colleague, who had taught him to play golf amongst other things, was a dour fighter and with his indomitable spirit, he just might pull through. Each day, fresh hope sprang—Bobby Charlton was now off the danger list and John Berry was putting up a hell of a fight to survive. 'Come on, Matt. Don't give up, you bugger. Don't give up,' he muttered to himself.

Ten days after the plane crash, standing in the gymnasium of English football's First Division champions, a well dressed young man sombrely gazed at the seventeen coffins that lay in line. He would be one of hundreds—thousands—who would wish to pay homage to the air crash victims. Having seen enough, he turned to go when a soft voice called over to him. It was Jimmy Murphy, the club's Assistant Manager, needing to discuss a matter of importance with him. Jimmy had not been involved in the plane crash as he had been on international duty in his capacity as Deputy Manager of the Welsh national squad on the weekend that players and officials of the club had flown out to Belgrade for their European Cup tie against Red Star Belgrade.

The young man knew the Welshman very well, having regularly trained with the club's players, and had developed a friendship with them and their staff, although he was not a footballer of the club. In his office, Jimmy explained his proposal as the young man listened intently. When he had finished talking, the young man readily agreed to help: 'Don't worry, Jimmy, I'll get what you need. There won't be a problem. I know who I have in mind. I'll get in touch with them straight away, then you can get in touch with them yourself, just to finish things off.'

Almost three weeks after what became known as the Munich Air Disaster, the telephone rang in the couple's household. The owner of *Rosebud* was outside, washing the dirt and grime from the metalwork and taking advantage of the sunshine to give the Vauxhall a polish. Dropping the chamois leather onto the bonnet, he marched into the house—this may be the call that he was anticipating.

Listening carefully to what he was being invited to do, he immediately agreed. He placed the telephone receiver on the rest and sat down trying to take in what he had just been asked. The young man had made the initial contact but receiving confirmation from Jimmy had brought home the enormity of the task that lay ahead.

'I cannot believe this,' he thought, 'this must be a dream.'

But it was not a dream. At the age of thirty-seven, the greatest ever amateur footballer, Bob Hardisty, was being asked to come out of retirement and put on his football boots to play for the club that had had its heart ripped out just twenty days ago—Manchester United.

Chapter Two
WIGTON

John Roderick Elliott Hardisty was born on February 1st 1921, son of proud parents, John and Mary of 6, Lynn Street, Chester-le-Street, a small but busy market town of Roman origin that bestrode the A1 in County Durham. He was a normal, healthy child and other than the usual childhood illnesses of chicken-pox and measles did not suffer any major ailments. Indeed, it could be said that his childhood was similar to that of scores of other children of that time who were able to dodge the nastier ailments of the time, such as rickets and scarlet fever. His parents were a fond and loving couple and when Mary Elizabeth Arkle from Morpeth had first met John—always known as Jack—Hardisty just after the war, a lifelong relationship was formed. As he looked down on his newborn son, he reflected that only four short years ago how distant such a day as this seemed, when he had been held captive as a prisoner of war and spent each day picking sugar beet from the Belgian landscape occupied by the German forces. Born in December 1897, he had lied about his age to join up for the army. He had not seen much in the way of action before his unit was captured and he ended up in a prisoner of war camp. Now, those dark days lay in the past, and the future held every happiness imaginable in rearing his son.

It was the midwife who was first to call the bouncing, bundle of joy, 'Bobby'. In her capacity as area midwife she had attended many births and could never remember every child's name, the consequence being that all of 'her' girls were called Mary and all of 'her' boys carried the name Bobby. Somehow, in the Hardisty boy's case, the moniker stuck, although it was soon shortened to Bob and as a result, the christened names of John Roderick Elliott Hardisty were mainly confined to the waste paper bin, except for official documents such as passports and medical records. That christening had taken place on 7th March at Chester-le-Street's Primitive Methodist Church.

Details of Jack or Mary's history remain elusive. There is little in the way of documentary evidence that gives any substance to either ones' background, although it has been possible to establish some conclusions from the contents of their son's birth certificate. Section six of this document seeks the 'Rank or Profession of Father', the handwritten completion by the Registrar reading: 'Constable—R.I.C.—ex army—(Theatre Manager)'. To decipher this complex conundrum, a certain amount of historical knowledge of that period can come in useful. World War I had ended less than three years earlier and there was continued political turmoil in parts of Europe and in particular, Ireland. To assist the Royal Irish Constabulary (R.I.C.), the British Government recruited veterans of the First World War from English and Scottish cities. These recruits were sent to Ireland in 1920 and formed a police reserve unit of the R.I.C.; Jack was such a veteran. Like so many others of his generation, wishing to serve King and Country, Jack had lied about his age to the recruitment officer when he joined the Yorkshire Rifles at Bramham, just outside Leeds, in 1915. The legal age for joining up was eighteen but he was just a few months short of this stipulation, although he did truthfully decalare that his occupation was that of a horse driver.

The military force formed at Chamberlain's request was known as the Auxiliary Division Force but is probably better recognized under its unofficial title of the 'Black and Tans', in some quarters, the most despised group of servicemen ever to set foot on Irish soil since Oliver Cromwell. During their time in Ireland, some (not all) members of the Division used extremely harsh and cruel methods on the local populace to secure their aims. I have obtained documentary confirmation that Jack Hardisty, working at the time as a theatre manager in Chester-le-Street, accepted the call by his government and went to serve in Ireland as a member of the Auxiliary Division Force, leaving Mary at 6, Lynn Street.[†] Mary was six months pregnant when Jack was appointed

---

†   Bob's birth certificate states that Jack Hardisty was a theatre manager but his R.I.C. records give his occupation as cinema manager

to join in. Other games would have involved playing 'canon' in the street or mischievously, 'knocky-nine doors'. A more sedate and seasonal pastime was collecting frog-spawn, or trying to catch fish from down by the riverbed of the River Wear, usually without much success. It was quite a trek from where Bob lived to the riverbed, which could only be reached by climbing down a steep hillside—the getting down was not so bad but the harsh climb back was very tiring, the more so if filled with the disappointment of failure to land any frogs, bullheads or eels.

Young Hardisty was a quiet lad with a pleasant disposition that enabled him to make friends easily and although he enjoyed the aforementioned games and past-times it was football that he loved the most. He would spend hours looking at pictures of famous players and was particularly interested in the pioneers of the game and the early stars, such as G O Smith and C B Fry who had played for Corinthians, wondering if he would ever play for such a successful club. Slight of frame, he was rather lanky in stature, perfect for any budding sportsman. He was able to show off his prowess on the football field to such effect that he became captain of the Cockton Hill Elementary School football team and was chosen to represent the county. On the academic side, he was a capable student and showed an aptitude for most subjects, particularly liking history and mathematics.

It was during Bob's schooldays at Cockton Hill that Jack and Mary Hardisty took the decision to open a florist and vegetable shop in Newgate Street, the main thoroughfare of Bishop Auckland. From all accounts it was Mary who was the driving force in taking this decision and it was she who had the business acumen for the venture to succeed. If it was raining or there was no after school game arranged on the rec then Bob would often call in to the shop when his school day finished and spend time helping make up the bouquets and wreaths that had been ordered that day. Now and again, his school friends would join in and lend a helping hand. It never ceased to amaze him the number of wreaths that people would buy just for one particular person that had died. Sometimes, one person could attract as many as thirty or forty wreaths to be made up. 'How could anyone receive such attention?' he would often think.

The shop soon attracted a lot of regular customers and became a notable landmark; anyone catching a bus into town need only request 'Hardisty's' for the bus to pull up there. The enterprise flourished and it was not long before the couple had established a profitable business. The shop itself was quite a small affair having no living quarters and consisting mainly of a front room where the customers were served and a backroom and yard where the produce was stored. A small room upstairs was used to prepare wreaths, bouquets and other flower arrangements for display.

As the business prospered, the name of Hardisty became well known throughout the town and surrounding areas and friendships were fostered with fellow shop-owners and associates. With prosperity came the opportunity to purchase those items that they could not have afforded beforehand and so it was that Jack and Mary decided upon buying a motor vehicle. Naturally, the roads were a great deal quieter than those of today as few people had the financial largesse to spend on such a commodity as a motor car. With the motor car came the opportunity to spend leisure time away from the shop and home and it was not long before the couple would spend their Sundays and early closing day afternoons visiting the coast or scenic countryside of the Dales. One of their favourite journeys, oft repeated, would take them to the beautiful Weardale towns of Wolsingham and Stanhope. From there they would travel over the spine of the Pennines to the sleepy town hamlet of Middleton-in-Teesdale, returning home via Barnard Castle. Sometimes, they would drive through the town, park by the side of the road and walk down a meandering path that opened onto the mighty High Force waterfall, which is particularly spectacular in winter. This was a time when playing football, or any sport come to that, on a Sunday was frowned upon and on the frequent occasions when no organized game was arranged to take place on the rec, Bob would look forward to the trips up to the Dales. He would be allowed to bring a friend along with him—and his football—and much of the afternoon would be spent having a kickabout, with Jack joining in, as Mary sat back reading a novel or just admiring the tremendous scenery. When the three grew tired of kicking the football, Jack would return to Mary whilst Bob and friend would wander into the undergrowth searching for rabbits or skylark nests and their hatchling eggs in the tussocks of grass. They always proved as elusive as the eels in the Wear.

The premises next door to the florist shop were occupied by The Society Of Friends, more popularly known as the Quakers. Often, Jack and Mary would be in conversation with their business neighbours and it was from such a relationship that Jack developed the idea to send Bob to a private school run by that organisation to further his education. Their son was showing ability at school and they wished to put his capabilities to the best of use. They had the money to meet the term fees that were required and were prepared to use it to further Bob's education but there was one slight drawback with this idea—there was no such educational establishment within the area. The ideal school was in Cumberland. How would Bob take to being told he was being sent to a boarding school seventy miles away?

The anxious parents need not have worried as Bob welcomed the idea of being educated away from Bishop Auckland. He understood that his parents were trying to give him a firm educational foundation but more than that—he would be going to a school that played football and cricket. In the meantime, however, a forthcoming engagement awaited father and son just thirty miles away.

Bob had supported his local Bishop Auckland throughout his childhood and now they were to face Wimbledon in the final of the Amateur Cup at Middlesbrough. Jack had obtained a couple of tickets and father and son helped swell the Ayresome Park crowd of 23,335. The game was a disappointment for the mainly partisan crowd, ending 0–0 after extra time. A week later the same pair caught the train to London and watched their favourites win the replay 2–1 in front of an even larger crowd of 32,774 at Chelsea's Stamford Bridge. When the team returned to Bishop Auckland two days later they were received by all of the townspeople gathered in the market place and lining the streets. Bob was amongst the throng, cheering his head off but the real thrill that he enjoyed most was actually touching the trophy when it had been placed on display a few days later at the local Doggart's store. 'Touching it is one thing but what must it feel like to actually lift it?' he wondered.

Wigton is a small town in Cumbria, perhaps best known as the birthplace of television and radio presenter, Melvyn Bragg. It is a beautiful town, in the heart of the Lake District with mainly Georgian style buildings, although it is dominated by the Gothic Catholic Church of St Cuthbert and a market cross stands sentry in the main street. It was in this Cumberland town that the founder of the 'Society of Friends', George Fox, delivered a speech in 1653. He made a return visit to the town but was forced to make a hasty retreat when the local populace took exception to his radical preaching. However, it would seem that the inhabitants of Wigton were a forgiving flock and when he returned to the town for a third time, some ten years later, he was received with a warm welcome. The Society of Friends became established in the town and surrounding area so much so that a school, fully supported by the organization, opened within the town in September 1815 (just three months after the Duke of Wellington had gained a glorious victory over Napoleon at Waterloo). Twelve years later the school moved to new premises on the other side of town, taking over a Georgian house at Brookfield, as the then current premises were inadequate to accommodate the increase in student numbers.

For over one hundred years, the school's students had entered the premises by way of the West Gate, two rather nondescript wooden gates over which hung an iron archway declaring 'Friends Society School' and it was in May 1935 that Master Bob Hardisty strode those same steps. The school was a fee-paying one, housing boarders but also accepting day scholars from the local communities, many of whom would return home after a hard day taking lessons to help out on their parents' farm or smallholding. It was here that Bob would spend the next three years of his life—a period that he always reminisced were the best three collective years of his life.

The school was run on similar lines to that operated by the grammar schools and the building had separate classrooms designated for each subject as well as a purpose built gymnasium and a woodwork room. To cap it all there was also a swimming pool, more of which later. The curriculum for all students was basically the same and included such subjects as Art, English, French, Geography, General Science, History, Mathematics, Scripture, Woodwork and Games, of which the latter consisted athletics, football and cricket for the boys: girls had netball, hockey, tennis and gymnastics. The more academically minded students were also encouraged to take up Latin. A spirit of competitiveness was engendered in the House system: all students were allocated membership of either *Dalton House* (named after the Quaker scientist John Dalton) or *Pardshaw House* (named after the small town in Cumbria where George Fox had once preached).

The school records show that Bob was a capable student without being a brilliant one. Not surprisingly, he was good at sport but also showed dexterity with his hands in the woodwork and metalwork class. Freddy Bell was the incumbent woodwork master (he also taught maths as well as being the sports master) and under his tutelage it appears that young Hardisty produced a metal bowl worthy of special praise. Regrettably, this chalice has been lost with the ravages of time and remains to be re-discovered!

Discipline at the school was strict and miscreants could expect punishment by way of the cane from Headmaster David Reed who, perhaps surprisingly, was a committed pacifist. Thus, it would be with leaden feet and a great degree of trepidation that a student would make his (or her) way to the headmaster's office when ordered to do so. As far as we know, our hero did not have to make such a walk.

The school day would start with boarders rising at seven o'clock from their respective male/female dormitories for a breakfast comprising porridge, bread, eggs, bacon, beans and tea. Local children would make their own way to the school on a daily basis to present themselves ready for Assembly attended by all scholars and teaching staff. As was the custom at Quaker schools, the only singing allowed would be for hymns: quite often it was not unusual for there to be no music at all (it was not until after Bob Hardisty left the school that Music formed part of the curriculum and a separate music department was established). The last lesson of the day would end at four o'clock whereupon students would have the tiring task of getting whatever homework had been set, completed. There would usually be time left for socialising with other scholars, especially of the opposite sex but such fraternisation was not allowed to extend to the dormitories where students had to return by seven-thirty in the evening, dependant upon seniority. Saturdays were slightly different: students would be required to attend 'Preparation', a form of homework that required diaries and journals to be up-dated, a process that lasted until lunch-time. Only when 'Preparation' was completed by all students did the school week actually end.

With the freedom of what remained of the weekend ahead of them, the fleet-footed would head for the all too few bicycles, having already obtained the pass-out necessary to leave the school premises, and make their way into Wigton or Waverton. The former may have been bigger and offered more in the way of shops but little Waverton had that shining oasis loved by all school boys—and girls—the tuck shop. Here is where the pocket money of school-children went … not on such trivialities as pens, pencils, rulers and good quality exercise books but on essentials like pear drops, liquorice, sherbet and stink bombs.

It was on such Saturday afternoons that the teenage Hardisty would bike away with his friends to sample the simple pleasures that the mountainous Lake District has to offer. It was not unusual to find him fishing with a simple willow rod and string using a worm for bait but, as always, he rarely caught anything other than the proverbial cold. There was always someone who knew a local farmer or resident who had a boat and on more venturous occasions Bob and his friends would row out on the River Waver, managing to capsize on more than one occasion.

Bob enjoyed the challenge of new subjects such as French and General Science but sport was always going to be his forte. He was soon able to put his best foot forward on the football pitch and prove himself an accomplished player even though he had not yet filled his frame and was rather lanky in stature. It was immediately noticeable to all concerned that he had outstanding ability, winning the ball in tackles and showing high quality in his distribution—Freddy Bell had no hesitation in placing him in the school team at right-half. However, it was during the summer months, when cricket had taken over from football as the major sports activity, that he claimed his most satisfying prize during his time at the school. At that time, the *News Chronicle* newspaper was running a feature that awarded a certificate of merit to the schoolboy whom they considered had put in an outstanding performance on the cricket pitch. To his everlasting delight, Bob was awarded such a certificate in June 1937 together with an autographed Herbert Sutcliffe cricket bat.

It was also in this year that an example of Bob Hardisty's immense modesty is worthy of mention. The Head Boy and Games Captain of that year, Raymond Peel, had been awarded the School's major honour of the Fenwick Prize, a year before he actually left the school. The Boys' Games Committee nominated as his successor, Bob Hardisty, who had been Captain of Dalton House. The prospect of carrying the honour of Head Boy weighed heavy on Bob's mind as he did not believe that he was deserving of the appointment. Headmaster, David Bell, invited the reluctant youth to his office for a friendly chat. There is no record of the actual conversation but the outcome was that Bob Hardisty was persuaded to believe that he did indeed possess all the credentials required for the post and he carried out his duties most meritoriously. Not for the first time would Bob need cajoling to accept a post of high honour.

Schooldays may well have been spent working with logarithm tables, evaluating quadratic equations and understanding declensions and intransitive verbs but the time spent at Brookfield gave ample opportunities to expand the innovative mind. Mention was made earlier that the school had a swimming pool. This is true—it was situated in the open air a little apart from the main building within the gardens. What the swimming pool lacked was the main element required for swimming—water! But why should a setback like that prevent the enjoyment of challenging youth? Every summer, boys and girls would dam the Black Beck that ran adjacent to the school gardens and when the water had reached a workable level would place a very long hose reel in the water linked to the pool. It may not have met any 'Health and Safety' principles that would apply today but it resulted in countless hours of enjoyment for the young scholars—and teachers—of Brookfield. Archimedes, no doubt, would have approved that his principal was still being put to good use some two thousand years after his death!

Pupil ingenuity did not end at the swimming pool: they also were able to form a toboggan run of sorts. The steep grassy slope leading from the gardens was often used as a sledge run and not only when snow lay on the ground. In the autumn months, students would be seen carrying buckets of water from the Black Beck to throw on to the dried grass to help make it slippery for the sledges and toboggans that were provided by the day-scholars attending the school. The danger was that once the sledges had built up a degree of steam there was no way of stopping, with the result that the trip could only be terminated with a sudden crash into the awaiting hedgerow.

Until now, Bob had not devoted much time as to what he was going to do when he left school. It was true that he expected to go on to sixth form study and then perhaps university but he had no real idea what he actually wanted to do or what he wanted to be. His time at Brookfield went a long way in helping him arrive at his decision. Members of the teaching staff there were well respected and held in high esteem by the one hundred and fifty students. The lessons were demanding and designed to test the students to their full ability but there was always time for the more pleasant side of school life, whether it be on the football field, cricket pitch, just doing physical exercises in the gymnasium—or better still, watching the girls in the gym! Many hours were spent weight-training to strengthen his arm and leg muscles. He had also become particularly fond of the cross-country runs that took him outside the school premises in to the Cumberland countryside. It was whilst on these country runs, when the mind was allowed to wander and unravel its contents, that the adolescent Bob arrived at the conclusion to become a teacher. Ideally, of course, he would have liked to have been a professional footballer but this was a time when that profession carried a maximum wage of just £2.00 per week—and that was for a First Division player. The teaching profession would give him job security and the opportunity of earning far more than he would as a professional footballer, together with the opportunity of continuing to play on an amateur basis.

School holidays would see Bob returning to Bishop Auckland, usually by train, through Carlisle, but never once did he feel homesick. True, he enjoyed being home, discussing news and politics with his parents and catching up with his friends and of course playing football on the rec but just as equally he enjoyed the school terms at Brookfield. He attended the Quaker school for four years but the time came when his education there could no longer continue: the school did not have a Sixth Form and as Bob, with the full blessing of his parents, wanted to progress with his schoolwork, the decision was made that he should return to Bishop Auckland and complete his studies at King James VI School. Bob Hardisty remembered his days at The Friends Society School, Wigton (but always known as Brookfield) with great affection and often returned in July or August to attend the annual reunion of former students.

And so it was that in June, 1938, Bob Hardisty enrolled for his final educational year to attend the school that was situated just a few yards from the football field where he would achieve so much acclaim.

'The days of our youth are the days of our glory'
Stanzas Written on the Road between Florence and Pisa, November 1821
(Lord Byron: George Gordon, 6th Baron Byron)

Chapter Three
DEBUT

1938 was an interesting year.

As Europe's war clouds formed, *Superman* was introduced as the first world super hero, *Snow White* was produced by Walt Disney as the first cartoon feature length film, *Time Magazine* of America appointed Adolf Hitler their *Man Of The Year*, Teflon was invented, Orson Welles brought panic to the streets of America with his rendition over the radio waves of H. G. Wells's *War Of The Worlds* and Bob Hardisty made his entrance on to the football stage playing for Bishop Auckland Reserves in the Darlington and District League.

The reserve team of Bishop Auckland Football Club was a free-scoring one for the 1938–39 season as was their first-team counterparts of the Northern League. At one stage the two sides had scored more than eighty goals apiece and there was a private competition going on to see who would be the first to reach the century. It turned out to be the first team that won that honour but the reserve players were showing that they were pressing for recognition and that no-one could rest on their laurels in the competition for first-team places.

At the age of seventeen, Bob was completing his education and also turning out on a regular basis for Bishop Auckland Reserves. Intriguingly, the school's Latin teacher, Gordon Leary, was also registered with the 'Bishops', playing in their first team. It was Gordon who had persuaded Bob to sign registration forms for the club with the full approval of his father. Every Tuesday and Thursday evening, Bob would either walk or cycle to the Kingsway, sometimes going straight from school, in order to train with other members of the Bishop Auckland team. Because of work commitments, it was not possible for all the members of the team to be there and it was not unusual for Bob to find himself running alone around the football pitch until colleagues arrived. With regular training exercises and the continued lifting of weights, Bob's fitness improved and his body began to fill his six-foot frame.

The 1938–39 football season kicked off with the spectre of war hanging in the air. Prime Minister, Neville Chamberlain, had assured the Free World that any problems concerning the German occupation of Czechoslovakian Sudetenland could be settled by diplomatic process. Britain, France, Germany and Italy attended a meeting in Munich to discuss the situation. Czechoslovakia was not invited to the conference and in its absence the *Munich Agreement* was approved by the four attending nations, allowing Germany to occupy the Sudetenland which heretofore was Czechoslovakian land albeit inhabited by a large number of German people. The Czechoslovakian Government was instructed by England and France it must accept the proposal or face German opposition alone, thus any existing cross treaties between the three countries would be disavowed. The Czechs knew that they could not face Germany alone and had to accept the betrayal with the greatest of reluctance. Twenty-four hours later, the English Prime Minister was witnessed by the news media of the day delivering his 'Peace in our time' speech. However, contingency plans were still being prepared should war arrive. The British Government informed all sports governing bodies that in the event of war, all sporting competitions would have to be curtailed. The Football Association and League had been warned!

With the threat of war on the horizon, the football season got under way and incredibly reached its end without mishap in May 1939 with the Cup Final featuring strong favourites Wolverhampton Wanderers and the much less rated Portsmouth. David defeated Goliath 4–1.

The prospect of war was far from the mind of the teenaged Bob Hardisty when that 1938–39 season commenced. He had been approached by C J 'Kit' Rudd, Secretary of Bishop Auckland Football Club, to sign for them and now, registered as a Bishop Auckland player, he was looking forward to regular football, week in week out. He had the exuberance of youth on his side and although his body was still developing, he was strong as an ox when it came to tackling for the ball. Following on from his time at Brookfield, he continued playing at right-half. Early newspaper reports of that time make frequent reference to Bob's displays and made note of his potential. The big break came on 5th November 1938 when he was selected to turn out for the first team at Billingham in a Northern League game. Bob felt so proud donning the dark and light blue halved jersey: his debut game for the first team and he felt a twinge of nervousness. He had trained and played with some of his team mates in the reserves but this was a proper first team game. The more experienced players tried to put him at ease with serious tactical talks whilst others used the opposite approach with ribald jokes. However, it was Carl Straughan who really put Bob at ease. Standing in the middle of the changing room, the club captain was in full flow telling a rude joke when he suddenly broke off and stared at the floor where Bob was hastily rearranging his boot laces.

'Bloody hell, Bob, what big feet you've got. Just have a look at these plates lads,' as he beckoned the rest of the team over. They all made their individual comment regarding the large size of Bob's feet. Every comment was funnier than the previous one and they were all laughing, helping put Bob completely at ease, all because of his size twelve feet.

It proved a difficult introduction, the opposing forwards being more experienced than he was used to dealing with but with the help of regular players such as Carl Straughan, Keith Humble and Bob Paisley around him, Bob came out of the game relatively unscathed. They even managed a 1–0 win to keep their league championship aspirations alive. Also playing in that game for the 'Bishops' was Ken Twigg who sadly passed away not long after my conversation with him:

I was quite fast in them days. I'm ninety-two now and not as quick! This was my first game for Bishop in my second spell with them. As a youngster I had played for Bishop Auckland and Willington Juniors. I must have been some good as I was awarded a county cap in 1931. I signed for Bishop Auckland when I was seventeen and played four or five games for them but they were such a good team that it was hard for a youngster to get a place, so I left and joined Willington for a season. I had signed for Spennymoor who were playing in the North Eastern League or Alliance when Bishop contacted and asked me to return to play for them as an outside-right. In a way, it was my first game but it was definitely a debut game for young Bob. Gordon Leary was either unfit or couldn't make it to the ground for some reason and so young Bob was drafted in, him being the reserve player for that position. I seem to remember that he found the pace of the game a bit quick with him being so young. It wasn't so bad for me because I'd been around a bit and had that little bit more experience. It was one thing to train with his team mates a couple of evenings a week but when it came to a proper game of football that's when the real test came. But he did all right. When he eventually became a first choice member of the team he was brilliant but he had a fault. With me being a right-winger and him being a right half-back we would have a lot of interplay together during a match. As I have said, I was quick … but Bob thought that I was quicker than I actually was and quite often he would overhit the ball that he wanted me to run on to. You asked me what he was like to play with: Bloody awful … only joking. He always liked to play forward and that was another reason I'd end up chasing the ball because sometimes he would just push the ball with that little bit too much pace. Or we would be working too close together as he loved pushing up in to the attack. As a consequence we would be that much closer together that we would be unable to form any worthwhile penetration. More often than not I was knackered before half-time just chasing the ball. But as I said, he was a brilliant footballer and I really loved playing with him … despite what I have just said. He was good as a youngster but when he grew up he was absolutely brilliant. Overall, he splayed out some splendid passes to all of us forwards and me in particular. I won't have a word said against him. Shame that he missed out on becoming a professional player.

Seven days later, Bob was in the team again, this time in place of the injured Straughan. South Bank were the visitors to Bishop's Kingsway ground. 'The Bankers' had been a decent side three years previously when they had finished league runners-up, then third in the following 1936–37 season but had failed to show anything like that form so far this current season. The first five minutes saw South Bank attempting to apply pressure with attacks from both wings but full-backs Kirtley and Humble snuffed out any danger to give goalkeeper Washington few headaches. The half-back line of Leary, Hardisty and Paisley began to take control of central midfield and it was not long before there was a cool, almost arrogant, confidence within the Bishop ranks. Bob made two very strong tackles to break up attacks and felt pleased with himself. Such was his confidence that he began to join in the attacks more as the game progressed and the goals started to go in. Inside-left Laurie Wensley gratefully accepted passes from recent signing Ken Twigg to score four times to make the combined contribution of the two new first team acquisitions all the more pleasing. However, as the game wore on and entered its closing stages it became apparent that this fine young Hardisty was losing some of his accuracy with regard to his passing and his tackling. Tiredness and cramp in his legs was beginning to take its toll. Those last ten minutes of that game seemed to go on forever for Bob Hardisty but when eventually the referee blew for full-time the 'Bishops' had won by a 7–1 scoreline. Bob was knackered but he had thoroughly enjoyed himself and did not think that he had let anyone down. Indeed he had not, but one of the spectators that Saturday was Bob's father. Jack took it upon himself to implore the club not to rush his son, believing that they would get the best out of him if he were brought along in stages, just giving him occasional outings for the first team. He need not have worried. Bob may have put in a satisfactory display that afternoon but it was clear to the Bishop Auckland observers that at the moment, he lacked the stamina of strong man Straughan. Hardly surprising as Bob was not yet eighteen and could not be reasonably compared with the far more mature captain.

With that game under his belt any thoughts that Bob was now a first team member were dashed when Gordon Leary and Carl Straughan resumed their customary roles. It was back to the Darlington and District League for Bob. If the disappointment of being returned to the reserve side bothered him he did not let it show—he knew that it was just a matter of time before he would be given another opportunity. A set-back of sorts came in a Durham Amateur Cup game—a competition that went on all season long and gave the younger brigade of players the opportunity to shine as any player who had played two or more games in the Northern League was ineligible. The match was against Witton Park and was a Seventh Round tie. With the reserve team almost picking itself, it was a confident Bishop squad that faced the 'Parkites'. That confidence seemed to be justified as goals came quickly and by half-time the 'Bishops' had a healthy 3–1 lead. Bob was having a good game and was winning the ball from the opposing inside-forwards with gleeful frequency, even finding the space and time to venture upfield and score one of the goals. However, by the end of the first half two of the Bishop Auckland players were carrying injuries and this had resulted in a more defensive action by the time that the referee brought the half to a close. Such increased defensive action allowed the Witton Park forwards greater possession of the ball and though the Bishop defence strove to repel the constant attacks, they began to wilt under the pressure. Three times in that second half the defence capitulated and Witton Park inflicted a surprise defeat by 4–3 to knock the favourites out of the competition.

Consolation for Bob Hardisty arrived with the news that he was to once again replace the injured Gordon Leary and that he had been selected for the first team—and not for just any old game! This was for the semi-final of the FA Amateur Cup.

Bishop Auckland had been drawn to play at Wallsend St Luke's in the First Round of the competition. On a dangerously hard, sun-baked pitch they had scraped through by a ten-minute goal from Slee. The Tyneside club had battled back determinedly in the second half and Washington had been made to make three good saves before the 'Bishops' class saw them through. South Bank had provided the opposition in Round Two, a game that was no more than shooting practice for the Kingsway outfit. Much to the disappointment of the home supporters they saw their team trounced once more by a repeated 7–1 margin.

A far more difficult foe had visited Bishop Auckland for the next stage in the form of Leyton. In front of 9,929 spectators the Londoners were defeated 2–0 in a highly charged match. The reward for that success had been a home tie with another London team, namely, Ilford. After going a goal behind, Bishop's supporters were relieved to have seen their team recover to come out 3–1 comfortable winners.

Now it was the semi-final and a trip to neutral Wimbledon beckoned where another crack London side, Leytonstone, lay in wait. With fourteen previous semi-finals behind them it was a confident squad that left the north-east for south-west London; they believed that they had history on their side. Bob Hardisty was eagerly looking forward to the challenge that lay ahead and received much support from the man whom he was replacing. In addition, captain Straughan and the other players had told everyone who would listen that their young right-half would be up to the task. Much newspaper print and ink was being used pointing out the fact that a pupil was taking the place of a master in such an important football match and that the game was to be played on April 1st. Bob Hardisty was out to prove that this boy was no-one's fool.

It is reckoned that more than 8,000 Bishop Auckland supporters constituted the 12,236 crowd that produced £740 in gate receipts. Torrential rain had soaked each and every one of them prior to the kick-off but that had not dampened their spirits. The rain had eased by the time the two teams came on to the pitch, Bishop being led out as usual by seven-year old mascot, Robert Wilson.

Leytonstone won the toss and began with an initial attack that fizzled out.

Bishop outside-left, Harry Young, went on a mazy run down his left wing to win a corner that proved fruitless and then Washington was called into action to punch over a thundering drive from Leytonstone centre-forward Genner. Another Leytonstone attack was halted but not before Bob Hardisty dodged a challenge from the opposing inside-left Bunce that could have seen the youngster in the back of his own goal net. All this within five minutes and Bob had not even touched the ball yet.

The pace of the game was frantic and the sodden pitch did not allow for pretty football with the heavy leather ball soaking in the moisture like a sponge. Both sides had skilful players but they were not given any time to develop constructive moves and consequently defences were comfortable in breaking up opposing attacks. The forwards of both teams were guilty of holding on to the ball too long thus allowing defenders time to make their challenges and dispel any dangers. However, even though the forwards were finding it difficult to obtain a breakthrough, Bob Hardisty was finding it difficult to get into the game. Much to his annoyance he was twice guilty of kicking the ball too far ahead of his willing forwards in his eagerness to impress. His light frame made him an easy target for the more muscular players of Leytonstone even though, man for man, the northern team had the taller players. Jim Kirtley, Ken Humble and the not-so-tall Bob Paisley were having fine games, as was Carl Straughan, and as a result were able to cover for their young co-defender.

On such a surface, though, it was only a matter of time before Bob's class would begin to show through and gradually he was able to adapt to the speed of play. He was all too aware that he was not being allowed the scope that he usually received in the Darlington and District League but once again his confidence was beginning to grow.

Then, in the last attack of the first half, Bishop's centre-forward, Mattie Slee, blasted the ball over the bar after a wonderful downward header from Young. The miss typified what had transpired in the first forty-five minutes.

A freshening breeze should have been to Leytonstone's advantage in the second half but each time they mounted a challenge on the Bishop goal their attacks petered out through overkicking the ball. In the forty-seventh minute Ken Twigg bamboozled three Leytonstone defenders to provide Young, not for the first time, with a scoring opportunity but the outside-left squandered the chance and full-back Black cleared the ball to safety. The next incident saw Leytonstone left-half Davies injuring his left ankle which resulted in him having to leave the field of play. As a consequence, his absence resulted in Bunce, the Leytonstone inside-left and thereby the man being initially marked by Bob Hardisty, being repositioned to the Leytonstone defence. This allowed the Bishop right-half a certain degree of freedom but he still found it difficult to construct that telling move that would breach the Leytonstone defence.

Play continued from end to end with a large improvement in the quality of play. Harry Young dribbled his way past two defenders and from a tight angle saw his shot squeeze the wrong side of the post before Lewis brought a flying fingertip save from Washington with a rasping twenty-yard free kick. The Essex side were gradually getting on top and even the calm Straughan was forced to kick the ball anywhere upfield to relieve the overworked defence. The ball was being returned to the Bishop defence with alarming regularity and it was only last ditch defending that saw the ball stay out of Washington's net. At the other end, Young once again failed to take advantage of a one-two passing movement with Slee that saw him firing tamely into Gregory's arms from fifteen yards. Then, right at the death, with Auckland's defence under siege once more, an attempt from Genner was goal bound before Bob Hardisty stuck out his long neck and headed the ball away from danger with a match-saving clearance. Fairy tale? Not quite.

Washington had only a couple of real saves to make, the majority of them from outside the penalty area, whilst his counterpart, Gregory, was troubled with greater frequency by the Bishop forward line. The fact was that both teams squandered chances and the second half became a replica of the first with the game ending goalless. There was no extra time and the replay would take place at Feethams Park, Darlington on the following Saturday. On a personal note, Bob Hardisty put in a committed display once he had been able to get into the game without it being a brilliant one. This had been his Amateur Cup debut and he would be more prepared for the next time he would be selected.

Harry Young had this to say of Bob's performance:

> The lad put in a good stint for one so inexperienced. Yes, it is probably true to say that he was not exceptionally outstanding on that occasion and that Carl Straughan and Jim Kirtley tried to protect him somewhat on the right side of the pitch but you can't carry a passenger all through a game and Bob Hardisty was no passenger … he was more than adequate. I didn't have a very good game myself, missing a couple of decent chances but it was a hell of a fast game with little time to be spent on the ball. This was the semi-final of the FA Amateur Cup and Bob proved that he was capable of playing at that level.

Alas for Bob, he was not selected for the replay, the club committee deciding to give reserve right-back, Ted Wanless, a chance at right half-back. Guest of Honour at the match was Secretary of the Football Association, Mr Stanley Rous.

Once again the game was a tight affair with both sides creating chances but not taking advantage of them. Gregory had to dive full length to keep out a Wensley effort before Washington fisted out a Joseph pile-driver. Twigg and Wensley looked effective in attack for Bishop whilst for Leytonstone, Bunce, Genner and the lively Moss on the right wing, always looked dangerous. Nevertheless, there was nothing to divide the teams and at half-time the score remained stalemate at 0–0.

The second half began with both teams sending attacking raids down the flanks—Harper, in the Leytonstone defence, was having a particularly good game as was Paisley for Bishop. Every player seemed to have an equally competent counterpart and although the play was always exciting, there was an air of certainty that extra time would be required. Play alternated from end to end with neither team shirking tackles. Shots began to rain in from all angles and both 'keepers were kept busy. One minute Gregory could be seen diving to his right to collect a twenty-yard shot from Bob Paisley, the next minute it was Washington's turn to sprawl full length to keep out a Joseph effort. With the goalkeeper out of position, Moss followed up only to send the ball inches over the bar, much to the relief of the Auckland defenders. The twelve thousand or so spectators were certainly getting their money's worth even if the game was light on goals.

With an hour of play gone, Bishop took the lead with a goal from Laurie Wensley. Paisley played yet another pass through to the inside-left channel whereupon Mattie Slee collected the ball and rounded a defender before putting in a menacing cross. Gregory came out of his goal to punch clear in a melee of attackers and defenders but the ball only went as far as Twigg who returned it into the penalty area for Wensley to score with a diving header. Gregory lay distraught, unhappy to have allowed such a sloppy goal.

That reverse, however, only spurred on the Leytonstone players and Bishop knew that they had a fight on their hands still and Washington was forced to make another flying save, tipping the ball over the bar.

Bishop's lead lasted only eight minutes. Wilson took on Kirtley and, as he rounded the defender, sent in a curling shot that struck the foot of the post. Bunce accepted the rebound and stroked the ball in to the net for the equalizer. There were no more clear cut chances and the score remained 1–1 after ninety minutes.

Extra time was played at a tremendous pace as both sides threw everything at each other but luck went Bishop's way and it was they who scored the all-important goal that brought despair to the four hundred travelling Leytonstone supporters. The identity of the goal-scorer is somewhat of a mystery as some reports give the credit to Wensley, whereas others give the decision to inside-left, Evans. Whichever of these two forwards actually applied the finishing touch, it cannot be disputed that the goal knocked the stuffing out of the southern outfit and Bishop were able to see out the remaining minutes without mishap. A 2–1 score-line had seen them through to the final.

After the game, Bob conversed with Stanley Rous whom he had been introduced to during half-time over a cup of tea. The pair talked about the match that had just taken place and exchanged pleasantries—thus from such an innocuous beginning a lifetime friendship was born.

Willington had defeated Norton Woodseats 1–0 in the other semi-final which meant for the first time in its history the FA Amateur Cup Final would be between two clubs from the Northern League. Bob wondered if he would be selected to play. He was making frequent outings now for the first team and thought that if he kept up his level of performance then he must be in with a chance. Disappointment, however, lay in store for him as Ted Wanless was again selected to play in the Final, which was being staged at Sunderland's Roker Park.

More than 20,000 spectators turned out to watch the two amateur clubs compete for the trophy and once again Bob Hardisty was amongst them, sitting in the grandstand.

Willington were much the better side in the first half, with central defender Sumby outstanding. He broke up any threat to Coe's goal and also created scoring chances for his forwards. Unfortunately, whilst the approach work was good, the finishing from the Willington forwards was woeful. Bishop's defenders were all over the place and as a result were unable to play with any fluency. If it were not for the ever dependable Straughan, the underdogs would have gone in at half-time with a healthy lead under their belts, instead of only being level at 0–0.

Bishop showed a vast improvement in the second half and gradually started to take control without really threatening Coe in the Willington goal. In fact,

Bishop's best effort was reserved until the final minute of normal time when Wensley brought Coe to his knees only to see his effort go wide.

It was in the thirty minutes of extra time that Bishop Auckland finally got the better of their workmanlike opponents and began to show their true form but the way that their opening goal came about was very fortunate. After ninety-two minutes of play, Slee saw his header fly into the net, the ball hitting the side-netting with such force that it rebounded shoulder height and allowing Coe to make some kind of save. The referee signalled for play to continue, claiming that the ball had not crossed the line. Slee and the other Bishop players were obviously aggrieved and attacked the Willington goal with ever more force. Exactly one hundred minutes of play had taken place when the unfortunate George Hewitt was involved in another controversial decision. Sumby believed he had heard the referee blow his whistle for an infringement and caught the ball for the free kick to take place. Referee Hewitt signalled a free kick to Bishop Auckland for hands, claiming he had not blown the whistle, and from the resultant free kick, Wensley saw his header enter the Willington goal. This time the goal stood. Two minutes later he added a second, again a header, and seven minutes after that, he dribbled his way through the static Willington defence to slot home a third to complete a memorable hat-trick. If Willington felt hard done by losing 3–0 in such circumstances and on such an important occasion then they did not show it, their players and officials accepting defeat with the grace that would have put some of the current-day football fraternity to shame.

In May 2004 I met up with Harry Young who, although being eighty-six years old, looked as sprightly as ever. I was researching for my book *Glory Days*, and for the benefit of those who have not read that work, I reproduce his comments again:

> With two northern teams in the final it was arranged for the final to be held at Sunderland. I think it was the third Saturday in April. We got there by Rolls-Royce, laid on by the club … not a Rolls-Royce each mind, just the one for all of us that needed it. There was about seven of us in it … ample room. It was the type that the Royal Family had. There weren't many cars about in those days, let alone Rolls-Royces. At the time, my hometown club, Newcastle United, signed me as an amateur. So long as you had only signed amateur forms then it was alright to play for another club. Newcastle had three clubs going at the time—the first team, the reserves and the 'A' team. Any professional that had been injured invariably came back through playing in the reserves or 'A' team first. As I was only on amateur forms it was me who would have to make way

for the professional to make his comeback. Training for us 'A' team players was held on Tuesday and Thursday nights. It used to happen quite often that I would be selected for Saturday's game on the Tuesday night, only for a professional to return and take my place. Still, never mind, that's the way it was.

Andy McCrombie of Newcastle recommended me to Bishop Auckland and I played my first game for them at the age of eighteen against Ferryhill Athletic. I never dreamt that just three years later I would be appearing in the Amateur Cup Final and gain a winners' medal. My brother has the medal now. You had to qualify to play in the cup, which meant that you had to be registered with the club for seven days and you had to have played at least one league game before being eligible for the cup-tie. The Ferryhill game was my qualifying match.

Mind you, we didn't travel by Rolls-Royce then. I had to go by bus from Newcastle to Bishop or whatever game was taking place. Bus fare was 3/3d (17p). It was a bind for a young lad like me, eighteen years old, as it would be gone half-past eight at night before I got home and I liked to knock about with my mates on a Saturday night. After every home match, some of the players would walk over to Gregory's Café in Newgate Street and have pie and chips and a cup of tea and then I would catch the bus from the market square to Newcastle.

We used to travel sometimes to away games in the Rolls-Royce—just the one remember—and as I said, it could fit seven or eight of us in comfortably. We used to play Whitby away on the opening game of the season and many is the time when we would be held up by the volume of traffic and have to strip off in the car and be ready to run straight on to the pitch. The Rolls would pick me up in Newcastle then go on to Sunderland train station where we would pick up Jack Washington, the goalkeeper, and Billy Evans, the inside-left—he was an insurance man—at the end of the taxi rank.

I worked as a printer for the newspapers and of course there was no such thing as a five-day week then. We had to work on a Saturday morning and then I would have to make it to the pick-up point, or if it was a home game, run for the bus to get to Bishop in time for the three o'clock kick-off. The Kingsway ground at Bishop might have a slope but the playing surface was the best anywhere. It was like a bowling green and was wonderful to play football on.

As I said, we travelled by Rolls-Royce to the 1939 final, picking up players on the way.[†]

This was to be Bob Paisley's last game in the famous two-blues shirt as he signed professional forms for Liverpool almost immediately. In addition,

---

[†]   The war years curtailed Harry's career, as it did many others, and he gallantly served his country in North Africa, Palestine and was at Anzio. A leg injury meant that his football days were over and he resumed his employment in the printing trade, working for *The Northern Echo* in Darlington until he retired. He lived in Bishop Auckland until his death in 2005.

Laurie Wensley joined Sunderland and from the Willington team, Bill Hindmarsh left to join Portsmouth for whom his first duty would be to watch them play Wolverhampton Wanderers in the FA Cup Final the following week. Nor were these the only players that had been courted by league clubs as it was widely acknowledged that none other than Bob Hardisty was being closely watched by a number of Football League clubs. Purportedly leading the way for his signature was West Bromwich Albion followed by Wolverhampton Wanderers, Leeds United and Middlesbrough as well as Scottish League clubs Rangers and Hibernian—he was becoming noticed and getting his name in the newspapers—but he wanted to finish his education and pending university course, before committing himself.

There was a wonderful camaraderie within the Bishop Auckland ranks and this was exemplified by Ted Wanless who, immediately after the game, offered his medal to the luckless Gordon Leary who had played in every round up to the semi-final. Gordon declined to accept but when Carl Straughan, the only member from the victorious 1935 side, made a similar gesture, the offer was accepted. Straughan did not miss out entirely—the Football Association gave two replica medals to the club, one of which was offered to him. The other went to Bob as he had played in the semi-final. Of course, there was an official reception and party for the victors and when the team and officials returned to the town a few hours later, it seemed that the whole of the north-east of England was present in the town square to welcome their heroes, including some Willington supporters from just down the road. Bob joined his colleagues on the team bus and reflected that four years ago he had been down there as one of the crowd, looking up from the streets admiring his heroes.

In the meantime, the football season continued as the Northern League fixture list had still to be completed. The Amateur Cup was paraded around the ground when Bishop Auckland played their next game at Tow Law a week later—as it would be at all of their remaining games—and Bob played his customary half-back role. Bishop Auckland were crowned champions of the Northern League, just a point ahead of runners-up, Shildon, whilst the reserves did even better, completing a league and cup double, winning the Darlington and District competitions. Personally satisfying for Bob, he had played twelve games and had established himself as an important member of the club. What's more, he had been awarded a Northern League Championship medal to go with his cup winners' one. The prospects of winning further medals looked rosy, a view that was echoed by the football correspondent of *The Sports Despatch* who proclaimed that the 'Bishops' had very few problems to worry about for the start of the next season, advocating that the club had quality replacements to fill the spaces left by Wanless and Paisley. The article went on:

> The position of left-half, made vacant by Paisley can easily be filled by moving Gordon Leary, who has been playing at right-half but is really a left-half, over to this position, and bringing in young Bobby Hardisty, a young half-back who has shown remarkable improvement in the past season or so and who attracted the attention of numerous league scouts towards the end of the season.

During the closing weeks of the 1938–39 football campaign, there was a slight change of direction for Bob inasmuch he was asked—and accepted—to turn out for Spennymoor United to help them complete their fixtures as they were unable to obtain the requisite number of players due to call-ups and employment difficulties affecting their players.

A postscript to this successful season came at the Golden Jubilee Meeting of the Northern League on 10th June when League Secretary J W Elliott praised Bishop Auckland for their achievements stating that they must be the best amateur side in the country to have not only won the FA Amateur Cup but to have won the Durham County Challenge Cup as well as the Northern League Championship Cup. Praise also went to Willington for the part that they had played in carrying the banner for the north-east. Mention was made of Bishop's great end-of-season performances when they were required to play eight games in a period of ten days of which they won six and drew the other two to deny Shildon the championship. In defeating professional club and the season's North Eastern League champions, South Shields 2–1 in the Final of the Durham Challenge Cup at Sunderland—a game in which Bob played at half-back—further proof was shown, if any were needed, of Bishop Auckland's wonderful achievements. Mr Elliott then took a swipe at the FA Selection Committee, pointing out that not one player from the two FA Amateur Cup teams had been deemed good enough to earn representative honours despite the defeats that each team had inflicted on other sides during their respective cup campaigns.

'Here and here did England help me: how can I help England?'
Home Thoughts from the Sea (Robert Browning)

Chapter Four

RECRUIT

Academia awaited young Hardisty.

School education behind him, the hot summer of 1939 saw Bob Hardisty taking his place at Bede College, Durham University where he was studying for his General Teaching Certificate, a two year course. Only being eight miles from Bishop Auckland, there was no problem him continuing playing for the 'Two-Blues'. He also became a regular of 'The College of the Venerable Bede Football Club' and as a result it was quite often that he would be playing three or four matches a week. Two other members of that team were bespectacled goalkeeper, Jack Dorman, who went on to be a Member of Parliament, and Lez Rawe, centre-half, who went on to play for Evenwood Town, Willington and later, Bishop Auckland.

With his future marked out, it was a confident Bob Hardisty that began the 1939–40 football season for Bishop Auckland's first team. A trip to Whitby began the campaign and the champions handed out a 5–0 drubbing to the home team and then four days later hammered Cockfield 7–0 at Kingsway with Bob getting his name on the score sheet. Astonishingly, Saturday saw the Bishop's demolish Billingham 8–0 and thus, with just three games played they had scored twenty goals and had yet to concede one. Nothing could stop them.

Perhaps nothing could stop Auckland's march on the playing field but a march of a more sinister kind would. Less than twenty-four hours after leaving the Kingsway turf with that 8–0 success, Bob Hardisty sombrely reflected upon what was about to happen in this chaotic world of ours.

The political state of Europe and the machinations of Adolf Hitler were about to have a profound and disruptive effect on every living person. Bob and his father, Jack, were browsing through that morning's papers whilst Mary was preparing vegetables for the Sunday dinner. As usual, it was the sports pages that had been read first but the front pages and their doom-laden headlines meant that they received a greater degree of focus than they would normally have done. Jack commented on the designs and ambitions of Herr Hitler and Bob chimed in with his opinion of Hitler's 'poodle', Benito Mussolini.

They were in mid conversation when the radio broadcast was interrupted. Prime Minister, Neville Chamberlain's wavering voice came through the airwaves.

I am speaking from the Cabinet Room of 10 Downing Street. This morning, the British Ambassador in Berlin, handed the German government a final note stating that unless we heard from them by eleven o'clock that they were prepared at once to withdraw their troops from Poland, a state of war would exist between us. I have to tell you now that no such undertaking has been received and that consequently, this country is at war with Germany.

You can imagine what a bitter blow it is to me that all my long struggle to win peace has failed. Yet I cannot believe that there is anything more or anything different that I could have done and that would have been more successful. Up to the very last it would have been quite possible to have arranged a peaceful and honourable settlement between Germany and Poland but Hitler would not have it. He had evidently made up his mind to attack Poland no matter what happened and although he now says he put forward reasonable proposals which were rejected by the Poles, that is not a true statement. The proposals were never shown to the Poles nor to us and though they were announced in the German broadcast on Thursday night, Hitler did not wait to hear comments on them but ordered his troops to cross the Polish frontier the next morning.

His actions show convincingly that there is no chance of expecting that this man will ever give up his practise of using force to gain his will. He can only be stopped by force and we, and France, are today in fulfilment of our obligations, going to the aid of Poland who is so bravely resisting this wicked and unprovoked attack upon her people.

We have a clear conscience. We have done all that any country could do to establish peace. In a situation in which no word given by Germany's ruler could be trusted and no people or country could feel itself safe, it became intolerable, and now that we have resolved to finish it, I know that you will all play your part with calmness and courage.

Bob and Jack sat silently, deliberating in their minds the broadcast, that had barely lasted three minutes, that they had just heard. All over the country, millions of people were, no doubt, thinking the same thoughts that they were pondering. War. Bloody War. This country had been at war just twenty years ago. Now she was to suffer the same agonies again. Had not that bloody conflict been the war to end all wars? Things would never be the same again.

Hitler had a lot to answer for and over the next six years the consequences of his actions would come to involve over twenty countries and all five continents of the globe. In the microcosm that is football his actions would also have significant ramifications.

The Football Association had no hesitation in bringing professional football to a close. The season had only been going for three weeks and it was hoped that competition would be resumed in a few weeks time. In the meantime, professional footballers were in fact laid off and faced an uncertain future. Some signed up for the Territorial Army or became police reservists whilst others awaited their call-up into the forces.

The amateur player was faced with similar problems but at least they did not depend on football as a (main) source of income and whilst inevitably there would be those called to the ranks, those working in what would become designated 'reserved occupation', working in essential industries, at least had the knowledge that they would continue their employment and maintain collecting a weekly pay packet.

The declaration of war brought about changes forthwith that affected everyone with the police having greater powers to enforce new laws and regulations. One such law that was imposed restricted the gathering of crowds and as a consequence attendances at all sporting events, not just football matches, were limited. Professional football clubs were sanctioned to restrict crowd attendances to half their grounds capacity or limited to 8,000 spectators. In certain circumstances, the Chief Constable could allow an attendance of 15,000 provided that the ground could, in normal circumstances, accommodate 60,000 on condition that tickets were purchased in advance. This and many more regulations were introduced in the opening weeks of the war. Perhaps the greatest disappointment—certainly for the amateur player and especially FA Amateur Cup holders, Bishop Auckland Football Club—was that there would be no Amateur Cup competition this season. Petrol rationing and crowd restrictions led the Football Association to abandon the tournament without a ball being kicked in anger—at least not on the football pitch. Thus, Bishop Auckland were denied the opportunity to defend the trophy: they would continue to hold the cup but this was in name only as it had to be returned to the FA headquarters in London for safekeeping.

Bob had the security of his college education to return to but it was with a heavy sense of foreboding that he continued his studies. In the meantime, the Northern League had to adopt those edicts issued by the Football Association to which they applied but hoped that they would be able to continue with the fixture list, at least for the foreseeable future. Cracks began to appear when Whitby United was forced to abandon the league, claiming that they were unable to continue with their fixtures due to the lack of petrol and suitable transport. Evenwood Town were forced to close due to similar reasons plus six of their players being unavailable due to the call-up. Brandon Social Club, recently elected to the Northern League, Billingham 'South', Cockfield (never to return), Ferryhill Athletic, Tow Law Town and Willington all followed within quick succession. Of the original fourteen clubs that had set out at the beginning of the season there were now just eight. The position had become intolerable and at a hastily convened Extraordinary General Meeting, it was decided, by the administrators, to delete all of the results from games played so far and to reform a new league competition effective from January 1st 1940 featuring the remaining clubs. Everyone expressed the hope that there would be no more resignations and assured all clubs that had been forced to leave that a warm welcome awaited them when the opportunity gave itself for their return.

With the depleted fixture list Bob found himself restricted to playing for St Bede's but kept himself fit with extended periods in the gym. When the occasion did come for Bishop's next game the venue was a bit of a surprise. Due to play Heaton Stannington away, the Newcastle-upon-Tyne club were unable to use their Newton Park ground for this Northern League Cup tie as it had been requisitioned by the military. Remarkably, Newcastle United offered the game to be played at their St James's Park. In front of 1,283 spectators, Bob put in a solid display, helping to create the approach work that led to Bishop's opening goal but there was to be no victory this time the game ending in a surprising 2–2 draw, much to the delight of the 'home' supporters.

Eight became six when Tow Law Town and Willington both resigned from the league on March 20th and as a result their scores were expunged from the official record. Bishop fought their way to the League Cup Final but were defeated 2–0 by a very good Shildon side, playing on their home ground at Dean Street, in front of over 2,000 spectators. The league table at the end of this truncated season showed Shildon as champions with 18 points from their ten official games with Bishop Auckland runners-up, having accumulated 12 points. That opening spell of three wins in which they had scored twenty goals without having one scored against them, counted for nothing—all such results were deleted from the record. Oh, yes … Adolf had a lot to answer for!

There would be no more Northern League football for six years. The League Committee had no option but to suspend any more competition until the war was over or at least until circumstances became such that a normal championship could take place.

It was with the knowledge that there was to be no further Northern League competition for some time that Bob Hardisty completed his teacher-training course. Like so many others of his age of that time, he did not go straight into teaching. Instead, he decided to 'do his bit' and join up.

The dark prospects of war had arisen throughout the 1930s but it was not until 1939 that it became almost inevitable. Neville Chamberlain's return from the Munich Conference in 1938 had given hope that war would be averted but the continued actions of Adolf Hitler in the proceeding months had, however, brought political observers and ministers to decide that it really was only a matter of time. The Football Association had shown an unfamiliar degree of foresight and preparation with its handling of the situation.

Mention has already been made that the 1939–40 season was halted after only three weeks of matches: the season had ended before it had got going properly. For three weeks there was no football. But the FA and the various football clubs had not been idle: they came up with a plan of dividing the country into regions and forming regional competitions. It was believed that, although there would be no Football League Division One Championship etc. at least the football fan would be able to watch his favourite sport. This disguised the fact that the supporter was unable to travel to the games and with crowd limits strictly imposed, for the professional game at least, attendances fell.

With many clubs, amateur and professional, seeing their players going off to war, it became impossible for them to operate with the same playing staff and some were forced to suspend football altogether. The majority, however, with the approval of the Football Association and the Armed Forces, carried on playing with the use of guest players. Clubs continued to play their games in a competitive spirit and on a league basis although it was not always based on the 'Two points for a win: One point for a draw: No points for a loss' basis. In 1941, because not all teams played the same number of games, league tables were calculated on a goal average principal.

Without the inclusion of guest players and the dispensation of any transfer fees, it would have been impossible for many clubs to operate. It was a system that in ordinary circumstances would have seemed chaotic yet nevertheless worked perfectly in wartime. It became the norm for clubs to have different players—amateur as well as professional—turning out for them each week, including international players such as Tommy Lawton, Joe Mercer or Peter Doherty. The clubs would just leave the space in the match programme blank and then announce 'team changes' over the tannoy or carry a board round the ground displaying the names of players turning out—the latter method became increasingly used as the war went on and paper for programmes became in short supply.

It became apparent to the Army that many of their new recruits required physical training on a major scale to bring them up to scratch. There were insufficient Physical Training Officers to do the job efficiently in training these raw recruits but when sportsmen (i.e. footballers) were called up it was obvious that they held an advantage in the fitness stakes as they were already well used to physical exercises. It was the visionary, Stanley Rous, Football Association Secretary, who saw a way of his organization helping out the Army. He proposed that many football players, coaches and trainers could perhaps, be used in helping train recruits. The proposal was taken up and as a result, many footballers became Army Physical Training Officers to meet the demand and were sent to the various army camps around the country, holding the rank of Sergeant. News travelled fast on the 'football telegraph' and whichever local football clubs were in that vicinity, they would invite those APTO footballers to play for them irrespective of whether they came from the amateur or professional ranks. Another of Mr Rous's proposals to be taken up was the donation from the FA to the Armed Forces of £1000 to be spent on footballs, there being insufficient number in army sports halls!

It was with this background that Bob Hardisty found himself called up on 23rd April 1941 to the Royal Corps of Signals. He had qualified from

Bede College with the prospects of a career in teaching but, for the time being, such a vocation would have to be placed to one side. He entered the Darlington Recruiting office as Mr Bob Hardisty but came out as Hardisty JRE, Signalman 2598259. Initially sent to a depot just outside Newcastle, he spent much of his time at various military bases throughout the north-east, including Catterick, that large army base just four miles down the road from Scotch Corner, set right next to the A1, that has forever been a landmark for all travellers, where he was readily accepted. Although he had come straight from university and had little knowledge 'of life', his amiable attitude and modesty helped him succeed in driving the new 'squaddies' to fitness level. Bob had always been keen on physical education and keeping himself fit. Well used to running distances and lifting weights he had few difficulties settling into the routine of getting the new recruits up to scratch. Hardisty drilled the men as hard as any APTO, pushing them to limits that they did not think themselves capable of. He earned the respect of those that he trained as well as a simple nickname—'The Bastard'. He became even more liked when he was able to show off his footballing skills on the playing fields, where he would be in competition against Football League players, including those from the First Division, who had been called up.

One onlooker at a particular match in which Bob was taking part was a stocky Scotsman. Like Bob, he was training new recruits in physical fitness but held a higher rank. He had played for Manchester City before being transferred to Liverpool in 1936 for the large sum of £8,000. Upon the outbreak of war, like a number of his fellow professionals, he had joined the King's Liverpool Regiment and was now stationed at Catterick, overseeing fellow APTOs. He admired the way that this six-foot tall wing-half seemed to glide over the rough army playing surface and made himself time to distribute the ball. 'Who the hell did he play for?' he wondered.

After the game, he made his way over to Bob and in his fine, almost lilting, Lothian accent, introduced himself: 'Matt Busby. Fine game. You're doing a grand job with the lads. Pleased to meet you. See you tonight in the bar.'

With that brief acquaintanceship, so began a friendship that would last a lifetime.

t was whilst he and Busby were stationed at Catterick that Bob was asked to turn out for Middlesbrough. Speculation exists as to how this came about but one theory is that it was Matt Busby who had recommended that he be included in the team. Matt was already a frequent guest player for Middlesbrough that season, occupying the right half-back berth, but he was equally adept playing in the left half-back position and had featured in the opening nine games of the season. Unfortunately, he was now injured and after using professional footballer, Ron Simpson, as a temporary replacement, Bob was selected by the Middlesbrough selectors to make his debut.

Bob's first game for Middlesbrough took place on Saturday 9th November 1940. It was a Football League (North) fixture and saw him line up with such luminaries as George Camsell (centre-half) and Wilf Mannion (inside-left). He had a good game but not good enough as Leeds won the match 2–1 in front of 1,500 spectators. The size of the crowd may surprise some readers, perhaps expecting a higher figure. The truth is that wartime football did not always attract the massive crowds that current day television programmes would have us believe. The football commentators of the twenty-first century often make reference to those massive crowds of the olden days when football was not up against other attractions that today may whet the public's appetite. There were no official attendance figures until the 1937/38 season but there was a general understanding that crowd numbers were in decline compared to those of the late 1920s. Figures for 1941 showed that attendances had dropped a further 35% against those of the 1939/40 season. Some of the attendance figures gleaned from official records are worthy of inspection e.g. 1939 Chelsea v Spurs (6,338), Manchester City v Manchester United (7,000), Derby County v Leeds United (2,500) and only 800 attended the Cardiff City v Stoke City game in December 1940. Larger crowds attended the internationals and War Cup Finals but even these figures are lower than one may have expected e.g. War Cup Final of 1940/41 between Preston North End and Arsenal was watched by only 60,000 at Wembley. Petrol rationing and the ancillary difficulty in travelling, crowd capacity restrictions, clubs being unable to play their registered players basing a reliance on guest players and the termination of a proper league system all played their part in the drop in attendances … some clubs even increased admission charges during this period. Gradually, crowds did return and attendances increased but it was a slow process.

After the Leeds game, Bob changed back into his civvies and made his way back to the railway station where he boarded the Darlington train. He was able to find an empty compartment that allowed smoking and had just made himself comfortable when the train began to pull away. He sat back, lit up a cigarette and reflected on the match. He was in that stage of quiet contentment when the carriage door opened and there stood a rather bemused soldier.

'Oi howp oive gorron the roight troyn, this toim. What a soddin' journey. This is the troin for Darlton and Callerick Camp, isn't it?'

Bob smiled, affably, recognising the Birmingham accent. 'Do you mean Darlington and Catterick?'

'That's it. Darlton and Catterick but it says Callerick on me pass.'

Bob engaged in conversation with the soldier who told him of his horrible journey so far, that had taken him from Birmingham to Manchester, where he had been delayed five hours, and then onto Leeds where he had suffered another two hour wait. They each moaned about the weather and talked about football, especially the demerits of wartime football with its absence of any real league competition and the situation regarding Birmingham and the refusal of the City Chief Constable to grant permission for home games to be played at St Andrews as a safety precaution, their games being played at Leamington or 'the bloody Villa'.

Bob took out the packet of Senior Service and offered one to his travelling companion, letting the conversation continue, just listening to the soldier and with typical modesty, not saying anything about his playing football that afternoon. Somehow, he did not think it right to let on that all the time that this young lad had been suffering the delights that only cold wintry railway stations could offer that he had been enjoying himself kicking a football around in front of a paying audience.

Darlington station soon arrived and much to the young soldier's amazement saw his travelling companion accompany him down to the bus stop from where they would proceed on their journey to Catterick.

'You a sojour, then?' he enquired, disregarding the wartime doctrinal warning about the need for secrecy over such matters.

'I am and yes, we are both going to the same destination. What's your name then, now that we have spent the best part of two hours company together?'

'Les. Les Rollinson, sir. Corporal. Yow one of us as well.'

'Bob. Bob Hardisty,' was the friendly reply, not exactly responding to the 'sir' bit.

'Bloody hell, oive heard of yow. Yow play football. Seen yer naim in the piypers with them others. The Albion are after you and Wuvrampton Wandrers.'

'Plus a few others,' thought Bob, as he went through the camp gates, leaving his Brummie friend to present himself to the guards for admission.

'Dalmahoy? Where in buggeration is Dalmahoy?'
     The ever avuncular Matt told his drinking partner exactly where the mysterious Dalmahoy lay, explaining it was where he originated from, or at least close by.

'Just outside Edinburgh. Loads of golf courses. Do you play golf, Bob? No? Then I'll teach you. You can be my caddy. I'll teach you as we go along. Should be plenty of time once we've exhausted our lads and put them right. And of course there's the races. We should be able to get to Lanark and Bogside if we play our cards right.'

Bob shook his head and wondered why they were leaving Catterick for Edinburgh. His friendship with Matt had flourished and he was pleased that at least he had a friend to accompany him. Although Matt was his senior officer there was a relaxed relationship between them—if authority had to come between them at anytime they each knew who was in command. For the meantime, their joint duties of getting the new recruits on the way to fitness remained the main priority and wherever they were required, so be it.

When they arrived in Dalmahoy, Bob was pleasantly surprised with the beauty of the area. He had known that Edinburgh was a much admired city but the peaceful tranquillity of Dalmahoy, just eight miles from the capital, gave an almost surreal air compared to the fighting that was taking place just a few hundred miles across the North Sea.

Matt was as good as his word. Whenever he could, he would escape the barracks and take Bob on to one of the local golf courses that surrounded Edinburgh. Bob wondered if golf was the official national sport given the number of courses that he could see dotted around the region. Golf, intermingled with training recruits, plus playing inter-regimental football matches, meant that Bob, Matt and the other APTOs had a strenuous, if not exactly dangerous, time in the army. True, they still had to learn about gun weapons and one-armed combat but, in the main, theirs was a relaxed survival compared to many other soldiers. It was this absence of being in the firing line that led to the only time that Bob ever feared for his safety, and it had nothing to do with avoiding enemy fire.

The decision by the Army to instigate the new intake of APTOs and give them rank of up to Sergeant, fresh from the sports organizations, to help get raw recruits fit, did not go down too well with some of the NCOs who had gained their stripes the hard way. Some of them saw these new upstarts as not worthy of such high rank. It was a Sergeant of this ilk who started to upbraid Bob one evening as he was walking back to his billet. The aggressor had clearly had too much to drink and started to pick an argument with Bob, whose mild-mannered demeanour did nothing to assuage the situation. The more Bob accepted the insults, the angrier the Sergeant became, to the point that he pulled back his arm and threw a right hook that Bob just evaded. Bob had decided that, perhaps now was the best time to make his exit. As he turned he fell over an empty oil drum that somehow rolled into the now splayed legs of the would-be Joe Louis. The contact with the drum knocked his assailant off balance and resulted in him crashing his head against the wooden stanchion of the barrack room building. This woke the occupants who came out to see what had happened. There, on the ground, lay the strapping sergeant, apparently knocked out by the spindly lad from Durham. The war had been going on for twelve months and Bob had been involved with his first bit of action!

Mention has already been made of the wonderful bush telegraph system that football clubs operated—their antennae were marvellously tuned; oh, if only the military had had the same to work with, the war may have been over in two years. Bob had not been at Dalmahoy long before he was asked to play for Edinburgh club, Hibernian. It may be that Matt had put in a word for him to the powers that be but there is no doubt that he became a firm favourite with the supporters.

When Bob was told that he was wanted by Hibs, he worried that he would not be able to get the time off to play. What would happen if he were required to watch over the sentries or something? It had not been a problem at Catterick as his immediate officer in command was a football supporter and so long as he obtained a ticket for the weekend match, then there was no problem. Remarkably, the same situation existed at Dalmahoy so that whenever Bob and Matt were required to turn out for any of the Scottish clubs, there was never any problem.

It was a home game for Hibernian at Easter Road that Bob starred in a remarkable match against Rangers. Mind you it was nearly a non-event for Bob.

He arrived at the ground in plenty of time and after being introduced to his new team mates, started unpacking his bag. To his horror he realized he had not packed his boots.

'Nae worry, Bob, we'll soon get yer fixed up.'

'Sure, we'll get some boots for you, Bob,' said the trainer 'What size?'

'Twelve.'

'Twelve?!?' enquired the trainer in disbelief. 'Bloody hell, ah dinna think we've got them that big', he cried as he went off in search of a suitable pair.

An hour later, just fifteen minutes before the kick-off, a rather exhausted trainer came scurrying into the changing room with a parcel under his arm containing a brand new pair of size twelve boots. 'Here you are, Bob. Hope these'll do. Had to go in to Edinburgh for the buggers. Got them at the second shop. Our usual supplier's didnae have any,' he explained, breathlessly.

As is the situation nowadays, Rangers and Celtic between them, generally ruled the roost in Scottish football. Only occasionally was this duopoly ever broken. To beat either or both of the 'Old Firm', as Rangers and Celtic are known, is a great feather in any lesser club's hat. On Saturday 27th September 1941, with Bob Hardisty at right half-back, Hibernian inflicted upon Rangers their heaviest defeat ever by the staggering scoreline 8–1. It does not matter to Hibs supporters that the result is not recognized officially by the Scottish Football League, that organization taking the view that wartime games were not worthy of official recognition but try telling that to a Hibs supporter … or a Celtic one if it comes to that. Just for the record, the Hibernian eleven that day was: Crozier, Shaw, Hall, Hardisty, Baxter, Kean, Smith, Finnigan, Milne, Combe and Caskie.

Bob turned out fifteen times in all that season for Hibs, in league games and made a further two appearances for them in the Southern League Cup as well as a further league appearance for them in the following 1942/43 season, when he also made twelve appearances for Middlesbrough.

The 1943/44 football season saw Bob living a somewhat nomadic army existence—football boots at the ready. In early August he returned to Scotland where on Saturday 11th September he turned out for Queen's Park in an away game against the now defunct Third Lanark. Playing in his customary right-half role he helped the eternal amateurs to a 3–3 draw. He played seven times in all for Queen's Park, his last game taking place on 13th November, a home defeat by 4–1 against Rangers.

All army personnel must go to where they are ordered and the very nature of Bob Hardisty's duties, both as Signalman and Physical Training Officer, meant he and others similarly placed, could be sent to anywhere in the country, or even abroad. As well as attending North Yorkshire (Catterick) and East Lothian (Dalmahoy) Bob Hardisty spent a great deal of his war time in the south of England at various posts in Kent (Wrotham), Essex (Brentwood), Hampshire (Lymington and Aldershot) and Berkshire (Reading). As usual, it was not long before he was requested to turn out for Reading. Matt Busby had come down earlier and had played three games for 'The Biscuitmen' in the 1942/43 season. It must have felt like old times for Bob and Matt teaming up together that 1943/44 season as Matt turned out for Reading on sixteen occasions, getting a goal and Bob turned out thirteen times scoring twice. The 1944/45 season saw Bob produce an identical record, resulting in thirteen appearances and two goals: Matt Busby also appeared thirteen times but without scoring.

It has been mentioned before that one of the vagaries of wartime football was the real uncertainty of who the spectator would see in action. Many Third Division clubs were able to field guest players resulting in a playing eleven of five or six international stars as playing guests. On one occasion, Aldershot fielded a team that included England internationals goalkeeper Frank Swift and centre-forward Tommy Lawton—they defeated Chelsea 5–1. However, there were occasions when the system worked the other way and teams were made up by volunteers from the crowd. It was on one such occasion of the latter variety that Bob met an old friend.

Reading were due to play Brentford at their Elm Park ground on Saturday 6th May 1944 in a Football League (South) fixture, the last game of the season and had expected to field a 'usual side'. Unfortunately, two players were late in arriving, having been on sentry duty at Aldershot that morning. Rather than ask the crowd for volunteers, Reading took the field with two men short hoping that their missing players would soon turn up. The match kicked off with Reading fielding nine men—Bob was in his usual right half-back role but because of the missing players was also having to work closer to the full backs as the Brentford forwards pressed for an early goal.

Only a few minutes of the game had elapsed, when Reading were awarded a throw-in on the right flank. Bob casually strode over to pick up the football when he heard a voice in the crowd call out 'Come on me babby, Bob.'

That caller, Les Rollinson, can take up the story:

I called out, 'Come on me babby, Bob,' and he looked up.

'Is that who I think it is, Corporal … Les?'

'Aye, it is, Sergeant,' I said, really surprised that he had remembered me from a couple of years before … perhaps my accent was something to do with it. We had only spent about two hours travelling together on the train and bus to Catterick from Leeds but I was only there for about four days and didn't see Bob during my short stay mending machinery. Six of us had been sent up to repair some machines or other but the other five had gone up the day before, leaving me to find my own way there. Anyway, there I am with the football match underway having a chat with the half-back, Bob Hardisty. Next thing he says 'Did you bring your boots along?'

I said the only boots I had were the ones that I was wearing to which he said 'They'll do if we haven't got anything better.'

He called over to the referee to tell him what was going on and that's how I came to play football with Bob Hardisty. He was a real gentleman, a smashing bloke. He had a senior rank to me, of course, in the army but on the football field that day it did not seem to matter. I think somebody else must have been roped in as we definitely had eleven players by half-time. My name is in the official record of Reading Football Club for that day even though they managed to spell it wrong—they have me down as Rawlinson, not that it matters. The two missing players did arrive so me and the other bloke expected to be brought off but they would have none of it. Anyway, I think that once you had started a game that was it. They could see how disappointed we would have been. Anyway, the rest of the team were happy with us. I'll never forget that day. Don't ask me if we won or lost, I haven't a clue … I couldn't care less really. I was just so thrilled. My mates couldn't believe what had happened and I got free drinks in the pub that night. Bloody marvellous it was. I always followed Bob Hardisty's career after that.

An illustration of the freedom of the use of guest players during this wartime football, if further evidence were needed, can be given by the study of Matt Busby. When war broke out in 1939 he was a Liverpool player. It is recorded that for that 1939/40 season (i.e. from the commencement date of Saturday 26th August, the three games that took place at the beginning of the season until war was declared on 3rd September, and the period when football resumed in the middle of September), he played a total of seventeen times for Liverpool plus a further four times for Chelsea without any transfer fee being involved. His wartime football career included spells at Middlesbrough, Bournemouth and Boscombe Athletic, Brentford and, of course, Reading. As mentioned earlier, without the operation of the guest system having the full approval of the Football Association and the Armed Forces (who agreed to release their soldiers in order for them to participate in such games) the whole structure of wartime football would have collapsed.

For the major part of the war, Bob was stationed at various army camps throughout the United Kingdom but in January 1945 he was sent to the Far East, disembarking at the east coast capital of India, Bombay (now Mumbai) before travelling inland to Deolali. This large town, with a population of over 40,000, was a major embarkation station for British soldiers returning to 'Blighty'. Unfortunately, soldiers were often forced to wait weeks at a time for their troop ship to leave port and some developed mental instability, almost bordering on madness, due to the intense heat and long delays following upon their military ordeals and as a result had to be hospitalised in the military hospital within the camp. Many years later, television and radio comedy writers, David Croft and Jimmy Perry, wrote the hit comedy series *It Ain't Half Hot Mum* about an army concert party set in Deolali, some of the episodes being loosely based upon many of the occupants' experiences.

Bob's purpose at the Deolali army base of the Officer Cadet Training Unit, where he was attached to the Royal Hong Kong and Singapore Signals holding the rank of Second Lieutenant, was to continue his duties as a Physical Training Officer, making sure that the troops did not get bored and that they remained fit, even under the baking hot conditions. It was not easy for him as he had to make adjustments to what had been his normal routine. It was impossible to have full-scale physical training sessions at the height of the sun in the afternoon and, therefore, many of the training exercises and football matches would take place in the cooler evenings.

It was during his term in India that Bob started to feel a pain in the area behind his right ear. He put up with the discomfort for a while, thinking it was no more than a flea bite but as the pain became worse the ear began to discharge pus and his hearing became impaired. When he visited the Medical Officer he was immediately diagnosed as having a mastoid infection that required urgent attention. If he had delayed much longer he would have run the risk of contracting meningitis or a brain abscess or developing facial palsy. Antibiotics were in their relative infancy in 1946 and not universally available; the only treatment he was offered involved penetrating the ear to access the *mastoid process* and sucking out the fluid that was the cause of the distress. He was warned that it was not a pleasant operation and that he would experience some pain.

As expected, it was indeed a very painful operation but the warning that Bob feared most was held back until the last possible moment—as the medical staff were about to start the operation, he was warned that if it proved unsuccessful, then his balance may be affected to such a degree that he may never play football again. One can only imagine the horror that was going through Bob's mind at the time that he was being informed of this—enduring all of that pain just to be told that his footballing days may be over. Thankfully, such fears were cast aside after the successful operation and a short period of rest and rehabilitation—during which time he learned to speak Urdu—and in no time 'The Bastard' was back, kicking a football and issuing orders.

Football matches would take place on any suitable area of ground large enough for a game to be played, although, whenever possible, 'local' football grounds would be utilised. Games between the different camps and battalions were a welcome respite from the ardour of warfare. During the latter stages of the war, visiting units comprising professional footballers serving in the army would tour military bases and stage matches against local army teams, thereby providing an opportunity for some relief to the engagement of war. Bob took part in as many games as he could during his time in India, Burma and Malaya and was even playing right up to the eve of his return to England in 1946, turning out for The Army against the Indian team, Tata Sports, at Bombay. Bob recorded: 'The Indians played in bare feet and beat us.'

With the war campaign now at an end—other than mopping up operations—Bob was able to relax a bit and looked forward to returning to England. His embarkation was some time away, however, and it came as a relief when he was asked to play football for a group of troubadours that was touring the Far East. The touring party, under the auspices of ISSECC (Inter Services Sports and Entertainments Command Control) also took in Burma and Malaya where they were rapturously received. Bob and his party stayed in the Far East until returning to England in August 1946 when he was demobbed. Incidentally, at the same time that Bob was entertaining the troops and locals in the Far East, his old friend Matt Busby was taking a similar squad out to Italy—the attraction of football never ceased.

Many soldiers who spent any time of their military career in the Far East returned to the United Kingdom with some form of illness, malaria probably being the most common. For Bob Hardisty it was something quite different.

It has been stated earlier that Bob was a very private person. On the one hand he was great at telling jokes and exaggerating stories and he loved to party and have a good time with his mates, but on the other he was never in the habit of talking about his personal life and kept whatever problems he may have been facing, to himself. He never let on if there was anything troubling him, following a similar characteristic of his father who kept very much to himself and never spoke much about his earlier experiences. Even in later years, when he could class every one of his playing colleagues as a friend and his circumstances had dramatically changed, he never revealed any confidences of his domestic life to any of them. Despite this, Bob let slip once that his premature loss of hair had been due to an illness whilst serving in India and that the burning heat of the country had exacerbated the degree of hair loss. He claimed that he received treatment for the ailment but he discontinued with it when the opportunity came for him to return to England and upon being told that its cause may have been psychosomatic.

It is not certain if this account is true as Bob was capable of exaggerating a story almost to the point of incredulity without blinking an eyelid. If, however, the story is correct, then it would indeed answer the question why he started to suffer hair loss at the comparatively young age of twenty-four.[†]

[†] This account is not as far fetched as it may seem. Sir Bobby Charlton's baldness is believed to be as a result of the mental stresses endured following the Munich Air Disaster.

PART TWO

'Their meetings made December June,
Their very parting was to die'
In Memoriam AHH (Alfred Lord Tennyson)

Chapter Five

RINGS

Normality for the human race was ready to return.

War had not ended by the spring of 1945 but victories in the European campaign led the British Government to relax legislation regarding sporting events, with a view to returning to some kind of conventional routine, much to the delight—and no doubt relief—of the football authorities. The transitional season of 1945/46 saw a number of Football League clubs unable to resume due to their grounds having suffered bomb damage or lack of players. The Northern League, for their part, made a valiant attempt to restore amateur football in the north-east and immediately started drawing up a fixture list. It was unfortunate that Heaton Stannington and Whitby United were unable to participate due to their grounds still being used by the military but to their credit, the league elected them with the status of non-playing members until such time they were able to compete.

Other changes to the league were the absence of Stockton, Cockfield and Chilton Colliery Recreation Athletic but there was an addition by way of Brandon Welfare, thus bringing the number of teams to twelve. In the meantime Crook Town had become Crook Colliery Welfare and Billingham (who had always previously been known as Billingham South) were 'replaced' by Billingham Synthonia.

With the war behind him, Bob sought a teaching position with the Durham Education Authority and was rewarded by being given a post at

The Bishop Barrington School, sited next to the market place in Bishop Auckland, teaching maths. With his modesty and friendly manner, he soon became a respected member of the staff and was well liked by the pupils, even those who did not like 'doing sums.'

He was still living with his parents and normally would walk home, sometimes calling in at his parents' shop in Bishop Auckland's main thoroughfare, along the way, unless the weather was inclement in which case he might catch the bus. It was on such a bus journey that he had an uncanny sensation that he was being watched. He was always being stared at or being pointed out in crowds and had become used to it to a degree—'That's Bob Hardisty, the footballer'; 'See him, he's played football with Tommy Lawton'; 'He's a friend of Matt Busby'; 'Would have been with the Toon if it hadn't been for the war' were frequent comments made in whispered tones. This time it seemed a little different. As he casually observed the other passengers, he wondered who it was—the woman wearing the green headscarf taking her young son home? The adolescent youth who would soon be receiving his call-up papers? The two men in gabardine coats discussing the return of football action? What about that beautiful brunette, intensely reading a magazine? He could go on forever. Was it his imagination? 'Pull yourself together,' said the voice in his head.

From time to time the sensation resurrected itself. It would happen when he was travelling on the bus but not every time. His was only a short journey of about a mile and usually took less than ten minutes to complete. He would often stand rather than take a seat and so was well able to look around, taking in the faces of passengers. After a while, by a process of elimination, Bob was able to conclude that he was not imagining it at all. Someone was definitely taking notice of him. He gazed about, trying to act nonchalantly and, on this instance, made direct eye contact with the person sitting three seats down from the back of the bus, next to the window. 'Bloody hell.' His heart missed a beat. 'Impossible. What the hell do I do?' he thought. It was the beautiful brunette who always had a magazine in her hand. Like a bubble bursting, Bob knew at that moment that he had not imagined it all. 'I must get to know her,' he decided.

And get to know her he did—in fact it would not be long before they would be working together at the same local school. Betty was two years younger than him and originated from Eldon, a small mining village just outside Bishop Auckland. The daughter of a mining family, she had attended the Girls Grammar School in Bishop Auckland where she had gained her

School Certificate and gone on to Leeds College but during the war had been evacuated to Scarborough. She was now a teacher of English at the school she had attended as a teenager. They went to the usual places that young couples go, cinema, theatres, pubs and clubs, anywhere just to be in each other's company. They had a courtship that would last three years during which Bob bought Betty a beautiful engagement ring. It seemed to have been written in the stars that the marriage would inevitably take place between John Roderick Elliott Hardisty, bachelor of Bishop Auckland and Miss Betty Laine, spinster, of Eldon.

Bob was serving abroad for the major part of the 1945–46 football season so played no part in Bishop Auckland's exploits that saw the club once again reach the Final of the Amateur Cup, staged that year at Stamford Bridge, Chelsea. A crowd of more than 54,000 saw an exhilarating game with Barnet. Gone from the Bishop ranks were the likes of Straughan, Kirtley, Wanless and Slee to name but a few. Goalkeeper, Jack Washington, was still there along with Ken Twigg, although he would not be available until later, due to work commitments, and Bob would also join up with them long after the football season was underway, but in had come new names that included Longstaff, Hadfield, Richardson, Teasdale and Farrer.

Barnet proved to be an obstacle too far. They were the better team on the day and duly deserved their 3–2 success in the sunshine. In the early stages of the first half, the Barnet forwards and half-backs overran the Bishop defence and the 'Two Blues' were fortunate to hold out for as long as the fourteenth minute, when the London side went ahead through Reilly. The 1–0 scoreline changed just a couple of minutes into the second half when Harry Teasdale scored a surprise equalizer. Bishop had not deserved to draw level but Barnet's inability to take advantage of mounting scoring opportunities had let them down. Any pretensions that Bishop held about raising their game and forcing a winning comeback were short lived when Barnet went 3–1 up through goals by Phipps and Kelleher—they could even afford the luxury of missing a penalty. Teasdale reduced the deficit three minutes from time but the scoreline detracted from Barnet's superiority.[†]

[†]   There is a little anecdotal curiosity relating to this game, as one of the players was registered to play for both finalists. Tommy Farrer, the Bishop Auckland left-back, originated from London where he was employed as a skilled machinist and played his

Another setback awaited Bishop when they were beaten finalists in the Northern League Cup, losing 2–1 to Crook Colliery Welfare, the game being played at Shildon's Dean Street ground. Nine defeats in the league meant that they finished a rather disappointing fifth in the table, behind runaway winners Stanley United, South Bank, Billingham Synthonia and Shildon.

Those two disappointments paled into insignificance over the coming months. The 1946/47 season had been under way with a number of new players registered to turn out for Bishop Auckland—it was recorded that the club had twenty goalkeepers alone to select from!—and in those opening weeks the club was on a helter skelter ride. On the opening day of the season they were roundly beaten at Whitby United 5–2 and followed that with another defeat, this time allowing Willington to win 3–1 at Hall Lane. Tow Law visited Kingsway and went away empty handed losing 6–2 and league minnows Heaton Stannington suffered a 5–1 defeat when they visited Kingsway. Shildon had knocked the 'Two Blues' out of the Bishop Auckland Hospital Bowl and when drawn against Crook Colliery Welfare in the Durham Benevolent Bowl, the 'Bishops' were knocked out of that competition after losing a replay on home soil. Furthermore, the team had just scraped through against lowly South Bank in a high-scoring game 5–4 and worse was to follow when Evenwood Town visited Kingsway and went away with the spoils having won the game 3–1. Fifteen goals had been conceded in Bishop's first three games and defensive frailties were there for all to see—an experiment to play Tommy Farrer at outside-left had carried over from the last two games of the previous season but had been abandoned after the opening defeats of the current season—and so far the team had been unable to prevent any opposition from scoring. The committee came under strong criticism from supporters who had seen their team play seven games without the same eleven players being selected for consecutive matches. The committee responded by asking the supporters to be patient and to give the new players, that had been brought in, more time to settle down. Team selection continued to be a bone of contention with supporters and during the early days of November, Bob Hardisty's name was missing from the team sheet,

---

football for Barnet. In 1943 he was transferred from London to Middleton St. George, just outside Bishop Auckland, and when hostilities had ceased, he and his wife Gladys, decided to stay in the area. He registered to play for Bishop Auckland whereupon he became a regular member of the side at left full-back but he also continued to register with Barnet every season in order that whenever he went down south he could get a game.

his last game being on Saturday 26th October in a 2–0 home win over West Auckland in which he wore the number eight shirt, playing at inside-right. Bob had missed some of the earlier games when the season commenced due to a delay with his demob and a slight groin strain and, once again, his absence was down to 'an injury' although it was not defined.

It was not until 21st November that the name of Bob Hardisty appeared again in the local press. Even then it was just a cursory note that gave no background to its foundation and yet was monumental in its message. Under the weekly diary heading 'Northern League Jottings' the news was announced amidst a variety of items:

'Bishop Auckland's Bob Hardisty has been transferred to Shildon.'[†]

That was it. No fanfare. No reference to his injury. Not a word of explanation in any shape or form. The fans deserved better from the club, the player and from their main source of information the local press, in this case *The Northern Despatch*.

Two days later, Bob Hardisty, having spurned the dark and light blue halved-shirts of Bishop Auckland, turned out at left half-back in the red and green quartered shirts of Shildon in a Northern League fixture against visitors Crook Colliery Welfare at the Dean Street ground. Match reports record that he had a good debut working alongside centre-half Bobby Davison but he could not get off to a winning start as the away side won 1–0.

The reason why Bob Hardisty decided to leave the 'Bishops' has been debated in pubs and clubs for the best part of sixty years but with no documentary evidence available to support arguments, has never been satisfactorily explained. Some would argue that he resented some of the new players who had been introduced at Bishop and that there may have been a clash of personalities between Bob and another player. Certainly the signing of Belchier as a half-back, who had played for Bolton Wanderers during the War may have given Bob reason to think that he was about to be replaced but on the other hand he was sufficiently experienced to know that he would have to fight for a place in the team anyway. On its own, this is surely a ridiculous notion given the number of players that Bob would have met in

---

[†] What was not known at the time was that Bob had also signed amateur forms for Darlington, thereby giving him a greater chance to 'get a game' should Shildon's be postponed due to bad weather; he continued this arrangement for the next three years and would turn out for the Division Three (North) club a total of six times.

the previous six years of army camps, where he would have come across all types and would have learnt how to get on with them.

A few have suggested that his girl-friend/fiancée did not wish to attend matches at the Kingsway but might be persuaded to go along to see a few games at Shildon's Dean Street ground, which was a little nearer to where she lived at Eldon. It is true that Betty attended a few of the matches in which Bob played at Shildon but she was no great fan of the game and did not attend any future games, even Cup Finals. I cannot accept that Bob Hardisty was so in love with Betty that he was prepared to forego playing for a club with a proud history and for whom he held great affection, just to play for one without any significant achievements in its record books—at least in the Amateur Cup which can only be the true yardstick. Moreover, I do not believe that such demands would have been placed on Bob by Betty. She loved Bob but disliked football. It was as simple as that. As for Shildon being significantly closer to Eldon than Bishop Auckland to make a difference of her attending matches—well the idea is just laughable.

Chris Foote Wood, in his book *Kings Of Amateur Soccer*, which records the history of Bishop Auckland Football Club, puts forward the view that Bob's leaving Bishop Auckland for Shildon was due to a falling out with one of the club committee members who had allegedly been heard to say that '… Bob Hardisty is too big for the club.' This may well have been the correct description of what happened but for the life of me I cannot accept it. What is there in that statement that could possibly offend anyone, especially the easygoing and fair-minded Bob Hardisty? Perhaps if what had actually been said was, 'Bob Hardisty *thinks* he is too big for the club', then that would put a different complexion on the issue and would give a more valid reason for Bob's professed actions resulting in him switching his allegiance. But we were not there to witness any such conversation and without proof it remains conjecture. Another mystery in the life of John Roderick Elliott Hardisty.

The majority view, certainly that held by the number of people that I have discussed the issue with, including Bob's friends, opponents and colleagues, is that he was offered more money by Shildon than Bishop were prepared to offer in the way of 'expenses'.

For what it is worth, I believe that it was a combination of factors that took Bob to Shildon. I think it likely that he was dismayed that the committee were changing the side from game to game and that he himself had been dropped—or euphemistically, told that he was in need of a rest—by the committee. He may not have agreed with the committee's assessment of his fitness and when Shildon came along with an offer he decided to talk to them. It is this writer's view that money was the deciding factor that took Bob to Shildon and that they were prepared to offer him more money in the way of expenses than the committee of Bishop Auckland Football Club were prepared to offer. Furthermore, I believe that once Bob had been seduced by Shildon's approach and agreed to register with them, he deemed himself honour bound to abide by that agreement and could not go back on it even if he had wanted to. Once he had signed the registration form that was it as far as Bob was concerned—he had become a Shildon player and was not prepared to change his mind.

To back up this view, I recall having a conversation with Bobby Davison who played for Bishop Auckland and Crook Town but prior to that had been with Shildon. Bobby was living in Alfreton, Derbyshire, at the time and had agreed to my interviewing him about his career. Anyone who had the pleasure of meeting Bobby will not need reminding that he was quite an outspoken person and prepared to give an opinion, whether it had been asked for or not—he was no shrinking violet.

> I knew Bob Hardisty well and we played alongside each other at Shildon, me at centre-half and him at either right or left half-back. Bob could play either side and he was a decent inside-forward too. He'd been and gone in a season and I soon followed a year or so later. Anyway, I can tell you now, that the Shildon committee were desperate to do well in the Amateur Cup, they wanted to win it and knew that they needed to improve the team. They had seen Bishop Auckland win the trophy just before the war and fail narrowly upon the resumption just after war had finished. Shildon had a reasonably good side in them days, always near the top of the league but the real money lay in the Amateur Cup where they had generally come unstuck. Just a season or so, before I joined, they had been thumped by a little Midland club who nobody had ever heard of, Boldmere St Michael, who played near Sutton Coldfield. There was decent gate money to be made, especially if you were drawn against one of the crack southern clubs. I was with Crook at the time and apparently had come to the attention of Shildon's scouts, whoever they were. As an 'incentive' to join Shildon, two of the committee members—I don't remember who—came to see me and asked me to sign for them. In return they offered me a job at the local railway sheds—good pay—plus the use, rent free, of a terraced house in South Church that was owned by one of them and not only that they would pay me an 'expenses allowance' of £2.10.00d (£2.50p) per game. They also promised me a bumper hamper of groceries every Friday for as long as I was with them. I said 'Where do I sign?'

Now if Bob Hardisty had been offered anything like those terms he would have been daft to turn them down, if Bishop were not prepared to match them. He would have still been living with his parents so wouldn't have wanted a house, not yet anyway as he wasn't married, so there would have been plenty more in the kitty by way of inducement to get Bob's signature. Bob Hardisty was no fool. Don't forget, First Division players would have been on about £4.00.00d (£4.00p) a game, so getting £2.10.00d (£2.50p) or £3.00.00d (£3.00p) as an amateur by way of expenses was canny. None of us used to talk about the money. We all guessed we were being paid the same so didn't bother. Southern clubs paid out more. Just after the '54 Final, Grays Athletic wanted me to sign for them—house, job, car, the lot. I talked it over with my wife but she wasn't keen leaving all the family up here, so that was that.

Bobby Davison transferred himself a couple of years later to Bishop Auckland, who by then had probably learned that the going rate for amateur footballers was not as low as they thought it was!

Another who argues that the cause of Bob signing for Shildon was financial, is Gordon Nicholson, who became Secretary of the Northern League in 1966 and who had served as Secretary for Shildon United prior to his appointment:

Living in a rather close community, both in footballing and social terms, I can remember the brouhaha that was caused when Bob went to Shildon. Everybody wanted to ask questions but no-one did. Rumours were rife but I was, and still am, convinced that it was money that took Bob Hardisty to Shildon. Quite simply, Shildon made him a better offer. Everybody was aware, even in them days, that the so-called expenses system was abused. All clubs did it, some worse than others, or better whichever way you look at it. Mind you, what the northern clubs paid in pennies the southerners paid in pounds—they were so much richer down there.

The image of the much revered Bob Hardisty accepting a bigger amount for expenses than that which would be considered reasonable, is no doubt anathema to some. All I can say is that if you prefer to believe that he did not accept what was termed 'boot money' then you are at liberty to do so. You would not be alone and can find support from Chris Foote Wood, who writes in *Kings Of Amateur Soccer*, on page 85:

… The Shildon players all got legitimate expenses but Hardisty refused even this small payment as he did throughout his career. Those players, even former playing colleagues at Kingsway, who took large amounts of 'boot money' or under the counter payments, he describes as 'sharks …'

One can pick holes in all of these suggestions and run around in circles trying to discover whatever real purpose Bob had in deciding to play for Shildon that season. Whatever, the fact remains that for that solitary season, Bob Hardisty played most of his football for Shildon FC. The irony could not have been missed when the First Round draw of that season's FA Amateur Cup competition pitched the two teams together for an eagerly awaited showdown at Dean Street. The general feeling was that Bishop Auckland undoubtedly had the history on their side but this time Shildon had a really good team to match that of their neighbours. Shildon supporters were adamant that with a half-back line of Atkinson, Davison and Hardisty, they would be more than capable of looking after the Bishop's inside-forwards of Edgell, Taylor and Teasdale. Those same supporters were more worried that the full-backs Husdane and Booth may not be able to cope with Auckland's tricky wingers, Twigg and Rutherford, who were lightning fast.

The week did not start well for Shildon. There was a fire at their ground and as a result, most of the club's players' football boots were burnt to a cinder. Thankfully, Bob Hardisty's size twelves escaped the blaze—he had taken them home to be re-studded. Shildon borrowed a set of white shirts and dark shorts for the game.

A bumper crowd was anticipated and *The Northern Echo* reported that there were over 3,000 in the ground thirty minutes before the start of the match. When the game did start this had increased to well over 6,000. The game was an open one but skilful football was absent due to the slippery surface on the muddy pitch. Bob had been looking forward to this one as playing against his old club made the challenge more exciting for him and he wanted to show Bishop what they were missing. Davison commanded the middle and every time Twigg or Rutherford sent over a high centre, he was always there to head the ball away, much to the frustration of Auckland centre-forward, Taylor. The Shildon defenders were equal to anything that Bishop threw at them and Bob was able to feed off clearances to set up counter attacks. He was having a solid game and was keeping Teasdale in check—which made it all the more galling to let the man who he was supposed to be marking, score the opening goal from Rutherford's cross. The reverse spurred Shildon on but they were unable to get the equalizer before the referee blew for half-time.

Bobby Davison says of that game:

> I gave the forwards a right go at half-time. I told them that they had to take
> on more responsibility and start attacking the Bishop full-backs. Bob Hardisty,

Atkinson and me had run around spending too much time in defence. The forwards had to do more with the ball when we supplied it to them and to be fair that's just what they did.

The Shildon forwards responded to Davison's demands and came out with all guns blazing for the second half and almost equalized when Derry was put through from an exquisite pass from Bob, only to see Jack Washington tip the ball around the post. From the resultant corner, Parkin saw his header safely collected by the Bishop 'keeper. The second half was all Shildon with Bob and Atkinson able to contribute with more attacking roles. The state of the pitch had deteriorated as the match went on and the muddy surface resulted in passes not reaching the intended target. It was just such an incident that led to Shildon's equalizer. Twigg tried to pass inside to Taylor but the pass was intercepted by Bob who had time to look up and assess the situation. Judging that outside-left Maddison was free and had the space to attack, Bob sent a superb pass forward for the winger to run onto and from his tantalizing cross, Parkin was able to prod the ball past Washington for a deserved equalizer. The goal had come just in time as a few minutes later the referee blew the final whistle.

Players and supporters alike could not wait for Saturday to come for the replay and the lucky 8,625 crowd witnessed a classic football match. Bob was in the thick of it right from the start, putting Parkin through who forced Washington in to a fine save. Another Shildon attack saw Bob bursting through the Auckland defence only to be tripped by the 'Bishops' captain and centre-half, Bert Hadfield. Bob took the free kick himself but his forwards were unable to make anything of it. Another free kick was awarded in the next Shildon attack. This time Bob had a direct attempt at goal but Washington was equal to it and pulled off a fine save. He had started well, and Bob was satisfied with his game, on his return to the ground for which he had so much affection.

It was an unusual incident that brought about the opening goal. Washington was penalized for carrying the ball too far.[†] It was not often that a goalkeeper was caught out for this offence but on this occasion the referee decided to take action and ordered an indirect free kick. Bob placed the ball and rubbed

---

[†] For the benefit of younger readers, before the law was changed, goalkeepers could only carry the ball by bouncing it every four steps, by this method they could reach the edge of the penalty area to gain maximum advantage in kicking the football upfield.

his left hand down the front of his left leg, a clear signal for Shildon full-back Robinson to get into the penalty area and be ready for the cross. It worked to perfection and Bob's delicate chip to the far post was headed past a rooted Washington. Thirty minutes gone and Shildon were ahead. After that it was all Bishop, with Robinson, Davison and Bob each in turn having to make last ditch tackles to prevent an equalizer.

The second half started where the first had left off with Bishop putting on all the pressure and within seven minutes Rutherford had put them level with a header. Undaunted, the visitors fought themselves back into the game without being able to score. Bob was having a fine game and despite the intensity of the play was showing a lot of composure and regularly gave the impression that he had all the time in the world to pick out the perfect pass. On the hour, he placed yet another pin point pass into the path of Maddison who centred the ball for Berry to put Shildon ahead again. Bishop were stung. They started to win the ball again with aggressive tackling and ten minutes after going behind, Edgill's attempt hit the post and rebounded for Taylor to slot home the equalizer. Taylor put his team in front five minutes later and Ken Twigg scored a fourth. Shildon had lost 4–2 and their record, in the competition that really mattered most, had not improved any.

This was Bob Hardisty's first of only two defeats that he would suffer on the Kingsway ground in the Amateur Cup. There would be no league honours either that season, Shildon finishing only three points behind the champions—Bishop Auckland, who had finished level with Crook Colliery Welfare on thirty-eight points but won the title on a play-off 5–1.

If Bob Hardisty's departure from Bishop Auckland had been a surprise, his return was not totally unexpected. There had been murmurings that he would be playing for the 'Bishops' again come the start of the 1947/48 season. Again, there is nothing in the way of documentary evidence but there is a very strong suspicion that this time, the committee of Bishop Auckland, having been stung by Bob's leaving twelve months previous, were prepared to pay the 'going rate', whatever that might be, for the prodigal son's return. Not that Bishop had fared badly in Bob's absence for by the end of the 1946/47 season they had reached the semi-final stage of the FA Amateur Cup, only to go down 4–2 to what many supporters thought was an ordinary Wimbledon side, and they had won the Northern League title after a play off against Crook Colliery Welfare.

To say that Bishop started the new season well would be somewhat of an understatement. Any team that wins its opening games away from home 9–2 (Whitby Town) and then 10–1 (Billingham Synthonia) spells serious trouble to all other contenders. Bishop went on their merry way right up to Christmas undefeated, during which course Bob was his solid dependable self. And guess which team inflicted the first defeat on Hardisty's eleven? That's right … Shildon, who beat the 'Two Blues' 1–0 at Dean Street on 27th December. The 'Bishops' got their revenge in the return fixture a few days later on New Year's Day winning 6–2 which included a goal by Bob.

In the FA Cup competition, Bishop saw off North Shields 3–2 in a Qualifying Round at Kingsway and were rewarded with an away tie in the First Round at Chester City. Situated next to the banks of the River Dee, more than 7,000 spectators crammed into Chester's quaint stadium amongst whom were almost five hundred Bishop Auckland supporters who had made the journey across the Pennines to support their heroes.

Within a minute, Bob Hardisty, playing at left-half, knew that he would be in for a tough time. Collecting the ball from goalkeeper, Jack Washington, near the half-way line, he turned with the ball only to be scythed down by Chester's big centre-half, Williamson. Five minutes later, Bob received similar treatment from full-back Wilcox. Chester had obviously done some homework and had highlighted Bob Hardisty as the main man to mark—literally. On each occasion, the referee did no more than order free kicks, not taking any further action against either Chester defender. The game became a bad tempered affair with the amateurs trying to play football but receiving no protection from the referee.

Chester led 2–0 after half an hour, much against the run of play but Bishop got a goal back when Colville felled Ken Twigg and Tommy Farrer reduced the arrears from the spot. Although, receiving yet more rough treatment, according to one journalist, Bob produced his best performance for the 'Bishops', during which he made an acrobatic goal line clearance at one end and then saw a blistering shot brilliantly saved by Chester goalkeeper, McLaren, at the other.

Chester broke away to score a third goal late in the second half to put the issue beyond doubt but in truth it was a strange result. At no stage of the game had the Football League team displayed form expected of them and with a stronger official in charge, the result may have been very different.

During this period, Bob had a few diversions to concentrate on. He had been selected to represent England in the forthcoming international which was in effect an Olympic trial match, the annual Amateur Cup competition was about to get under way, with Bishop one of the favourites to win it and finally there was the not insignificant matter of his forthcoming marriage to Betty, scheduled for August.

The initial diversion, in this short list, concerned Bob's old Army colleague, Matt Busby, who, like so many other budding and established footballers, had seen their career cruelly curtailed by the war. Considered too old to continue playing (he was thirty-six) in 1945 he had been offered a post of assistant coach at the club for whom he had been a registered player, Liverpool. For Busby, however, the post did not offer any control or responsibility of the playing staff. Manchester United were looking for a manager at the time and heard that Busby would be available. They approached him and Busby accepted on the condition that he would have total control of all matters relating to the players. Matt Busby was his own man and knew exactly what he wanted. Although he was not readily available, as his demob from the army was not due for a further six months, the Manchester club was prepared to wait until he could take over the reins, which he duly did in September of that year.

Notwithstanding the responsibility that he carried holding such a position for the First Division club (who were not as famous then as they are today), the Football Association contacted Busby and sought his agreement to take charge of the Great Britain Olympic Football Squad for the forthcoming 1948 Games to be held in London. Busby was delighted and agreed, subject to his usual demands that he would have total control of the squad and would have sole responsibility for team selection. Busby got his terms although it was agreed that the Amateur Football Association, who had the machinery and personnel in situ to observe the form of the amateur players up and down the country, would select the primary twenty-two players that would make up the squad. Other than that, Busby was free to control the players as he wished.

It may seem remarkable today, looking back upon sixty years, that a manager of a First Division (Premier League) football team would be willing to take on the dual role of manager of an international squad and an amateur one at that. Can you imagine Alex Ferguson managing Manchester United and at the same time being responsible for a Great Britain football team? Yet, that is exactly what Matt Busby had agreed to do. He had some idea of the type of players he wanted, having seen the standard of performance that amateurs could produce with and against their professional counterparts, during the numerous games that took place during the war, and he knew the perfect person to be captain of the team. Bob Hardisty would be twenty-seven, just a shade too old, in Busby's estimation, to begin a career as a professional footballer but he would be perfect for the leading role in the amateur game.

Bob Hardisty's first England cap was awarded when he played against Wales at Bangor, North Wales, on 24th January 1948, less than six months before the Olympic Games were due to start. England coasted to a 7–2 victory and Bob acquitted himself satisfactorily. Playing centre-forward for England that day was Harry McIlvenny of Yorkshire Amateurs who would later become a Bishop Auckland player.[†]

Two weeks later, Bob was wearing the England shirt again, this time against Ireland in Belfast. The Irish were comfortably defeated 5–0 with Bob scoring his first international goal. Further games followed but were not as successful for the England team. They were surprisingly beaten at Shrewsbury 3–4 by Wales and a month later had a 0–2 defeat inflicted on them by France at Ilford. Matt Busby had seen enough, however, and decided by then to make a telephone call to his old friend.

Telephones were not a universal commodity in the 1940s like they are today and if anyone wished to speak to Bob on the 'phone they would ring his parents' florist shop and leave a message where Bob would often call in if he had decided to walk home from the school. Matt and Bob had kept in touch since their army days and had corresponded by letter. On this particular day, Bob walked into the shop to be greeted by Jack; 'Bloody phone's been going all day with people wanting orders ... and Matt Busby has rang a couple of times. Perhaps he wants to sign you up at last and take you off to Manchester.'

Brr ... brr ... brr ... Ring ... ring ... ring.

'There it goes again,' he moaned, raising his eyebrows in exasperation.

[†] W. D. Reed, in his book about Bishop Auckland Football Club, writes on page twenty-three, in respect of season 1945/46: 'Hardisty and Teasdale were capped for England.' I am loath to contradict this statement but it would appear to be incorrect as according to the Football Association minutes for that season, neither Bob Hardisty nor Harry Teasdale was selected for any of the four representative games that took place. Many unofficial games took place, amateur as well as professional, between footballing countries on an unofficial basis during this time and it is probable that Mr. Reed was referring to such a game. It is likely that the game to which he was referring was held in 1949.

Jack took the call and immediately raised his hand to beckon Bob to speak to the caller. 'Bishop Auckland 163, Jack Hardisty.' A slight pause, then he whispered, 'It's Matt Busby.'

Bob and Matt exchanged pleasantries and then the Scotsman came to the point and explained to Bob that he wanted him to be captain of the Great Britain Olympic Football team. Matt had not wished to put the offer in a letter. Ideally, he would have preferred to have met Bob face to face to discuss the proposal but the demands of their separate employment made that option difficult. Matt had taken the only personal route left—telephone. Bob was taken aback. How could he be captain, he enquired? He had never been captain of Bishop Auckland, that was Tommy Farrer's claim and he had never thought about holding such a responsible position. He was honoured but did not think that he deserved the captaincy. Matt would have none of it and made it clear that he believed Bob was the right man for the job and would not take 'No' for an answer. It went through Bob's mind that he had been in a similar position ten years ago when his headmaster had gone to great lengths to explain to him the leadership qualities that he considered he held.

'Okay, Matt. Thank you.'

Bob Hardisty replaced the telephone to the cradle with a big grin on his face and turned to his mother and father who had been able to assess the meaning of the conversation that had just taken place. Bob looked at his watch. The shop would be closing in half an hour.

'Need any help?' he offered as two late shoppers entered the premises. The newly appointed captain of the Great Britain Olympic Football Team was not too proud to put a bouquet of roses together.

Away from the international scene, Bishop Auckland continued producing their usual brand of winning football in the Northern League. They, and the rest of the clubs were, however, in for a shock as a surprise challenge to the league title had emerged in the form of Ferryhill Athletic who had finished mid-table the previous season. Right from the outset, Ferryhill had been up there with the pace and it soon became obvious that the title would rest between them and the 'Bishops'. Both teams won their away game with each other, Bishop winning 3–2 at Darlington Road but Athletic winning 3–2 at Kingsway near the end of the season, in a match that went a long way in deciding the championship. Bishop had four remaining fixtures but only took one point out of a possible eight, thus allowing

Ferryhill to take only their second championship in the club's history. Given the close rivalry between the clubs that year, it seems remarkable that when they were paired against each other for a Second Round tie in the Amateur Cup, Ferryhill went down 0–6, choosing an inopportune game to produce their worst display of the season in front of a record home crowd of 9,051 very cold spectators. If it was Ferryhill's worst showing, in contrast it was probably Bob Hardisty's best to date. As early as the first minute he showed his skill with a defence splitting pass for Teasdale to open the scoring with a glorious shot into the roof of the net. The Bishop mid-field players became inspired by Bob and were able to take full advantage with the wind behind their backs. Countless attacks were made on the Ferryhill backs who relented time and again, so much so, that by half-time they had conceded five goals without so much as one shot at goal in reply. Ferryhill tried to make best use of the conditions in the second half but Bishop were in complete control with Hardisty and Farrer sewing things up on the left side of the field whilst Webb, Smith and Tulip took care of any danger on the right. Centre-forward, Taylor, added a sixth goal to complete the rout.

Further success followed in the Amateur Cup when Bishop defeated Norton Woodseats 5–0 in front of their own supporters who had seen them record a First Round success over Penrith 7–3. An expected tough Fourth Round tie looked in store when the draw was made, although they would have home advantage against a very useful Wycombe Wanderers, who had suffered a recent dip in form, which had resulted in them dropping to near the bottom of the Isthmian League.

To win any game 6–2 is an achievement. To win by such a margin against top class opposition makes that achievement even more meritorious. Wycombe were soundly defeated by such a scoreline and it was with maximum confidence that the 'Bishops' found themselves in the semi-finals of the Amateur Cup for the fourth consecutive time, including the successful 1938/39 season. The game would be played at Ayresome Park where they held a particularly good record, having never lost there. The whole team was confident and even the eternally modest Bob Hardisty could not help thinking that this time he would get to play in the final. A five-star shock lay in store.

Opponents, Leytonstone, were a class act at Ayresome Park and it was Bishop Auckland's turn to be handed out a footballing lesson by the current holders of the trophy, in front of 34,673 paying spectators, going down 5–0 to the southern outfit and thereby gaining revenge for the semi-final defeat inflicted at Darlington nine years earlier. Bob was so disappointed. In the last round he had been able to distribute the ball with the accuracy of a rifle and had played a part in two of the goals and defensively he had made at least five well-timed clearances including two off the goal line. This time it was as if everything he tried failed to come off. He had launched himself at a Twigg cross only to injure himself in the attempt. They were already three goals down at the time so it probably made little difference, he thought. He was not alone. His team mates had all had an off day. Even Tommy Farrer, stand-in captain and perfect penalty taker, had seen his spot kick effort easily saved by Jarvis. As for Bob, it was his own performance, however, that he was critical of and it was a dejected set of northerners who left the Teesside cold.

'Nomad' of *The Northern Echo* spoke to Bob Hardisty about the defeat a few days later and they both agreed that Leytonstone had deserved their victory. As ever, Bob pointed out his own shortcomings and apologized that he was never able to support the usually tricky Alan Gilhome. In addition, however, Bob was not slow to recognize that the southern teams, who were mainly richer and could afford to employ managers with football coaching experience, generally had better training facilities and methods than their northern counterparts and that the north was playing catch up. It was up to the teams of the north to put their own house in order if they were to compete successfully against the south.

The end of the domestic season saw Bob picking up a runners-up medal from the Northern League but for him there would be no rest. He would be putting aside the Bishop's mitre and stepping out towards the Five Rings of the Olympic Games Movement.

I t is fair to say that not all countries held the prospects of staging such an international tournament as the Olympic Games with any high degree of priority. War had only just ceased and money was in short supply as were the other essentials of life—food, clothing, property etc. The Olympic Movement had other ideas, however, and took the view that the people of the world needed a bit of cheering up after the catastrophes of the previous six years, and the aftermath of war. If only they could get a country to stage the games. The 1940 Olympiad had been scheduled for Tokyo but obviously had been cancelled as had the games due for 1944 for which the venue would have been London. There were four other serious candidates to hold the 1948

Games, namely Lausanne and the three American cities of Baltimore, Los Angeles and Philadelphia but London was selected and once the decision had been confirmed, there was a hushed sigh of relief from the British Government, who now saw a means of improving the national economy through ticket sales and tourism. It was anticipated that hotels and hostels, bus and train services and shops would benefit with the increase in customers, both domestic and foreign, and that there would be a boom in sales of British products. Immediately the International Olympic Committee had given the go-ahead, with the cooperation of the British Government, plans were put into action for the XIV Olympiad to be held in the capital, with Wembley Stadium being the central arena. It was no surprise that Germany and Japan would not be participating but there was an air of disappointment that the USSR refused to send a representative team—the Cold War wind had started to puff if not exactly blow.

The majority of sporting events were to take place at the Empire Stadium, Wembley, but other venues outside the capital were utilized to accommodate other sports e.g. Tweseldown Racecourse staged the equestrian events, water polo took place at Finchley in North London, and the yachting tournament was watched at Torbay. Not all of the football matches could take place at the Empire Stadium and the eighteen competing football nations would have to play their football at a variety of venues comprising, Highbury (Arsenal), Griffin Park (Brentford), Selhurst Park (Crystal Palace), Craven Cottage (Fulham), Champion Hill (Dulwich Hamlet), White Hart Lane (Tottenham Hotspur), Cricklefield Stadium (Ilford) and Green Pond Road (Walthamstow Avenue) as well as The Old Goldstone Ground (Brighton and Hove Albion) and Fratton Park (Portsmouth).

The various participants of the competition were housed in an asssortment of buildings. Respective foreign embassies vied with the British Government to find the best accommodation for their athletes but some were more influential than others. Schools and colleges were transformed into makeshift hostels and even spartan army barracks were used to full effect. Uxbridge RAF camp would be the home for the Great Britain squad, not exactly the height of luxury.

Twyford Hall was a rambling mansion set close to Sunningdale Golf Club and in 1948 could have done with what we would politely describe as 'a lick of paint and some tender loving care'. It may have been in need of a lick of paint but the building was more than adequate to serve the purposes of the Great Britain Football squad. It had enough rooms to house the twenty-four players plus the training and coaching staff and was in a quiet setting with large gardens. Physical training drills would take place here but to break any risk of monotony the players could be taken to the White City Stadium, which had excellent training facilities and a running circuit next to the greyhound track.

Leading up to the games, Busby had been busy. He had taken Manchester United to the runners-up spot in the First Division, losing out to Arsenal, the same position they had finished the previous year when Liverpool had pipped them for the championship. In consolation, however, he had had the satisfaction of seeing his team lift the FA Cup when they defeated Blackpool 4–2 in a memorable final. He would now have to concentrate on forging a winning team for the Olympics—from a bunch of players, with the exception of his old friend Bob Hardisty, he did not know and had never met. He started by organizing weekends at United's home, Old Trafford, for the squad of players that the Football Association had selected, and endeared himself to all of them with his knowledge of tactics and of the game. The players would be put up at the Midland Hotel and from there would be taken for their daily workouts at the Old Trafford ground, which still showed signs of bomb damage suffered during the war.

It was especially uplifting for the amateurs when any of the United first team players would turn up and join in to support them. Every Friday night these amateurs would make their way from all points of the compass by bus and train to Manchester and by Sunday evening, after a gruelling two days, would make the return journey with an individual fitness programme laid out by Busby. For those players who lived close to professional clubs, he insisted that they approach the club to carry out the training programme that he had set. Busby's thinking was that by working with professionals his amateurs would develop professional ideas and standards. Irrespective of whatever work commitments the players had, it was their responsibility that they adhered to the programme and kept themselves fit.

Following Busby's programme to the letter, Bob would train every evening with Bishop Auckland utility man, Johnny Wright, and 'sponge man', Jack Sowerby, doing the stretching and running exercises that Matt Busby had scheduled for him. It meant that these dedicated amateurs got little in the way of leisure time during these weekends as they would have jobs to return to on Monday mornings but it would be worth it if Busby could gel the squad together. He worked them hard and got them to improve their fitness

Bob Hardisty's birth certificate showing the puzzling Section 6.

Bob aged three.

Bob as captain of the 1931 Cockton Hill Elementary School Team.

Wigton School photo from 1936. Bob is standing to the left, sporting a dark tie.

Bob and his mother circa 1936.

The certificate awarded to Bob in 1937 following an outstanding batting performance.

Bob is seated second left in this 1938 photo of the Wigton School XI whose colours were green and brown.

The successful 1939 Bishop Auckland team with Bob seated cross-legged at front left and a youthful Bob Paisley seated cross-legged extreme right.

St Bede's College Football Team 1939 with Bob third from right on back row. Lez Rawe, Bob's long-time friend, is seated extreme left.

A rare picture of Bob's parents, Mary and Jack Hardisty.

Bob playing for Reading against Fulham in 1944. Bob wrote home that they had won this game but records show that the result was 1–1.

Leading out an Army team in the Far East.

Bob in India.

Second Lieutenant Hardisty of the Royal Hong Kong Signals.

Bob is arrowed in this photo of his last game in India before embarking for England.

Bob as a member of the teaching staff of Barrington School with Betty seated second right.

Showing how it is done … 'You put your right foot in, your right foot out …'

Playing for England in a friendly against Holland in Amsterdam prior to the 1948 Olympic Games.

Training for the Olympics.

Bob, second left—next to Harry McIlvenny—relaxes with a cup of tea as the Great Britain football team take time off from training.

The 1948 Great Britain Olympic Football team with Manager Matt Busby in the centre, and Bob to his left. Harry McIvenny is behind Bob.

Bob in action for Great Britain against France during the 1948 Olympic games.

levels and speed of thought. But there was a limit to what he could achieve in such a short space of time and privately he did not give the team much chance of progressing in the competition. As he watched this variety of teachers, accountants, pipe-fitters and all other occupations, doing their best to carry out his instructions, he wondered how could they compete with the likes of Sweden, a country whose footballers were all amateurs but had grown up together: or Yugoslavia, a country that clearly took the amateur ethics of the Olympian ideal to a level that bordered on cheating, conscripting its best players into the army who could, therefore, be paid as soldiers and who were trained by the best coaches available—they were, in Busby's eyes, professional in all but name.

Bob enjoyed these weekends with his old friend as they gave the opportunity to form new friendships and renew acquaintances with others he had played football with during the war, such as Andy Aitken and the droll Jim McColl, both from Queen's Park. Unlike Matt, thought Bob, at least I know a few of the players. Yet it was Bob's previous friendship and playing experience with Matt Busby that gave the manager the idea of a surprise element for the forthcoming games. Busby would have Bob playing as a forward at inside-right and not in his accustomed position linking defence to attack at right-half. Bob had played in this position at times with Busby during their period together at Reading, and the Scotsman remembered how Bob had taken to the change of role that the position demanded. He also knew that he was capable of scoring goals. Hopefully, the other international teams would not be aware of this positional change, or at least if they were, then they would have little time to adjust their play to counteract it.

Busby approached the Football Association with the suggestion that it may be worthwhile to have the players together for a longer period than just the weekends that he had organized. He felt that having all the squad together for a longer length of time, before the Games, would be experience for them and would also bond the players together as a unit. However, he still harboured thoughts that his team was not good enough to progress far—they had just suffered a heavy defeat in a friendly match against the Netherlands who would be sending a team over to London. The Football Association approved Busby's idea and the players were requested to present themselves, if possible, to the Grove Hall Hotel, just outside Reading, for a fortnight of training, tactics and fitness. To their credit, all of the players attended, even though they were not compensated for loss of earnings.

He had said his goodbyes to his parents and had seen Betty the evening before. She had told him not to return with a broken leg—their wedding plans were completed and the big day was less than two months away. She would prefer her bridegroom not to be walking down the aisle with his leg in plaster, she had told him. He smiled as he reflected on that conversation as the train pulled out of Darlington railway station and made its way past countless fields towards King's Cross station and the capital.

Matt was as jovial as ever when Bob arrived at Uxbridge and greeted his footballing captain with a huge grin and hearty handshake. 'Still trying to find the winners, Bob?'

'Aye, Matt. That Harry Carr might be the Queen's favourite but he buggers about whenever he rides one that I fancy,' came back the jovial response.

Training got under way the next day and Matt, with trainer Tom Curry alongside him, eyed every one of his squad, the pair taking in every nuance that each player had, looking to see who needed weight exercises, which ones required speed training and who needed to improve ball control. Under his eagle eyes the players went through the routines of exercises and programmes to which they had been set. Of course, by now, Matt had seen and studied them all. He had a general idea of what his best eleven would be but he doubted that they would be good enough to take on the Swedes or Yugoslavia. Not yet, anyway. It was his job to get them to the level where they would be capable of such a task. For Bob, this was an enjoyable part of football—the keeping fit. He loved it and he and his fellow players never shirked any of the demands made by Matt Busby and his staff. He thought what a good squad it was that had been put together and that there was a good relationship between all of the players. After training they would all relax and fool about together making fun of each other and exaggerating each others faults. Eric Lee was a real comedian and would not look out of place in the theatre, thought Bob, with his endless stream of jokes and impersonations.

As the weekends had progressed, Bob had been particularly impressed with centre-forward, Harry McIlvenny, and had even thought how good he might look in a Bishop Auckland shirt. Bob could see him scoring a lot of goals for the 'Bishops' if only the Yorkshireman could be persuaded to leave Bradford Park Avenue. Meanwhile, he wanted his star centre-forward to score for the Great Britain side on Saturday, after tomorrow's opening ceremony at the Empire Stadium.

I t was only 10:30 a.m. on Thursday 29th July 1948 and already the sun was beating down. Bob Hardisty, resplendent in his official Great Britain black blazer, tie and white Oxford bag trousers stepped onto the bus, one of more than two hundred that had been requisitioned to take competitors to the Games over the next two weeks. He jokingly cursed to Jim McColl about the uniform that they were wearing. 'Who the hell decided on us wearing berets?' he asked generally. 'Makes you wonder if the French will all be wearing bowler hats.' No doubt similar comments were made by the rest of the squad, even if just to rid themselves of any nervous tension that they may have held. The opening ceremony was always a highlight of the Olympics with dignitaries and royalty from around the globe in attendance and no-one wanted to let their country down, especially when 100,000 pairs of eyes were on them and that was discounting the viewers who would be watching on the newfangled television sets.

The bus journey from Uxbridge to the Empire Stadium was a relatively short one, the distance being a little more than eight miles, but on that morning the bus seemed to take forever to reach its destination. The opening ceremony was not due to start until 2:00 p.m. with the parade of each nation's competitors not due to begin until an hour later. In the meantime, competitors would have to stay at their point of disembarkation from the bus, until their time to participate in the parade. As host nation, Great Britain would be last and, therefore, would not parade until about 4 o'clock, some four hours hence. As time passed by, the ever continuous snake of buses kept arriving to deposit more and more competitors from all nations at the holding area outside the stadium, until at one point there were more than 3,000 of them all congregating about waiting for the parade to start. Everyone tried to gain some sort of vantage point but the number of trees that would have offered welcome shade in the sectioned off area was minimal and had already been snapped up by those countries that had arrived early. It was natural that each country kept to themselves at first but with each passing minute under the hot sun, metaphorical barriers were broken and the athletes started conversations with whoever they happened to be next to. Bob, Bill Amor and Ronnie Simpson were talking about the pending ceremony and football in general, making jokes when possible to ease the tension. Bill Amor had a hatful of funny tales to tell relating to his time of occupation as a policeman over at Reading and the various drunks and ladies of the night that he had been forced to move on or take in to custody. Ronnie was younger and told of his teenage start in football when at the tender age of fourteen years and ten months he had made his debut in the Scottish First Division for one of Bob's old clubs, Queen's Park.

Ronnie was just getting to an interesting point in his tale when Bill interrupted and motioned for Bob to stand perfectly still. Bob raised his eyebrows but played along, not saying anything, expecting Bill to swat an errant wasp or spider from his shoulder. Bill did nothing but as he continued to stand in the same pose, Bob started to grow weary and altered his stance slightly, all the time wondering what was in Bill's mind. The trio continued talking until Bill repeated his request. This time, Bob began to enquire what the hell was going on but before he could finish a rather small oriental gentleman scurried from behind and presented himself with an apologetic bow. In broken English, he explained that he was not used to such a hot sun and had found the tall Englishman to be the perfect height to provide him with the right amount of shade. He had taken advantage of him and did not wish to offend, after which explanation he made a quick exit and returned to his fellow compatriots.

'Bugger me, I never thought when I was picked for the Olympics I'd be used as some kind of parasol,' laughed Bob.

During the opening ceremony, some of the competitors, who had entered the stadium at the head of the parade, fainted due to a combination of the intense heat and the emotion of the occasion and had to receive medical attention. The Great Britain athletes, being the last to enter the stadium, had at least been able to take things a bit easier until their time arrived to take their place at the rear of the parade and did not have to endure standing still on the spot for the best part of an hour in the baking temperature.

The roar that greeted the host nation as its competitors emerged from the tunnel and entered the arena was tumultuous. Bob always reckoned that he felt a lump in his throat at that moment, such was the emotion that had been generated by such a spontaneous roar. The whole stadium was a sea of white shirts and blouses with everyone clapping and cheering at the tops of their voices. He had never experienced anything like it and at that moment felt very proud to be British. Bob attempted to take in all that was going on around him as he, along with over three hundred of his co-athletes, saluted King George VI and Queen Elizabeth up there in the royal box.

The Great Britain contingent completed their part in the parade and took their appointed place to hear the closing speeches in the stultifying heat. As he stood in his allotted position, Bob could not help hoping that the weather would be a little kinder for Great Britain's opening game against Holland, in forty-eight hours time, at Arsenal's Highbury Stadium. He stared at the five coloured rings that formed the Olympic design and imagined them as five footballs. Yes, he thought—five goals would do very nicely.

M att Busby had decided upon his starting eleven and gave them a team talk on the eve of the match. Only a few weeks earlier the teams had met in a friendly in which the Dutch had come out convincing winners. Despite that setback, Busby was of the opinion that his set of players had improved since then and were a better all-round unit with greater team spirit and, with reasonable fortune, were capable of gaining revenge in the match that mattered.

The hopes for milder conditions went unanswered and when Bob led his players onto the Highbury turf, the sun was beating down once more when 2:00pm kick-off time arrived. In front of 21,000 spectators, the two countries put on a fine display, producing end-to-end football that had the sweltering crowd on its feet from the word go, although to many observers, the Dutch players were allowed to get away with some rough play by a very lenient referee, Laursen of Denmark. Netherlands were first to score but MacBain equalized in the twenty-first minute. The Dutch players were very strong in the tackle and continued with some high challenges for the ball. Outside-right, Tommy Hopper, came in for some nasty treatment from the no-nonsense tactics of full-back Schijvenaar and centre-half Terlouw, so much so that he required treatment after one challenge and was forced to leave the field for a while, blood streaming from his face. On the positive side, Bob was relishing the game and generally was coming out on top in his duel with left-half De Vroet. In the Great Britain defence, however, Eric Lee, centre-half, was having a torrid time trying to contain centre-forward Appel and it was the Dutchman who scored his second goal to equalize just three minutes after Bob had put the 'home' side ahead. Dennis Kelleher put Great Britain ahead again but five minutes from time Holland found another equalizer and extra time was called upon. With the score tied at 3–3, it was Harry McIlvenny, the Bradford Park Avenue goal machine, who broke the stalemate. After a strength sapping one hundred and eleven minutes he popped up to settle the issue. At that precise moment, Tommy Hopper, who had returned to the field heavily bandaged around the head, collapsed, his bandage soaked with blood.

This time he left the field not to return. The ten men of Great Britain had to hold out for a further nine minutes but with great courage and a bit of luck they did so.

It had been a hard fought battle by both sides and it was a weary two sets of players that left the field of play. A delighted Matt Busby shook Bob Hardisty's hand and greeted his battered and bruised players as they left the field. In the dressing room, Bob looked around at his colleagues who had all played their hearts out. McIlvenny and Lee started a sing-along and everyone else joined in. It had not quite been five goals but four was sufficient.

The Games had only been under way a few days before Buckingham Palace hosted a reception for all the nations participating. In an aid to achieve some level of equality, each nation was requested to limit the number of guests to nine, thus resulting in an overall head count of just over five hundred. As captain of the football team, Bob was an automatic choice for one of the places. He was thrilled to be included and at last would have the opportunity of meeting their Royal Highnesses. One member of the royals had already attracted his attention and he was hoping that that person would be in attendance. In his daily sealed postcard to Betty, of Tuesday 3rd August, a mischievous side of his character is revealed in a few lines that convey love as well as humour:

> Tuesday morning
> Darling I love you—last night I wrote you telling you of tonight's visit to Buckingham Palace. Well, I didn't have the story exactly right. Evidently the King is inviting 9 people from every country competing which means there will be about 450 of us. Will be thinking of you and you alone at 6 o'clock even when I wink at Princess Liz.
> Again and always
> I love you,
> Rod

Two days later, Bob shook hands with his French counterpart at Craven Cottage, Fulham, for the next stage of the competition. The game itself was an anti-climax compared to the adventurous one against the Netherlands. Bob failed to get his men going and it was fortunate that France were just as poor. Bob scored the only goal of the game but on the principal that winning was everything, the Great Britain players were jubilant at the final whistle.

After this success, in his next letter to Betty, Bob wrote:

Tuesday night

Darling,

One card is not enough so here goes no.2.

Tomorrow we train all morning and afternoon and are in bed for 9 o'clock—then the next battle Thursday—we must win Darling, if it means playing twice at Wembley, if we reach the semi-final.

Wed. morning

Have got a Dutch newspaper of Saturday night's game—will keep it for us Darling. Are all the arrangements tied up for the wedding yet, love—will we be OK for a honeymoon? Am writing to Queen's Park today for whisky.

Keep loving me Betty—I can feel it way down here—My love, I love you—Rod

In another communication Bob wrote:

This morning I rang home to put a bet on for the boys. Matt Busby got a tip for it and as they—or I should say me—couldn't find a bookmaker, I rang it up to 163. I suppose they did it and of course it lost. (I had 5/- each way on it) so it's not so bad. Hope Grandad didn't do it.[†]

In a further post card, the camaraderie of the players and staff and the developing team spirit shines through:

… We have been told that the Yugoslav's are a big burly team who do a lot of kicking without the ball so we are preparing ourselves for another blood match. Matt Busby, Andy Aitken and I went up to see Tommy Hopper tonight. The specialist arrived and examined Tommy while we were there. The result was disappointing. Tommy can't come out until Monday and then no football for a fortnight but his presence down here will be a tonic to us all.

By the way, Darling, Tom Curry the trainer has promised us a couple of white towels from his club, Manchester United. I thought it was a nice gesture.

Tomorrow we start heavy training for Wednesday's game—we are having two hours in the morning and light work in the afternoon …

'Afore warned is 'afore armed. Bob Hardisty and his ten colleagues knew what to expect. Matt Busby and Tom Curry had done all that they could. Expectations of the previously ambivalent public had been raised. The football supporters of Great Britain had not expected their team to reach the semi-finals but there they were. There was no denying that whichever of the

---

[†]   163 refers to the telephone number at Bob's father's shop; 5/- represents 25p in modern currency.

other three semi-finalists Bob Hardisty's team had met—Sweden (trained by ex-Aldershot winger, Englishman George Raynor) and Denmark (trained by ex-Huddersfield and England full-back Reg Mountford) were contesting the other match—an extremely difficult tie would have lain in store.

Bernard Joy, football correspondent of *The Star* reported:

> It is worth noting that there is no professional football played in Denmark, Sweden or Yugoslavia, which no doubt accounts for the very high standard of their amateur sides. In Great Britain, as we at home all appreciate, an outstanding amateur player invariably has the English clubs seeking him. More often than not, probably because he wishes to play in the very top-class, he does turn professional. Of the present Great Britain side only three men, Harry McIlvenny (Bradford Park Avenue), Peter Kippax (Burnley) and Eric Lee (Chester), have had much experience in English League football.
>
> The Swedish, Danish and Yugoslav teams arrived in Great Britain with a great advantage over the home side. They had, as their country's representative side, played many times together before. The Great Britain eleven, however, drawn from the four home countries, had, in many instances, met for the first time at their training camp. That they have succeeded in reaching the last four is a tribute to their football, a fact their opponents will be the first to appreciate.

A crowd of more than 40,000 attended the Empire Stadium to witness Great Britain take on the favourites for the competition, Yugoslavia, who earlier in the year had defeated Bulgaria 3–1 and Czechoslovakia 6–3. Matt Busby had already warned his players of their opponent's skill and impressed upon them the necessity to shoot on sight, pointing out that the Bulgarians had at least scored three against them. He had warned that whenever the Yugoslavs had possession of the ball they generally were patient in building their moves and were not afraid just to play across the field until an attacking opportunity presented itself. He likened it to a cobra mesmerizing its victim until delivering a deadly strike. His parting words to his players as they left the dressing room were, 'Best of luck, do your best … and take care of yourselves.'

Regrettably, their best wasn't good enough. The Yugoslavian players were quicker to the ball and once they had it they kept it, just as Matt Busby had warned. There was no denying that they were a good side and Busby suggested afterwards that they would be the equal of any First Division side—another disguised remark aimed at their convenient amateur status.

The defence of the Great Britain team had been breached in the nineteenth minute by inside-left Bobek but Frank Donovan equalized a minute later. The respite was short, however, as centre-forward, Wolfl, put the Yugoslavs ahead 2–1. Bob and his fellow inside-forward, Dennis Kelleher, strove hard to create an opening for centre-forward, McIlvenny, but the Yugoslav defenders gave little away and covered the empty spaces, thereby stifling the limited attacks that the home team devised. A third goal was added just after half-time and a rather dejected Great Britain squad trooped away to the dressing room whilst the east Europeans cavorted around the pitch and hugged each other in delight. They had proven the better of the two teams but in the final would meet their match when they would lose 3–1 to Sweden.

Three days later, Great Britain and Denmark contested for the bronze medal and produced another goal feast. This time the Danes came out on top winning 5–3, Bob Hardisty getting one for Great Britain who, for the second time in three days, had lost on Wembley's lush turf. Prior to the game, Matt Busby had expressed a real desire for winning the bronze trophy but he also wanted to include players who had not yet made an appearance, as a sign of gratitude for their commitment and faith in him. It was, therefore, not the first eleven that he would necessarily have chosen but nevertheless it was a team that he believed was well able to inflict a defeat upon the Danes. It turned out that his team lost but it was a proud manager and an equally proud captain that said goodbye to the Olympic Games and those five emblematic conjoined rings. In forty-eight hours, Bob would be presenting a far more important ring than any of those stood for.

The bells of the magnificent twelfth century St Andrew's Church, Bishop Auckland rang out on Wednesday 18th August 1948 as the sun shone through the stained glass lancet windows. Miss Betty Laine had now become Mrs Betty Hardisty and there was no prouder man than the one by her side who had placed the gold ring on the third finger of her left hand. In his dress coat and pin-striped trousers, John Roderick Elliott Hardisty could not believe that such a beautiful woman as Betty was now his wife, as he stood next to his best man, Harry McIlvenny who wore a grin as wide as the Humber estuary. He gazed at her and thought how radiant she looked in her bridal gown and veil, as she held a small bouquet of flowers (supplied by Hardisty's of course) with a childlike innocence.

The night before, he had contemplated that perhaps he had been selfish in going off on all of those weekends and then leaving her to finalize the arrangements for today. She was not a fan of football but had accepted his involvement in the sport and his absences that they brought about, right up until almost the wedding day itself, with a grace and equanimity of which he was not worthy. Now, here they were, walking down the aisle as one—the happiest couple in England. He attempted to take in the hushed tones of congratulation that friends and relatives were passing on as he and his bride walked down the aisle, the organist continuing with Mendelssohn's 'Wedding March' in that sharp vibrant pitch that only that instrument can reach but he was oblivious to it all.

They exited the church to a snowstorm of confetti thrown by those who had waited outside or sneaked out of the ceremony early. The couple were amazed. To Bob and Betty, it appeared as if every one of the thirty-thousand inhabitants of Bishop Auckland had given up their Wednesday afternoon just to see them and wish them well. Everywhere they looked men, women and children were cheering for them.[†]

They posed for the never ending stream of photographs and patiently waited for mums and dads, brothers and sisters, uncles and aunts and anyone else, to ready their box brownies for 'one last shot, please.'

After a reception at 'The Queen's Hotel' the happy couple made an early departure. They honeymooned in Scotland where they spent a delightful week just walking and taking in the beautiful Lanarkshire scenery. Bob pointed out to his new wife, the barracks, where he and Matt had put new recruits through their paces, and the golf courses that they had walked together. They spent time in Edinburgh where they admired the beauty of the classical buildings and the city's castle but also attended many of the varied events that compiled the second ever Edinburgh Festival. They enjoyed walking up to Arthur's Seat and they found time to shop in Princes Street. And when they had finished with Edinburgh, they left it behind and toured further north, staying in a crofter's cottage from where they were able to take in the beautiful scenery that Scotland has to offer whilst sipping the malt whisky that Queen's Park had generously supplied by way of a wedding present. They were happy. They were in love. Nothing else mattered.

[†] Such was the admiration that the town had for their local hero that a collection had been proposed for the wedding couple. It was suggested that donations were to be restricted to 6d (equivalent to 2.5p) in order that as many people as possible could be involved. The total sum collected was used to buy a table and cabinet from a local furniture store as a present to Betty and Bob from the town's inhabitants.

'Who can control his fate?'
Othello (William Shakespeare)

Chapter Six
FATED

B ob and Betty started their married life at 'The Laurels', Princes Street, Bishop Auckland—officially it was number thirteen but superstition dictated that it be given a name or become 11a. Sometime in the past, someone had decided upon 'The Laurels'. It was a big house and, at first, the newly-wedded couple shared it with Jack Waine and his wife Joanna (but always known as 'Jonny' to her friends), Jack being the son of Bishop Auckland Football Club committee member, George Waine. The Waines occupied the upper floor of the house whilst Bob and Betty had possession of the downstairs. The arrangement may seem a bit strange to the modern-day reader but sixty years ago it was common for large houses to be split horizontally in order to accommodate more than one family. Within five years, however, the Waines had relinquished their share of the house and the Hardisty family took over exclusively. Jack later died of cancer and 'Jonny' would not survive much longer, suffering a brain haemorrhage a few years later.

The property is no longer standing and was demolished in 2008 to make way for a new development.

The Hardistys had a comfortable lifestyle. They were not what could be considered 'well off' but as they were both securely employed, they were able to afford more things than the majority of young couples who had just been married could. They both enjoyed music and the theatre, so whenever any of the big name artists came to the Sunderland Empire or Newcastle's Theatre Royal they did their best to obtain tickets. They had a close network of friends, some from the football club, such as the McIlvennys and the Majors and, of course, there was always their amiable landlords, the Waines, with whom Bob and Betty got on particularly well. They frequented the local golf club, becoming members, where Betty especially liked the sedate and friendly atmosphere, being able to socialise with other lady members, with the man she loved on her arm. Another venue of a sporting nature where she would often accompany Bob was the cricket ground. Betty found the relaxed nature of cricket, like golf, more to her liking, far removed from the robustness of football. She and Bob were regular visitors to the cricket club where the playing area formed a major side of the Bishop Auckland Football Club's pitch.

On the football scene, the 1948–49 season was a disappointing one for Bob and Bishop Auckland supporters. The club, who had reached at least the semi-final stages of the FA Amateur Cup for the past four consecutive seasons, were eliminated 3–2 as early as the First Round by, of all teams, Shildon and there was little achievement in any of the domestic competitions: they lost 6–1 to Stanley United in a catastrophic League Cup game and the nearest that they came to achieving anything like success was when they finished runners-up in the league to champions, Evenwood Town. On a personal note, Bob had at least the satisfaction of being selected for the three amateur internationals that England played. In January, he played a major part in the 4–1 defeat of Wales at Swindon and a month later travelled to Norwich where Ireland surprisingly won 1–0. He was also on the losing side when Scotland won their home fixture 3–2 in April. The game at Swindon was a particularly pleasurable one for Bob as it gave him the opportunity to congratulate his old friend, Stanley Rous, on becoming a Knight Bachelor in the New Year's Honours List, it being the first occasion that the pair had met since the Olympic Games.

One of the most enjoyable games that Bob took part in was held on the evening of 14th April at Kingsway. It was a Grand Charity Match between Bishop Auckland and King James I Grammar School Old Boys. All proceeds went to the Old Boys Memorial Fund the purpose of which was to provide a memorial for those Old Boys who had made the supreme sacrifice in the two World Wars. Forty-five Old Boys were killed in World War I and sixty-three in World War II. There was a great sense of pride for those who had been selected to play in this match and many of the Bishop Auckland players went out of their way to impress that they would be 'available if required'. Both teams contained the best amateurs playing in the north-east of England:

Bishop Auckland
Outhwaite—Coxon, Farrer—Harburn, Davison, Stones—
Murray, Major, Teasdale, Gilhome, Steele

King James I Old Boys
Bond (Howden-le-Wear)—Rawe (Willington), Coulthard (Shildon)—Hardisty
(Bishop Auckland), Peacock (Evenwood), Towers (Willington)—Turnbull
(Eldon Albions), Tate (Manchester United), Whitfield (Wolverhampton
Wanderers), Wensley (Spennymoor United), Austin (Chilton)

Bob is recorded as playing for the Old Boys but in fact he swapped sides at half-time together with some of the other players who were similarly eligible for both teams. Such an occasion gave Bob the opportunity to meet up with old colleagues and it is understood that the celebrations after the match, that took place in the cricket club, went on well into the night. He did not need much persuading to attend a party. The Bishop Auckland players were due to leave for London on an Easter tour the following day so no doubt there were some sore heads on that journey and for a few days, thereafter. Nevertheless, they were able to put out a team capable of taking on the likes of Ilford, Erith and Belvedere, Tooting and Mitcham United, and Hayes. It must have been a very tired party that returned to County Durham a week later.

The failures of 1949 were soon forgotten when the new season got under way and in one of those early games Bob was on the score sheet five times as the 'Two Blues' demolished poor Heaton Stannington 11–0. Such a scoreline, even against a weak team like Heaton Stannington, sent out a clear warning that the 'Bishops' meant business and were out for the title. The other clubs had been warned. Winning the Northern League title was one thing: winning the Amateur Cup was an entirely different kettle of fish. That was the competition where the money lay and now that Wembley had become the venue of the Final there was an extra incentive to lift the trophy. It was recognised, however, that wresting the Cup from current holders Bromley, who had won the initial Wembley Amateur Cup Final, and staving off the challenge from the southern clubs would not be easy. In his excellent book, *Northern Goalfields*, Brian Hunt quotes Bishop Auckland Chairman, Councillor Jack Waine, at the time as saying: 'Northern clubs are not up to Amateur Cup standard. Until the quality of the Northern League is much higher than it is today, we have no hopes whatsoever of winning the Cup, this is clear when you see southern teams in action.'

Notwithstanding their Chairman's thoughts, the Bishop Auckland players had other ideas when they set off on the cup trail against South Bank, a club, like Bishop Auckland, that had been a founder member of the Northern League. On paper, this First Round tie looked a formality for the 'Two Blues', even though they were playing away from home, if the league form of the two teams was anything to go by. League leaders Bishop had scored fifty goals so far and had earned twenty-three points from a possible twenty-six (two points for a win, remember) whilst the 'Bankers' had gained a paltry five points out of a possible thirty, having been beaten twelve times. There was to be no shock score. Harry Teasdale returned from Auckland's injuries bench to play at inside-right—some line-up reports of this game have Bob at inside-forward but he was in fact at centre-forward and had one of those days when everything he tried came off.

In the opening encounters, South Bank goalkeeper, MacDonald, saved point blank from one of Bob's specials and a few minutes later it was full-back Bradley's turn to deflect a goalbound shot from the nimble Hardisty. After fourteen minutes of non-stop Bishop Auckland pressure, centre-half Wilson tripped outside-left Palmer and Bobby Davison promptly despatched the ball into the net to give the 'Bishops' the lead from the penalty spot. Midway through the half, Bob took on the South Bank defence single-handed and waltzed his way to the six-yard line before slotting the ball past a bemused MacDonald. There was no more scoring, due to a combination of woeful finishing from Auckland's inside-forwards and spirited defence from South Bank's defenders and in the end Bishop Auckland had a comfortable victory rather than a spectacular one, but that did not matter so long as the 'Bishops' were on the Wembley trail.

Round Two saw Bishop Auckland pitched against Isthmian League Ilford who were fourth from bottom in that division. Nevertheless, the Bishop Auckland players were aware not to underestimate their opponents. Supporters of the 'Two Blues' were given a bit of a surprise before a ball was kicked when they were made aware of the decision by the selectors to play Bob at centre-forward. The week before, Harry McIlvenny had made his debut for the club.[†]

[†]   Bob had been singing Harry McIlvenny's praises to 'Kit' Rudd for over twelve months urging the club to sign him. He had scored lots of goals for Yorkshire Amateurs and the Football League club to whom he was registered but when he scored for Bradford Park Avenue against Newcastle United in an FA Cup tie, Bob always believed that that goal was the clincher in finally convincing the Bishop Auckland Committee that they should try to prise him from Yorkshire Amateurs. McIlvenny could not turn out again this week as he was not qualified for the competition.

The Auckland players were right in treating their visitors with respect as it was only after a very hard fought tussle that they won through after extra time by 3–2.

The Midlands provided opposition in Round Three by way of Moor Green who played their football in the Birmingham Combination. The two teams had met each other twice in the past with Bishop coming out on top on both occasions. They made it three with a satisfactory display at Kingsway, the 3–1 scoreline not exactly indicative of their superiority. Harry McIlvenny, now qualified to play in the competition, spearheaded the Bishop attack with Bob as his partner at inside-right. The game is probably best remembered by those who witnessed it as one of the few occasions when Bob Hardisty 'lost his cool'. He had a very good game and had opened the scoring with a stunning header from Taylor's cross after seventeen minutes but within two minutes Moor Green had drawn level. Continuous Bishop Auckland attacks were repelled with some crude tackling and more than once the referee had to speak to the midland club's defenders. Bob, especially, came in for some rough treatment and was fouled whenever he received the ball. The referee was doing everything he could to keep the game flowing but he was not being helped by the aggressive style of play from the Moor Green players who must have thought that they had performed meritoriously when the half-time whistle went with the scores at 1–1.

Three minutes after the restart, Moor Green went a goal behind. With the visitors trying everything they knew to curb Bishop's attacks, centre-half Chadwicke found Palmer too quick for him and promptly despatched the flying winger into the crowd as he cut in to the penalty box. The Moor Green players were incensed at the referee's decision to award a penalty and tried to get him to change his ruling. The official would have none of it and once again Bobby Davison drove the ball home from the penalty spot. When play resumed, Bob was crudely kicked from behind by a Moor Green defender and turned as if to retaliate. Only the intervention of Harry McIlvenny prevented a punch-up that would have inevitably resulted in Bob's sending off. Bob was severely spoken to by referee Power and warned that any further action of a similar nature would see his dismissal.

Bob was furious that he had been made the perpetrator rather than the victim of the incident and, when Moor Green defender, Rooney, tried to dribble his way out of the penalty area, he went in hard with a challenge that caught the defender high up on the shin. The referee blew his whistle for a foul but took no further action, much to the relief of the Bishop Auckland supporters but to the obvious anger of the Moor Green players. Five minutes later it was centre-half Chadwicke's turn to receive the Hardisty treatment when he was sent into the crowd with a strong tackle. Much to the surprise of everyone, spectators and players alike, the referee allowed play to go on, declaring Bob's challenge a fair one.

If Moor Green's plan had been to rattle the Bishop Auckland players, particularly Bob Hardisty, with strong-arm tactics, then it had backfired on them. Now that they had received a taste of their own medicine they caved in and a further goal was added before the referee blew for full-time. Afterwards, Bob Hardisty told Harry McIlvenny that he never thought that an English amateur club would have players that would deliberately kick opponents when the ball was at the other end of the pitch. He had faced the Yugoslavs in the Olympic Games but he reckoned that Moor Green could have taught them a trick or two!

Finchley, from the Athenian League, were Bishop Auckland's next opponents and confidence was high in the Kingsway camp that they could gain another victory at Summers Lane. The Athenian League was not considered as strong as its Isthmian companion, even though it housed the likes of Bromley, Hendon and Barnet as well as Hayes and Tooting and Mitcham. Bishop Auckland supporters could have extra reason for optimism insofar as their team had a forward line that could be selected from such players as Jacky Major, Harry McIlvenny, Fred Palmer, Alan Gilhome, Harry Teasdale, Ken Murray and Bob Hardisty and therefore need fear no-one. Add to that a defence as strong as that held by the likes of John Coxon, Tommy Farrer, Bobby Davison, John Taylor and the season's new signing, Jimmy Nimmins, it could be argued that the 'Bishops' had the best squad of players in the amateur game.

There was a little surprise in store for both teams ten days before the game when it was announced that BBC television would be covering the second half of the match.

Bob had warned his players that Finchley's danger man would be outside-left George Robb, who was on Tottenham Hotspur's books and whom Bob knew well, as they had played together for England. Robb was an accomplished winger and liked to take on defenders but was culpable of overdoing the dribbling. Prior to the game, Bob had a word with captain, Tommy Farrer, and it was agreed that a concerted effort would be made to starve the supply line to the outside-left. In fact, the plan was not needed. Star of the show,

Alan Gilhome, who had been drafted into the team from the reserves, scored Bishop's opening two goals and laid on the third for Palmer. It was only near the end that Finchley scored a consolation goal. After the game it was revealed that Auckland goalkeeper, Storey, had suffered a broken hand.

Joe Gibson was one of the Bishop supporters who attended that match:

> I was working on the railway at the time, at Shildon, and because of the job was entitled to free rail travel. Me and my mates went all over the place following the 'Bishops'. We went down to London to watch Bishop take on Finchley. It was in the early days of television—black and white—and the BBC outside broadcast was covering the second half; not that many people would have had a television I suppose in them days and most of them would have been down south—I think it was the Coronation that made people want one, a few years later. When the game had finished and we came out of the ground, people were coming out of their houses to tell us that they had seen the goals. I said to one of them, 'You may have seen them but our team actually scored them!'

Wycombe Wanderers were to be Bishop Auckland's opponents in the semi-final at Brentford and although the southern club may have felt that they held the advantage, in not having to travel as far, Bishop players and supporters were full of confidence. There was the added spice of once again there being the strong possibility of an all-northern final and a repeat of that of 1939, as Willington were in opposition to Leytonstone in the other semi-final game, at Middlesbrough.

Drama entered only four days before the semi-final when Bob twisted his knee in a training session at Kingsway on the Tuesday evening. It seemed innocuous at the time, as all Bob had done was turn to collect a ball but in the space of a few minutes it was obvious to Bob and the other players present that it may be serious. Bob tried to stand but a needle-like pain seared through his knee. Dr Donald Prescott, the club doctor, was called and he inspected the knee. For twenty minutes a cold compress was applied, Bob being told to keep his leg immobile as the other players carried on with their exercises. Forty minutes had elapsed and by now Dr Prescott felt that he could ask Bob to apply a small amount of pressure to the leg. He asked Bob to stand, holding on to him as a crutch, advising him to take things slowly and just let the blood supply run through at its own rate. The doctor could have saved his breath; Bob had been carrying out training courses for long enough to know not to rush things. If it was ligaments that had been damaged then he would be out of football for a considerable time but if it was only a nerve that had been harmed then it could be a short term injury, perhaps only hours.

For the next three days, Bob continued to receive treatment from Dr Prescott. By Friday, despite the knee showing little sign of outward damage, Bob's ability to play in the next day's semi-final remained in the balance. His absence would be a massive blow to the team and the club did everything possible to get him fit. On the morning of the game, Dr Prescott and members of the committee put Bob's fitness to the test with some demanding exercises. At the end of twenty minutes, Dr Prescott was shaking his head—he was uncertain if Bob could get through the full ninety minutes. The committee formed a huddle. Then, after deep conversation, the huddle broke up and everyone returned to the meeting room of their hotel, whereupon the remaining members of the team were summoned.

The situation as to Bob's fitness and the results of the tests that he had just undertaken were made clear to the players. Dr Prescott sat with the committee members and repeated his assessment. To a man, the players declared that they wanted Bob to play, even if he was not fully one-hundred per cent fit. In their eyes, an eighty per cent fit Bob Hardisty was better than most other players. It was now up to the committee and after another huddle, a few moments later they declared that Bob would be playing. Bob, who had sat stone-faced slumped in a chair, was clearly moved by his team mates' faith in him and tried to thank them. For once in his life, he was tongue-tied. The best way that he could thank them was by not letting them down on the playing field.

Jack Washington had returned to keep goal and yet again Bob was to link up with McIvenny who was proving as good a signing as Bob had predicted. A crowd of over 30,000 saw a hard fought gruelling encounter, as one would expect for a semi-final, on a surface devoid of any grass, except in the four corners. Once again, the match was being televised by the BBC and to make viewing easier the Football Association had given permission for a white ball to be used (oh, the power of television).

Early stages of the game showed Bishop on top with Bob continually prepared to take on the Wycombe defenders from his inside-right role, his injured knee standing up to the early strain. Only the intervention of centre-half Krupa prevented one of his centres being converted. Both sides pressed hard for the advantage but defences remained on top with the light ball proving troublesome for both sets of forwards to control. The opening goal came after half an hour's play when Alan Gilhome was brought down by a Wycombe defender. Ever reliable Bobby Davison scored yet again from the spot with a shot that entered the net via a post. Jacky Major, Alan Gilhome and Bob Hardisty continued to link up well and consistently put the Wycombe defence under pressure but no further goals came in what had been a storming forty-five minutes.

The second half started with Wanderers striving for an equalizer and for a while, the Bishop Auckland forwards had very little service. Bob Hardisty found himself playing in the role of half-back to try to ease the pressure on the defence and as a result the forwards were relying on scraps. Slowly but surely, the Wycombe raids became more stereotyped and gradually the Bishop defenders began to gain the upper hand and start counter-attacks. After ten minutes of sustained Wycombe pressure, Bishop caught the Wycombe defenders out of position. Bob broke up yet another Wycombe attack and passed the ball to Jacky Major. An immediate return ball back to Bob and Jacky was speeding down the wing for a quick return. The pass from Bob was precise and with an equally inch perfect pass, the outside-right supplied Riley, who ran on to slam the ball past Lodge, with an unstoppable left foot shot.

Birdseye, playing at outside-left for the southern team, created a danger in the Bishop defence but it was again Lodge who had to save his team from going three down. Wycombe did, however, reduce the deficit when left-half Way was allowed to join in an attack and he calmly stroked the ball past Washington. A minute later and Washington pulled off a fine save with a dive to his right to foil inside-left Mikrut. It was end to end stuff now with both teams fighting for every ball. Lodge pulled off two saves from McIlvenny and Riley, whilst at the other end, Washington was forced to dive at the feet of Mikrut, just as the Wanderers player was about to shoot. The Bishop Auckland goalkeeper safely collected the ball and cleared it upfield where Bob Hardisty collected it and ran towards the goal. He passed two defenders and supplied the ball inside for outside-left Riley to send in a blistering drive that Lodge saved brilliantly. That was the last chance of the game; Bishop Auckland had made it to Wembley and Bob's knee had withstood the test, much to the relief of everyone, especially Dr Prescott.

Meanwhile, three hundred miles to the north, Willington were inflicting a 2–1 defeat over Leytonstone. The north-east of England, with County Durham in particular, had its wish. In five weeks time the FA Amateur Cup Final would be played out between two Northern League clubs, the same two clubs that had fought out the last pre-war final. This time, the venue would not be a relatively local Roker Park but a more distant and grander arena—Wembley Stadium awaited.

Ironically, the two clubs were destined to meet in another cup-tie before the Wembley showdown. Willington's Hall Lane ground was where the semi-final of the Durham Benevolent Bowl would be played. Bob Hardisty was injured for this game which ended goalless.

All of the north of England was abuzz with the forthcoming final. Interest lay not just in the fact that perhaps this would be the year that Bob Hardisty earned his winners' medal but there were deep concerns, especially from those in power in the south of England, that perhaps holding the Final at Wembley might prove to be a disaster, given the distance that supporters of both clubs would have to travel. It was even mooted that the game should be transferred from Wembley Stadium to Roker Park, Sunderland, such was the concern that a prestigious FA Final may only attract a small crowd. Such narrow-mindedness was given short shrift by supporters and players alike of the two clubs. Bob Hardisty came out and declared that every club that had entered the competition had done so with the hope of reaching Wembley. Now that two clubs from the far north-east corner had attained that goal, he argued that the opportunity of playing at the revered stadium should not be denied to those players that had made it through. Having already experienced the thrill of playing football at Wembley, Bob had described to attentive reporters what a proud feeling it was to walk out of that stadium's dark tunnel into the bright sunlight and witness a deafening crowd. 'Why should that moment be denied to anyone because of a matter of geography?' he enquired. The sentiment was echoed by more than one northern newspaper correspondent—supported by the national newspapers—and the accusation went up once more of southern bias being rampant in the powers of football. Dare the Football Association decide that Wembley finals would only host southern clubs? The debate went on and, no doubt, helped sell a few more newspapers as more passion was thrown into the argument by eager correspondents, but the matter subsided as the big day drew nearer and was gradually laid to rest.

Bob did his best to get Betty to attend the Final but she was adamant that football was not for her. She had no wish to spoil Bob's big day by not being in attendance but she argued that she did not want to spend all the time travelling and in the company of people whom she did not know. Bob tried to change her mind, suggesting that the other players and their wives and girlfriends were a great bunch and good social company but she would not be moved. Football was not for Betty—she would be quite happy entertaining some of her golf club friends at home or content to have a round of golf and a social drink afterwards, thank you very much, whilst her husband kicked a ball around a field!

Only five miles separates the small town of Willington from its larger neighbour, Bishop Auckland, so it was inevitable that players and supporters alike took part in a lot of friendly banter once the teams had made it through to the final. In pubs, clubs, cafes, shops, buses, trains or at the workplace, the constant subject of conversation was the impending final. As a schoolmaster, Bob was daily questioned and ribbed by his erstwhile students and would tell them that he hoped that he would soon be able to show them a winners' medal—then he would tell them to get on with their studies.

Wherever one looked, whether in Willington or Bishop Auckland, walls and windows were decorated with bunting, ribbons and banners in the club colours. Blue and white bedecked every property from The Burn Hotel the whole length of Willington's main high street down as far as the two public houses each named, unimaginatively, The Black Horse, in Low Willington. Every cake in the confectionery shop seemed to be topped with blue and white icing. It was as if every inhabitant of the town wanted to be associated with the club and its success. Bishop may have the star players but Willington supporters knew that their lads would not let them down. What is more, the players were confident that they had devised a plan that would find out their more famous neighbours on the big day.

It was the same in Bishop Auckland. Shops and offices were draped with ribbons and banners wishing its football club players every good wish and demanding that the FA Amateur Cup be returned to the town. Jack and Mary Hardisty played their part and dressed their shop window appropriately, with blue irises and forget-me-nots.

The days leading up to the final saw supporters of both camps setting out for Wembley, not all of whom had had the foresight to book a room in advance at any of the hotels and guest houses that filled north and central London. They would make do as best they could. At first it was just a trickle but the exodus slowly gathered momentum and by Friday every bus, car and train seemed to have only one destination in mind—Wembley. The private bus companies were on to a winner right from the start with whole fleets being used to cater for the demand and the LNER laid on hundreds more carriages for their special trains that had been commandeered for the big day. Not many people could afford a car in those days but those fortunate to have one were carrying friends and family down the A1, so the result was that on that April Saturday, the streets were almost completely devoid of traffic around that part of County Durham.

Bob and his fellow players, together with the Bishop Auckland officials, travelled by train from Bishop Auckland to Darlington from where they caught the connection that would take them to King's Cross station on the Friday evening. As Bob gazed out of the carriage window, taking in the scenery, he wished that Betty had been going with him but she was not for changing her mind. The train would take the party to King's Cross from where they would travel by taxi to the Great Eastern Hotel in central London.

Bob took his place in the middle of the team line-up leaving the dressing room. Team captain, Tommy Farrer, was at the head.

'Not much longer now, Bob, till we get our hands on that pot,' said Alan Gilhome in his strong Northumbrian accent, trying to ease the tension. Bob smiled in return at the man immediately in front of him. Behind him, Harry McIlvenny started to jump up and down on the spot, trying to warm his muscles but equally just as much to settle his nervousness. The Willington eleven exited from their dressing room led by their captain, Eddie Taylor, and as the two teams lined up side by side in the tunnel under the east terracing, the order to take the field was given. As the players entered the arena in glorious sunshine more than ninety-thousand throats exploded in unison.

Officials of the Football Association were presented to the players as they lined up in front of the royal box and, when Sir Stanley Rous shook hands with Bob, there was a slight hint of extra encouragement to his old friend.

The teams were:

Bishop Auckland (Red shirts, White shorts)
Washington—Coxon, Farrer—John Taylor, Davison,
Nimmins—Major, Hardisty, McIlvenny, Gilhome, Palmer

Willington (White shirts, Navy blue shorts)
Snowdon—Craggs, Howe—Lewthwaite, Yeardley, Dodd—Robinson,
Ernie Taylor, Larmouth, Armstrong, Rutherford

Referee: A Murdoch of Sheffield

What transpired in the course of the following ninety minutes of football was one of amateur soccer's greatest upsets, played in a spirit of sportsmanship almost unequalled in a game of such importance and in a contest that produced a quality of football barely imaginable in the amateur ranks. It was Bishop Auckland's thirteenth final and, in this case, thirteen was definitely an unlucky number for them. Bishop Auckland were the odds-on favourites to lift the trophy with regular England players in the team including Hardisty, McIlvenny and Farrer; Willington on the other hand had no-one of such stature, although a number of their players had represented their county in the amateur championship.

From the kick-off, Willington played with a style and fluency that decried their standing as the underdogs. Bishop were outplayed and outthought in every department for half an hour, during which time Willington had scored three good goals. Bishop tried to play the short passing game but the eager Willington half-back line broke up every move. They used a different approach, getting the ball wide out to wingers Joe Robinson and Stan Rutherford, who had played for Bishop Auckland in the 1947 semi-final against Wimbledon, with repeated regularity and then centring the ball to put Bishop's defence under pressure and in particular, their goalkeeper, Jack Washington who at only five feet six inches was one of the smallest goal minders in the league, although he was a brilliant shot stopper. The use of Wembley's wide spaces was the plan that Willington had hatched on paper and in their training at Hall Lane and now they were putting that plan into action. In addition, the plan depended upon the ability of wingers Rutherford and Armstrong to place as much pressure as possible on the Bishop half-back line of Taylor, Davison and Nimmins, all of whom were strong in the tackle but considered vulnerable when faced with true pace.

Both teams were able to create chances in the first ten minutes but the tall, thin Jackie Snowdon in the Willington goal smothered efforts from Major and Hardisty whilst at the other end, Tommy Farrer blocked an Armstrong effort.

Willington deservedly took the lead after twelve minutes with a goal from Eddie Taylor. Armstrong's shot went wide but the ball was retrieved by Joe Robinson who delivered an accurate cross from the right to present his captain with a scoring chance. Taylor's header from the six-yard line right in front of the goal easily beat Washington as the goalkeeper dived in vain to his left.

To their credit, Bishop were not disheartened and manned two counter attacks before Willington went further ahead, this time through Stan Rutherford whose left-foot thunderbolt into the roof of the net gave Washington no chance.

Ten minutes later, the 'Bishops' went further behind when centre-forward Bill Larmouth crashed the ball through a crowded penalty area after good work once again from Stan Rutherford. Bishop Auckland supporters could not believe what they were seeing—neither could those of Willington. Nor could the Bishop Auckland players who tried to encourage each other with every pass. They were not used to taking such a beating from any of their northern rivals.

Five minutes before half-time a ray of hope presented itself to Bishop when Bob Hardisty collected an errant pass from Lewthwaite but his shot at goal was punched clear by the diving Snowdon who was having a fine match and stopping anything fired at him.

The half-time team talk by Tommy Farrer to his shocked troops would have been interesting. Tommy remembers the disenchantment within the Bishop Auckland dressing room that day:

> We could not believe it. We knew we were a good team and were used to beating any opposition put in front of us. All I could do was tell the players to try harder. We had given the ball away a couple of times—me included—that had led to goals but other than that we had not played badly. Bill Larmouth's goal was just one of those that nobody would have stopped. I told the lads that if we got an early goal in the second half then we would be in with a chance and I believed that. What we could not afford was to let in another goal.

Farrer's team talk had some effect and the Bishop Auckland forwards applied more pressure on the Willington defence in the early stages of the second half. Bob had another effort at goal that skimmed the crossbar and a third effort just went wide of Snowdon's goal. The goalkeeper was repeatedly in action and brought off a string of further saves from Major, McIlvenny and Bob Hardisty again. Snowdon was having one of those games that every goalkeeper must dream of. Here he was facing some of the best players in amateur football and they were unable to get the ball past him. He was saving everything that the Bishop forward line could offer. Just twelve moths ago he had been playing in front of thirty people in a game at Howden-le-Wear and being barracked and now here he was in front of ninety-thousand, having a 'blinder'.

Armstrong broke away in another flowing Willington movement to score a fourth goal and when Palmer's header rebounded from the crossbar, the Auckland players knew that they would not be getting anything from this match.

When the referee blew his whistle for full time, the first person Bob shook hands with was Jackie Snowdon. Bob congratulated him on putting up such a fine display. Jackie recalls that occasion:

We went down by Pullman Coach from Darlington station on the Friday afternoon. We stayed at the Imperial Hotel. Wives, girlfriends, mothers and fathers went down on the ordinary supporters' trains and they stayed in different hotels but after the match they all came round to see us. When we arrived at King's Cross a waiting bus took us straight to the stadium for a pre-match look. It was just vast and I thought 'Blimey!'

I remember everything about the match but what struck me was the quietness—we walked out from the tunnel and it was just one grey mass. It was impossible for me to pick out anyone because we were so far away from the crowd and I swear I did not hear a thing. We were used to playing in front of much smaller crowds, of course. We would get five or six thousand at Willington but this was 88,000 at Wembley. With the much smaller crowds you could hear every spectator's comments, good or bad, throughout a game. I remember one incident when I played for Wolsingham at Howden-le-Wear in front of about eighty people. Standing in my goal area, I was about to collect a high ball when I heard a woman say, 'I bet that long bugger misses it.' You hear things like that but you don't let them bother you. You just get on with it.

In the Cup Final I managed to make a few saves, one from Bob Hardisty, and when the referee blew for full time I went over to shake his hand. I said to him 'Bob, you'll play worse than that in a Cup Final and win' and I was right. He was a superb player: the best; a master.

We didn't experience the thrill of victory until afterwards, when we were sat down in the dressing room. Then it dawned on us on what we had achieved. All of us were delighted, of course, but we were just, well, flabbergasted. We were the underdogs, you see. They had seven internationals in their side. Before the game some people had enquired, 'What are you bothering going all the way to Wembley for?' They just expected us to get beat.

In the evening we went out to Finnegan's Bar, which is where the Bishop Auckland players went to whenever they had a game in London. They were there then and Bob and I had a good natter. We knew each other, of course, not only through football but also through our jobs—I was with the County Planning Department. After the celebrations we all went along to King's Cross station to see the trains off, packed with supporters of both clubs. We travelled back the next day and received a tremendous reception being feted up and down the town.

A few days later I broke my collarbone playing in our next game. As a result I had to give up my international call-up and Bennett, the Southall goalkeeper, took my place.

Dave Marshall had joined Bishop Auckland as a full-back whilst studying to become a teacher at Bob Hardisty's old college, Bede. He was a great friend of Bob and recalls the feeling of awe and disappointment at Bishop Auckland's defeat:

> It was such a surprise. Everyone wanted Bob to get a winners' medal. He was approaching thirty and it was generally believed that he may not have many more chances after this. He was well liked in the town and was a local hero. Willington deserved their success but Bishop had only themselves to blame. They expected to win with a degree of confidence bordering on arrogance. Do you know that the committee had already made the timetable and arrangements for the winning celebrations two weeks before the final? It was all kept secret so as not to offend anyone but I think word got out and that put an extra step into Willington. The town was in shock for days whilst just up the road at Willington they didn't stop partying for weeks.

It is a sorry reflection upon the state of England's Football Association selection procedures at that time prior to the Final that not one of the twenty-two players that had graced Wembley's hallowed turf with a superb display of football and sportsmanship, had been called upon to represent their country during that season, such was the bias within the ranks of the FA favouring the southern clubs. Perhaps not a surprise when one realizes that seven of the eight members who formed the selection committee were southern based. Not even Bob Hardisty, who was not without a few friends in the halls of the Football Association, had been selected, nor had Tommy Farrer, the best left-back in amateur football. The situation was remedied immediately after the Amateur Cup Final when Willington's Jackie Snowdon, Stewart Howe, Eddie Taylor and Stan Rutherford, along with Bishop Auckland's John Taylor, were selected for an FA XI that were due to tour Scandinavia. Fate, however, played its ugly hand when Snowdon and Taylor had to withdraw.

It was a sad and disappointed Bishop Auckland troupe that returned home to a very subdued welcome. There was no band, no procession and there was very little ribbon left on the town's shop windows. The players made their way home either by car or taxi that the club had provided. Bob did not have so far as many to travel, his home in Princes Street being only a few minutes from the football ground.

Betty greeted him with a loving smile and commiserated with Bob on his disappointment. Bob, accepted her loving words and as he kissed her, murmured, 'Well, Betty, there's always next year.' He placed his hand in his jacket pocket and pulled out a medal, the one that he had received in the royal box from Sir Stanley Rous, only a few hours ago. 'There. I don't want too many of these.'

Bob's football season was not over yet and just over a week later he played in the game at Kingsway that saw the 'Bishops' defeat Willington by a lone McIlvenny goal, in the semi-final of the Durham Benevolent Bowl. Jackie Snowdon was missing from the Willington goal, having suffered a broken collarbone in Willington's previous game, only five days after his heroics at Wembley. Fate can play a very cruel hand as he had been selected for the recently announced England squad. Whilst sympathies went out to Snowdon from all football supporters the question on the lips of those following the 'Two Blues' was a simple one about their team: 'Why, oh why, couldn't they have produced that result in the game that really mattered?'

That was not the last time that the players of these two fine teams met during a cup tie as the final of the Durham Benevolent Bowl was held at Spennymoor United's ground where Bishop's opponents were Ushaw Moor, whom they defeated 3–1 to lift the trophy. However, the main trophy on display that afternoon was the Amateur Cup, which was paraded around the ground by the Willington players themselves, before the game. Bob and the rest of the Bishop Auckland players could only stand and applaud their conquerors once more.

Bob was on the Amateur Cup trail again the following season but before that campaign began he played a part in the FA Cup First Round tie against York City. Bishop Auckland had won the right to stage a home tie against the Third Division (North) side by beating Horden Colliery Welfare 1–0 in a Fourth Qualifying Round match. A crowd of more than 10,000 watched the Northern League leaders take on the Football League outfit.

Bob was selected to play at right half-back, Bishop Auckland having signed Scottish international Willie Anderson at the beginning of the season to play at inside-right. His partnership with Bobby Davison (centre-half) and Jimmy Nimmins (left-half) produced a formidable midfield line. York had a reputation as a no-nonsense team but were not having the best of seasons, currently labouring in the lower half of their division.

The York defence was soon put under pressure when Bob collected a pass from full-back Dave Marshall and took on two defenders before passing a through ball for Anderson to shoot just wide. Three minutes later he again won the ball in a tackle with York forward Cooper and pushed a pass forward for McIvenny to run onto but his shot was saved by Ashley. It was all Bishop with their half-back line picking up every loose ball in the midfield area. The York defenders were under constant pressure and after fifteen minutes were forced to concede a penalty that Bobby Davison easily converted. The pressure was maintained on the York goal but it was the away side that scored the second goal of the game when Patrick was allowed too much room to slot a well worked goal past White. Undeterred, Auckland continued with their fluent passing game with Bob and Jimmy Nimmins combining with the inside-forwards to create chances that were not taken. It was against the run of play that York went ahead after Linaker laid on an opportunity which Brenen gratefully accepted, sending an unstoppable header past goalkeeper White.

Roared on by a partisan crowd, Bishop continued to attack while the Football League side placed their dependence on breakaways. It was outside-left, Benny Edwards, who scored a deserved equalizer eight minutes from time but the York defence held out for a rather fortunate draw, much to the disappointment of the home supporters.

Four days later the replay took place on a quagmire of a pitch at York's Bootham Crescent ground in front of 6,875 rain-soaked spectators. Torrential rain leading up to the game had reduced the centre of the pitch to a mud bath and it was touch and go whether or not the referee would allow the match to start. Pools of water lay on the pitch as kick-off time approached, despite the efforts of workmen pumping water off the ground. The conditions meant that Bishop Auckland's brand of flowing football, that relied upon short, sharp passing movements, would be heavily compromised and as it turned out, York were better able to take advantage of the playing surface. Right from the outset, York played the long passing game, getting the ball out to wingers, Linaker and Patrick, for them to run on to the long passes. Bishop on the other hand were unable to develop moves with their wingers, Major and Edwards, who were continually facing their own defenders to receive the ball.

York City's plan to use the long ball and to starve Bob Hardisty and Jimmy Nimmins of possession began to bear fruit. The Auckland defence was always under pressure with Bobby Davison in particular finding it hard to contain centre-forward, Alf Patrick, brother of York's outside-left. Bob Hardisty was not having too fine a time of it either. On the previous Saturday he had been able to find the time to construct moves and create chances but on this much more difficult surface he was having to defend more and link-ups with his inside-forwards were in short supply.

Under sustained pressure, the Bishop Auckland defence held out until the fifty-second minute when Patrick broke the deadlock. He again got the better of Davison to double the lead and it was only two minutes from time that McIlvenny reduced the deficit to 2–1. York had deservedly won a tense encounter. As for Bob Hardisty and Bishop Auckland, well, at least they could concentrate on the Amateur Cup now.

It was during this period of his football career that Bob achieved one of his ambitions. As previously stated, he had always been keen on keeping fit and playing football, a combination that always brought him the greatest satisfaction. During his time in the army, as well as guesting for Football league and Scottish League teams, there had been numerous inter-battalion and inter-service matches. He had participated in a great number of these and had made a lot of friends, including professional footballers such as Matt Busby, Joe Mercer and Tommy Lawton but also fellow amateurs, one of whom was Walter Winterbottom. Born in Oldham, Winterbottom played amateur football before being noticed by Manchester United for whom he signed in 1936, when he was twenty-three years old. He only played twenty-six games before a spinal injury ended his career. Walter had served in the RAF, carrying out a similar role to that of Bob and, indeed, had played against Bob in games between the Army and RAF. The pair had struck up an instant friendship that would last the rest of their lives. After the war, in 1946, Walter was appointed National Director of Coaching by the Football Association, and a year later he became England manager, the arrangement being that the FA would select the squad from which Winterbottom would chose the eleven who would actually play. It was natural, therefore, that Bob and Walter would renew their relationship once Bob was selected for the international squad.

Walter had visited the Great Britain training camp when Matt Busby had been putting the team through their paces for the 1948 Olympic Games. It was over a cup of tea that Walter suggested to Bob that he should become a fully qualified FA Football coach. Walter stressed that there would be no requirement for Bob to give up the playing side and that it was an opportunity for Bob to pass on his skills to others. The overall strategy of the FA was to achieve a general improvement in the standard of football players and coaches in England. Bob was impressed with Walter's enthusiasm and took up the challenge. The course was a combination of football skills and knowledge which Bob was able to complete over a period of a few weeks. Having attained the standard that the qualification required he became a certificated FA Coach, one of only six in the country at that time, and took up every opportunity to coach others. Coincidentally, Bob did not have far to travel to conduct these courses as they were held at his former place of education, Bede College, where one of his first pupils to attend the coaching course was his old playing partner, Ken Twigg.

January brought the customary start of the FA Amateur Cup trail and in Round One Bishop did not have to travel far, being drawn against fellow Northern Leaguers, Evenwood Town. The teams had met a fortnight before when Bishop had won 2–0 but the home team had been handicapped as right-half Jordan had been forced to leave the field after twenty minutes, suffering from concussion, and did not return.

The Evenwood players could have been excused for having that *déjà vu* feeling as Bishop again won 2–0, McIlvenny scoring an opportunist goal and Bobby Davison slotting one home from the penalty spot. Bob had a steady game but had time to study the commanding performance given by Evenwood's centre-half that day. He held his midfield together and marshalled his defence to cope with Bishop's constant attacks as well as any other team had so far managed that year. He made a sound impression on Bob and the rest of the Bishop players, even McIlvenny, who considered himself fortunate to have got his name on the score sheet. The young centre-half in question was Corbett Cresswell, who would become a great friend and playing colleague of Bob Hardisty within the next two years.

Rounds Two and Three saw Bishop Auckland playing in front of their home supporters. Shildon provided the opposition in the first of these games, losing 3–1 and in the second, Whitby Town suffered a 7–2 drubbing— Davison getting one of the goals from the penalty spot.

Walton and Hersham of the Athenian League provided a third home game for the 'Bishops' in Round Four and in front of 12,116 spectators earned themselves a surprising 2–2 draw. Almost inevitably, Bobby Davison scored one of Bishop Auckland's goals from the penalty spot—did he ever miss one?—whilst inside-left Hogg scored the other. Seven days later, however, Bishop returned to their true form and won comfortably 4–1.

Once more, Bob Hardisty was looking forward to playing in a prestigious semi-final. The game was to be played at Elland Road where he had turned out for Middlesbrough eight years earlier, when making a Football League debut as guest player for the Teesside club. This time the opposition would be Athenian League members and current cup holders, Bromley.

More than 20,000 spectators saw an evenly matched game with neither side playing to anything like their full potential. In the first ten minutes, Bob had tried to make four passes to his forwards but two had been wasted and the other two were intercepted. The Bromley defenders seemed to anticipate everything that was coming their way, whilst the forward line was putting the Bishop defenders under tremendous pressure. Bobby Davison broke up an attack down the middle with a well timed tackle on centre-forward, George Brown, whilst Bob made three clearances to stem the tide. Defensively, he was showing his usual skill and composure but he was unable to set up any meaningful attacking moves. It was no surprise when Bromley took the lead after twenty-three minutes when Brown beat Davison to a cross and thumped the ball past White. Bishop returned with an attack of their own and when the ball was cleared by full-back Len Wager, Hardisty collected it on the edge of the centre circle and returned the ball with venom. Tommy Fuller completely miskicked his attempted clearance and when the ball fell invitingly to Anderson, the Scotsman coolly slotted home the equalizer.

Remarkably, a minute later, Bishop were handed a gift when experienced centre-half Charlie Fuller inexplicably handled the ball in the penalty area. Bobby Davison stepped up and, of course, he scored. Auckland were all over Bromley after that and Bob was able to play a more attacking game, almost becoming a sixth forward. The pendulum had not stopped swinging, however, and the fourth goal of the game went to Bromley when Brown once again escaped the attentions of Davison and headed home the equalizer.

There were worried looks on the faces of the Bishop Auckland supporters now as Bromley threw everything at the northerners' rearguard but Tommy Farrer marshalled his defence well and it was Bishop that scored the decisive goal, seven minutes from time, with a winner by the scoring machine from Yorkshire, Harry McIlvenny. Positioned on the edge of the Bromley penalty area in the inside-left slot, Harry collected a through ball and in one balletic moment, flicked the ball up with his left foot and spun round to fire an unstoppable right foot drive into the far top corner of the Bromley goal. Bishop supporters were ecstatic, as were the players. In an era before footballers celebrated goals with wild antics and kissing, Bob ran towards Harry and picked him up with a hug. Other players joined in and for a moment McIlvenny was smothered by his colleagues. Composure returned and the teams lined up for the remaining six minutes of play, which saw the 'Two Blues' holding on to their precarious lead. Bishop Auckland were in their fourteenth Amateur Cup Final and, for the second year running, would be making an appearance at Wembley. Their opponents would be the relatively unknown Pegasus.

A few days after the defeat of Bromley, a surprising but very welcome letter was delivered to the Hardisty household. It was from the Football Association and informed Bob that he had been selected to play for England in the forthcoming international against Scotland at Hampden Park, Glasgow. Betty was pleased for Bob but enquired of him why they should chose him now after omitting him from the team for the past two years. Bob simply had no answer. He could not believe it. Here he was at thirty years of age and had been selected for the England squad. He noticed that also included in the list of players was his own club team mate and captain, Tommy Farrer, as well as Bromley centre-half, Charlie Fuller but there was a more interesting choice at outside-right where Potts of Pegasus had been chosen. It would be interesting to see him play, thought Bob.

The selectors had done right in selecting Bob. True, he was thirty years of age but his was a football brain and he had skill and composure in abundance. The form that he had shown on the football field had been as good as ever and northern supporters needed no convincing that he was worthy of the selection. His inclusion did, however, resurrect the perennial argument of north versus south when it came to the selection of international players. Northern clubs had always thought that the southern clubs received favouritism whenever an international squad was due to be selected. The majority of selectors (seven) were southern based with the north having a sole representative—and he was expected to cover the whole area north of Birmingham to the Scottish border!

More than one newspaper correspondent had claimed that for a northern-based player to be recognized by the selectors, it was essential that they had either already played for a southern club (e.g. Tommy Farrer who had previously played for Barnet), had played for a Football League club or were on their books (e.g. Eric Lee of Chester City) or they played for a club that had at least reached the semi-final stage of the FA Amateur Cup. The last point had been driven home the previous season when neither Willington nor Bishop Auckland had any of their players selected to play for England until after the Final itself had taken place. Arthur Appleton, in his best-selling book about football in the north-east of England, *Hotbed of Soccer*, reiterates this view when he repeats that clubs from that area must reach at least the semi-final for its players to be noticed by the selectors and that an outstanding player in a club that does not get that far has no chance of gaining a cap.

One could now point to the return of Bob Hardisty to the international scene to re-enforce this view but not for the last time would such sentiments be expressed by northern based correspondents, club officials and supporters alike.

On Friday 6th April, Bob and Tommy Farrer travelled by train to Glasgow station from where they caught a taxi that took them to where the rest of the England party were staying, the Central Hotel. The other members of the squad were already there, most of them having travelled the almost nine-hour journey by train from Euston. Walter Winterbottom welcomed the pair with a strong handshake and introduced them to the other squad members. Jack Neale of Walton and Hersham, who had played for Great Britain during the Olympic Games, was the only member that Bob had actually played alongside although he knew the Bromley lads, Charlie Fuller and John Gregory, from their recent semi-final encounter.

Bob and Tommy had discussed on the train the inclusion of a Pegasus player in the squad and had agreed that they should make a concerted effort to get to know him—to be sociable but also try and find out where their Cup Final opponents may have a weakness. They were a bit taken aback, however, when not one but two Pegasus players introduced themselves. Jimmy Potts was accompanied by Ben Brown who had been drafted into the squad when Jarvis, the Leytonstone goalkeeper, had been obliged to withdraw due to injury. Any plans of outnumbering Jimmy Potts went clean out of the window, it was now two versus two and each pair knew exactly what the other was trying to achieve. At one point, Tommy and Ben were conversing together whilst Jimmy and Bob swapped football stories. As the evening progressed, and numerous cups of tea and half-pints had been quaffed, amid tactical plans directed by Walter and conversational chit-chat petered out, the players made their way to their rooms. When Bob reached the door of his room he heard Tommy behind him.

'Well, three hours of gassing away and we didn't tell them anything that they would not have known already,' Tommy whispered satisfactorily to Bob.

'I agree,' said Bob, 'but do you know what we learnt?'

'No, what's that, Bob?'

'Absolutely fuck all. Cagey bastards.'

The following day, after a light breakfast, the players relaxed by reading the Saturday newspapers or played a few games of table tennis. Bob scanned the runners and riders and picked out four horses for a yankee bet (selections that are combined in six doubles, four trebles and an accumulator totalling eleven bets) that were guaranteed to win and produce a great payout, which he telephoned through to Bishop 163. His father took the call and wished him well for the game, promising to place the bet. Luncheon was at twelve-thirty and after a further relaxation period the bus collected the officials and players for the short journey to Scotland's major football theatre, Hampden Park.

With its dark terracing and vast open spaces, 12,000 spectators were lost inside Hampden Park's giant amphitheatre that could house well over 130,000. The rain came slanting down as the crowd greeted the teams making their way onto the Scottish turf.

Bob Hardisty and Tommy Farrer were not the only Bishop Auckland players on view as Tommy Stewart and Willie Anderson had been selected for Scotland. Jim Lewis opened the scoring for England after only six minutes but Grierson found an equalizer before half-time. Bob played a competent game showing great skill on the slippery surface, keeping his balance when others were sliding about. He was able to take a hand in Lewis's second goal, linking up well with Stroud who created a perfect cross and later in the game helped the Walthamstow Avenue player complete his hat-trick. Scotland scored a second goal through Bruce but the final score saw the 'Sassenachs' victorious with a 3–2 score-line.

Of the two Pegasus players, Brown had shown a command of his goalmouth area and pulled off a couple of fine saves. Potts had proved a thorn in the side of Scotland's full-backs and had shown a willingness to take on defenders with speed and dribbling skills. He had come in for some strong tackles but had never shirked the issue. Bob and Tommy made mental notes as no doubt did Tommy Stewart and Willie Anderson. The next time the two Bishop Auckland players would meet the 'Cagey Bastards' would be in a fortnight's time in the Amateur Cup Final. As for those horses—all four lost.

Pegasus Football Club was a phenomenon. Less than three years old, it had been formed—perhaps created is a more apposite description— by Dr H W Thompson F.R.S. Fellow and Tutor of St John's College, Oxford, and some of his colleagues to help stem the flow of schools towards adopting rugby football as their main sport as opposed to continuing with association football. The idyll was that the club would play honest, attractive football with full appreciation of its 'Laws of the Game' and in doing so would play at all times in a sportsmanlike manner—very much like Corinthians had played some eighty years before. Membership of Pegasus Football Club was restricted to players who had played for either Oxford University Centaurs or Cambridge University Falcons. In his wonderful book *Corinthians and Cricketers*, Edward Grayson tells us that the name for the club was the brainchild of Dr Thompson's wife, Grace, who had studied classics and suggested that the new club be called Pegasus, after the winged horse of mythology as it would be an amalgam of the Centaur (the horse with a man's head) and the Falcon (a flying bird). Dr Thompson and his fellow members were suitably impressed and the name was immediately adopted. The newly formed football club would play their games at Oxford University's athletic track at Iffley Road, where Roger Bannister in 1954 would break the four-minute barrier for running the mile.

Although the team players were strictly amateur they did allow themselves to receive coaching from professionals, to improve skills and tactics. Don Welsh of Charlton, and Leslie Compton of Arsenal, were pioneer coaches to the club whilst Bill Nicholson, right half-back of Tottenham Hotspur, was a frequent visitor to the Oxford members whilst his club coach, Vic Buckingham, took on the responsibility of coaching those based at Cambridge. Tottenham Hotspur manager, Arthur Rowe, was approached even though he had a full-time post with the Second Division club striving for promotion; he nevertheless took up some coaching sessions with the amateurs.[†] A bond developed between the

---

[†]   Tottenham Hotspur landed the Second Division Championship in season 1948–49 and twelve months later were crowned First Division Champions, pipping Manchester United for the title.

clubs and not long after, when Vic Buckingham had taken over from Rowe, he coached the Pegasus players at the Football League club's Cheshunt training ground. Buckingham showed them how to adopt the way that 'Spurs' played with short, sharp passing movements on the ground and players moving into space—much similar to the style that Bishop Auckland played.

Within three years of its creation, Pegasus had captured the imagination of the football public, both amateur and professional. The club's very first match had been against an Arsenal Reserves team on 8th December 1948 which they had won 1–0. Since then, their players had earned international recognition having been selected for England and they had entered the FA Amateur Cup, despite not playing in any organized league and relying solely on friendly matches. Surprisingly, they had reached the Fourth Round of that 1948–49 competition. The following season they had been eliminated in Round Two, away from home, by one of the south's best teams, Walthamstow Avenue, going down 3–1. This season, they had fought their way to the Final without playing a home game after winning away games at Gosport Borough Athletic (Round One 3–4), Slough Town (Round Two 1–3), Brentwood and Warley (Round Three 2–3), Oxford City (Round Four 0–3), Hendon (Semi-Final at Highbury, Arsenal 1–1 and then the replay at Selhurst Park, Crystal Palace 3–2).

The players of Pegasus did hold an advantage over a lot of clubs insofar as they were allowed to delay their entry into the Amateur Cup competition until the Fourth Qualifying Round, the FA upholding a request from the club to be exempted due to their players otherwise having to take time off from their studies and exams. The Football Association allowed the request, turning two completely blind eyes to the players of those clubs that had to lose work to turn out for their clubs, when forced to play in earlier qualifying games. Notwithstanding such favouritism it has to be conceded that the playing principles and results of the Pegasus Football Club were good for the game and that they had earned their place in the Final against the far more experienced Bishop Auckland, with a brand of football that was pleasing to the eye and had newspaper correspondents drooling—even though it could be argued that they had shown more than a nod away from total amateurism by allowing themselves to be coached by professionals. Needless to say, the 1951 FA Amateur Cup Final was eagerly anticipated.

Against this backcloth, the Bishop Auckland players got on with the task of training for the forthcoming encounter. Neutral sentiments were with the

Pegasus camp but the Durham side were confident that this time, having already played in front of a 90,000 crowd, they would be able to lift the trophy once again for the first time in twelve years. This time, an even larger crowd was guaranteed—only a few standing tickets remained two weeks before the day's event—such had been the demand from an excited public.

With the Final barely a week away, Bob Hardisty would have felt embarrassed had he been aware that Pegasus's plan for victory was centred around him, or rather his containment. Just as Willington had hatched a successful plan twelve months before, based on the speed of wingers, Robinson and Rutherford, this time Pegasus devised a plan that they hoped would be equally effective. Buckingham's plan was that whenever Bob Hardisty had the ball and was attacking the Pegasus defence, Donald Carr would not fall back to assist the defence but would remain upfield. This would result in Bob Hardisty having more room to attack but such was the confidence within the defensive ranks of Pegasus that Buckingham bargained that there would be times when his defenders would be able to retrieve the ball with quick tackling. Having won the ball, a telling pass into the gap created by Hardisty's leaving, would result in greater freedom for Carr and his co-forwards. Buckingham was convinced that it was worth the risk taking on the attacking role of Hardisty.

Vic Buckingham arranged that Pegasus should have a full work out and organized a match between the University side and his Spurs side that consisted mainly of the full first eleven that had won the Second Division Championship, at the League club's nursery ground in Cheshunt. The game took place on the Wednesday, just three days before the Cup Final, with the main aim being to practice the plan that would result in Bob Hardisty being caught out of position in the Final itself, ultimately bringing about the downfall of Bishop Auckland. Pegasus lost this practice match 3–1 but the result was immaterial—what really mattered was that each and every one of the players knew exactly how they had to play and what they had to achieve.

Most of the experts agreed that a good game of football looked in prospect, with the majority deciding that Bishop Auckland were favourites to win. They had the experience and had two current England internationals in Farrer and Hardisty and two Scottish internationals in Anderson and McIlvenny. They were well accustomed to their style of play and were rarely flustered even when going a goal in arrears. Pegasus, on the other hand, were the newcomers and had only limited experience, even though in such a short space of time they too had four internationals in their squad, namely Brown, Cowan, Tanner and Potts. It was contended that their biggest handicap was that they played their football without the competitiveness that is only generated within a league system. Their style of play would be a joy to behold but the mighty 'Bishops' would have too much in their armoury to combat them. Such were the views of the respected men of the press.

At four minutes past nine on a sunny Friday morning the train pulled out of Bishop Auckland for the short journey to Darlington. Bob sat next to his buddy, Tommy Farrer, and discussed the prospects of the forthcoming match with Pegasus. The club officials and their wives sat together in one group whilst the players and their wives—Betty was absent again—sat likewise. Twelve months ago they had made a similar journey full of expectation but had fallen badly at the final hurdle. This time they were slight favourites once more but with public sentiment once again on the side of the underdog, the university students of Pegasus. After a short wait on Darlington station, the Pullman coach drew in and took the party to King's Cross, whereupon the club officials and players were transported to Wembley Stadium. The wives, girlfriends and children in the party were taken to the Royal Hotel in Russell Square to await the return of the players.

The Empire Stadium was resplendent in the sunshine and as the group were ushered through the tunnel onto the greyhound track that formed the perimeter of the lush green playing area, the players noticed that the Pegasus team were there also. The two sets of players kept apart and other than a friendly wave from one or two, no verbal contact was made. Pegasus departed from the stadium first, leaving the Bishop Auckland entourage to take in the surroundings all alone. Twenty-three souls tried to take in the enormity of what was about to take place in twenty-four hours time. Just twenty-three; tomorrow there would be one hundred thousand.

That evening, all of the club representatives and families were taken to the Victoria Palace Theatre where Bud Flanagan and The Crazy Gang were appearing. After the show, the players were introduced to the great comedian and other members of the Gang. Bob and Bud had met before, at Buckingham Palace, during the Olympic Games, and Bob was amazed that Bud remembered him. They got on really well and Bud promised that he would be rooting for the 'Bishops'.

Family members returned to the Royal Hotel but the players spent the night in Weybridge, Surrey at the Oatlands Hotel. The reason for the splitting of the party was to allow the players complete rest and to afford time during the early Saturday morning for relaxation and to discuss tactics. After lunch, the two parties departed from their respective hotels for the journey to Wembley.

As the team bus approached the stadium, a steward opened the giant green doors to allow entrance. The players were ushered into the allotted dressing room with its long windows. Telegrams lay on a table.

'Bloody hell, there must be hundreds of them,' exclaimed Bill White, the goalkeeper. There were.

Some of the players that had played at Wembley before strolled around the dressing room as they picked up the messages of goodwill whilst those new to the experience stood in admiration trying to take it all in. Ken Williamson and Benny Edwards were nervously chattering away as others admired the size of the room, painted in neutral colours of fawn and green with its massive plunge baths, much to the amusement of the waiting attendants who were ready to cater to the players every need before and after the game.

Having played at Wembley three times before, Bob was relatively accustomed to the place and was more relaxed than some of the others. He said a 'Hello' to a steward and strolled over to the pile of telegrams, selecting those addressed to him, before finding a place on one of the benches, and started to read them. Friends, family, supporters, some he knew, lots he didn't, all wished him and the club well. No doubt over the other side of the tunnel the Pegasus players were going through the same motions. After one or two, he noticed that Dave Marshall had come to sit beside him as he too read his telegrams. 'Don't worry, we'll get that bloody medal for you today, Bob, you see,' said the six-footer, in his soft northern voice.

'Thanks, Dave,' muttered Bob, slightly taken aback by the young man's confidence in helping him obtain the only medal absent from his collection. Much had been written in the newspapers that Bob Hardisty had won every trophy and winners' medals except an FA Amateur Cup medal and that time was running out in his quest to obtain one.

Dave Marshall was making his first appearance at Wembley and it struck Bob how calm the twenty-three year-old full-back appeared. He had been with the club two years and earned a regular place in the team with some outstanding performances. He seemed devoid of any pre-match nerves and was undaunted that he would be up against England's outside-left, Jimmy Potts.

'What will be, will be, Dave. Fate will decide who lifts the Cup.'

Bob looked up and around him at his team mates as they all began to change into their colours and wondered if the other members remaining from the eleven who had played in last year's final, Tommy Farrer, Harry McIlvenny, Jimmy Nimmins and Bobby Davison, were carrying the same singular thought that was in his head. He did not wish to endure defeat again in a Cup Final. Not again. Never again.

The players donned their new shirts displaying the traditional dark and light blue halves and as they sat waiting for the signal to leave the dressing room, Harry McIlvenny started to issue last minute instructions and words of encouragement to his players but before he could finish, a steward put his head round the door and requested that the team line up in the tunnel next to the Pegasus team. Some of the players uttered a sigh of relief. Not long to go now.

Two sets of eleven players left their dressing rooms and lined up side by side. Harry McIlvenny, captain of the team, stood behind Alderman Waine, Chairman of Bishop Auckland as Denis Saunders, captain of Pegasus, took his place behind his club Chairman Dr H W Thompson. Bob took up his position behind Harry and the remaining nine players took their places. There was a slight delay and then, all too quickly, the order came to walk into the arena and make way to face the Royal Box. As the sun beat down, the two columns came out of the darkness of the Pageant Tunnel in to Wembley Stadium's bright glare to be received by a mighty roar.

The teams were:

> *Bishop Auckland* (Dark blue and Light blue halved shirts, Black shorts)
> White—Marshall, Farrer—Hardisty, Davison, Nimmins—
> Taylor, Anderson, McIlvenny, Williamson, Edwards.

> *Pegasus* (White shirts, Navy blue shorts)
> Brown—Maughan, Cowan—Platt, Shearwood, Saunders—
> Pawson, Dutchman, Tanner, Carr, Potts.

> Referee: Arthur Ellis of West Riding, Yorkshire

For twenty minutes, Bishop Auckland battered the Pegasus door but could not break it down. Somehow, the Pegasus goal remained intact and somehow the Bishop forwards contrived to squander golden opportunities to score. After five minutes, Benny Edwards showed clear signs of nerves when he shot hurriedly from seven yards and missed the goal by a wide margin. Alarmingly, he repeated his error ten minutes later with a similar effort when he only had Brown to beat, his shot going well wide of the goal. The 'Bishops' would regret missing these two cast-iron chances but during those first forty-five minutes, Edwards was not the only culprit. Twice, McIlvenny, usually so dangerous in the air, wasted goal scoring chances with headers over the bar and when Hardisty placed a sublime pass into the path of Willie Anderson, the Scotsman's tame effort was readily saved by Brown.

Not that it was only Bishop Auckland delivering the attacking moves. The Pegasus plan of drawing Hardisty towards their goal and then replying with quick counter-attacks was working well but without reward. Potts became the main danger man with his speedy raids down the left wing and Marshall did well on two occasions with well-timed tackles. Pawson, on the other flank, saw an effort blocked by Tommy Farrer and only another strong tackle from Hardisty prevented Dutchman from opening the scoring. The Pegasus inside trio were causing problems for the Bishop defence and on more than one occasion, Bobby Davison was lured from his central position, necessitating Hardisty or Nimmins to plug the gap.

Both defences were put under pressure but coped adequately. Pegasus defenders had to deal with the more aerial approach of the 'Bishops' whilst the Auckland defence had to cope with the quick passing game of the Pegasus players.

On the half-hour mark, the dangerous Tanner was dispossessed by Hardisty who took the ball to the edge of the Pegasus penalty area before releasing the ball to McIlvenny. Steadying himself, the Bishop striker delivered a strong shot to Brown's right that just went wide of the far post. It was the closest that Bishop had come to scoring yet. At the other end, Tanner, Dutchman and Carr combined with an inter-passing movement that was only thwarted by a fine save from Bill White. If the first twenty minutes had belonged to Bishop Auckland then the latter twenty belonged to the academics of Pegasus. Only two further fine saves from the 'Bishops' goalkeeper prevented the 'Two Blues' from going behind when Arthur Ellis blew his whistle to bring the half to a close.

The second half began like the first. Bishop threatened the Pegasus goal but were unable to achieve the most important result of getting the ball into the net. Jimmy Nimmins and Bob Hardisty became extra forwards but, even with a seven-man attack, Bishop were unable to score and, inevitably, became vulnerable at the back. From a Pawson corner, White jumped to collect the ball but made a howler of it and the ball was hooked off the line by Bob who, like all good defenders, just happened to be in the perfect position at the right time. Pegasus players screamed for the goal to be allowed but referee Ellis would have none of it. The university side, however, had given fair warning of their capabilities and it was no surprise when, after fifty minutes, they broke away to score.

A Bishop attack was foiled and the ball was quickly sent wide to Dutchman who advanced down the right-wing. He took one look up and saw Jimmy Potts running into the penalty area beyond the recovering defenders, Hardisty, Farrer, Davison and Marshall. Potts launched himself to produce a magnificent diving header that resulted in the ball arcing into the far corner of the Bishop Auckland goal with White well beaten. Bob had run back, realizing the danger all too late and, although he was on the goal-line, Potts's fine header evaded him. The Pegasus plan had come off.

Bishop responded with further attacks. Nimmins became a resident sixth forward, with Bobby Davison and Bob Hardisty running the Bishop mid-field operation. The Auckland players became aware that the catalyst for gaining the equalizer lay in the skills of Bob Hardisty and everything of merit that had been created so far had come through him. As the game went on their reliance on him became greater. After exactly an hour, Bob placed a free-kick perfectly for Benny Edwards to knock the ball down but the usually productive McIlvenny shot hurriedly and his effort went inches wide. Two minutes later the Bishop Auckland play-master sent Edwards down the wing but his effort was foiled by Maughan and then Hardisty provided McIlvenny with another golden opportunity which the centre-forward once again squandered, sending his shot straight into Brown's grateful arms.

There were only ten minutes remaining when the second goal of the game was scored. Once again a Bishop attack was broken up and with defenders caught out of position, Tanner and Pawson combined with fluent passing for the England international to put the universities team two up.

It was now or never for the 'Bishops' if they did not wish to return empty-handed to the north-east for the second year in succession. Bob Hardisty did everything possible to assist his forwards and played a magnificent game. With only six minutes left he collected the ball midway in his own half and dribbled to the edge of the Pegasus area, leaving three Pegasus players in his wake. He looked up and played a perfect pass for McIlvenny who inexplicably miskicked the ball and the danger passed. Within two minutes, another Bishop attack broke down at the expense of a corner. Bob placed the ball in the quadrant and composed himself, taking in the positioning of attackers and defenders. Only Jimmy Nimmins looked as if he had space to attack the Pegasus goal. The corner from Bob was perfect. The ball curled to the right of Jimmy who stuck out a leg to direct the ball past Brown with an overhead kick. It may have been a fortunate goal but it was no more than the northerners deserved.

Pegasus were holding on now and defenders just cleared the ball anywhere to safety. As a throw-in was about to be taken, Bob stood next to Arthur Ellis and enquired how much longer to go. 'Time enough for a goal, Bob, but not much more,' came the official's response.

The throw-in was taken and ten seconds later, Bishop were awarded a corner. This time Bob did not take it but placed himself on the far corner of the penalty area, readying himself to run in and attack the ball should it come his way. With the crowd roaring, the ball came over, missing the heads of defenders and attackers alike. Bob rose with Cowan to make contact but the ball evaded Bob's bald head by a whisker. As he fell to the ground and the ball went out of play, Arthur Ellis blew for full time. Pegasus had won a thrilling match 2–1.

The Bishop Auckland players sportingly congratulated their victors who could not believe what they had achieved. Bob Hardisty shook hands with his opponents and then with his own players. Disappointment was etched on the faces of all his team mates. Jimmy Nimmins who had been standing near the centre circle, hands on hips, a picture of total abjection, walked towards his colleague.

'Let's go, Jim. Let's pick up our medals.'

'You know, Bob, I'm beginning to hate this fucking place.'

'Plus ça change, plus c'est la même chose'
(The more things change, the more they stay the same)
Les Guêpes (Alphonse Karr)

Chapter Seven
CHANGES

The bright morning sun bounced off the pale green wall.

Betty Hardisty opened her eyes and gazed up at her admiring husband. She felt weak and wanted to go home. Her mouth was dry and her stomach felt as if it had been stretched like an elastic belt.

'Won't be much longer now, darling. You'll be out of here and back home soon. Look at all of the letters and cards that have been sent you.'

'Where is he?'

'He's only next door. You'll be able to see him again in a moment, she's just gone to fetch him.'

They looked at each other, their faces full of love.

Four years ago, John Roderick Elliot Hardisty, was the happiest man in the world. He had never thought then that he could be as happy again. How wrong he had been. Betty had delivered a beautiful bouncing baby boy and the joy that he had felt four years ago was incomparable to this. The footballing disappointments of the last twelve months were cast aside. Nothing could better these precious moments that he was sharing with the woman he loved.

A small, slightly rotund nurse appeared, carrying a tiny bundle swathed in a blanket and delivered the firstborn to the mother.

'And how is the proud father today?' the nurse enquired.

'Speechless,' replied Bob, leaning over to gaze on his son's face.

'You've got a fine son there, Mr Hardisty,' she remarked, leaving Betty and Bob to enjoy the gift of their love.

Jonathon Robert Stanley Hardisty continued sleeping as his proud parents gazed down at him unaware of the problem that he was about to present to his doting parents.

It was usual in those days, for mothers who had just given birth in hospital, to remain in the ward for a few days in order to recover from the ordeal. The onus of registering the baby's birth was, therefore, usually the responsibility of the father. Bob duly went along to the Register Office the day after his son was born and had the birth certificate completed. When he presented Betty with the certificate she was not best pleased—Jonathon was fine, as was Robert but they had never agreed upon Stanley. Bob tried to argue that it was a fine name and that many people had been given the name in the past—including the current football hero, Stanley Matthews—but Betty would not budge. No son of hers was going to have the name Stanley.

It was too late to do anything about the innocent baby's birth certificate but when he was christened, three months later, his name was given as Jonathon Robert Adrian Hardisty.

Bob reflected on all that had happened during the previous twelve months or so.

It had been a time of change for Bob Hardisty since the disappointment of losing to Pegasus at Wembley the previous April. A month after that Amateur Cup Final defeat, Bob had been selected to play for England against Finland at Swindon. The game was one of a tournament that celebrated The Festival of Britain. The match attracted 15,000 spectators and on a sunny spring evening, the visitors had been defeated 3–2 with Bob the man of the match. Five days later, he produced another creditable performance against Norway at Ayresome Park, Middlesbrough, England winning 2–1.

The game against Norway was Bob's eleventh for the national team and with him being thirty years of age many people, Bob included, believed that it was to be his last. His performances for club and country had been of the highest standard but age was not on his side and with the Olympic Games about to take place in a little over twelve months time, there was a feeling that the time was right for bringing some new blood into the England team. Bob must have resigned himself to thinking that his England playing days were over, especially as he was unable to make the next international game against France in Cherbourg.

The first few weeks of the Northern League Championship campaign

had begun with champions, Bishop Auckland, once more leading the race
but there had been significant changes to the side. Len Wilson had been
appointed Secretary in 1948, taking over from 'Kit' Rudd. He was an amiable
man with an eye for quality players. Whenever any of the Bishop players
reported on an opposition player's performance that merited special praise,
he would take note and, where possible, see for himself. He and 'Kit' were
responsible for acquiring the services of many of Bishop Auckland's finest
players of the 1950s. Len had followed Bob Hardisty's advice and helped bring
Harry McIlvenny to the club as well as Jimmy Nimmins from Spennymoor
and Willie Anderson from Newcastle, who had been playing for the Army at
Catterick. Reference has already been made earlier of Corbett Cresswell's fine
game for Evenwood some eighteen months ago and now Len had moved in
to claim the services of the mobile centre-half. The signing would not have
been required, however, had it not been for a dispute within the club that was
not revealed to the public.

Bobby Davison explained to me the events that led to Corbett Cresswell
coming to the 'Bishops':

> All of the players were training at Kingsway one Tuesday night when I was
> called inside by 'Kit' Rudd. 'Kit' was the messenger who passed on the decisions
> that had been made by the committee. He told me that for the next game on
> Saturday, the club wanted to try me out at right-back and play Bob Hardisty
> at centre-half. I said to 'Kit', 'What the hell do you want to do that for? Bob's
> alright at half-back and I'm fine at centre-half and what's more, young Dave
> Marshall's fine at right-back.'
>
> 'Kit' said that the committee wanted to see how good Bob would be in the
> middle of the field, instead of at wing-half, where he had always played in the
> defence. I went ballistic and told 'Kit' that I was not prepared to be part of an
> experiment. He said a few words to the effect that I should be more reasonable
> and that it was inevitable that tactical changes must be made from time to time.
> The way he put it I felt that it was me in the wrong and not the committee.
> Nothing more was said about it and I carried on training with the rest of the
> lads. I said nowt about it but all the while I was seething up inside. I must admit
> that I thought some nasty things about Bob in those moments because I felt that
> I was being used just for his benefit. I suppose I was jealous.
>
> I left training early and went for a pint in The Castle. Who should come in
> after a few minutes but Bob Middlewood, Chairman of the club and the main
> voice of the committee. He came over to me all smarmy as if butter wouldn't
> melt in his mouth and offered me a drink—he could see that I had a full pint in
> front of me. I decided to take the bull by the horns and asked him straight out
> what the committee were trying to do in moving me away from the centre-half

position in favour of Bob. He tried to sweet-talk me, saying it was for only this once. They thought that Bob might be slowing down and that he would be more effective in the middle away from the speedier inside-forwards and wingers. What a load of shite! Bob Hardisty was playing better than ever. He had a footballing brain that was far better than anybody else's and had been brilliant in the Pegasus match just a few months before. He had even been picked for England since then.

I told Middlewood that I did not believe him when he had said that it was just an experiment for the one game and told him that if the club went through with the change then I was finished with them. He told me not to be so hasty but I repeated what I had told him—either I continue at centre-half or I would go!

Come the Saturday—I forget who we were playing—half an hour before the match is due to start we were all in the dressing room chatting away and preparing to get changed when in walks 'Kit' Rudd confirming the team. I was at right-back, Bob was at centre-half, Dave Marshall at half-back I think. None of the others said anything. They accepted the changes just as if nothing was going on. I looked up at 'Kit' and said, 'Are you sure that's the line-up, 'Kit'? He nodded and at that I picked up my bag and left.

Three days later I signed for Crook and Bishop had a new centre-half in Corbett Cresswell. Do you think it was all planned? Do you think that the club wanted to get rid of me knowing that if they signed up another centre-half I would have left anyway, as I would not have stood for it? I was a hot-head at times then and would always speak my mind—still do. Word was passed round that I was ready to leave Bishop—you know how it is—with Darlington, Hartlepool, Carlisle, Hull and Berwick Rangers all wanting me to sign professional forms with them but I wasn't interested—I was making far more than they could have come up with. The irony is that the very next week I turned out at centre-half for Crook and Corbett turned out for Bishop—we were playing each other and drew 2–2. But I'll never forget that night in The Castle and Bob Middlewood's ingratiating air. Bishop Auckland was a fine club. 'Kit' Rudd and Len Wilson were smashing fellas but the rest of the committee were shite, absolute bastards the whole lot of them.

Bob Hardisty was saddened by the nature of Bobby Davison's departure. The pair had established a formidable half-back line with the inclusion of Jimmy Nimmins and they got on very well, even though they were entirely different in character. Bob was the mild-mannered, easy-going type who accepted change readily and hated falling out with anyone. He was the one who could see the best in everyone, wanting to be liked and loved having a good time at the bar or at parties. He had never turned an invitation down whether it be to present awards at a school or athletics club, a reception at the local Women's Institute or musical society, or anything—Bob could not say 'No'. Bobby Davison had a more forceful personality, not afraid to air his views and not caring who he upset. Some people branded him a big head, too confident of his own capabilities and self opinionated. He wasn't bothered if people took exception to what he had to say. He and Bob were two people from two completely different moulds but there was no arguing that they had built a relationship on the playing field that was the envy of other clubs.

When I interviewed Bobby Davison, he acknowledged that for a while he resented the special treatment that he believed Bob Hardisty was receiving at Bishop Auckland and for a period he refused to speak to his ex-playing partner. Time mellowed his opinion and he accepted that his behaviour had been childish. Bob Hardisty had not sought to take the centre-half position away from Davison but it was sad that the machinations of the all-powerful Bishop Auckland Football Club committee had resulted, for a time, in the breakdown of a friendship between two playing colleagues.

The local newspaper, *The Sports Despatch*, was lagging behind in the developments that were going on at the club. News travelled fast of Bobby Davison's rift with the club but clearly, dealings that were being negotiated with Corbett Cresswell were being kept under the tightest of wraps, as can be seen by the following report taken from *The Sports Despatch* of 8th September 1951:

> Bishop Auckland, although they have not lost a game, appear to be in the depths of despondency. They have not yet got a settled team, though there are prospects of new blood being introduced into the side in the course of the next few weeks.
>
> The majority of last season's players are still available but the departure of Bobby Davison has beset the committee with a difficult problem. Centre-halves, especially of the Davison calibre, are very difficult to get these days but the 'Bishops' no doubt will be able to solve their difficulties in their own way.

Even as the article was being prepared for printing, Corbett Cresswell was being registered as a Bishop Auckland player.

The introduction of Cresswell to the club resulted in Bob reverting to the right half-back role and normal service was resumed. Results on the field continued to please supporters although the style of play had the doubters voicing concern. Bob dismissed the criticism and advised all who would listen that Bishop Auckland's chief target was, as always, the Amateur Cup but before that tournament began, the FA Cup proper had started, in which

Bishop had received a bye to the First Round. It was usual for the winners of the Amateur Cup to be awarded a bye to the First Round of the competition but as Pegasus had not entered, the honour was given to the 'Bishops' as runners-up.

The Bishop Auckland players and supporters would have hoped for a more glamourous tie against a Football League club than that which the draw gave them but at least there was a lot of local interest in the away game against Blyth Spartans who played in the North-Eastern League. They were not having a particularly good season and the Bishop Auckland players went to Croft Park full of confidence. The two clubs had never met before although when Auckland was in its infancy in the 1890s it had met a team from Blyth that soon after disbanded. Years later, the club had been reformed as Blyth Spartans.

In a bruising encounter, Blyth came out the winners 2–1. Bob Hardisty and Jimmy Nimmins had been Auckland's best players but the home team showed superior movement in front of goal and the visitors were on the back foot for most of the game. It was only when they were 2–0 down that Bob created a first scoring opportunity for Harry McIlvenny, which went wide. Bishop's goal came five minutes from the end when McIlvenny's effort was deflected into the net off a Blyth defender.

Better luck followed in the more realistic target of the Amateur Cup when Bishop comfortably defeated Rawmarsh Colliery Welfare in the First Round. The game was transferred to nearby Rotherham United's ground because of the limited capacity of the Rawmarsh ground. Such was the interest generated for the game that more than 6,000 spectators turned up to watch the minnows take on the crack amateurs. A 5–1 victory by the 'Bishops' had seen the 'Two Blues' through to the next round which saw them pitched against Hendon who were leading the Athenian League. This was a much tougher tie and the northerners did well to come away from Hendon's Claremont Road ground with a 1–1 draw. The following week Bob Hardisty and his colleagues disposed of the London club in convincing fashion 5–1. This was a magnificent performance by the 'Two Blues' as Hendon had five international players in their team—Avis, Stroud, Adams, Topp and Evans—thus equalling Bishop Auckland's quintet of Hardisty, Farrer, McIlvenny, Major and Anderson.

Dexter Adams, Hendon and England centre-half remembers that defeat, some fifty-eight years ago and Bob Hardisty's performance:

Bob Hardisty was inspirational that day. Everything he did was so perfect and composed. He seemed to have all the time in the world to look up and find his man with an accurate pass. He was majestic. He had a brilliant football brain and carved us to pieces. He may not have been the captain of the team but by God he was the one who the Bishop players looked for if ever they were in trouble or a tight situation. I seem to remember that he played the ball quite often to his winger [Jacky Major] but even though we knew what to expect, Laurie Topp and I had a gruelling time that day.

With Hendon out of the way, Bob Hardisty could have been forgiven for thinking that the New Year might turn out more rewarding than the last two. He had a beautiful wife who was carrying his first child and once the travelling backwards and forwards to Carnegie College was over he had a new job lined up. The football team was, he believed, as good as ever with not a weak link to be found. Walton and Hersham, whom Bishop had knocked out of the competition, last year, were the opponents for Round Three and prospects looked good, especially as the game would take place at Kingsway, where the 'Bishops' had not lost an Amateur Cup tie in eighteen years. He knew not to count his chickens before the event but he could not help feeling confident.

At four-thirty in the afternoon, on Saturday 9th February 1952, Bob Hardisty stood in the goal mouth area of the Walton and Hersham defence and shook hands with Arthur Braithwaite, left-back of the victorious visitors. He watched, as eleven thousand disappointed fans traipsed out of Kingsway, whilst a small band of less than a hundred cheering fans threw their red and white hats and scarves in the air, shouting in delirium, in praise of the shock result that their team had just achieved. By beating the mighty Bishop Auckland on their home soil 3–1, surely this was the shock of the round.

Try as hard as he could, Bob Hardisty had done his best to bring his team mates through but Walton had deserved their win after going a goal behind. Once again, Bob had become a sixth forward in pursuit of goals but everything that the Bishop Auckland attack came up with was repulsed by a stoic defence. Wembley would have to wait at least another year.

Hopes were raised when it was announced two days later that Bishop Auckland were to protest against Walton and Hersham's win, as they had fielded an ineligible player and that the club was confident of the outcome.

Under the rules of the competition, clubs had to send a list of its players to the opposing club at least five days before the match. If either club had any objection against any player then it had to lodge such objection no more than twenty-four hours prior to the commencement of the game. As Secretary of the club, it was Len Wilson's responsibility to lodge the objection which was based on the grounds that the Walton and Hersham player, John Taylor, had in the past been registered as a professional for North-Eastern League club Consett. John Taylor (not to be confused with his namesake, the fine musician, who played for Crook Town and Bishop Auckland in the 1950s) therefore, was not a true amateur but a 'permit' player, argued Len Wilson.[†]

The protest failed as the FA Amateur Cup Committee ruled that Bishop Auckland had breached the procedure by not making their protest within the specified time-scale.

The failure of the appeal was greeted with ambivalence by the players and the majority of supporters who shared the view that Bishop had been defeated by a better team on the day and that it had not been due to the inclusion of one player. Letters to the club and to the press conveyed the feeling of disapproval towards the objection. W T Chester, a Bishop Auckland supporter, wrote the following, expressing sentiments shared by many:

> As one who has followed the interests of the Bishop Auckland club for many years and who also saw the game last Saturday, I feel that this protest, even though it may be upheld, is not in keeping with the best traditional sportsmanship of the Bishop Auckland club. Anyone who saw the game last Saturday must surely agree that on the day's play, Walton were the better team and this was not caused by any one player but by the splendid co-ordination of the team as a whole. Bishop Auckland have a wonderful record and I am sorry that they should have made this protest.

The day before the verdict was announced, Bob Hardisty was asked by a newspaperman if he was confident of the result being overturned. In answer, Bob reiterated the views of all of his playing colleagues when he said that

---

[†] The Amateur Cup rules stipulated that the competition was only open to amateur clubs: clubs who allowed ex-professionals to play for them—permit players—were excluded, without exception. This accounts for the broad base of amateur clubs in the north-east of the country and in the south, as midland clubs, generally, allowed ex-professionals to register with them. Thus, it was not until the introduction of the FA Trophy and FA Vase that such players could aspire to ever having an opportunity of gaining a chance of playing at Wembley.

Walton and Hersham had been the better team on the day and had deserved their victory. He would not wish to progress to the next round of the competition on a technicality that, in his and his team mates' opinion, had no bearing on the final outcome of the match. He ended his statement by wishing the Walton and Hersham players all best wishes for the remaining rounds. It was notable that he had made no direct reference to the actions that Bishop Auckland Football Club and its committee had taken.[†]

With the cup exit behind him it was left to the domestic titles to sustain the footballing interests of Bob Hardisty for the remainder of the season. The Northern League Championship would be retained and the club would be successful in winning such trophies as The Durham Benevolent Bowl, The Durham County Challenge Cup, The Durham Hospital Cup and The Bishop Auckland Nursing Cup. The club would also be successful in travelling to the Channel Islands and winning the Guernsey Victory Cup. Bob would have a few more medals to put away but 'The Big One' remained elusive.

Barrington School had lost the services of two fine teachers, Betty to become a mother, and Bob, who had left to take up a more senior position. Twelve months earlier he had received information from George Metcalf, head of the Durham Education Services, that there were prospects of a vacancy coming up in a year's time, within his physical education section. The position meant Bob having to attend Carnegie College, Leeds for a year but it would be worth it as he would be appointed Area Physical Training Organizer within Durham County. The position was not office-bound and gave the holder the flexibility of working all over the county, although the centre of administration would be at the relatively small town of Houghton-le-Spring, midway between Durham and Sunderland. The higher salary was obviously attractive as was the inclusion of a car, which could be exchanged for a newer model every two or three years, but what appealed to Bob most was the opportunity to work full-time within a sporting environment and not be confined to a classroom.

It was with this dual vision—the future of fatherhood and the bright

---

[†]   Walton and Hersham defeated Crook Town 2–0 after a 0–0 draw in Round Four but were beaten 3–0 in the Semi-Final by eventual Amateur Cup winners Walthamstow Avenue.

dawn that a new job brought with it—that Bob Hardisty viewed the coming spring-time and summer of 1952. A surprise lay in wait.

In October of 1951, Bob had been selected to play for the Northern Counties—at centre-half!!!—in an amateur international Trial Match at Carlisle against the Southern Counties. He had a decent game and played as well as any other on the field. On this occasion, however, he did not progress to the full England team and it was generally accepted that at the age of thirty, his involvement with international football would now be over although he would continue to represent his county as captain and right half-back.

Bob had not been forgotten, however, and was very much in the spotlight of the Football Association.

On 14th January 1952 the 'Selection (Amateur) Committee of the Football Association' convened a meeting to discuss the forthcoming Olympic Games to be held in Helsinki. It was recommended that the responsibility of selecting, training and sending a team to represent Great Britain would be undertaken by the Football Association and that Walter Winterbottom was to be appointed Manager of the Olympic Team, with Jack Jennings of Northampton Town Football Club being the designated Trainer.

Two months later, on 22nd March, the Committee selected 'Mr J R E Hardisty as Honorary Team Manager' of the England team for an amateur international against France at Norwich on 5th April. At that same meeting the names of twenty-five players were nominated to 'undertake the training and match play programme in connection with the Olympic Games.'

Well satisfied with Bob's industry in carrying out these duties, at a further meeting, held on 2nd May, the Committee selected Bob as 'Team Manager' for a Continental Tour to be made by an Olympic Trial Team. Matches were arranged to be played against a West German Amateur XI at Dusseldorf and Nurnberg on the 14th and 18th May respectively.

On 31st May the Committee pruned the final party of twenty players to go to the Olympics—one of the personnel to go as a player was none other than Bob Hardisty himself, in addition to his capacity as Assistant Manager.

It is difficult to imagine what the feelings of Bob and Betty were at this particular juncture of their lives. A proud and busy mother with her firstborn undoubtedly required a lot of love and affection as well as help in the house. Bob had a full-time job within the Education Department which carried a lot of responsibility and the hours of which extended beyond the normal 'nine to five' routine. To add to this, much of his 'spare' time took him away from the home: Saturdays and regular mid-week football matches for Bishop Auckland could be classed as routine but interspersed with the regular Northern League games were the various County competitions as well as the Amateur Cup games and of course the international games. Just two weeks earlier, he had travelled to Guernsey with the rest of the Bishop Auckland players to take part in a football tournament organized by the Channel Isles Football Association. Bob had been inspirational and helped the club win the tournament and trophy, The Guernsey Victory Cup. Now, just when it was feasible to assume that his involvement playing for England was drawing to a close, he was to be appointed Assistant Team Manager of the Olympic Football Team, second in command to Walter Winterbottom. Throughout his career, not only was Bob's time taken up by his football interests but many evenings were taken up accepting invitations and appeals to attend prize-giving celebrations, various sporting clubs and institutions or be guest of honour at a function, all met with an affirmative response—Bob did not wish to let anyone down by refusing an invitation and right now, even at this very hectic time of his and Betty's life, he did not want to turn down the opportunity to work within the framework of the Football Association. His sporting interests and activities did not stop at the football field. He was a regular visitor to the local snooker hall and he loved cricket. He was an accomplished batsman and could turn his arm when called upon and as a result he became a regular member of Bishop Auckland Cricket Club's XI which took up his Saturday afternoons during the summer, and of course he loved golf. He was a member of the town's Golf Club and this was one venue where Betty did like to attend and accompany her husband. She had made friends with many of the lady members and if there was one place outside the home where Betty and Bob socialized it was at Bishop Auckland Golf Club. For all Bob's various sporting interests, if Betty had any grievances regarding Bob's absences from home she kept them to herself and never once expressed disapproval, even during the latter stages of her pregnancy when, perhaps, she would have appreciated the presence of her husband most.

And so it was that on 11th July 1952, a York aircraft lifted off from Bovington aerodrome, with Bob Hardisty and his Olympic colleagues on board, bound for the Norwegian capital. It was billed as the greatest airlift in British sport at the time and was the first ever of its kind to the Olympics. At regular intervals, until 27th July, a further fourteen flights followed, taking the two hundred and ninety-one competitors and fifty-eight team officials, coaches, masseurs, grooms and boatkeepers as well as horses for the equestrian events. Return journeys were planned from 24th July, before the games were over, for those competitors that had taken part in earlier events or had been eliminated from their chosen events. Bob Hardisty did not envisage being on one of those early return flights.[†]

One of the surviving members of that Olympic Football Team is Bill Holmes. During a long and distinguished career, Bill had played for Morecambe, Lancaster, Wolverhampton Wanderers, Leeds United, Doncaster Rovers and Blackburn Rovers. He was with Blackburn Rovers at the time of his selection for the Olympics and had featured impressively in the semi-final match of the FA Cup against Newcastle United, three months earlier. The clubs had initially played out a 2–2 draw but Newcastle won the replay and went on to win the Cup by beating Arsenal in the Final 1–0. Bill did not play in the semi-final replay defeat due to a knee injury incurred during the first game. It was a similar injury that kept him out of the team to meet Luxembourg in the Preliminary Round of the 1952 Olympic Games.

> Bob Hardisty and Walter Winterbottom had us trained to the peak. We knew that we would have to be good to beat the likes of Sweden and Yugoslavia if we were to win the competition but we were fully expected to get through against Luxembourg. Walter taught us all of the tactics and instilled us full of confidence, telling us to fear no-one. Bob was Walter's assistant and put us through our paces in the gym, around the track and on the field. Obviously, he joined in as well, him being one of the players. God he was fit. Six foot tall and slender as a pea-pod—not thin mind you, just slender. I bet he never weighed much over eleven stone. The players respected him and some of us wondered why he had never turned professional. There could not have been a fitter set of players. Having said that, I had to miss the game, of course, as I had an injured leg but would have been fit for the next one.
>
> What happened in the game was unbelievable. All of us who weren't playing sat on a bench next to the pitch with Bob and Walter sat together at the front. Just along from us, in the crowd were a bunch of English sailors and soldiers, come along to give the team some support, believing that we would rattle up a cricket score They did a lot of singing and shouting. By half-time, they were doing a lot more than just shouting. They were really angry with the performance by the team for all that we were winning one-nil through an early goal by George Robb but the football we displayed was poor. We were lucky to be ahead and the little Luxembourg players had the support of the 3,500 crowd. Luxembourg!

[†]   The British Olympic Association had taken out personal accident insurance cover of £1,000 for each team official and competitor for the return journey.

They weren't supposed to be any good at football. Whatever the lads tried that afternoon, nothing went right. Passes went astray at critical moments and if we made an opportunity to score, the shot would go wide, or hit a defender and go safely into the goalkeeper's hands. Other than the opening goal, everything went against us that day.

At the end of ninety minutes it was 1–1 but in the next fifteen minutes or so they were leading 5–2, Bill Slater having scored one for us. Jim Lewis scored a third for us two minutes from full-time but Luxembourg had won 5–3. That was the end of the road for us. Beaten before we had even started—we were out of the Olympics. It wasn't good and those forces lads gave us some stick when it was all over.

What a let down. Bob was devastated. The English press were scathing. There was no second chance for the team. In those days, there was no mini-league system that gives a defeated team an opportunity to gain ground by winning later matches. This was straight forward win or out and Great Britain, one of the fancied teams to at least make the semi-final stage, were out of the tournament.

The players and officials held a meeting shortly afterwards and voted to stay on at the Games to support the other athletes but in their hearts they knew that they had failed.

Bob Hardisty had become accustomed to failure but that didn't make the burden any easier to bear. He suffered another dose just a few months later when the two major cup competitions—the FA Cup and the FA Amateur Cup—got under way.

Bishop Auckland did not have to enter the FA Cup until the Fourth Qualifying Round and were drawn to meet Spennymoor United. A creditable 1–1 draw was earned at Spennymoor's Brewery Field and four days later victory was achieved in a hard fought win 2–1. Selby Town provided the opposition for Round One and they were beaten 5–1 to put the 'Bishops' into Round Two where they would meet Coventry City who were riding high in the Football League Division Three (South).

The demand for tickets for the Coventry game was phenomenal. Everywhere that Bob went he was besieged by fans asking for tickets, as were the other players. Bob tried to explain that he only had a limited allocation and that it was impossible for him to satisfy everyone. He estimated that he alone had received over a thousand written or verbal requests for tickets, such was the interest in the match.

There was a scare for Bob, just two days before the tie, when he slipped down a flight of stairs in the Education Offices in Houghton-le-Spring. Carrying a pile of books, he tried to read the cover of one as he descended the steps but at a bend in the stairway his right ankle caught a railing, causing him to stumble. Fortunately, he did not fall, as his reflexes reacted but in his attempt to maintain balance he twisted his right knee. Within seconds, the ankle began to balloon up with swelling and his knee became puffy. He had remained remarkably free from injuries on the football field, where stud marks on legs from flying tackles delivered by burly defenders were second nature, and he felt a bit stupid catching his ankle over something as innocuous as a stair rail, just forty-eight hours before such an important game, so far removed from the playing field.

He returned to his office and nursing his leg with both hands, dropped into the chair by his desk. Slowly bending the leg, he felt for any signs of injury and prepared himself for the sharp pain that would tell him that ligaments had been damaged. By fractions at a time he eased the joint. He repeated the process half a dozen times, gradually increasing the pace of the movement. Luckily, he was able to fully bend the knee without any sharp twinge of pain and he was satisfied that there was no real damage to the knee but the ankle gave cause for concern. He decided against calling the club doctor and asked for a member of staff to bring him a bucket of cold water, immediately. The strange request was answered and Bob slowly began to remove his shoe and sock. For the rest of that afternoon, Bob sat at his desk with his trouser leg rolled up whilst his right foot was implanted in the bucket and at the same time a cold compress was applied to the knee.

He sat at his desk for what seemed ages. Writing a few letters and reports helped to kill the time but all the while he was wondering if he was doing the right thing and questioning his decision not to seek immediate medical advice. He could be stubborn at times. He was desperate to play against Coventry in such an important game but did not wish to let his team mates or supporters down. He knew that he would need to be one-hundred per cent fit and right now he could see his hopes of playing disappearing over the horizon. Three hours later, the swelling on his ankle had subsided and he felt confident enough to stand up and put his weight, rather gingerly, on his foot. He placed his hands on the arms of his chair and took a slow pace forward. The foot left a wet imprint on the office floor. He took another step, then another. Nothing happened. He was able to walk without any noticeable limp. No pain. He would be okay.

He carefully rolled his sock back on and then put on his leather brogue. Looking round his office he decided to leave for the safety of home. Those books could wait.

Bob was able to put the ankle scare behind him and turn out for Bishop Auckland against Coventry City but was unable to help his team to victory. The Football League side were far quicker to the ball and asked a lot of questions of the Auckland defenders. Bob and his fellow forwards received scant reward for their efforts but with supply lines being continually blocked, the Bishop attack was only of limited threat to the midland side. In front of 16,319 spectators—Bishop Auckland's record attendance—Coventry put on a convincing show and won 4–1.

With the FA Cup out of the way, the more realistic target of the Amateur variety presented itself. Round One saw the 'Bishops' inflict a convincing 7–2 defeat upon Shildon, away from home, and as a result they were drawn to visit Southall, members of the Athenian League. Southall were a useful team but without any stars—Ted Bennett, international goalkeeper, was probably their best known player. It was Bennett who had taken the place of Jackie Snowdon in the 1950 England touring team of Scandinavia when the unfortunate Willington goalkeeper had broken his collar bone just days after the Amateur Cup Final.

If Bishop were confident of progressing to Round Three and beyond they were in for a shock. Tommy Farrer had suffered an attack of jaundice on the morning of the game but, after resting, decided that he was fit enough to play. Unfortunately, Southall pressed the Bishop Auckland defence throughout the game and Bob Hardisty—playing at inside-right—and his colleagues received limited service from beleaguered half-backs. Southall won 2–0 and Bob had the unhappy experience of missing a penalty. Tommy Farrer would have been the usual nominee for such a spot-kick but due to his illness had passed the responsibility on to Bob. Usually so reliable, Bob fluffed the chance and Bishop Auckland would have to wait another year for the chance to visit Wembley.

'Why were they proud? Again we ask aloud,
Why in the name of Glory were they proud?'
Isabella or The Pot Of Basil (John Keats)

Chapter Eight
EPIC

With his international career well and truly behind him, Bob Hardisty returned to the 'domestic' scene of the Northern League for his football. As always, the priority for Bishop Auckland Football Club and himself was winning the Amateur Cup. A good run in the FA Cup was always welcome but they were never going to win that. He was nearing the end of his career, according to those that knew—after all he was now thirty-two and those legs of his could not go on for ever, even just playing amateur football. There would not be many more opportunities for Bob Hardisty to gain that missing medal, declared more than one media reporter.

The new season got under way with some significant changes to the Bishop Auckland squad. Tommy Farrer and his wife Gladys had decided to return to their roots in north London, where Tommy continued playing amateur football with Walthamstow Avenue. His replacement would be the Scottish international full-back, Tommy Stewart, who had been pushing Farrer for a regular place in the team. Willie Anderson had left, as had Ken Williamson who had decided that he preferred rugby union football to the association kind. Harry McIlvenny, regular scorer of important goals, had decided to hang up his boots and concentrate on his second love—cricket. The record books show that he turned out for the 'Bishops' eighty-nine times and had averaged a goal a game, scoring ninety goals in just a little over three years. Finding replacements for these quality players would be difficult—if they found one half as good to replace McIlvenny then they would have done well, was the opinion of more than one Bishop Auckland supporter. Yet that is just what Len Wilson and 'Kit' Rudd set out to do, and they came up with a stack of aces.

Bob Hardisty was not one of the club party that left for Rhodesia in the July of 1953. Family and work commitments meant that he could not justify leaving his wife and young son behind on this occasion for such a tour, which had been arranged following an invitation from the Rhodesian Football Association. The tour lasted almost a month and involved playing eight games, under hot conditions, within a period of fifteen days. Bishop Auckland were the first amateur side to visit the country for such a long period and were following in the footsteps of nearby neighbours, Newcastle United, who had visited the country twelve months previously as FA Cup holders. And so, whilst Bob stayed at home and got on with his domestic and employment duties, his team mates sweated it out against the likes of Broken Hill (won 4–0), Matabelina (won 2–1) and Mashonaland (won 6–2). Bishop Auckland won six and lost two of the eight games, a highly commendable record given the hot climate and amount of travelling involved to and from the different venues, not to mention the number of official parties and functions that they were required to attend.

Although many of the Rhodesian supporters were disappointed not to see the legendary Bob Hardisty, the Bishop Auckland players were applauded wherever they went. They may not have appreciated it at the time but they were in fact witnessing the moulding together of a new squad of players that would prove to be the best in the history of the club. Harry Sharratt had joined the club at the back end of the 1952–53 season and had displaced Bill White and his young understudy, Geoff North, between the posts. In October 1952, he had entered Blackpool's record books when he became the first amateur goalkeeper to turn out for the famous club in a First Division game against Tottenham Hotspur. Harry was destined to become one of the best-loved players ever to turn out for the 'Bishops', admired by supporters and opponents alike. Already an international, having been capped for England against Wales, he would earn further caps and build a reputation whereby many considered him the best goalkeeper in the country—amateur or professional. As every football fan knows, his name would become indelibly associated with Bishop Auckland with his magnificent goalkeeping and his rather eccentric behaviour—he may have been the last line of defence but Harry saw himself as an outfield player and would frequently try to venture upfield to 'assist' his forwards whenever the fancy took him.

Replacement for Harry McIlvenny was Ray Oliver, who had been prised from the clutches of Whitley Bay, and was prepared to play for Bishop Auckland despite the attentions of almost every club in the First and Second Divisions, including Newcastle United, Sunderland, Middlesbrough, Manchester City, Luton Town and Darlington. He was happy to play for the 'Bishops' and hoped to win an Amateur Cup winners' medal—that was his goal, and turning professional did not play any part in his plans. This magnificently built centre-forward, not overly tall at 5'11" and weighing just over 13 stone, had the physique of a Malcolm MacDonald and had a similar never-say-die attitude, giving little respite to opposing centre-halves but he was much more than a 'bull-at-a-gate' battering centre-forward—he also had skill and could turn on a sixpence. Ray made his living as a railway porter but was also a member of the Royal National Lifeboat Institution and performed acts of bravery throughout his time. When he was only eighteen, he was instrumental in saving the lives of three men who had been swept into the water at Cullercoats, his home town, on the Northumberland coast. Without any thought of danger to himself, he dived into the heavy sea and helped in the rescue.

Ray had previously blitzed Bishop Auckland in an opening game of the season encounter, when the Northumbrian team beat the 'Bishops' 5–2. Ever since then he had been coveted by Len Wilson, who had him marked down as a likely replacement whenever Harry McIlvenny called it a day. He was a proven goalscorer with a heart as big as a lion's.

To replace Willie Anderson, Len Wilson had obtained the services of Whitby Town's speedy inside-forward, Les Dixon, who could score goals as well as create them. To add further punch to an already potent attack, Len had gone north of the border to Queen's Park, from where he had already coaxed Tommy Stewart, and had triumphed in bringing a certain Seamus Cyril Patrick O'Connell to Kingsway. Although he had a name as Irish as the Blarney Stone, twenty-four year-old Seamus was as English as they come: his father had come over from County Derry and settled with his wife in Carlisle, where he started a successful cattle business which now Seamus helped to run. Proud of their Irish ancestry, the O'Connell's had christened their children with good old fashioned Irish names—Seamus's sisters being Maureen, Eileen and Patricia. Seamus had an abundance of skill that had not gone unnoticed by professional clubs, including Middlesbrough and Chelsea of the First Division. Len Wilson must have had a very persuasive tongue to get a player of his proven talent to join the Kingsway amateur ranks.

Len had the vision to see this superlative trio benefiting from the creative skills of Bob Hardisty, and foresaw his forwards as the archetypal goal machine. It was, therefore, a sad loss when he died in his sleep, at the comparatively young age of fifty, at his Bishop Auckland home in the summer of 1953, his death resulting in 'Kit' Rudd once more taking over the post of Secretary at the football club.

The Rhodesia trip was an exercise in team bonding before such a term existed. It enabled the established players to get used to the new ones and vice versa: if there was a better way to prepare for the new league and cup campaigns, then the Bishop Auckland committee could not think of it. And all the while, back home, was the added bonus of the best amateur player of them all, resting himself for the rigours of the new season. Wembley was the vision. Wembley was the goal. Len Wilson and 'Kit' Rudd had never prepared for a forthcoming season on such a scale before.

On Saturday 19th December 1953, Bob Hardisty set off on the Amateur Cup trail that led to Wembley Stadium's Twin Towers. Drawn away to I.C.I. (Alkali) of the Mid-Cheshire Football League, he and the rest of the team headed off for Northwich, where the game was to be played. The tie held no fears for the players although the I.C.I. programme notes claimed of the home team that '… we are confident that we can put up a really first class performance.'

If Bishop were not worried beforehand, they had cause for concern after less than a minute. In running back for the ball, left-back Tommy Stewart, injured his foot and was forced to leave the field to receive treatment. During his absence, Jimmy Nimmins and Harry Sharratt got themselves in a pickle and it was only quick thinking by the left-half that saw the ball cleared to safety. Stewart returned after ten minutes and was able to run off his injury, although the next day his foot was swollen, and he required further treatment throughout the week.

It was Bob who provided the first piece of skill for the 'Bishops' when he latched on to a back pass from Seamus O'Connell and sent in a thundering drive that rebounded from the crossbar. The opening gave fresh confidence to the, up until now, faltering Bishop defence, and five minutes later Jacky Major linked up with Hardisty again, a move that resulted in the outside-right forcing Southern, in the ICI goal, to make a fine save. Unfortunately, his effort was in vain as it rebounded to O'Connell who slotted the ball home to put the visitors ahead. Bob found himself with a lot of freedom after that and time and time again was able to venture forward in search of a second goal. After twenty minutes, Bobby Watson waltzed down the left-wing and sent a well placed cross over but this time Bob's effort was cleared off the line by the well positioned Barlow.

ICI were always on the defensive and it was only a matter of time before O'Connell was able to increase the lead, then just before half-time, Jacky Major and Les Dixon both got their names on the score sheet. Four nil up at half-time and the 'Bishops' were coasting. Bob Hardisty was having the time of his life. It seemed such a long time since he had had such freedom in a football match. The longer the game went on, the more controlled became the play from the northerners. Bob was able to attack more than he had to defend and was unlucky when he had a goal-bound shot deflected for a corner. O'Connell completed his hat-trick, Major added the final nail in the ICI coffin and at the end of ninety minutes, Bishop Auckland had gained a comfortable 6–0 success. 'A few more games like that and we'll be okay,' remarked Bob, as he trooped from the field with Dave Marshall.

'Yes, that would be nice, Bob,' replied the full-back.

Bob got his wish, when the draw for Round Two was made just two days later. The draw immediately provided an intriguing clash of southern clubs when Wycombe Wanderers were first out of the hat to be given a tough-looking home tie against Leytonstone. Walton and Hersham followed with a seemingly equally difficult home tie against Woking and when Dulwich Hamlet were paired with Barnet, northern supporters could have been forgiven in thinking what a good draw it was turning out to be. Six fancied southern clubs pulled out of the hat had created three wonderfully difficult ties. Bishop Auckland's name followed and when the name of Ware came out next, home supporters must have been believing that their club's name was already on the Amateur Cup for the current season. Those views were extended when local Northern League side, Crook Town, were handed an extremely difficult away tie to Romford. After the draw had been made, one local correspondent for *The Northern Echo* newspaper wrote:

> In view of their great form, Bishop Auckland look a 'football certainty'. They are
> scoring goals left and right (27 in the last three matches) and their supporters are

confidently looking forward to another visit to Wembley. Ware are not a strong club and on the face of it will do well to hold the Northern League leaders to two or three goals.

The forecast proved correct on this occasion but again there was a setback for the 'Bishops' when the local press announced that Tommy Stewart was unfit to play, due to his foot injury. 'Kit' Rudd sent an SOS message to seventeen-year-old Barry Wilkinson, who was a registered Bishop Auckland player serving in the forces, requesting permission for him to play. Neither Wilkinson's commanding officer in the RAF at Yatesbury, Wiltshire, nor another club for whom he was registered and had played for in the FA Cup, Liverpool, held any objections to his participation and so it was that Barry Wilkinson was set to cover for Jimmy Nimmins in the left-half position, Nimmins moving to Stewart's full-back slot. 'Kit' Rudd's actions in getting the best possible player as a replacement was testimony to his desire to win the Amateur Cup this year—for himself, for the club and its supporters and for Bob Hardisty.

Much to 'Kit' Rudd's annoyance, he received a telegram from Barry Wilkinson within hours, which read: 'Sorry, unavailable. Notification too late.' Instead, Wilkinson had chosen to play for Liverpool against Tottenham Hotspur.

'Kit' Rudd's dissatisfaction was made perfectly clear when he claimed: 'I am extremely disappointed. We have first claim on the player.'

Early editions of *The Northern Echo* proclaimed that Tommy Stewart would now, amazingly, be fit to play and that the team would be the same one that defeated ICI (Alkali) in the previous round. In fact, there was further confusion when it was decided, fifteen minutes before the game was due to get under way, that Stewart was, once more, declared unfit and over the tannoy it was announced that Kenneth Pooley would be playing at left-back, with Jimmy Nimmins in his customary position of left half-back.

Ware had travelled from their Hertfordshire base on the eve of the match, staying at a Darlington hotel overnight before travelling on to Bishop Auckland—their two hundred supporters arriving by train on the morning of the game. They had no star names amongst their players but were trained and coached by ex-Scottish international and Chelsea left-back, Tommy Law, who had represented his country in the late 1920s. He had been a member of the Scotland team that thrashed England 5–1 at Wembley in 1928, a victory that earned members of the team the nickname of 'The Blue Devils' … and of course, it had been an opportunity to remind the English of Bannockburn!

After only ten minutes play, Ware were already heading for the exit door. Goals had rained in from the first minute, with O'Connell and Dixon getting a pair each to put the 'Bishops' 4–0 up. Bishop were relentless. Bob and Jimmy Nimmins were in control of everything in the mid-field and were able to play the game in the Ware half of the field. Ware tried to battle back but were guilty of giving the ball away too much to the eager Auckland half-backs. Centre-forward, Long, was penalized attempting too robustly to regain the ball and from the resultant free kick, Bob Hardisty crashed a thirty-five yard piledriver against the Ware crossbar. The crowd gasped at the audaciousness of the Bishop Auckland half-back for attempting such an effort from so long a distance from goal. Harry Sharratt had only back passes to deal with and the tie was as good as over when visiting left-back, Pedder, put through his own goal with a misdirected pass back to his goalkeeper.

The second-half was an anti-climax. Bishop eased off and became sloppy in their passing and it was no surprise when the visitors scored a consolation goal through their best forward, Hibbert, although his shot did take a deflection off Marshall's leg. Ten minutes from the end, Harry Sharratt was hurt when he was forced to rush from his goal area and make a spectacular clearance. He fell awkwardly and got up clutching an elbow. Play was held up whilst he received attention from the trainer but it was only when in the dressing room after the game that the club doctor diagnosed a dislocation, which he assessed he would be able to reset. Before that, though, on the field of play, Bob Hardisty weighed up the situation with his captain, Jacky Major, and the two men asked Harry to retire from the field. The game was almost over and Bishop held a comfortable lead. Bob would play the last nine minutes or so in goal. Harry would have none of it and resisted all attempts for him to leave. Foolhardy? Courageous? It was neither, it was just typical Harry Sharratt.

In the meantime, Ray Oliver got his name on the score sheet in the last minute with a header from Marshall's centre to give Bishop a very comfortable 6–1 win over the Spartan League side and send the majority of the 7,100 spectators home, happy.

It had been another easy and satisfying performance from the Bishop Auckland players and by Bob Hardisty in particular. At no stage of the game were Bishop ever in danger of defeat but what was impressing Bob more and more was the combination of Seamus O'Connell and Ray Oliver in attack.

He could not resist the thought that this time, perhaps, he might just get that elusive winners' medal.

Bishop Auckland landed another home tie in Round Three when Yorkshire League side, Hallam, would provide the opposition.

The pitch was bone hard with a few icy patches and it was apparent to everyone that the team that was first to master the conditions would be the likely winner. That honour fell to Bishop Auckland and in particular to Bob Hardisty, who was able to call on his skill and composure to develop attacking moves with ease. In the ninth minute, Bob stole the ball off a Hallam forward and went on a jinking run towards the visitors' bye-line. A quick look up and there was Seamus to nod an exquisite cross home. Four minutes later, Ray Oliver added a second and five minutes after that, Les Dixon made it three. Bishop were well on top and Bob was able to play his natural attacking game in the opposition half of the field. He was a constant threat to the Hallam defence, whether it be from incisive passing, taking on defenders with accurate dribbling or shooting from distance. The visitors' defence had no answer to his varied skills.

After twenty minutes, Bishop were awarded a free kick on the edge of the Hallam penalty area. Bob collected the ball and placed it deliberately. Everyone knew what was coming, including the defenders, who tried to form a wall. Bob strode up and hit a thunderous shot over the defenders heads. Salt, the Hallam goalkeeper, flung himself high and to his left. In that instant, the sound of the roaring crowd was replaced by the thud of the football crashing against the Hallam crossbar. The ball was cleared to safety as Bob Hardisty, hands on hips, stood looking at the mark that the ball had left on the paintwork. For the third time in as many Cup ties, he had hit the woodwork.

The Hallam defenders may have thought that they had got away with Bob's effort but it was only a short respite as Ray Oliver and Jacky Major scored additional goals before half-time. In the second half, Auckland took their foot off the pedal and failed to add to their tally, although Bob had two terrific efforts brilliantly saved by the unfortunate Salt.

The Northern Gazette's reporter is quoted as saying: 'Highlights from the Auckland angle were the goals piled on by Ray Oliver (2), Seamus O'Connell, Leslie Dixon and Jack Major, and a brilliant display of ball control and distribution by the evergreen 'Rod' Hardisty.'

The draw for Round Four gave Bishop Auckland another home game, this time against Hounslow Town. The Corinthian League side—a league generally considered inferior to the Athenian and Isthmian Leagues—had disposed of fancied Wycombe Wanderers 3–0 in Round Three and, with England international Alan King at centre-forward, were expected to prove a tough nut to crack.

Hounslow put the Bishop Auckland defence under pressure straight from the kick-off and even the usually composed Bob Hardisty was twice forced to make 'haymaker' clearances, kicking the ball into touch to break up attacks from the speedy Hounslow forwards. After twenty minutes of play, that had seen the visitors much the better side, Bob was put under pressure sufficiently for him to lose control of the ball and was dispossessed by the dangerous King. As Bob tried to recover, King beat Cresswell with a dip of the shoulder and sent a brilliant twenty-five yarder past a despairing Harry Sharratt.

For the first time in the competition, Bishop were behind and threw everything into attack. Such was their urgency to get back on terms that Harry Sharratt was even taking throw-ins and it was from such a move that Bishop drew level. Bob collected the ball from Harry and combined with Les Dixon who supplied the final pass from which Seamus O'Connell drilled home the equalizer past Percy Edwards, the Hounslow goalkeeper.

Bob continued to supply Jacky Major for sorties down the right wing, as did Jimmy Nimmins on the left side of the field, who provided Benny Edwards with the opportunity to take on full-back, Emmins. In the twenty-seventh minute, Bishop got their reward for all their purposeful play when Ray Oliver accepted O'Connell's pass and put the 'Bishops' ahead. It was all Bishop Auckland now and the Hounslow defenders did well not to concede any further goals before half-time, especially as centre-half, Briggs, was injured in a collision and had become a passenger on the wing from the thirty-eighth minute. It was, therefore, surprising that Hounslow found an equalizing goal to draw level just before half-time. With Bob Hardisty and Jimmy Nimmins up in attack, Hounslow defender Cope, hoofed the ball upfield. The ever dangerous King latched on to the ball and squeezed it past Sharratt to score.

Despite the setback of conceding a sloppy equalizer, Bishop continued pressing forward. Bob and Jimmy decided that Bob should continue in his attacking mode and that Jimmy would hold back and play a more defensive role. This had the effect of minimising the dangers of the Hounslow attacks, and gradually the 'Bishops' managed to get on top. In one particular driving movement, Bob combined again with Jacky Major only to send his cross-shot wide of the far post. In another, he saw a similar effort tipped round the post by Edwards, and just after that he provided Ray Oliver with a headed chance that just went wide. Finally, the Hounslow defence was breached again by a stunning piece of skill by Bob. Outside-right, Jacky Major, collected a pass for the umpteenth time from Bob, and as full-back Emmins made his challenge, returned the ball to the attacking wing-half, who dribbled past two defenders. Full-back, Rickard, who had been forced to deputise at centre-half due to Biggs's injury, prepared to get in a third tackle but Bob glided past him and placed a sublime pass for Major to run onto and slot the ball past Edwards.

Remarkably, with only five minutes play remaining, Bob made an error similar to that which had provided Hounslow's opening goal. Having won the ball from an opponent, Bob decided to dribble the ball clear, out of his defence. The ever alert King won the ball back but with only Sharratt to beat, surprisingly placed his effort wide. Harry had a few choice words to say to Bob who accepted the admonishment, apologising for his error. Two minutes later, Ray Oliver outjumped the Hounslow defence to put the issue beyond doubt and Bishop were through to the next round of the competition by the slightly flattering score-line 4–2. They had not played as well as they could and Bob Hardisty had had one of those 'in and out' days. Nevertheless, they were through to the semi-finals and who knows what could happen, now?

I t is remarkable that an innocuously simple task of drawing names out of a hat, for the purposes of deciding the ties and venues for the semi-finals of the FA Amateur Cup competition, could generate a high degree of controversy. Yet that is exactly what happened in March 1954.

The north had always believed that southern clubs received favouritism from the southern based, biased FA whenever possible, and in particular whenever they were drawn against their northern cousins, no matter how slight that favouritism may have seemed. In 1947, the semi-final draw of the Amateur Cup had resulted in Leytonstone meeting Barnet at Brentford and in the second tie, Wimbledon were drawn to meet the only northern survivors, Bishop Auckland, at Dulwich Hamlet's ground. Northern fans were angry that both games were to be played 'down south'. In response to the north's protestations, the FA issued an explanation, declaring that as Wimbledon had been drawn out of the hat first they were the *de facto* home club, and the practice was to stage the semi-final on a ground as near as possible to the 'home' club, in this case the home club being Wimbledon. If ever there was a case of juggling the facts to arrive at a preconceived conclusion this was it.

Seven years later, the semi-final draw resulted in the following ties:

Crook Town v Finchley or Walthamstow Avenue
at White Hart Lane, Tottenham
Bishop Auckland v Briggs Sports or Pegasus at St James's Park, Newcastle

As soon as the draw was made, Pegasus and Briggs Sports objected to the choice of St James's Park. Northern supporters feared the worst—the FA would find reason to select an alternative venue nearer the south, and thereby mean more travelling for northern supporters, although, in truth, Bishop Auckland had not had to do that much travelling this campaign. Crook Town also made it known that they were unhappy with the choice of venue should their tie with Walthamstow Avenue have to be replayed, and that they would be lodging a protest immediately.

Bob Hardisty was asked about the situation and diplomatically replied that he and his fellow players did not mind where their game was to be played, whether it be in the north or down south. He did wonder why Newcastle's ground had been chosen rather than that of Sunderland's, the only senior club in County Durham. True, Sunderland had been originally set to play Preston North End at home in a First Division fixture on March 13th, the day of the semi-final, but as Preston were due to play an FA Cup game that day, the situation resolved itself. Bob expressed the view that Bishop Auckland supporters, however, would be quite happy to cross the Tyne and play at St James's. He went on to say that he hoped that Crook Town would overcome their semi-final opponents and thereby provide the country with another all-northern Amateur Cup Final.

The other tie was also not without criticism. Crook Town had no qualms about meeting Walthamstow Avenue at White Hart Lane but they strongly objected to the venue for any replay—Boothferry Crescent, Hull. 'Where was the local interest in that?' questioned Crook Town supporters and officials. They suggested that any replay should take place at Roker Park, Sunderland, which would be available on the date for any replay, as Crook fans would not have as far to travel. They also argued that playing any replay at Roker Park would be in accord with the 'home' principle evinced by the FA seven years earlier. Crook were supported in their objections by the Durham Football Association as well as Bishop Auckland Football Club.

A rather beleaguered Sir Stanley Rous informed the press that objections to the draw had been received by three clubs and that the issues raised would be considered by the appropriate committee within the next few days.

On the following Thursday, Pegasus and Briggs Sports were informed that they had been unsuccessful in their objection (the FA showing a remarkable support for the north but in truth were probably vexed by the two clubs—one of whom, Pegasus, had received every encouragement from the Football Association in the past few seasons, having been allowed to miss earlier rounds of the competition—and did not wish to see their authority questioned) and that the tie would take place as originally planned.

Crook Town, on the other hand, were more successful in their appeal and the FA showed an equally remarkable degree of support for the northern club when they agreed to any replay being played at Roker Park, Crook Town's original choice of venue.

Bishop Auckland prepared for the semi-final with three days intensive training under the tutelage of a specialised trainer/coach, namely George Ainsley, considered to be one of the best FA coaches in the game. His playing career had been as an inside-forward for Sunderland and Leeds United, and as recently as last season he had been coaching the Pegasus players. Up until now, this current season he had been looking after Yorkshire Amateurs but when Chairman, George Waine and Secretary, 'Kit' Rudd came a' calling, he was happy to transfer his services to help the south-west Durham club. His first look at the Bishop Auckland players was at Ayresome Park, where Bishop took in a practice match against a Middlesbrough XI which the home side won 2–1. The purpose of the match was to introduce the players to a playing surface equal in size to that of St James's Park: the Bishop Auckland committee were determined to reach Wembley and would leave no stone unturned in their efforts. Briggs Sports were the underdogs and considered to be the outsiders of all the teams in the semi-final draw but Bishop would take no chances, especially as Briggs had knocked out Bromley and cup holders Pegasus in previous rounds, both of whom had failed to score.

A crowd of more than 54,000—paying an incredible gate for an amateur game of £7,856—turned up to watch the match, the majority, of course, cheering on the 'Two Blues'. Surprisingly, for a semi-final game, Bishop found themselves easily dominating their southern opponents and twenty-five minutes had elapsed before Harry Sharratt was called upon to make the semblance of a save, by which time the 'Bishops' held a commanding 3–0 lead. Goals from O'Connell, Oliver and Watson had wrapped the game up although Briggs' left-winger, Green, pulled one back after twenty-six minutes.

Bob Hardisty had had a comfortable game. In defence, he was easily foiling the threat of inside-forwards, Kempster and Smith, whilst in attack he was able to split the Briggs defence and feed his forwards. Called upon to take a free-kick on the edge of the Briggs penalty area, he saw his drive headed clear by Bradford, who could have known little about it. Bob and Jimmy Nimmins had been able to control the centre of the field and with Corbett Cresswell blocking out sixteen-year-old centre-forward sensation, Les Allen—who would go on to make his mark in League football, as would his son, Clive—every Bishop Auckland player and supporter was confident of the outcome.

In the second half, Bob and Jimmy continued to dominate proceedings, although it took a while for them to orchestrate a fourth goal. Feeding Seamus O'Connell with a delightful pass, the former Queen's Park forward delivered a stinging shot that was only partially saved by Goddard. The ball would have spun into the net without Ray Oliver's assistance but it was the lifeboatman's goal. Les Dixon added a fifth and at the finish, Auckland were deserving 5–1 winners. Wembley was ready to receive the 'Bishops' once more.

The whole north-east of England had an anxious wait for it to be settled whether or not there was to be an all-Durham Amateur Cup Final for the second time in four years. Crook Town had earned themselves a replay in the other semi-final with a 1–1 draw, Walthamstow Avenue surviving a late onslaught by the Northern League club. The replay at Sunderland was a triumph for Crook centre-forward, Ken Harrison, who scored all of their goals in a 3–2 win. Seven days after Bishop Auckland had cruised their way to the final, near neighbours Crook Town had followed suit. The north had been granted its wish.

For the next three weeks, players from both clubs were inundated with requests for tickets and invitations to speak at pubs and clubs throughout the area. Bob Hardisty was more used to such appearances than most of the other players and was in great demand to air his views upon the perceived outcome of the Final. During the day, his employment would take him all over the county and wherever he went he was met with the same question: 'This time, Bob?' A polite smile was usually enough for an answer. Requests for his appearance throughout the north-east were never ending and he did his best to attend every one of them. On some evenings he would attend two or even three events just so that he did not let anyone down by having to refuse. Occasionally, he would be in attendance with a Crook player at the same venue and in such circumstances there would be a more lively debate about the Wembley outcome but he would never be drawn into making any firm prophesy. At every meeting, he always ended the evening by saying that he expected a tough match and that it made little difference that Bishop Auckland had already won both Northern League games that season involving the two clubs. He hoped that the best team would win and that it would be Bishop that carried off the trophy—that is as far as he would go. Bob would not tempt Providence—he had become suspicious of Wembley.

It was widely held that the two best amateur teams in the land had made it to the final. There was little between them in the Northern League, although Bishop Auckland were slight favourites as they were top of that league and, as already stated, had recorded two successes already over their closest rivals.

Crook were only two points behind the 'Bishops' and their players were confident that it would be a case of 'third time lucky'. Theirs had been an interesting passage to Wembley. A 3–0 away win at Shildon in Round One had been followed with a 1–1 draw against a tough Romford team. The replay had resulted in a very comfortable 6–0 home win and in Round Three they had thumped a dangerous Walton and Hersham side 5–0 at the Millfield. Another home tie in Round Four had seen the score of the round. On the day that Bishop Auckland were struggling to knock out Hounslow at Kingsway, and Willington were losing at home to Pegasus, they hammered unfortunate Hitchin Town 10–1. Then had come the semi-final games against fancied Walthamstow Avenue and eventual victory at Sunderland. Clearly, this Amateur Cup Final was no foregone conclusion. Bishop Auckland might have the pedigree in the competition to have reached fifteen finals and had already contested two Wembley finals but they had yet to win there, and Crook had every reason not to be daunted. A team from Crook had won the trophy as far back as 1900–01 when they defeated King's Lynn 3–0. The current club was a resurrection of a previous one and in reality this was the club's first appearance in the final and, of course, at Wembley.

Four years ago, the small mining town of Willington had been caught up in cup fever and had surprised the football world, when trouncing the favourites 4–0. This time it was the turn of Crook, a town built on the mining industry, situated just two miles from Willington and six from Bishop Auckland. Their team had made it to Wembley without the cushion of a reserve team and had used only a total of fifteen players. Every shop, pub, school and office was bedecked with black and amber bunting and banners, proclaiming allegiance to their heroes, although one or two brave souls within the town did venture to voice their support for the 'Bishops', including this writer's father!

Bishop Auckland supporters had been enthusiastic with the arrival of George Ainsley as a recognized trainer but Crook produced a trump card when it was announced that Joe Harvey, manager of Newcastle United, had been given permission by his club Chairman Stan Seymour, to take charge of Crook Town's training programme. Crook President, Billy Parkin, and Secretary, George Charlton, were clearly throwing down the gauntlet for Bishop Auckland Chairman, George Waine, and Secretary, 'Kit' Rudd—they meant business. Under Joe Harvey, the Crook players would be introduced to the large St James's Park pitch and its floodlights. Harvey must have worked a miracle on the Crook players as he had them playing against a Newcastle XI which resulted in an 8–1 win for his amateurs. Not surprisingly, Crook were full of confidence.

Ironically, it should have been Bob Hardisty and company being tested at the St James's Park ground as Newcastle had invited the players and officials of Bishop Auckland to practice on their ground as soon as they had despatched Briggs Sports in the semi-final. The Bishop Auckland committee accepted Newcastle's offer but when Crook Town beat Walthamstow Avenue in the semi-final replay, a similar offer of help was made to them by Stan Seymour. Newcastle did not see any reason for controversy in offering a helping hand to two local teams but when Joe Harvey was confirmed as the coach to assist Crook in their Cup Final efforts, George Waine made a diplomatic statement saying 'Owing to unforeseen circumstances we have decided not to play at Newcastle. We consider it unwise to continue with the game and have written to Newcastle United on our decision.'

For once, the committee were correct in their unanimous decision: it would have been tactical suicide to play a Newcastle side, even behind closed doors, at the very home of Crook Town's new coach.

To finalize their training, Bishop Auckland turned to their old allies, Middlesbrough, who once again provided the 'Bishops' with extra training facilities and a full scale practice match. They were not hospitable hosts—they trounced the amateurs 7–3!

More than two hundred private coaches and twenty special trains made the journey from south-west Durham to the metropolis, as well as thousands of cars making their way down the A1 in the early hours of Saturday April 10th. Whole families formed part of the exodus that would result in the streets of Crook and Bishop Auckland being comparatively deserted. Many had left as early as Wednesday to stay with friends and relatives but there were many who had no idea where they would be staying the nights before the match. All that they were interested in was getting to Wembley, match ticket in hand. The LNER had taken the decision that Crook supporters travelling by train would be channelled to Marylebone Station, while the Bishop Auckland supporters would be taken to King's Cross. Both teams left for London by train on the Friday morning.

Within both towns, many shops and businesses closed down for the whole weekend, not opening until Monday morning, and it was reported that some benevolent firms in the area had given their employees financial aid to help meet the travelling costs involved in making the trip to Wembley. Those businesses that did remain open had either a wireless or television installed, in order that workers and customers could keep up with the game. In Bishop Auckland Town Hall, a local television dealer was to 'demonstrate a television projector set' on the Saturday afternoon, and anyone unable to attend Wembley was invited to come along and watch the second half, which was being broadcast by the BBC. Elsewhere, at Bankfoot Coke Works, just outside Crook, *The Northern Gazette* reported that workers unable to get to Wembley because of shift work would be able to see the television broadcast, as a local firm would be installing a television in the works rest room.

Bob Hardisty and Jimmy Nimmins sat on the same bench that they had occupied three years ago when Pegasus had defeated them. Each one was hoping that this time the result would be different and that they would taste the sweet smell of success. Jimmy asked Bob about his father and said how proud he must be, sat in the Royal Box as a committee member, ready to watch his son play on Wembley's hallowed turf again. It would not be the first time that Jack Hardisty had watched him play at the home of English football as he had attended the other Amateur Cup Finals that Bob had played in but he had told his son, this game would be different. 'You'll be playing the second best team in the country, Bob,' had said Jack, just a few hours before 'but just remember, you are playing for the best team in the country. Do your best and everything should be all right, this time, barring accidents,' not knowing just how prophetic the last two words of his statement would be.

The players were summoned from the confines of the dressing room to line up in the tunnel and Bob fell in line behind young Ron Fryer for the parade on to Wembley's luscious turf. He was well used to the proceedings by now and just wanted the game to get under way. As he gazed out of the mouth of the tunnel into the sunlight, he could just make out the crowd filling the distant West Stand behind the goal. 'How are you feeling, Ron?' he said, to his diminutive left-back, who had been chosen to replace Tommy Stewart who had gone down with chicken pox earlier in the week. This was his first visit to Wembley as he had never been before, not even as a spectator.

'I'm fine, Bob. Can't wait to get out there,' responded the nineteen-year old. 'I just hope I don't let Tommy Stewart down—he is such a great player. It certainly won't be for the want of trying.'

'That's the spirit, Ron. You'll be okay. Treat it like any other game but try to conserve some energy for the last twenty minutes—this pitch can sap your strength before you know it,' advised Bob, hoping he did not sound too much like the school master that he had been.

Before any more conversation could take place, the other dressing room door opened and out strode Crook Town captain, Bobby Davison and the rest of the Crook team.

Bobby Davison recalls:

We had had a good long talk in the dressing room. Ken Williamson, our inside-left, had been carrying a leg injury and news had leaked out about it a few days before the Saturday. Joe Harvey wanted Ken to play. To test out his leg, Ken had played a game of squash on the Thursday. Joe Harvey wanted to make sure, though, and when we got to London, he and Ken went straight to Highbury where the Arsenal physiotherapist and Joe put Ken through some very strenuous exercises. Ken passed the examination. John Taylor, who like me had played for Bishop against Pegasus in 1951, had been nursing an injured ankle at the beginning of the week but he was deemed fit to play come the Saturday. There was a fear that Bill Jeffs, our right-half might struggle if his groin injury flared up again. He had injured it before the semi-final and had been given special treatment from the Billingham Synthonia trainer, Fred Robson, who knew exactly how to put things like that right. So we had a few worries, right up to the last minute, but we were confident that if all went well, we were capable of winning the cup. Bob might have to wait another year for his winners' medal.

When I led the lads out from the dressing room, the first player I set eyes on was Bob. He looked calm and was talking to a young player, Ron Fryer, no doubt trying to put the young lad at ease. He wished me all the best and I did likewise then I went and stood next to Bishop captain, Jacky Major, at the head of the line. Each of us was joined by a member of our committee who would lead the teams out. For Crook it was Billy Parkin and for Bishop it was George Waine. I seem to remember that the majority of Crook supporters were on the side of the Royal Box while the Bishop fans were on the other side, to our left as we came out in to the blazing sunlight. The next few minutes was just a blur, it all happened so quickly. One minute we were in the quiet subdued light of the tunnel, the next minute we were marching out to 100,000 supporters producing the most amazing crescendo of noise you ever heard and I'm shaking hands with the dignitaries, one of whom was the Lord Mayor of London, Sir Noel Bowater, another being Sir Stanley Rous. I don't remember much else before the referee, the one-armed Alf Bond, set proceedings under way.

The teams were:

Bishop Auckland (Dark and Light blue halved shirts, White shorts)
Sharratt—Marshall, Fryer—Hardisty, Cresswell,
Nimmins—Major, Dixon, Oliver, O'Connell, Watson

Crook Town (Amber shirts, Black shorts)
Jarrie—Riley, Steward—Jeffs, Davison, Taylor—Appleby,
Thompson, Harrison, Williamson, McMillan

Referee: Alf Bond of Middlesex

Alf Bond was one of the Football League's most respected referees but had it not been for an accident he would not have become one at all. He loved football and had hoped to make a career of it but, when aged nineteen, had suffered a factory accident, resulting in the loss of his right arm. Undeterred at not being able to play, he had taken the whistle and climbed his way up the footballing ranks. Moving from junior football, he progressed to the Football Combination and then on to Football League games, initially taking charge of games in the lower divisions, and then eventually on to the First Division and internationals. He argued that his physical disability was no handicap and always reckoned that, so long as a referee had a whistle and a finger, there was no need to have two hands. He was a pragmatic person but carried a superstition: in his early career, he had apparently had a bad match—bad-tempered players, contentious decisions, disputed goals etc. As he sat in the dressing room after the match, he took notice that the laces on his boots were old and dirty. He decided, there and then, that he would always take to the field with a new pair of white laces. Unfortunately, this most amiable of men, would fall into disfavour with the supporters of one of today's clubs, in making one of the most controversial decisions in an Amateur Cup Final.

Bob Hardisty took up his usual position at right-half, facing the tunnel from where they had just emerged, and prepared himself for the next ninety minutes, barring extra time, that would determine the outcome of the 1954 Amateur Cup Final and decide upon whether or not he would leave this stadium with a winners' or a losers' medal. What was to follow would go down as one of football's most epic encounters in the history of the game.

Ken Harrison kicked off for Crook but the move broke down when Ray Oliver intercepted his pass and set up a counter-move with Bobby Watson that came to nothing. Bob's first involvement of play was in the second minute, when he gained the ball from a misdirected Jeffs pass. He combined with Les Dixon before playing a daisy-cutting pass to Jacky Major. The usually so reliable wingman completely mistook the pace of the ball and the move fizzled out, with the winger unable to take proper control of the football.

Two minutes later, after a series of end-to-end play, Bishop were awarded a free kick, which Bob took. He deliberately placed the ball and looked up. His target was centre-forward, Ray Oliver, who rose to accept the delivery. He was impeded by Crook's Bobby Davison and the header was not a strong one, going well wide of the goal but Bobby Watson retrieved the situation only to send a weak shot past Jarrie's near post.

Only five minutes play had taken place when tragedy struck the 'Bishops'. Jimmy Nimmins, so tough and so strong, went down in the centre circle without an opponent being near. He had gone to turn and somehow injured his leg; it was the type of body movement that ninety-nine times out of a hundred would not produce an injury of any kind. This was the hundredth time. Fred Scales, Bishop Auckland trainer, was on the field to offer medical assistance and gauge the situation. A quick inspection of Jimmy's leg and it was obvious that he would have to leave the field—hopefully, only a temporary measure but for the time being it would mean the 'Two Blues' would be playing with only ten men.

Jacky Major took signals from George Ainsley and quickly ran over to Bob, at the same time beckoning Seamus O'Connell to join them. The three huddled together for a few moments, in total concentration at what was being proposed. Seamus was to take up Jimmy's vacated position at left-half and Bob was to act as a roving mid-field link man with the remaining forwards. Jacky's parting words to Seamus before play resumed were: 'If in doubt, Seamus, give it to Bob or just kick it out. With any luck, Jimmy will be back soon and we'll be able to resume as normal.'

Seamus accepted his new responsibility with enthusiasm and every tackle that he produced was cheered by the mass of Bishop Auckland supporters.

After ten minutes, Crook's outside-right, Eddie Appleby, took on the Bishop defence but was adjudged to have fouled Seamus. A free kick was awarded well inside the Bishop Auckland penalty area. Seamus would take the kick and Bob made a move to support his forwards, who were lining up midway in the Crook half. Jacky Major, anxious that the free kick might come to no avail and that Crook would then launch a counter attack, called to Bob to stay back. Bob was disappointed, as he thought that the free kick might just throw up a scoring opportunity. He was right.

From Seamus's long, hopeful ball, Les Dixon outpaced the Crook offside trap and raced to the edge of the penalty area where his right foot connected with the football, sending it screaming under Fred Jarrie. Against the odds, the ten men were a goal to the good and what a stunning effort it had been.

Within two minutes, Crook were level. From a John Taylor throw-in, the ball was flicked on to Ronnie Thompson. The Crook inside-forward had spent some time with the 'Bishops' prior to joining Crook but had been unable to command a regular place. He took his revenge on being discarded—with a neat bit of control with his right foot he sent a scorching left-footed drive that beat Harry Sharratt to the Bishop goalkeeper's left. Only twelve minutes had gone and already this was turning into a classic encounter.

Bishop were encouraged when Jimmy Nimmins returned to the fray after twenty minutes but his participation was restricted to that of a passenger and he played the rest of the half out on the left flank, with Bobby Watson playing a deeper role than that to which he was accustomed. However, Seamus O'Connell was proving a natural in Jimmy's position and time and again broke up Crook attacks on the left side of the field. If it was Crook's plan to play mainly down their right flank, in order to put pressure on raw full-back,

Ron Fryer, then that plan was coming unstuck due to the cool display from O'Connell, playing immediately in front of the youngster.

Just after Nimmins returned, it was Crook's supporters turn to feel dismay. Ken Williamson—the former Bishop Auckland inside-forward who had returned to the association football code, after a spell playing rugby union—went down, clutching his left foot. Crook sponge man, Charlie Peart, helped Williamson from the field and administered treatment sufficiently for the inside-forward to return after four minutes.

With play passing from one end to the other, both teams' defences were put under intense pressure, even though each side had a man short in attack. Ken Harrison had a great chance when Corbett Cresswell slipped, but with only Harry Sharratt to beat, the centre-forward shot wildly over the bar. Another Harrison opportunity went astray, thanks to the timely intervention of Seamus and then immediately afterwards, Bob Hardisty blocked a Jimmy McMillan drive that was goalbound. Bishop were riding their luck during this spell of the game.

Two minutes later, the 'Two Blues' were ahead again, the result of an amazing piece of skill by Ray Oliver. The ball was won, yet again, by O'Connell, who supplied the effervescent Bobby Watson who, in turn, looked up to see what his options were. He immediately sent a searching pass to Ray Oliver, who collected the ball out on the left. Bursting through, Oliver beat three defenders before delivering a stunning volley from the edge of the Crook penalty area. Jarrie got both hands to the ball but such was the force at which it was travelling, that it still found its way into the goal.

Crook responded immediately and were unlucky not to draw level when, from a free kick on the half-way line, Harrison headed the ball past Sharratt in a crowded goalmouth, only for Alf Bond to rule out the goal due to a foul on the Bishop goalkeeper—a let off for the 'Bishops'.

There was plenty of action in the remaining ten minutes of the first half but there were no further goals and with a one goal lead, it was the Bishop Auckland players that left the field, slightly happier than their county neighbours.

In the sanctuary of the dressing room, Jimmy Nimmins was given a hasty examination whereupon it was decided that his day was over—he would have to go to hospital. He leaned over to Bob as he was despatched to the waiting ambulance:

'I told you Bob—I hate this fucking place. Best of luck, lads.'

During what remained of the half-time break, George Ainsley dispensed words of encouragement to his players. Each one of them was spoken to and reminded of his specific role.

'If in doubt, give the ball to Bob.'

'Bob, you are the link between defence and attack.'

'Corbett, keep it tight with Harrison.'

'Ron, you are doing fine. Don't try anything fancy. Play your normal game.'

'Jacky, keep talking to the lads out there.'

'Ray, the lads will supply you as best as they can. Don't give up.'

'Seamus, why have you been wasting your time as an inside-forward?'

The attendant pushed his head round the door and called the players to return to the pitch for the second half. The two sets of players returned to thunderous applause and when they lined up, Ray Oliver got the second half under way.

Williamson had been on the treatment table in the Crook dressing room during the half-time break but it was clear that he was not fully fit. He took up a position wide on the Crook Town left, with Jimmy McMillan moving to the inside-left spot. It was McMillan who was instrumental in the first attack of the second half. Feeding John Taylor, the half-back was allowed to approach the Bishop penalty area where he fired a shot at goal. Harry Sharratt was forced to make a diving save and only fully recovered the ball at the second attempt.

Bishop retaliated when Bob Hardisty collected a Dave Marshall clearance and, seemingly for the thousandth time, passed to Jacky Major. The wingman took on Bobby Davison and, having rounded the giant centre-half, looked certain to score but Fred Jarrie was equal to the task. A goal then and in all probability, Bishop would have been in the clear and gone on to win the game. As it was, Major's miss was to prove costly as Crook scored in their next attack. Williamson, Thompson and Appleby weaved a wonderful combination of passes down the Crook right wing, which ended with Williamson taking the ball to the bye-line, where he pulled it back for the grateful Appleby to send in a thumping shot from ten yards out, leaving Sharratt helpless.

Undeterred, Bishop came back with three attacks in the space of as many minutes. First, Davison cleared a Bob Hardisty header, then he foiled Dixon with a well-timed block and a minute later it was Davison again when he twice prevented Ray Oliver adding to his tally. However, it was Crook who went closest to scoring again when, with only five minutes of normal time remaining, Cresswell let in Harrison, who beat Sharratt all ends up, only to watch his effort crash against the underside of the crossbar and rebound into the safe hands of the relieved Bishop Auckland goalkeeper.

It was turning out to be a magnificent spectacle between two fine sides, neither of which could gain supremacy over the other. Bob Hardisty was forced into conceding a corner when McMillan easily beat him on the outside but Thompson's effort was easily collected by Sharratt. The Bishop goalkeeper, however, was brought in to more dramatic action when Williamson was allowed room in the penalty area to send in a terrific shot. Sharratt had anticipated the ball going to his right. Instead, Williamson's goalbound strike was to his left. Amazingly, Harry twisted his body in mid-air and brought off an incredible save that even had the Crook fans applauding.

Not to be outdone, Fred Jarrie brought off a fine save from Oliver's header; it may not have been as spectacular as Harry Sharratt's save a few minutes earlier but it was just as important. Then, in the dying seconds, the Crook goalkeeper brought off another fine save when he kept out a Bobby Watson lob. After ninety minutes, the score was 2–2 and now there would be an extra thirty minutes on Wembley's strength sapping surface.

In the brief few minutes before extra time got under way, George Ainsley could be seen cajoling his players for more effort; Joe Harvey, his Crook Town counterpart, was doing the same. George had his players in a huddle and urged them to adopt a different style of play for the extra thirty minutes.

Dave Marshall, Bishop Auckland full-back, recalls:

> George Ainsley had us all together. He repeated what he had said individually to us at half-time but with one major change. Up until now, Seamus had been deployed in a defensive position, taking over from the injured Jimmy Nimmins. Now, George instructed Seamus and Bob to play in a more attacking role. He reasoned that the Crook defence would be tiring now and that they would be suspect against the pressure that the pair of them would apply, working with Les Dixon and Ray Oliver, as they had done throughout the season. Don't forget, that including the Rhodesian tour, the three of them had scored a stack of goals. By the end of that season, including the Rhodesian tour, Jacky Major had scored 25, Les Dixon 48, Ray Oliver 50, Seamus O'Connell 65 and Bobby Watson 11—199 in all.

Les Dixon was given the first opportunity to score, when he raced through a static defence only for Bobby Davison to stick out a leg and deflect the ball for a corner, over Jarrie's crossbar. Bob Hardisty took the corner but Davison outjumped Oliver and the ball was cleared but only to Seamus, waiting in the midfield. The ball was swiftly returned and this time, Oliver took it under control, only to see his shot punched out by a diving Jarrie.

It was all Bishop now, even though they were a man down. True, Crook were handicapped by the limping Williamson but at least he was still on the field of play and had proved himself to be a lot more than just nuisance value. Seamus and Bob were the joint creators of Bishop's moves and they kept the supply line going by feeding Ray Oliver and Les Dixon. Les was still able to show his speed against the failing legs of the Crook defenders but the goal that would give the 'Bishops' victory and Bob Hardisty his winners' medal would not come. Time and again, shots hit valiant defenders or went wide of Jarrie's post with the Crook attack offering little in return. It seemed certain that the ten men of Bishop Auckland would pull through but, at the end of one hundred and twenty gruelling minutes, these two magnificent teams had failed to provide a conclusive result.

When Alf Bond blew his whistle for the last time, twenty-one players shook hands and took in a deep breath. It had been one of the most exhilarating games to watch and would have been more exhausting for the players, who had given everything for their clubs and supporters. Respected BBC Radio and Television commentator, Kenneth Wolstenholme, who had delivered the game that afternoon to the television and radio world said: 'I have just witnessed the finest two hours of entertainment that I have ever seen.'

South-west Durham had served up another banquet for the football aficionados, with a little touch of history—for the first time, a Wembley Cup Final would require a replay. Wolstenholme was not alone in issuing fulsome praise, as every member of the pressroom voiced similar epithets. Every member of the two teams had played right up to their merits but in selecting a 'Man of the Match' *The Northern Gazette* correspondent was in no doubt that the mantle should go to Bob Hardisty:

> The outstanding figure of this magnificent game was the veteran, Bob Hardisty. Oh, how he strived for that elusive cup-winners' medal. His football was excellent and, in extra time, he looked one of the fittest players on the field, proof of the thorough way he has trained this season … He looked as if he had been training for 120 minutes instead of the usual 90 and showed the England selectors that at thirty-three he is still England's best right-half.

Two hours later, Bob and his colleagues were joined by those family members that had made the journey to London, at their hotel, The Great Eastern Hotel. It was a sober affair, with the players unsure whether to celebrate a magnificent performance in procuring a draw with only ten men, or to be grateful that they would have another chance of winning the trophy in ten days time, when the replay would be held at St James's Park. The mood became significantly brighter when Jimmy Nimmins returned from hospital, accompanied by his lovely wife, Lillian. His right leg was in plaster and he was on crutches. The doctors had diagnosed a fractured fibula as well as ruptured ligaments to his knee and ankle, and the plaster would have to stay for at least eight weeks.

After the usual 'celebratory' meal, some of the players and families remained in the confines of the hotel but Bob had other ideas. He just wanted to get away and found two willing allies in Jimmy and Lillian. They visited the regular 'watering hole' of Finnegan's Bar, where they were later joined by Ray Oliver and Seamus O'Connell. Having sampled the delights of Finnegan's, Bob looked at his watch and casually remarked that the trains would be leaving at regular intervals now, to return the Bishop and Crook supporters. In that instant, it was decided that they would order a taxi to take them to King's Cross, where they would hope to talk to some of their supporters, before they began their long journey home.

It was a gesture that was much appreciated by those supporters fortunate to meet Bob and company. Many of them were cheered to see Jimmy, resplendent with his crutches, and all wished him a speedy recovery.

The unofficial send off party remained at King's Cross until well past midnight before making their weary way back to the hotel.

'St James's next, Bob,' said Seamus, back at the Great Eastern. 'At least we have a bit of experience at that ground,' he continued, referring to the semi-final victory over Briggs Sports.

'Aye, and so have Crook,' responded Bob. 'Don't forget that Joe Harvey has had them training there every day for the past three weeks. It will be like a home game for them.'

Ten days later, the two teams lined up to do battle once more for the honour of winning the coveted Amateur Cup. In the event of another draw, the Football Association had decided that the game would take place at Ayresome Park, Middlesbrough, in three days time—it was hoped that such arrangements would not prove necessary.

Both sides had been forced into making changes. Ron Fryer, who had put up such a fine performance on Wembley's testing turf, was brought back down to earth when he sprained his right knee ligaments in a Northern League game at West Auckland on the Good Friday, just three days before this Cup Final replay, and would be unfit to play. The good news, however, was that Tommy Stewart was over his bout of chicken pox and ready to return. Barry Wilkinson, still on National Service, was drafted in to take Jimmy Nimmins's place, Seamus O'Connell reverting to his customary position of inside-left.

In the Crook camp, the brave Ken Williamson had announced his retirement from football immediately upon returning to the Wembley dressing room, acknowledging that his right knee was no longer up to facing the rigours of competitive football. Aged only twenty-five, his was a sad loss to the game. His place was to be taken by John Coxon, another Crook player who had previously spent some time with the 'Bishops'.

The teams were:

Bishop Auckland (Dark and Light blue halved shirts, White shorts)
Sharratt—Marshall, Stewart—Hardisty, Cresswell,
Wilkinson—Major, Dixon, Oliver, O'Connell, Watson

Crook Town (Amber shirts, Black shorts)
Jarrie—Riley, Steward—Jeffs, Davison, Taylor—Appleby,
Thompson, Harrison, Coxon, McMillan

Referee: Alf Bond of Middlesex

On the stroke of six o'clock, on a beautiful sunny Easter Monday, Ray Oliver kicked off the proceedings. Four minutes later, he had repeated the act a further twice. Incredibly, Bishop Auckland were two goals down and Bob Hardisty had only twice touched the ball—he was watching his dream of a winners' medal falling over the horizon with its backside on fire!

Despite having the benefit of the kick-off, Bishop had lost the ball to Ronnie Thompson who robbed O'Connell of the football. Thompson, who had spent some time with the 'Two Blues' in 1952 and had been wanted by Fulham, played a delightful pass to Ken Harrison. The Annfield Plain schoolmaster made no mistake and netted with a looping drive to Harry Sharratt's right.

Incredibly, Crook scored a second when a long punt upfield cleared the Bishop Auckland defence and Harrison was on hand to slot the ball past a bemused Sharratt. The cup favourites were losing 2–0 after only four minutes. It could have been even worse as Thompson sent a shot wide, when tackled by Bob Hardisty in the fifth minute.

Like a heavyweight boxing champion caught by a sucker punch, the Auckland players strove to clear their heads and bring some kind of sense to the proceedings. Gradually, Bob and Corbett Cresswell brought a measured sense of calm to the defence and were able to break up the Crook attacks down their left flank, Bishop's right. Things were a little different on the left side of play, however, where Tommy Stewart was having a torrid time against the speedy Appleby, who was always proving dangerous with his link-ups with Bill Jeffs, Ronnie Thompson and Ken Harrison. Fortunately for Bishop, no more goals were forthcoming from the Crook forwards but equally, they had shown little in attack to give their supporters encouragement for the remaining seventy-five minutes or so of the match.

Things looked decidedly brighter for the 'Two Blues' and their supporters when, after twenty minutes, Hardisty easily beat Coxon to the tackle and played a through pass for Ray Oliver to run on to but the centre-forward's shot went wide. It was the first threatening move that the Bishop midfield had created and turned out to be the only real chance of the half.

When Alf Bond blew for half-time, the Crook defence had shown themselves to be well on top and satisfied to play a holding game, with the cushion of a two-goal lead. The Bishop Auckland defence had woken up after a disastrous start and Corbett Cresswell was now proving a commanding figure in the centre of defence, ably supported by his two wing-halves. Creatively, though, Bishop had been disappointing. Bob Hardisty had been forced to spend more time on defensive duties and had not been allowed the freedom that he had experienced at Wembley—other than the opening that he had carved out for Oliver, he was having a quiet game. Collectively, the Bishop Auckland players had endured a frustrating forty-five minutes, unable to produce their usual free-flowing style, they had been regularly finding themselves cramped for space. As a result, they had been pressured in to making hasty passes, showing little in the way of composure.

Like a wounded tiger, the Bishop Auckland players came out fighting for the second half. Urged on by frantic supporters shouting themselves hoarse, they mounted one attack after another upon the Crook rearguard. Bobby Davison and his fellow team mates stood solid as each attack was repulsed. Fred Jarrie, who had previously spent some time with his home town club,

Hartlepool United, may have had an easy time in the first half but now he was being called upon to do his duty. First Oliver, then O'Connell, fired in shots that he was able to collect without much trouble but after sixty-nine minutes, the break that Bishop had struggled so hard to achieve, was made.

Bob had come more into the game in the second half. With the Crook defenders playing further back (either through choice or because of the sustained Auckland pressure was unclear), Bob was able to present a more domineering figure and it was from his cultured feet that Bishop's best moves came, although the goal itself came from a free-kick.

As he had done on many occasions before, Bob deliberately placed the ball and steadied himself to deliver an accurate cross. He sent over a long, curling ball into the Crook goalmouth that Ray Oliver was unable to control. The Crook supporters breathed a sigh of relief when Davison cleared the danger, but the ball was swiftly returned. The ever alert Oliver collected the ball and, before John Taylor could get in his challenge, delivered a right foot volley past Jarrie who was rooted to his goal line. It was just the fillip that the 'Bishops' needed.

From that moment on, Bob Hardisty took control of the game by the scruff of the neck. With a successive stream of crunching tackles and piercing passes, he became the central figure that would orchestrate every meaningful Bishop attack. The Crook defence had been put under terrific pressure for those last thirty minutes at Wembley and now they were in for a repeat of the same. For all their attacking moves, Bishop were fortunate to survive a Harrison effort that thundered against Sharratt's crossbar but largely, it was Bishop Auckland who looked the more likely scorers at this stage of the game. From right and left, whether it be through Jacky Major or Bobby Watson, the Bishop inside-forwards were constantly fed a series of passes and scoring opportunities. Shots were blocked, diverted or saved by an obdurate Crook rearguard. Every one of that 56,008 crowd had the same combined thoughts running through their minds: 'Can the Crook defence hold out? Can the Bishop attack get the equalizer?'

The question was answered with only nine minutes of regular time left. Barry Wilkinson, who had had a slow start but got better with each minute, collected the ball in the Bishop Auckland half and sent a pass down the left side of the field. The willing O'Connell collected the ball and saw Ray Oliver perfectly positioned to run on and take his pass. With a powerful low drive, the lifeboatman made no mistake, leaving Fred Jarrie diving helplessly to his left. By now, Fred Jarrie's opposite number, Harry Sharratt, and his defensive colleagues were only having to deal with sporadic Crook raids and Bishop were finishing the game well on top.

The next nine minutes saw more of the same with Bob supporting his forwards but the Crook defence held out and another thirty minutes was called.

Crook made a tactical change for extra time, Coxon swapping his inside-left position with full-back, Tommy Riley, in an effort to put extra impetus to the Crook forward line but it was the 'Two Blues' who should have gone ahead. O'Connell had a wonderful chance in the first minute of extra time but his headed effort went wide of the goal. Crook displayed more determination through the extra time period and looked just as likely to score as Bishop. However, there were few clear cut chances carved out by either team and at the end of another gruelling two hours of play, the contest was still undecided.

Bobby Davison remembers the end of that game:

> Bob came over to me and shook me by the hand. 'How much longer can we go on, Bobby?' he said.
>
> I said to him, jokingly, 'You can always withdraw, Bob, and concede the match.'
>
> 'I'll think about it,' he said with a grin.
>
> It was mind boggling really. There we were, having played four hours football and still we couldn't decide which was the better team. Both teams gave everything. Each one of us must have been so fit. Marvellous really when you consider that we were part-timers and not able to train every day.

Three days later, the final instalment of this magnificent saga took place in front of a crowd given as 36,727.[†] The FA had decreed that, in the event of a draw after ninety minutes play, there would be no extra time. The twenty-two players would be presented with a medal, suitably inscribed as 1954 joint holders of the FA Amateur Cup, and that the two clubs would share ownership of the trophy for six months each—no-one at the FA had come up with the idea of having a penalty shoot-out to find a winner!

---

† Les Dixon, Bishop Auckland inside-right and keen Middlesbrough supporter, always questioned this official figure. He regularly attended Ayresome Park and believed that there were at least 45,000 spectators in the ground that night.

It was with the certainty of an outcome, in whatever shape or form, that the two teams took to the Ayresome Park pitch just before six o'clock on a dry, balmy April evening.

The teams were:

Bishop Auckland (Dark and Light blue halved shirts, White shorts)
Sharratt—Marshall, Stewart—Hardisty, Cresswell,
Wilkinson—Major, Dixon, Oliver, O'Connell, Watson

Crook Town (Amber shirts, Black shorts)
Jarrie—Coxon, Steward—Jeffs, Davison, Taylor—
Appleby, Thompson, Harrison, Riley, McMillan

Referee: Alf Bond of Middlesex

Bob Hardisty entered the arena knowing that the next ninety minutes of football would truly decide the outcome of his quest for an Amateur Cup winners' medal. He was fed up of reading newspaper reports that he had the sympathy of the whole country in his attempt to gain the elusive medal. If it happened, all well and good: if not, then it would not be the end of the world. Who knows, there may even be one more opportunity left, if this one was unsuccessful.

It was probably a case of familiarity breeding contempt for, it had to be admitted, this third meeting, in so short a space of time, did not live up to the standard set by the two previous encounters. Yes, it was exciting for the fans and was not without controversy but the skill element was of a lower quality in this third game, not helped by a light ball bouncing on a bone hard surface. There was drama and commitment from both sets of players but such incidents were infrequent and large sections of the game took place in the relative safety between the two penalty areas, in what is now commonly referred to as midfield.

Auckland held the upper hand for the opening fifteen minutes or so, during which period they had a perfectly legitimate goal disallowed—that is if you are a Bishop Auckland supporter: if you are a Crook Town supporter then, no doubt, the correct decision was made.

The Oliver–Davison battle had been one of the many highlights of this protracted duel. It was the classic encounter of a strong, robust England international centre-forward against an equally strong, robust England international centre-half. Both players had earned praise for their performances in the preceding two games, neither asking for, nor expecting, any quarter. It was unfortunate that both players would be embroiled in a bitter difference of opinion for the rest of their careers, and long after that.

Bob Hardisty had begun the move that resulted in Jacky Major winning a corner for Bishop after ten minutes. Major swung the ball over and there was Ray Oliver, timing his run to perfection, sending a bullet header into the bottom corner to Fred Jarrie's left-hand post. As Ray circled away in delight to receive the congratulations of his players, he was brought to an abrupt halt. Referee, Alf Bond, had blown his whistle and disallowed the goal, claiming that Oliver had climbed on to Bobby Davison's back to gain an unfair advantage. The Bishop Auckland players could not believe it—neither could some of the Crook players. The Bishop players totally disagreed with Mr Bond's decision but the Crook players—at least when they realized that the goal had been disallowed—took the opposing view and believed that the correct decision had been made.

Ray Oliver: 'It was a perfectly good goal. Nothing wrong with it. I had headed the ball and it was going in the net before I touched Bobby Davison. The cameras showed that I didn't foul Bobby—just look at the photographs. I had a clear run at the goal from just outside the penalty area and he wasn't anywhere near me—surprising when you think of it as he was supposed to be marking me. We had been like limpets up to now in the first two games. Now, when he had left me room to score, I took advantage and did just that. No way did I climb on his back. Nowt wrong with the goal,' he summarised, in his strong Northumberland accent.

Bobby Davison: 'It was definitely a foul. The referee blew his whistle straight away and gave a free kick to us. Of course Ray fouled me. If you look at the photos I am almost doubled up, my head almost touching the floor as a result of Ray climbing on my back. I would never have allowed him that much room if I hadn't been pushed. The Bishop lads were upset with the referee's decision and, yes, we were glad that he had ruled out the goal but in the end he was right.'

Alf Bond: 'There was no doubt in my mind that it was a foul. I saw the foul a second before the goal was scored and blew my whistle for a free kick. Two years after the event I was in the Isle of Man and met Ray Oliver. Ray said to me—"You were quite right about that goal. I did bump the centre-half as we went up to head the ball, but I'm sure you were the only man who saw it." I am sure that by saying these words, Ray was admitting the foul.'

Ray Oliver: 'Yes, I did meet Alf Bond a couple of years later but in no way was I admitting to the foul. What I said was "… I'm sure you were the only man who saw it *as a foul*"—something entirely different to what he had said.'

As a result of that decision, Mr Bond would ever after be known as 'The One-Armed Bandit' by Bishop Auckland supporters, even now, some sixty-five years later.

Notwithstanding this setback, Bishop continued to play the ball down their right flank with Bob Hardisty supplying Jacky Major with the opportunity to send in some dangerous crosses but the tall Davison, who was turning out to be the best player on the pitch, snuffed out any apparent danger with timely clearances.

By the time forty minutes had passed, Bishop were slightly on top but Crook were beginning to put a few telling passes together and, against the run of play, they took the lead. Outside-right, Eddie Appleby, centred the ball in to the Auckland goal area and as the ball was cleared to safety, the Bishop defenders started to move out. The ball was quickly returned, catching the defenders off guard. Harrison was just onside and was able to lob the ball over the outstretched hands of the advancing Sharratt, who had seen the danger all too late.

The second half got under way with Bishop showing more purpose to gain the equalizer but the spark was missing. Seamus O'Connell, who one would have expected to be able to put on a good performance as a result of his Middlesbrough connection, was particularly disappointing, and when Bob Hardisty supplied him with a scoring opportunity, he wasted it with a looping header that Jarrie easily coped with. Not that Crook were exactly threatening to score a second goal. Their forwards were finding it just as tough to get the ball in the net. Cresswell was having just as good a game as Davison but by his side, young Barry Wilkinson had begun to tire in the later stages of the second half, whilst Bob Hardisty had played himself to a standstill and was suffering the consequences when the final whistle went.

There was to be no more goal-scoring and Bob had to stand and watch with the rest of his team mates, as Bobby Davison took possession of the Amateur Cup, presented by Alderman T Meehan, Mayor of Middlesbrough. As he stood, only a few feet away from the Crook captain, he could not help thinking what might have been had not Alf Bond disallowed Ray Oliver's tenth minute header. The other Bishop Auckland players held similar thoughts but there was no denying that Crook deserved the trophy, having fought their way through the most gruelling and dramatic of contests. It had been an epic encounter.

'Never mind, Bob, there's always next year,' said Dave Marshall, trying to add a few words of solace.

'I'm not sure these ageing legs of mine can take much more of this,' Bob replied.

'Don't be daft, Bob,' joined in Ray Oliver, 'we'll be back and you'll be with us.'

PART THREE

'Whence are we, and why are we? Of what scene the actors or spectators?'
Adonais (Percy Bysshe Shelley)

Chapter Nine
GOALS

The beautiful Ayrshire coastline greeted Bob, Betty and young Robert in the summer of 1954. Grateful to see the back of what had been a long and tiring football season, the couple were looking forward to taking a relaxing break with their two year old son, breathing in the Scottish air. Neither of them had visited this part of Scotland before but they had heard a lot about it and they were delighted with its wide open spaces, beautiful scenery and open skies.

They had driven through the romantic town of Gretna Green—perhaps contemplating how many knots had been tied over that blacksmith's anvil, ahead of a chasing father-in-law—and stopped for a short while at the attractive town of Moffat, with its towering St Andrew's Church and quaint streets, before arriving at their destination, the fishing port of Girvan, where fishermen landed their daily catch.

Long, sandy beaches were where the Hardistys and their 'wee wain' spent a lot of their time, with young Robert trying to understand why the sand sifted through his tiny hands, while his father was able to build simple sand castles with a bucket and spade. If the beach became too noisy with holiday-makers, the family would retreat to their car and move along the coast to another peaceful spot, or they would just drive around the region, admiring the scenery and views. One of their favourite sites was Culzean Castle, dominating the Ayrshire coast from its precipitous setting atop coastal cliffs.

Betty particularly enjoyed the splendour of the oval staircase, supported with Ionic and Corinthian pillars.[†]

Bob could not resist the temptation of visiting Turnberry, where he had heard there was a beautiful golf course looking out on to the Irish Sea, where the spectacle of Ailsa Craig, the volcanic knob of granite, rested upon the horizon, just ten miles away. He never got to have a round of golf but it was enough for him to stand on the coast with his beautiful wife, admiring the sunset, before driving back to their Girvan hotel, with young Robert oblivious to it all, fast asleep in the back seat of the car.

Seven days was not enough for the young family but it was soon time to return to County Durham. Not wishing to arrive home too early, Betty convinced Bob that it would be a good idea to make a more southerly journey for their return. She had fallen in love with the region and suggested that they travel through what is now known as Dumfries and Galloway, an area that includes the old county of Kirkcudbrightshire.

It was sometime mid-morning when Bob parked the car in one of Kirkcud-bright's side streets and extracted Robert's pushchair from the boot. They intended to stay for about an hour, to sample the town's offerings. Bob and Betty took turns with the pushchair, stopping almost every five minutes to call in at the numerous antique stores that formed a main part of the town's business. They strode up to the ruins of MacLellan's Castle and came across even more shops, before wending their way to the town's charming harbour, by which time young Robert's face was covered, yet again, with another sampling from the contents of an ice cream cone. At the harbour side, they came across the welcoming oasis of a tea parlour that advised prospective customers that 'real' fish and chips were served there. The Hardistys had built up an appetite and replenished their empty stomachs before returning to their vehicle.

Six hours after arriving in Kirkcudbright, Bob started the car engine to begin their journey home. They had enjoyed their detour to this part of Scotland and both wished each other that they would return again, one day.

[†]   In appreciation of General Eisenhower's part in helping overcome the Nazis in the Second World War, the owners of the castle had granted the would-be United States President the top floor of Culzean. The castle has been much improved over the past decades and has been a country park—Scotland's first—since 1969.

Four months later, Bob Hardisty, once again, set out on the road that he hoped would end in that elusive Wembley victory—amazingly, his club was fighting for the honour on two fronts, as they were still in the FA Cup, as well as the Amateur version.

Bishop had been granted a home draw for the First Round of the FA Cup, their opponents being the semi-professional club, Kettering Town, members of the Southern League. This was the first ever meeting between the two clubs and Bob had warned his team mates that they faced a tough task and that their opponents would be no pushover. Two goals each from Ray Oliver and Les Dixon, plus one from Jacky Major, had seen the 'Two Blues' record a surprisingly easy 5–1 victory. The 'Bishops' feared no-one on their home ground.

Two weeks later, Bob Hardisty and company lined up at Selhurst Park, Crystal Palace, for their Second Round fixture against the Third Division (South) side. Bishop Auckland were able to field a strong side but there had been a few changes to the playing personnel since the defeat in the Amateur Cup Final replay, the previous April, at Middlesbrough. Frank McKenna had been noticed putting in some good performances, playing on the right wing for North Eastern League club, North Shields, and was duly snapped up by 'Kit' Rudd, thus allowing Jacky Major to play at inside-forward, when required. On the opposite flank, Benny Edwards had been persuaded to return from Horden Colliery Welfare, another North Eastern club. In addition to these new signings, Seamus O'Connell was being frequently selected to play in the First Division by Chelsea, thereby necessitating regular line-up changes to the Bishop Auckland forward line. However, even without the absent Seamus, it was a confident Bishop Auckland team that was led out by Jacky Major on to the frosty Selhurst Park pitch on a bright, albeit cloudy, December Saturday afternoon, to the applause of 20,155 fans about 500 of whom had made the long journey from south-west Durham.

The teams were:

> *Bishop Auckland* (Dark and Light blue halved shirts, White shorts)
> Sharratt—Marshall, Fryer—Hardisty, Cresswell, Nimmins—
> McKenna, Dixon, Oliver, Major, Edwards
>
> *Crystal Palace* (Claret and Blue shirts, White shorts)
> D MacDonald—Edwards, Greenwood—Belcher, Briggs,
> H McDonald—Berry, Choules, Tilston, Thomas, Hanlon
>
> Referee: L G Leafe of Nottingham

Tommy Stewart had to cry off at the last minute, when he went down with influenza and Ron Fryer stepped in to take his place. It was apparent from the beginning that the professionals' plan was to play as much as possible down their right flank. This would have two objectives: firstly, pressure would be put on stand-in full back, Ron Fryer, and secondly, Bishop's main creator, Bob Hardisty, would be starved of the football.

The plan appeared to be working as Bob Hardisty saw little of the ball in the opening ten minutes. He had to watch and wait on the right side of midfield as play took place on the other side—if he had been drawn in to help out, he would have run the risk of leaving a large gap for the Crystal Palace left flank to receive long through balls.

Twice within three minutes, Harry Sharratt had to show why he was rated the best amateur goalkeeper in the business, as he saved from Berry and then Tilston. The centre-forward fired in another drive that skimmed the crossbar and then, with only twelve minutes gone, Berry drove the ball past Sharratt to open the scoring.

Jacky Major and Bob both clapped their hands in support of their team mates not to become disheartened. Within ten minutes, Bishop were level. A free kick was awarded and Bob—Auckland's regular choice to take free-kicks—placed the ball to send a perfect cross to the far post, where Ray Oliver knocked down a simple header, which Benny Edwards converted. It was a classic free kick and goal, so simple in its deliverance and execution.

Slack marking—for which Bob Hardisty later blamed himself, for not getting his tackle in earlier, so as to prevent the cross—let in Choules, who beat Fryer and Sharratt to the ball with Cresswell out of position, to score with a fine header only two minutes later, thereby restoring Palace's lead. The home team were well on top now and the Bishop defence were repeatedly placed under pressure by the slick combination moves created by the Palace forward line. Only the brilliance of Harry Sharratt prevented more goals from being scored by the home forwards who were threatening to run riot. Amazingly, the home team failed to add to their tally and it was the visitors who had the best chance of all to score, after thirty-five minutes of play, when full-back Briggs inexplicably handled the ball in his penalty area. Bishop Auckland supporters could not believe it; here they were about to witness their team draw level 2–2, against the Third Division (South) side. Bob Hardisty and Jacky Major were both good penalty takers and the supporters fully expected one of them to take the spot kick. Much to their surprise, it was Ron Fryer who took the kick and, alas, he drove his effort wide of the goal.

A missed penalty would have deflated most teams but through the urgings of Bob Hardisty on the right, and Jimmy Nimmins on the left, it was the amateurs that ended the first half the stronger, although Hanlon did cause some panic in the Auckland defence following a breakaway that ended when Sharratt bravely collected the ball, diving at the feet of Tilston. In the final two minutes, MacDonald was forced to make saves from Oliver and Hardisty, before the referee blew the half-time whistle.

Within two minutes of the restart, Major got a second goal for Bishop. Bob Hardisty won a tackle in the Bishop half and passed inside to Corbett Cresswell. Running in to space, Bob collected a return pass and, looking up, saw that Jacky Major had a couple of yards of space off his marker. A quick pass found the inside-right who took on a static defence and thumped the ball past MacDonald, from twenty-five yards, into the top corner of the net. Two minutes later, Bob Hardisty ran with the ball and passed to Frank McKenna who sent in a low, hard cross that Major tapped into the Palace net. Remarkably, five minutes later, the diminutive inside-right completed his hat-trick to put the visitors 4–2 up.

Crystal Palace supporters could not believe it. They could not understand how their team could have let such an opportunity slip. For the last twenty-five minutes of the game, they were treated to an exhibition on how to retain control of a winning situation. Palace attacks were repeatedly broken up by the Bishop defenders who would look up and pass the ball on to their talisman, Bob Hardisty. He was now showing the class and composure for which he was renowned. With implacable temperament, he made light of tackles from the now tired Palace inside-forwards and it was only a touch of good goalkeeping and bad marksmanship that prevented the score line from being even more decisive.

Of this remarkable result, Jimmy Nimmins said:

> The boys had an inferiority complex at the start but as soon as they found that the first man to the ball had an advantage on the hard ground, they gained more confidence. When Jacky Major got the second equaliser, we were right on top and we finished that way.
>
> We played as a team; every man pulled his weight and that is what matters in football today—I don't believe in stars. A team pulling together, as our boys are, will beat all your stars. It was a fine sporting game and Crystal Palace were sporting to the end.

The more 'usual' type of game awaited the victors of Selhurst Park, just seven days later, when Bishop Auckland travelled to Bromborough, near Birkenhead, Cheshire, to take on Stork in the First Round of the Amateur Cup. Stork were a works team—as in Stork Margarine—and played their football in the First Division of the West Cheshire League. They had won Cheshire Amateur Cups and other minor trophies in their history but were not expected to pose much of a danger to the cup favourites.

There was an unfortunate incident, prior to the start of the game, when a home supporter suffered a heart attack and died.

Stork were not used to the high speed football that Bishop Auckland generated and they had little of the ball for the opening ten minutes, during which time Bob Hardisty had fed his forwards three good chances, all of which had been squandered. Deciding that his forwards had been unduly wasteful, he decided to take on the Stork defence himself, and promptly despatched the ball in to the net. Stork found their feet a little better as the game went on and dug out an equaliser when centre-forward, McCallum, was able to latch on to a through ball and lob over Harry Sharratt.

The game became more even in the second half with Sharratt called on to pull off some fine saves but slowly the Bishop midfield regained more and more of the ball and after eighty minutes, Bob Hardisty scored direct from a free kick before Frank McKenna wrapped things up.[†]

Ever on the lookout to improve its playing squad, Bishop Auckland signed one of its finest ever players, Derek Lewin, just a few days after the win over Stork. The arrival of this England international from Lancashire, engendered a great deal of excitement among Bishop supporters, who saw the addition of another goalscorer as proof that this was to be the season when Wembley would be conquered. Derek had played most of his football for Oldham Athletic in the Football League but had turned down all overtures to turn professional. He and his father ran a bacon company and Derek was not short of a bob or two and therefore had no need to 'turn pro'.

There was more than a touch of coincidence attached to Derek's first match for the 'Two Blues' as it was at Dean Street, against Shildon—the club for whom he had guested during his army days—the traditional Christmas

---

[†] A hundred miles north, on the other side of the Pennines, Willington caused a shock, knocking out cup-holders Crook 1–0 with a stunning away victory.

Day fixture, where he played at inside-right, linking up for the first time with Bob Hardisty. It was apparent from the beginning that it was the perfect partnership and that success was only a matter of time—and luck. Bishop ran out 3–2 winners, a result that put them at the head of the Northern League table, just ahead of second placed Crook Town.

The first major match that saw Bob Hardisty linking up with his new inside-forward was the FA Cup Third Round tie at Portman Road when the amateurs from the north took on Ipswich Town of the Football League Second Division. It was a draw that had brought sighs of disappointment from many Bishop supporters as Ipswich were not a fashionable club and another long distance journey was involved. Bob Hardisty told the fans not to worry as he was confident that the team would get a result, at the very least he expected the 'Bishops' to come away with a draw. 'Kit' Rudd was a little more ambivalent about the outcome; a few days before the Ipswich game he commented:

> We couldn't care less about our opponents, in fact we won't lose any sleep if we get knocked out of the competition at Ipswich. We know that we will not win the FA Cup. This does not mean that we won't go flat out; we always play to win but our real target has to be the FA Amateur Cup and we'd rather beat Erith and Belvedere on January 22nd than Ipswich. We will sacrifice anything for that trophy.

The teams were:

Bishop Auckland (Flame shirts, White shorts)
Sharratt—Marshall, Fryer—Hardisty, Cresswell, Nimmins—
McKenna, Lewin, Oliver, Major, Edwards

Ipswich Town (Black and White hooped shirts, Black shorts)
Parry—Malcolm, Feeney—Fletcher, Rees, Parker—Reed,
Grant, Garneys, Phillips, McLuckie

Referee: George McCabe of Sheffield

To the surprise of the football world, Bishop Auckland obtained the draw prophesied by Bob Hardisty. They suffered the handicap of going a goal down as early as the second minute, when centre-forward, Garneys, was allowed to poke in a corner from five yards. Urged on from midfield by the probing Bob Hardisty, Bishop put incessant pressure on the Ipswich defence, earning three consecutive corners. The equaliser came from the third corner when

Ray Oliver outjumped Welsh international goalkeeper Parry, and with two defenders rooted to the goal line, scored with a towering header.

Bob became the play maker and with his usual composure began to dictate proceedings, feeding his inside-forwards with well timed passes. Twice, he was able to provide Ray Oliver with scoring chances but on each occasion, Parry brought off commendable saves. The Ipswich goalkeeper was beaten for the second time, however, when Bob fed Frank McKenna with a peach of a pass and the right-winger scored with ease to give the amateurs a 2–1 half-time lead. In the second half, the Bishop defence was put under constant pressure and Bob was forced into playing a much more defensive role. It looked as if the amateurs would hold out but three minutes from time, tragedy struck when a Reed header was deflected by Corbett Cresswell past a helpless Harry Sharratt to give the League side a somewhat fortuitous 2–2 draw.

In the Portman Road dressing room after the game, Bob Hardisty offered a few words of condolence to his young centre-half. To Bob's and everyone else's surprise, Corbett was unrepentant about scoring the own goal. Corbett Cresswell recalls that incident and proclaims:

> I remember the incident very well. Harry should have come for the ball and it was left to me to pick up the pieces. Ipswich were throwing everything into attack. This time, the nippy outside-right, Reed, who was a Welsh international, managed to get his head to the ball and send it goalwards. I stuck out a leg to clear it but it was just that too far for me to get to with any purchase and as a result it went spinning past Harry. In my opinion it would have gone in to the goal anyway, even without my help. That's my side of it and I said so to the lads immediately after the match. There was no need for Bob or the others to console me as I don't think that I was responsible for the goal. I told them to 'Piss off!' and they all just laughed, don't know why!

Bob Hardisty had predicted that his team would achieve at least a draw and he was adamant that Bishop were capable of defeating the Football League side in the replay, which was scheduled for the following Wednesday afternoon.

On a snow covered surface, the game was played in a deceivingly cold temperature, despite the sunshine, but the 9,000 Bishop supporters would be warmed by their team's performance. Playing brilliant football on the surface, Bishop held the upper hand over their opponents from the beginning. The Ipswich defenders found Bishop's inside trio impossible to contain and when they did happen to get the better of them and mount an attack they found Corbett Cresswell in impeccable form. His was a man-of-the-match performance and nothing got past him. Atoning for his own goal in the first match, he restricted centre-forward, Garneys, to two long range efforts which Harry Sharratt fielded away with contemptible ease.

Playing with controlled calmness, Bob Hardisty was his majestic self, although on this occasion he was outshone by Cresswell. Frank McKenna was a constant threat to the Ipswich defence and seemed to skate over the slippery surface. He scored the opening goal in the second half with a looping header, after receiving attention for an injured ankle. McKenna's second came when he was put through by Jimmy Nimmins to score with a low drive from outside the penalty box. Parry dived to his left but was well beaten. Three minutes later, Major scored a third with a drive to Parry's right that left the goalkeeper stranded and sealed a magnificent team effort. York City would visit Kingsway for Round Four but in the meantime Erith and Belvedere were due to visit this little corner of County Durham for a Second Round Amateur Cup tie.

Sitting in the dressing room with Jacky Major, about to dip into the plunge baths, Bob Hardisty congratulated his team mates on a magnificent performance. Jacky turned to Bob and said, 'Well, Bob, it looks like this to me. You've gone without a winners' medal in the Amateur Cup for so long that I reckon the powers that be are going to grant you two medals this year—one for the Amateur Cup and the other for the FA Cup.'

The sentiment was greeted with wild cheers of approval and then there was one mad dash to jump into the plunge baths that were full of welcoming warm water.

Three days after an all-conquering performance over Ipswich Town, Bishop Auckland handed out a 5–0 drubbing to Erith and Belvedere of the Corinthian League. Volunteers had cleared all of the Kingsway surface and large mounds of snow lay around all four sides of the pitch.

Two minutes in to the game and Bob Hardisty was thankful for the snow as Erith centre-half, Fuller, sent him hurtling over the touch line with a hefty challenge. It could have been nasty but Bob just picked himself up and brushed the snow from his shirt and shorts, as the crowd bayed for more action from the referee. Five minutes later, it was Derek Lewin's turn to receive the Fuller treatment and this time referee Tuck cautioned the centre-half.

Fortunately for the 8,500 spectators and the game in general, the nastiness went out of the game after Tuck's reprimand and Bishop were able to play their usual game. After twelve minutes, O'Connell put the home team in front, and then Lewin escaped his marker to score with a brilliant header from Major's corner. O'Connell scored his second, ten minutes from half-time, with a cracking long range drive but before then he could have had a hat-trick as he had a header cleared off the line by full-back, McCullough and goalkeeper, Andrews, tipped a volley over the crossbar.

The Erith defence was no match for the incessant probing of Bob Hardisty and Jimmy Nimmins and it was a minor miracle that Bishop only managed two goals in the second half. Tommy Stewart had smacked a penalty against the crossbar and Bob himself had missed two clear cut chances. As it was, a goal each from Jacky Major and Ray Oliver ended the scoring.

When the teams retired to their respective dressing rooms, after the referee had blown for time, Bob sat down and removed his shirt. To his surprise, Corbett Cresswell pointed out a six-inch cut across Bob's midriff, with blood seeping from it. The players who had not yet jumped in to the plunge bath came over and inspected the cut. Bob appeared as surprised as anyone and could not think of how the injury may have initially happened. He then thought and decided that it must have occurred when he had hit the snow bank early in the game as a result of Fuller's challenge and perhaps there had been a sharp stone or nail in the snow. He had been fortunate that the offending object had not produced a more serious injury. Doctor Prescott, who looked after the players, decided that stitches were unnecessary and that the wound required no more than the application of elastoplast. Bob's altercation with the pile of snow had been almost two hours ago—he had played throughout the match, without any pain, with the bleeding gash in his stomach. What was more surprising was that his shirt had not been punctured by the incident.

York City, like Bishop Auckland, were recognized giant-killers for this season's FA Cup competition. They had come through Rounds One and Two with predictable wins over Scarborough (3–2 at home) and Dorchester (5–2 away) but had earned the giant-killer tag as a result of their win over Blackpool 2–0 on the First Division club's Bloomfield Road ground. Only two years earlier, Blackpool had won the FA Cup when defeating Bolton Wanderers 4–3 in that memorable 'Matthews Final'.

For Bob Hardisty and four of his colleagues—Dave Marshall, Jimmy

Nimmins, Jacky Major and Benny Edwards—it was an opportunity to gain some kind of revenge over the Third Division (North) club in respect of their cup defeat by York in 1950–51.

The teams were:

Bishop Auckland (Dark and Light blue halved shirts, Navy blue shorts)
Sharratt—Marshall, Stewart—Hardisty, Cresswell,
Nimmins—McKenna, Lewin, Oliver, Major, Edwards

York City (Red shirts, White shorts)
Forgan—Phillips, Howe—Brown, Stewart, Spence—
Hughes, Bottom, Wilkinson, Storey, Fenton

Referee: J Jepson of Mansfield

Fortune did not smile on the amateurs and for the third time that the clubs had met each other in the competition, it was the Football League club that, once again, came out victorious. More than 15,000 spectators filled every inch of Kingsway—temporary 'stands' were erected, made up of beer crates and trestles, none of which would get through today's strict safety measures. Bishop Auckland Football Club Treasurer, R W Cail, was no doubt pleased with the takings that totalled a record £1,727.0.0d.

In the opening fifteen minutes, Bishop were the better side, able to produce their high brand of powerful football on a difficult muddy surface, before the League club could get to grips with the conditions. During this opening spell, there was a nasty incident, however, when Arthur Bottom made a decidedly ugly attempt to get the ball from Dave Marshall. The full-back went down clutching his ankle, with the rest of the Bishop players, as well as supporters, incensed at the viciousness of the challenge. Marshall was already of the opinion that Bottom was a 'dirty bugger' and had little reason to change his mind now.

 Notwithstanding Marshall's injury, which he was able to run off after some attention from sponge man Jack Sowerby, Bishop started another attack. Unfortunately, Spence intercepted Bob Hardisty's intended pass to Ray Oliver and the left half-back forwarded the ball to his winger, Billy Fenton. The York wingman had enough experience behind him to know that he should not give an injured player a decent break, and took on the limping Marshall. He was able to round the full-back with ease and from his pin-point cross, Sid Storey coolly placed the ball past Harry Sharratt, to open the scoring.

The amateurs, undeterred, threw everything into attack straight from the

*Young Tommy Gartland congratulates
Bob and Betty on their marriage.
Tommy would go on to be registered
as a Bishop Auckland player
under the tutelage of Bob.*

*Looks like Bob and Betty are
about to go rob a bank as
they appear to act out their
fantasies as Bonnie and Clyde.*

Bob (number 4) strives for a goal in the role of attacking wing-half.

This time, Bob is on defensive duty and heads a clearance away from danger.

Captain of England v Ireland, Norwich, 1949.

Bishop Auckland v Willington, Amateur Cup Final, 1950. The lanky Jackie Snowdon beats Bob to the ball as another Bishop attack fizzles out. This was probably the finest game that Snowdon ever played as he helped Willington overcome the favourites 4–0.

Bishop Auckland v Pegasus, Amateur Cup Final, 1951. Bob and goalkeeper Bill White are helpless to prevent Potts (out of picture) putting the universities side ahead.

Bob looks anxious as a Pegasus attack is just foiled by Bill White.

Betty shows off young Robert (nice set of wheels, too).

Although not captain of Bishop Auckland, Bob was regularly called upon to captain various representativ sides. One such occasion was this game, playing for Durham against Lancashire at Kingsway, Bishop Auckland in January, 1954. Jimmy Nimmins is in the background.

Les Dixon opens the scoring for Bishop Auckland in the 1954 Amateur Cup Final against local rivals, Crook Town. This was the start of an epic encounter, watched by an accumulative audience of almost 200,000.

Bob and Corbett Cresswell manage to block out a Crook attack this time.

Harry Sharratt is about to collect the ball as Bob covers.

Seamus O'Connell, Bishop Auckland coach George Ainsley and Bob.

June Laverick.

Derek Lewin and Bob, 1955.

Bob's ungainly header ends a Hendon attack in the 1955 Amateur Cup Final at Wembley Stadium.

Sharratt and Cresswell look on as Bob relieves the Hendon danger.

The winners' medal at last and Bob is proud to show it off.

Jimmy Nimmins, Bob, Derek Lewin, Les Dixon, Dave Marshall, Ray Oliver and the prize—the FA Amateur Cup—following the win over Hendon.

Last chance for autograph hunters to get Bob's signature as the train prepares to carry Bob and his victorious team mates back to the North.

The whole town comes out to greet the winners as the Amateur Cup is paraded on the return to Bishop Auckland.

From the Town Hall balcony, Bob shows off his winners' medal ... or was it?

restart. Ray Oliver kicked off and passed to Derek Lewin who laid the ball back for Bob Hardisty to supply a probing pass to Frank McKenna. The right-winger swung over a beautiful centre that Benny Edwards met, racing in from the left, to fire in the equalizer. The move could not have been bettered had it been executed on a chess board.

Buoyed by the goal, Bishop placed even more effort into getting in front, but York's defenders were not giving way so easily a second time. Oliver was unlucky to see his shot skim across Forgan's goal, the ball scraping the far post, but the Division Three side gradually recovered ground and for a while Bob was forced to play a more defensive role, as York persisted in playing their attacks down their left wing, in an attempt to place further pressure on Marshall. By half-time both teams had landed blows in equal numbers and the 1–1 score line was just about right.

Any prospects that the amateurs had of handing out another defeat to a Football League side were dented when Bottom and Tommy Stewart challenged for the ball after only two minutes of the second half. Bottom's challenge looked high and ugly to many supporters and Stewart fell to the ground nursing his knee, as the ball went out of play for a throw-in to the 'Two Blues'. Bottom stood with his arms open wide, as if pleading that the coming together had been an accident. None of the Bishop Auckland supporters had any doubt that it was a malicious tackle but the referee disagreed and merely ordered the throw-in to be taken.

With both full-backs having been injured—although Marshall was now moving more freely, following attention during the half-time break—York started to pile on the pressure. Stirling work from Bishop's half-back trio thwarted a number of attacks as York came on to the 'Two Blues' defence like a red tide but when the York forwards did happen to break through, there was the brilliant Sharratt to foil the raiders. Twice he was forced to dive to his right and fingertip the ball around the post for a corner and on another occasion he brought off a world class save, palming Wilkinson's header over the bar. Then, after seventy-six minutes, with the home supporters hoping that their team might get a worthy draw, York got the goal that their superiority deserved. Once again it was Fenton, with some delightful wing play, who took on Marshall and this time provided Bottom, the villain of the show, with a scoring chance that he did not cast aside, much to the delight of the travelling York supporters.

Bishop were unable to respond and it was York who finished the game on top. They got a third goal when Tommy Stewart was adjudged to have fouled Billy Hughes as the winger forced his way in to the Auckland penalty area. With Bishop Auckland supporters hissing and seething, a York player strode forward to take the penalty—yes, it was Arthur Bottom. Placing the ball on the spot, he took five paces back and without looking up ran forward to strike the ball. Harry Sharratt leapt to his left and got both hands to the football only to see it rebound from the upright in to the goal. Much to the chagrin of Bishop supporters, Bottom was on top, and they could not help but feel that the 3–1 score did little justice to the efforts of their team.

Bob Hardisty, with the rest of the Bishop Auckland players, was philosophical about the result and the way that it had been achieved. Publicly, he refused to castigate the methods used by some of the York City players and their perceived rough tackles. He wished York City all the best for their next venture in the Cup and in their quest for promotion to the Second Division. In some newspaper accounts, Arthur Bottom was singled out for praise in his notable efforts in helping his team to obtain the victory. If Bob held any opposing views he kept them to himself. As for Dave Marshall, in his view, Arthur Bottom would always be a 'dirty bugger'.

At the usual mid-week training session, Bob Hardisty warned his colleagues about the difficult task that awaited them in south London in four days time for their Third Round Amateur Cup fixture. Kingstonian were rated one of the south's leading clubs and had been tipped by some respected pundits as possible winners of the Amateur Cup. He singled out the wingers for attention, Fruin and Adams, and warned Tommy Stewart and Dave Marshall that they could expect to be taken on by the wingmen: the Bishop Auckland full-backs had been warned. Jimmy Nimmins and Corbett Cresswell were made aware that Davies, Whing and Coates were a dangerous looking inside trio, well able to put the best defences under pressure.

Bob, with the assistance of his good friend Jack Sowerby, continued with the training session that consisted of only a handful of first team members as well as a mixture of reserve players and youngsters, and led them through a variety of exercises—a practice that he had been carrying out since his days as England's Assistant Team Manager, under Walter Winterbottom. The disappointment of York City had now to be put behind them and the more attainable target of the Amateur Cup remained the 'Holy Grail' for Bob and Bishop Auckland.

Arthur Caiger DCM, was leading the record crowd with thirty minutes Community Singing before the match got under way, when Bob's warnings were repeated in the dressing room at Kingstonian's Richmond Road ground. Seven days ago, they had faced a tough York City and had lost out, now they had to brace themselves for what would seemingly be just as tough a task against the Isthmian League side. What followed was one of the most remarkable football scores in the history of the FA Amateur Cup competition, given the status and ability of the teams involved.

The teams were:

Bishop Auckland (Dark and Light blue halved shirts, Navy blue shorts)
Sharratt—Marshall, Stewart—Hardisty, Cresswell,
Nimmins—McKenna, Lewin, Oliver, Major, Edwards

Kingstonian (Red and White hooped shirts, Black shorts)
North—Johnstone, Foss—Crook, Reeve,
Wood—Fruin, Davies, Day, Coates, Adams

Referee: S B Stoakes

As far back as 1921, the two clubs had met in the competition, with the 'Two Blues' winning 2–0 before going on to win the trophy when defeating South Bank 5–2 after extra time. Goalkeeper and captain for Kingstonian that day was E J North, father of today's Kingstonian custodian, Geoff North. Geoff had previously been a regular for Bishop Auckland's reserve team and had made a sprinkling of first team appearances—he was still officially registered as a Bishop Auckland player—but had moved to London to attend Westminster College. The Bishop Auckland Committee had granted him permission to play on loan for the Isthmian League club, not fully expecting that their paths would cross in such a way.

The Bishop Auckland players received a boost before the game when it was announced that Kingstonian regular centre-forward, Whing, was unavailable and that full-back, Day, would take his place and that Johnstone would fill Day's regular right-back position.

Kingstonian gave their supporters reason for a successful outcome in the opening minutes with dangerous looking raids but they came to nothing and in the fifth minute, Ray Oliver provided Derek Lewin with a scoring chance. The Lancastrian made no mistake and sent a low drive into the left-hand corner of North's goal.

Three minutes later, Bob Hardisty received the ball in midfield and was allowed to advance to the edge of the Kingstonian penalty area before he fired a shot that skimmed North's crossbar. The warning went unheeded and in the twelfth minute, Seamus O'Connell was allowed to receive a pass from Benny Edwards and take his time to turn before firing home, giving North no chance.

Twice, Kingstonian tried to set up attacking moves but were caught offside each time and so far Harry Sharratt had only to deal with back passes from Cresswell and Marshall. Bob Hardisty and Jimmy Nimmins were totally dictating play in midfield and were able to play their game in the Kingstonian half of the field. When Bob supplied Ray Oliver with a chance after seventeen minutes, North was extremely brave and brought off a fine save to prevent the centre-forward scoring. The save only delayed the inevitable, however, as O'Connell scored in the next minute and then sixty seconds later North received all-round applause when he brought off a stunning save to tip an O'Connell header over the crossbar.

By now the Kingstonian defenders were being completely overrun and, had it not been for the brilliance of their goalkeeper, they would have conceded far more goals.

Kingstonian did not let in another goal until the thirty-fourth minute when Bob collected a cross-field clearance from Tommy Stewart and looked up to see Seamus O'Connell preparing himself for a run in to the Kingstonian penalty area. With a perfectly flighted pass, Bob played the ball in to the stride of the cattle-dealer who reached his hat-trick with aplomb. A minute later he had scored his fourth from Jacky Major's cross.

It was proving all too easy and, eager to get his name on the score sheet, Bob tested North with a stunning twenty-five yard drive, which the goalkeeper saved brilliantly.

Referee Stoakes blew for half-time with the visitors comfortably leading 5–0. During those opening forty-five minutes, Harry Sharratt had been forced into action just once, on the stroke of half-time, when Day had been presented with a scoring opportunity that the makeshift centre-forward muffed, with only the goalkeeper to beat.

The second half was very much the same as the first. The Kingstonian players could not keep possession of the football and, therefore, the Bishop Auckland midfield had an easy time setting up attacks one after the other. Only four minutes after the restart, Ray Oliver rose to meet Jacky Major's inch perfect cross and headed the ball past North for Bishop's sixth. Within the space of ten minutes, North pulled off three good saves to foil Lewin,

Edwards and Major but, despite his heroics, he could not prevent Oliver scoring his hat-trick goal on the hour mark.

Lewin was on hand to tap in Auckland's eighth before Oliver was allowed to twice waltz through the remnants of the Kingstonian defence to score goals nine and ten. By the eighty-fifth minute, the 'Two Blues' had recorded a dozen, number eleven coming from a grateful Cresswell, who received a pass from O'Connell who was standing on the Kingstonian goal line, and number twelve was scored by an almost apologetic Derek Lewin—eleven of the twelve goals had been scored by the inside-forward trio. Len Wilson would have been proud.

With only five minutes remaining, Harry Sharratt decided that he wanted to get his name on the score sheet and wandered upfield as far as the Kingstonian penalty area, leaving his own goal area unguarded, save for right-back, Dave Marshall. Because of Harry's wanderings, Kingstonian were allowed to rattle in three goals in those closing minutes. Day got a brace and Coates netted a third, with Sharratt hopelessly caught upfield on each occasion.

The final score was 12–3 and Bishop Auckland had played the perfect game of football, notwithstanding the aberrations of Harry Sharratt in those closing minutes.

Ray Oliver, scorer of five of Bishop Auckland's goals recounts: 'Near the end of the game, I recall the ball coming over from the wing. I was just steadying myself to shoot when I was pushed out of the way. It was Corbett. He said, "Give some bugger else a chance, you've got five already." We all felt so sorry for young Geoff, in the Kingstonian goal. Everything we tried just came off for us, that day.'

Dave Marshall says: 'In those final twenty minutes or so I was wandering around at the back like a lost soul. Everybody else was upfield, trying to score. Even Harry Sharratt was further forward than me! I think he saw himself as an inside-right.'

Bob Hardisty was quoted as saying: 'We were absolutely sensational that Saturday. I had warned the lads that Kingstonian would pose a real threat to our challenge for the Amateur Cup. They really were a good side but it was as if our lads had listened to everything that they had been told and were determined not to take any chances. Make no mistake, without Geoff North's heroics, we could well have scored twenty, really. He pulled off some magnificent saves that even Harry Sharratt would have been proud of. Geoff had nothing to be ashamed of.'

Chairman of the club, George Waine, later commented: 'In my long experience with the club, I don't think I have seen a team work with such precision as last week against Kingstonian.'

As a result of Bishop's demolition of Kingstonian they were made even stronger favourites for the Cup and yet, as so often happens in football's contrary world, after having put on such a magnificent performance in Round Three, they struggled to overcome Athenian League team Finchley at Kingsway in Round Four.

Finchley were not given much of a chance when drawn to meet the 'Bishops' and their Chairman had been quoted in a national newspaper as saying: '… I hope more than anything that we steer clear of Bishop Auckland.' The Londoners had struggled to beat Evenwood Town and only won through by virtue of a last minute goal. When asked by a pressman what he thought of Finchley's chances against Bishop Auckland, Evenwood's Treasurer, Horden, replied: 'Judging on Finchley's display against us, Auckland should win easily.'

Snow was removed from the Kingsway pitch a few hours before the three o'clock kick off and on a slippery surface, Finchley showed their intentions from the outset. They would pack their defence and allow the Bishop attack to come at them, and then raid on the counter attack. This was a dangerous ploy given the form that the Auckland forwards were in, yet the plan worked. Bishop's inside trio received support from half-backs, Bob Hardisty and Jimmy Nimmins but were unable to pose any threat to the Finchley goal and after twenty-seven minutes the Londoners stole a lead. On a rare breakaway, Sharratt dropped the ball, allowing Finchley's inside-right, Head, to score, a lead which they held on to when half-time came.

The 'Bishops' came out for the second half full of intent and Barham in the Finchley goal was made to produce a fine save from the previously quiet Hardisty. For some reason, Bob, like his colleagues, was struggling to play anything like his usual commanding game. The more he tried, the more mistakes were made. Sometimes, football can be like that. Then, after fifteen minutes of the second half, Bishop were awarded a free kick following a foul on Ray Oliver. Bob took it and shot at goal. Barham was equal to the task and pulled off a fine save but Bob's effort was the spark needed to put some fire in to the attack, and from then on the Finchley goal looked vulnerable.

The equalizing goal came with only ten minutes remaining and what a stunner it was. A Finchley raid was broken up and the ball was passed to Jacky Major, standing twenty-five yards out from the Finchley goal. Barham never saw the ball as it sped in to his net.

The winning goal proved elusive and, try as they might, Bishop's forwards could not find the net again and it was a somewhat subdued eleven that bathed in the Auckland dressing room afterwards. The general consensus among the players was that they could not possibly play as badly again. Finchley would be forced to change their tactics on home soil and Bishop's forwards should be able to take advantage—at least that was the theory.

Theories are not always proven correct but on this occasion, that of the Bishop players turned out to be true. Seven days later, on an icy surface at Finchley's Summers Lane ground, Bishop Auckland produced their true form. Bob Hardisty had had a poor match in the drawn game at Kingsway but this time he was once again the Grand Master. He orchestrated the midfield and made light of the difficult conditions where others floundered. Gone was the indifference and hesitancy of a week ago: now he produced the assuredness and purposefulness for which he was renowned. He had the confidence to take on defenders and, of the game, *The Sports Despatch* recorded: 'Two events of note were Hardisty beating three men in as many yards and Wastell winning his opening duel with Oliver … With Hardisty paving the road to goal, a touch of finesse was creeping into this tough game.'

Bishop won 3–1, and Bob Hardisty was the undoubted star performer. Benny Edwards had opened the scoring with a brilliant thirty-yard free kick into Barham's top right-hand corner and Oliver added a second from Seamus O'Connell's pass. Oliver scored his second before Gedder pulled one back for Finchley but the day belonged to the northern raiders. They would not know the name of their opponents until the Wycombe Wanderers–Pegasus replay was settled but whichever of those two highly talented teams they were destined to meet in the semi-final, they feared no-one.

Although Pegasus had travelled to Wycombe Wanderers and held them to a 0–0 draw in the first match, on their home soil at Iffley Road, Oxford, they were beaten 1–2 in the replay and when the result came through to the Bishop Auckland players and supporters, there was an air of quiet optimism in their combined ranks.

Doncaster Rovers' Belle Vue Ground was the venue for the semi-final— the FA once again showing a profligate attitude and a seemingly lack of geographical knowledge to the so-called 'home' advantage that Bishop should have had, being first out of the hat—which proved to be every bit as tough and thrilling as the forecasters had predicted, and the 24,800 crowd were treated to a stirring match.

The opening fifteen minutes was a cut and thrust affair, with both sets of forwards scorning chances, but the best opportunity fell to Tommy Stewart when Ray Oliver was fouled in the penalty area, and referee Kirk awarded a penalty. The usually reliable full-back sent his spot kick wide of the goal, much to the consternation of Bishop's travelling supporters. Then it was Wycombe's turn to attack, and only a fine interception from Bob prevented the Wycombe forwards from opening up the Auckland defence. Play continued end to end, with players flying in with strong but fair tackles. The referee, Kirk, was having a fine game and was to be congratulated in allowing play to carry on when other referees may have been constantly blowing for free kicks—this was a semi-final, after all.

No goals were scored in the first half and for the opening thirty minutes of the second, play continued in the same vein. Both goalkeepers were called upon to pull off saves and defenders were forced to just kick the ball to safety when such action was merited. There was a setback for the 'Bishops' on the hour mark when Dave Marshall was injured in a tackle with inside-left Truett and was forced to leave the field for attention. Bob filled in temporarily for Marshall's absence but fortunately the full-back returned to the field after only five minutes. His return seemed to introduce fresh spirit into the Bishop players and within thirty seconds of Marshall's return, Oliver received a long ball from Bob Hardisty. The centre-forward played a ball to Jacky Major who took on, and beat, two defenders before sending a rasping shot that beat goalkeeper Syrett all ends up, only for the ball to thunder against the crossbar and bounce back in to play.

Wycombe were on the defensive now and were relying on breakaways. After seventy minutes they were almost successful, when outside-left Bates had only Sharratt to beat but took too long in preparing himself to shoot and Cresswell was able to get in a challenge and clear the ball upfield to the waiting O'Connell. Seamus took the ball forward and drew his marker before playing the ball inside for Ray Oliver to breast down and flick the ball past Syrett, despite the close attention of Wicks. The 'Two Blues' had their nose in front.

The goal knocked the stuffing out of the Wycombe players and Bishop were able to play out the next twenty minutes with an air of authority, although they were unable to add to Oliver's single goal. When the referee blew for full-time, the Bishop Auckland players all went to their talismanic right-half as if to say, 'This one's for you, Bob.'

Bob Hardisty and his Bishop Auckland team mates had made it to

Wembley again where, it was learned later, that their opponents would be Hendon, who had just defeated Hounslow Town 2–1 at White Hart Lane.

As before, the town of Bishop Auckland, as well as the whole of south-west Durham, was filled with anticipation. Wembley beckoned yet again. There was added 'local' interest this time in the shape of Newcastle United, who had also made it to the FA Cup Final where they would meet Manchester City. The whole area was once again caught up with cup fever and the prospect of a 'Cup double'. Much was made of the fact that Bob Hardisty—and Jimmy Nimmins—would be making their third appearance in a Wembley Final and were yet to be successful. Bob was his usual affable self and dryly commented: 'The game will be won by the team scoring the most goals. How many appearances Jimmy and I have made previously will have no bearing on that fact. It is totally irrelevant.'

Bob did not make the traditional journey to London with the official Bishop Auckland party but travelled down on the Thursday before the big game with Seamus O'Connell, Tommy Stewart, Derek Lewin and Corbett Cresswell. They would meet up with the remaining members of the party on Friday afternoon. In the meantime, they were to attend the BBC studios in West London where the two captains, Tommy Stewart and Dexter Adams, would appear on that evening's television programme, *Sportsnight*, with host Peter Dimmock. On the programme, Stewart declared that he would be fit to play on Saturday as he had fully recovered from an aggravated ankle injury, whilst similarly, Dexter Adams also claimed that he was fully fit following a thigh strain and that Hendon would be at full strength. Naturally, both captains were confident that their respective team would carry off the Cup.

The whole football world was aware that Bob Hardisty was at Wembley, yet again, in search of his winners' medal. Every newspaper had stated the fact that this would likely be his final opportunity to gain it, as 'Olde Father Time' was catching up with him. The neutrals may have been willing him to succeed but there was a small corner of north London that had other ideas. Hendon supporters were full of confidence that their team would be able to smite down the mighty 'Bishops' and they were more than happy to leave fairy tale endings to the sentimentalists.

The road to Wembley from Hendon was factually only three miles but in the football world it had been a very long journey. They had been in existence since 1908 under the name of Christchurch Football Club and, having had a succession of name changes, had been known as Hendon Football Club since 1946. This was the club's first appearance at Wembley Stadium and also their first appearance in the Amateur Cup Final. They had defeated Dartmouth 2–1 in a First Round replay, after drawing the opening game away from home 3–3. Round Two saw them have difficulty beating Cambridge City 4–3 on home soil and then the short journey across north London resulted in a 1–0 away win over Walthamstow Avenue. A difficult obstacle lay ahead, in the shape of Wimbledon, in Round Four. The clubs drew 1–1 before Hendon won the replay at their Claremont Road ground with a convincing 4–1 score line and then semi-final opponents, Hounslow Town, were beaten 2–1 at Tottenham.

On the face of it, Hendon's form did not appear as good as that of Bishop Auckland's, but more than one journalist pointed out that since putting on that exemplary display against Kingstonian, Bishop had failed to produce anything like that form in subsequent rounds, including the well merited win at Finchley.

At exactly eleven minutes to three, Arthur Caiger dismounted from his podium in the centre circle, his stint at conducting the 100,000 crowd in twenty minutes of Community Singing at the Amateur Cup Final, over for another twelve months. As he descended the steps, the crowd raised the volume two or three notches, in expectation of the teams emerging from Wembley's famous tunnel. Within minutes, in glorious sunshine, Dexter Adams and Tommy Stewart had completed the long walk with their respective team mates, to the front of the Royal Box, where they were to be presented to today's dignitaries, chief amongst them being Field Marshall Viscount Montgomery of Alamein. Sir Stanley Rous was not far behind 'Monty' and had his, by now, customary question for the Bishop Auckland number four: 'This time, Bob?'

'We'll see, Stanley.'

'Best of luck, Bob.'

With the preliminaries out of the way, the two teams peeled away for the shoot-in before the referee called the captains to the centre circle.

Bob Hardisty strode forward and thumped the football as hard as he could past a startled Harry Sharratt who just stood and waved it in to the net. As he turned round, a beaming Jimmy Nimmins called out: 'Now all you have to do Bob, is repeat that in the next ninety minutes, in the actual match.'

'Aye, let's get on with it, Jim. Best of luck.'

The teams were:

Bishop Auckland (Dark and Light blue halved shirts, Black shorts)
Sharratt—Marshall, Stewart—Hardisty, Cresswell,
Nimmins—Major, Lewin, Oliver, O'Connell, Edwards

Hendon (Green shirts with White sleeves, White shorts)
Ivey—Fisher, Beardsley—Topp, Adams, Austin—Saffery,
Hvidsten, Bahler, Cunningham, Parker

Referee: R H Mann of Worcestershire

All eyes were on Bob Hardisty as the game got under way with Ray Oliver's kick off but Hendon gained the ball and Sharratt had to be alert to collect Saffery's cross. Another Hendon attack, just two minutes later, brought the crowd to their feet, following a mistake by Jimmy Nimmins. Erwin Bahler was a Swiss 'B' international and played for Young Boys of Berne. He was a very fast centre-forward with excellent ball control and had been flown over from Switzerland that morning. Dispossessing Nimmins, he homed in and it looked inevitable that he would score. Once more, Sharratt proved why he was rated the best goalkeeper in the country with a terrific diving save to his left. Bishop supporters could heave a huge sigh of relief.

Bob was in action on Auckland's next raid, when he combined with Jacky Major, but the move ended tamely with a weak shot from O'Connell. Benny Edwards was also wasteful when his lob was easily dealt with by thirty-nine year-old policeman, Reg Ivey, in the Hendon goal.

The opening twenty-five minutes had seen both sides create chances but forwards were wasteful in missing them. O'Connell was having a particularly frustrating time, and only Lewin of the Bishop Auckland forward line seemed to be playing with any composure. It was he who gave Bishop the lead, when, after twenty-six minutes, he received a through pass from O'Connell who had drawn Adams out of position. Lewin raced towards the Hendon goal and, as Ivey came out, the Bishop inside-right lobbed the ball over the Hendon goalkeeper's head to score with consummate skill. Pat Austin raced back desperately in a failed attempt to clear the ball.[†]

[†] Nearly all newspaper captions to the photographs of this goal mistakenly place Dexter Adams as the luckless defender trying to retrieve the ball, much to the Hendon centre-half's annoyance.

For a minute, Hendon were rattled and Bob Hardisty created another attack only for O'Connell to shoot wide. On a counter attack, Bahler did get the ball in to the Bishop goal but it was correctly disallowed for offside—this was the only time that Hendon were able to mount a raid during this spell of the game. Bishop were the more dominant force and the team's confidence grew, thereby enabling Bob Hardisty and Jimmy Nimmins to control the midfield. Cresswell was having a good game and, other than allowing Bahler's early missed chance in the game, he was putting in a solid performance.

The first half ended with Bob and Seamus combining well but the latter shot straight at Ivey who made a comfortable save.

Coming out for the second half, Tommy Stewart warned his team to be on guard against the expected onslaught that Hendon would attempt, to get themselves on equal terms. Surprisingly, perhaps, it was Bishop who played with more clarity and purpose. Bob received the ball from a throw-in, standing in the outside-right position, and carried on going down the wing. As he neared the bye-line, he looked across to see O'Connell about to make his run into the penalty area. Delivering a perfect cross, Bob had the agony of watching Adams clear, just as Seamus was about to connect with the ball. A few moments later and it was Seamus again, this time seeing his header go just wide of the goalpost. The Bishop forward line continued to receive piercing passes from Bob and Jimmy, whilst Corbett kept things under control at the back and Harry Sharratt was not seriously troubled by any of the Hendon forwards, who found it increasingly difficult to get in any shots. In the space of two minutes, twice more O'Connell was put through by Hardisty passes but on both occasions his efforts were blocked by frantic defenders.

After sixty-six minutes, Bishop were rewarded for their perseverance with a second goal and it was something of a tragedy for Ivey. Seamus O'Connell sent over a shot-cum-centre that the Hendon goalkeeper caught. As Ivey moved to dodge a shoulder charge from the onrushing Oliver, he was simultaneously charged by Derek Lewin. This resulted in Ivey dropping the ball as he fell to the ground. In an instant, Lewin spun round and smacked the loose ball into the net, as Hendon defenders tried to recover. The goal would not be allowed these days but this was still in the era when goalkeepers could legitimately be shoulder charged. Nowadays, of course, they are a protected species.

The Bishop Auckland supporters went wild. Two goals up with less than twenty-five minutes to go and Hendon now looking as if they had been pole-axed.

But the Hendon players gradually fought back and decided that, as time was running out, it was best that they throw caution to the wind. With defeat staring them in the face, they tried all that they could to get a goal back. Bahler was robbed of the ball by Stewart when about to shoot and Bob Hardisty had to be alert when Cunningham attempted an audacious back-heel. Suddenly, Hendon had hope and their attacks, albeit belatedly, became more fluent. Bob was forced back to do more defensive duties with Corbett Cresswell and the full-backs, Dave Marshall and Tommy Stewart. Marshall was particularly fortunate when Parker overran the football and it went out for a goal kick.

The minutes ticked away—anxious Hendon supporters checked their watches as time seemed to be standing still for those supporting the team in blue. During the closing ten minutes, Bob Hardisty was brilliant. On one occasion he was able to supply Benny Edwards with a perfect pass but the opportunity was spurned and then, with amazing footwork, he created a scoring chance for O'Connell which was similarly missed.

It was obvious by now that, barring a catastrophe, Bob Hardisty was going to get his medal, and that his long wait was over. The Bishop Auckland supporters were shouting and singing at the tops of their voices, knowing that victory was theirs.

When the final whistle went, many supporters wept unashamedly. Bob Hardisty would now receive his winners' medal and they were here to see it. Life was good.

Jimmy Nimmins and Bob hugged each other in delight. The first Hendon player to congratulate Bob was Hendon captain, Dexter Adams:

> I was standing close to Bob when the referee blew for full-time. I can see him now, looking so proud and yet there was no smugness about him. He had won his medal and obviously he was pleased but he said to me 'Dexter, I could not have done it without these lads—they are the best in the business. I'm so glad for Jimmy,' meaning Jimmy Nimmins.

Tommy Stewart led his team mates up Wembley's Royal Box steps and gratefully accepted the Amateur Cup from Field Marshall Montgomery. As he was doing so, Sir Stanley Rous was relaying his congratulations to his old friend, Bob Hardisty, as the rest of the team waited in line to receive their medals.

Supporters of both clubs applauded the winners, as one by one the medals were issued, and when it was the losers' turn to ascend those thirty-nine steps, the noise was just as raucous. Hendon had played their part in a thrilling but by no means classic football match. Five years ago, when Willington had vanquished Bishop Auckland, Jackie Snowdon had told Bob Hardisty that Bishop would play worse and win the Cup. He was right, as today's performance was testament to that prediction. Bishop had played better football against Willington, and Pegasus and Crook but in all of those Finals they had come off second best. Now, when they had failed to play to their full potential, they had won. Football could be a funny game.

Stewart preceded his warriors down the exit steps of the Royal Box and upon returning to the playing pitch, with a hand movement worthy of an illusionist, passed the silver trophy to Bob, who raised it above his head to the acclaim of Wembley Stadium's masses. Now he remembered that day twenty years ago, when he had first set hands on this piece of shining silverware in a Bishop Auckland department store. Then it was a desire, a dream; now it was reality and he was never going to forget this fleeting moment, as the cheering massed ranks of the Bishop Auckland fans and remaining Hendon supporters rang all around Wembley Stadium.

Photographers were swarming around the players, using up rolls of film as if it was going out of fashion, with Bob being the main attraction, closely followed by Jimmy. With the cameramen still scurrying to get the best picture, a steward requested that the Bishop players move on to begin their lap of honour. At that moment, Bob caught the sight of the Hendon players, dejectedly coming down the steps with their losers' medals, and disconsolately leaving the arena for the dressing room. He knew all about the disappointment that they were experiencing at that precise moment but now was the time for him to take in the sweet smell of success. As the team proceeded around the stadium, each player carrying the Cup in turn, as the Bishop Auckland supporters whooped in delight and adoration, he believed these to be the best moments of his career.

In the dressing room, an old team mate presented himself—Tommy Farrer, who asked Bob just one simple question: 'What took you so bloody long?' Another visitor was Harry McIlvenny, who was thrilled to bits that his old friend, and Jimmy Nimmins, had won their winners' medals after all those failures.

More than one very reliable source has advised me that Wembley Stadium had a surprise visitor that day to witness Bob's triumph—Betty. She had been persuaded to leave Robert in the care of friends and had travelled down to Wembley on a 'special' with some colleagues, having left Bishop Auckland railway station at five-thirty in the morning. The train had delivered its passengers directly to Wembley Station just five hundred yards from the famous stadium.

Having watched her husband achieve his goal and met him after the match, she and her colleagues made a hasty return to Wembley Station, where they boarded the train for the long journey home. Betty must have been the most sought after passenger on the train, as all of the others beseeched her to show off her husband's winners' medal that he had given to her just a few short hours ago.

However, there are major flaws with this account which will be explained shortly.

Later that evening, at the celebratory dinner held at the team's hotel, the Great Eastern, each player had congratulatory telegrams to open. The first that Bob opened was from Ted Wanless, the player who had replaced him way back in the 1939 Cup team and went on to earn a winners' medal. He looked along the banqueting table and his gaze fell on Jimmy Nimmins, who twelve months ago, had entered this room on crutches.

'What do you make of Wembley now, Jim?' enquired Bob.

'Fucking marvellous, Bob. Fucking marvellous,' came back the not altogether unexpected response.

Before returning by train to County Durham on the Monday after their success, the Bishop Auckland players were shown around the House of Commons by the town's Member of Parliament, Hugh Dalton, who had witnessed the club's victory.

Seven hours later, the players were standing on the balcony of Bishop Auckland's Town Hall, looking down on a throng the likes of which had not been witnessed before. Everywhere that the players looked it was just a mass of smiling, cheering, joyous faces. The tumultuous ovation that the crowd gave their heroes touched all of the players, recognizing that this was an occasion that would live with each of them forever.

One by one, the players were introduced to the crowd by Councillor

J Murphy, and in reply each player gave a short speech. When it came to Bob's turn, the crowd's excitement reached new heights and he was so moved that his prepared speech was abandoned in place of just fifteen emotional words: 'I have only one short sentence to say. I have got it at long last.' Then, to even louder applause and cheering, he raised his left hand that held a winners' medal. The roar was deafening.

But whose medal was it that he held aloft, that night, on Bishop Auckland's Town Hall balcony? Was it really his? Surely his own medal had been given to Betty after Saturday's match and it was in her safekeeping at their Princes Street home, if those reliable sources were to be believed. Had Betty delivered his medal to the Town Hall earlier that day, in order that her husband would be able to hold it at the Town Hall reception? This hypothesis is extremely unlikely, given how precious the medal was to the Hardistys—it is inconceivable that Betty would have let it out of her sight, if indeed she ever had possession of it in the first place! Or had Bob been obliged to borrow a medal from one of his team mates, as a temporary replacement, in order to show it off to the townsfolk of Bishop Auckland? Regrettably, the mystery remains unresolved as players, friends or family members have been unable to come up with any solution to the conundrum. Attempts to come across anyone who was travelling on the train with Betty and saw her showing off the medal have proved fruitless and, in the circumstances, this writer does not believe that Betty attended the match. She would have much preferred to have stayed at home, looking after her child with her select golf club members, over a coffee morning get-together, than watch twenty-two men kick a football around a field.

Not that any of this speculation matters—Bob had his medal at long last and that was the main thing.

At the end of season Football Writers' Awards, senior BBC sports correspondent and commentator, Raymond Glendenning, selected the eleven-man squad that would comprise his 'Dream Team' for the season. When it came to selecting his right half-back, he overlooked such leading professionals as England's Billy Wright and Ireland's Peter Doherty, opting for the amateur, Bob Hardisty, instead. In Glendenning's view, 'Bob Hardisty has shown everyone just how to play the game of football and that perseverance does have its rewards. He is a credit to us all.'

'O, let the hours be short,
Till fields and blows and groans applaud our sport!'
King Henry IV (Part One) (William Shakespeare)

Chapter Ten

RENAISSANCE

Surprises have an uncanny knack of turning up at the most unexpected times.

Bob Hardisty received his surprise just days after lifting the Amateur Cup, when he, Betty and young Robert were sat around the table having breakfast. There was a clatter at the front door, as the postman delivered the mail, and on the hallway floor lay an envelope, carrying the Football Association insignia. Thinking that it was just a standard letter of congratulation on winning his winners' medal, Bob laid the envelope aside on the mantelpiece in the living room—and forgot about it.

The letter was still there when Bob returned home that evening from work, and it was only when Betty reminded him, that he took the trouble to read it. He could not believe it—he had been selected for the forthcoming international against France in Brest, in three weeks time. Naturally, they had a drink or three that evening in celebration.

Not only had Bob made it back in to the England squad but also included were fellow Bishop Auckland colleagues, Corbett Cresswell and Seamus O'Connell. In addition, Dave Marshall and Ron Fryer had been informed to stand by, in case of injuries, that would result in their selection. All of this was further proof to the northern sceptics, if any was still needed, that to be recognized by the selectors, northern clubs had to reach at least the semi-final of the Amateur Cup competition, for their players to be placed in the spotlight, in order to receive international recognition.

In the communication from the Football Association, Bob was reminded that:

1. Each player must have a valid passport.
2. Under the present currency regulations, no individual may take out of the country more than £10 sterling. It is not permissible to spend any of this amount whilst abroad.
3. Individual members wishing to have funds of their own whilst on tour, can make application for foreign currency through their bankers in the usual way.
4. Members of the party are advised to take with them a suit for travelling, and a dark lounge suit for evening wear. Members should also take soap and towels for personal use.
5. Each person will be responsible for his own baggage when passing through customs.

Three weeks later, on Friday 6th May, Bob travelled with Corbett Cresswell by train to London and arrived in the evening at the Lancaster Court Hotel, Paddington, where he joined up with the England Team manager, Norman Creek, and the rest of the England players. Included in the squad were the Hendon pairing of Dexter Adams, surprisingly selected to play at right-back instead of his usual centre-half position, and Eric Beardsley, selected for the left-back spot. Playing at inside-right was a young man who would have his career tragically cut short, through injury, in a couple of year's time—Alex Jeffreys of Doncaster Rovers. Although neither Dave Marshall nor Ron Fryer had made it to the party, Bob was pleased to renew his acquaintance with Tommy Farrer, who had been chosen as a reserve player. After a good night's rest—there was no visiting Finnegan's Bar on this occasion—the party were taken by taxi to Blackbushe Airport, situated on the Surrey–Hampshire border near Camberley. The flight took the party to the Hotel de France, Rue de Lyon, in Brest.

That afternoon, the players were put through a light training session, led by Bob and trainer, Jack Jennings, for two hours, before the squad was allowed to return to their base and spend the evening strolling around the French town.

Sunday morning began early with a light breakfast, before the Mayor of Brest received the England players and officials at the Town Hall.

The game took place on a blustery Sunday afternoon. It was a satisfactory affair insofar as the players from both sides produced a really closely fought match. Bob had a comfortable game, as did the majority of the England players, without exactly being exceptional. He had played better but when the game ended he was reasonably satisfied with his performance, having helped his country gain a meritorious 1–1 draw.

The players arrived back in London on Monday evening but Bob decided not to travel back straight away to Durham, preferring to stay overnight in the capital and spend time with some friends that he knew.

The return to the international scene gave Bob the resolve to continue his playing career with renewed determination. Not that he was contemplating hanging his boots up just yet. He had seen the arrival of the mercurial Derek Lewin as the final piece to the jigsaw that was Bishop Auckland Football Club. The best goalkeeper in the country was between the sticks, in the shape of Harry Sharratt; the defence was as solid as ever with dependable and experienced players of the calibre of Dave Marshall, Tommy Stewart, Ron Fryer, Corbett Cresswell, Barry Wilkinson and Jimmy Nimmins. The forward line, he saw as the best in the country with not a fault in view. Jacky Major was moving on to play for Hull City but in his place was Frank McKenna and on the left wing was Bobby Watson, two players who had the wit and the speed to turn defenders inside out. The inside-forwards were formidable—Derek Lewin, Ray Oliver, Seamus O'Connell and, on stand-by, the speed merchant and goal scorer, Les Dixon. With an array of talent like that within the club, Bob rightly reckoned that now was not the time for calling it a day. Any thoughts that he may have been harbouring about retirement had been displaced when the Amateur Cup had been won and he walked off Wembley's green lawn on that sunny day in April. They had won the Cup and each and every one of them truly believed that they were capable of repeating the feat. A further international cap had added extra ethos to a most successful year and if he was back in the sites of the selectors, then good for him.

England played Ireland at Cliftonville on 17th September, 1955 and Bob captained the team. Also in the side were Corbett Cresswell and Seamus O'Connell, with Derek Lewin and Harry Sharratt travelling as reserves—the latter kept out of the playing eleven by Mike Pinner of Pegasus. England won 4–1 and *The Times* correspondent reported that, 'Hardisty gave a grand display at right-half—one of the best seen by an amateur on an Irish ground.'

The game was a trial, with a place in the Great Britain squad, for the following year's Olympic Games that were being staged in Melbourne,

Australia, the prize. For these forthcoming Games, the title 'Great Britain' was something of a misnomer as none of the other home football federations took part. The Football Associations of Scotland, Wales and Ireland had decided that the cost of paying for players to travel 11,850 miles to Melbourne was prohibitive and also, they did not wish to provide players who would otherwise be playing in their respective League programmes that would have been well underway in the northern hemisphere. The England Football Association was, therefore, to provide all of the players and officials for the 'Great Britain' team and would also meet the total estimated costs of £15,000, in flying the party out to Melbourne.

A 4–1 winning margin was a good result and yet in some quarters it was seen as much less than an overwhelming success. Bob Hardisty's inclusion in the team had drawn criticism initially but his performance had silenced the doubters, at least for the time being. Much was made of England's slow, methodical pace that some observers saw as out of date, claiming that such a style of play would fall into the hands of the Continentals, who preferred a quick passing game.

Great Britain had been drawn to meet Bulgaria in a Qualifying Round for the Olympic Games tournament and from the outset their chances of making it to Australia were recognised by the press as minimal. Bulgaria, like many other continental sides, had a different interpretation of the word 'amateur' when it came to sport, and football was no exception. The Bulgarians were as good an outfit as one could wish to see and were quite capable of holding their own against the best professional countries. Their players were drafted in to the military and as a result would spend months at a time honing their footballing skills and techniques. They were no more an amateur team than Arsenal or Spurs were. However, because the players were in the military forces in a country that did not accept professionalism as we may know it, they were able to comply with the Olympic standard of amateurism, in the way that Eastern Bloc countries had done in previous Olympiads. The Great Britain squad knew that a tough test lay ahead of them when the first leg of the tie would be played in Sofia, in October.

To their credit, the FA did their best to get the Great Britain team up to scratch, and arranged a mini-series of trial games against professional football league clubs. The performance of the players as a team was the most important thing in these games, rather than the actual results. The first had been against a strong Arsenal side, just three days before the Ireland international, and for all the Division One side won 2–1, the amateurs came out of the game with a lot of positives. 'Pangloss', reporting in one of the southern newspapers, claimed 'Bob Hardisty has never played better, even in the hey-day of his career'.

West Ham United proved a far more difficult obstacle and came out 6–1 winners. Queen's Park Rangers won 2–1 and Luton Town inflicted another 2–1 defeat, Bob's stylish performance in the latter game drawing the comment from one noted southern correspondent as '… a joy to watch the academic calm of Bob Hardisty'.

It was hoped that the experience of playing against professionals would bring on the amateur Great Britain squad but playing five competitive games, interspersed with practice matches—that not all of the squad could attend, due to inability to be granted time off from work—was an ineffective answer to the force that the Bulgarians would pose.

Immediately after the Luton game, Bob Hardisty, Derek Lewin and Harry Sharratt, along with the other Great Britain players selected for the trip to Bulgaria, returned to the Lancaster Court Hotel in London. The next day was spent watching films, provided by the FA, of continental football teams in action. One of the newsreels was that showing the first defeat at Wembley by a foreign side, the 6–3 thrashing of England, handed out by Hungary in 1953—a team that included the likes of Ferenc Puskas and Lev Yashin—whom the Bulgarians had defeated in a recent international. When that newsreel had finished, all tension in the room was removed when Derek Lewin turned to Bob and dryly commented, 'Well, that's certainly cheered me up, how do you feel, captain?'

If Derek's mockingly black-humoured remark had a touch of realism, it was nothing compared to the rather defeatist attitude of Team Manager, Norman Creek. Norman was well liked by the players and carried a lot of respect but for this match his team talks to the players lacked any of the 'Agincourt spirit', and definitely failed to give any confidence to the squad. He had told the press that he thought the defence would put up a good show but the attack needed to improve, much to the annoyance of the chosen forwards. He went on to say: 'If we only lose 1–2 in Sofia, some real English spirit might see us through in the return game in England, next May.' This was not exactly a Henry V speech akin to 'Once more unto the breach, dear friends, once more …' and the English newspapers picked up on this lack of positivity from the Great Britain Team Manager.

The players had a training session that afternoon at Greenford, where

Bob and Jack Jennings put the team through some vigorous exercises, but the evening was spent in more pleasant surroundings when they attended a cocktail party at the Bulgarian Legation. Bob was introduced to the Bulgarian Minister and his wife, Madame Halova, and later said how charming he had found them. Madame Halova, in particular, had taken the time to tell him about Bulgarian culture, that the whole of Bulgaria was looking forward to the football match and that the Great Britain players would be made most welcome in Sofia.

Following Norman Creek's assessment of the game's outcome, Sir Stanley Rous attempted to deflect any notions of defeatism by issuing a more positive statement. On the eve of their departure from Blackbushe Airport, the players had a low-key practice match against Aldershot and spent the night at their hotel, watching a television broadcast of England 'B' beating Yugoslavia 'B' 5–1. Buoyed by the result against a team that were expected to be a major force in the Olympic Games, Sir Stanley, in an interview after the broadcast, gave a more positive forecast about Great Britain's amateur squad. He predicted that the game against Bulgaria would be a close one and he was confident that Bob Hardisty and his team mates would come away from Sofia with at least a draw, in this first ever game between these two footballing nations.

The Halovas were not wrong. The reception given to Bob and his players, as they took to the field in Sofia's Letvy Stadium, was an experience that he never forgot. True, the stadium was not as attractive as Wembley—renowned correspondent Harry Carpenter likened it to a 'concrete saucer'—and did not have any distinguishing features like Wembley's twin towers, but it did have the ability to convey the warmth and passion of the Bulgarian people towards footballers in general. This feeling of 'welcomeness' was heightened when each of the teams lined up for the national anthems, prior to the game, and every Great Britain player was handed a bouquet of flowers from schoolgirls wearing traditional dress.

As well as Great Britain played, they left the stadium a defeated team, although the 2–0 score line was an honourable, if not unexpected, defeat. Right from the kick-off, the visitors made their plans known with a defensive formation. Before the match, Norman Creek had heaped praise on his backs and now they were showing him why. Time after time, Bulgaria's forwards surged towards the visitors' goal but every time they were turned back. Bob Hardisty was impeccable and played a captain's role. Leading by example, he made timely, rock-hard challenges and helped build counter attacks. Shouting commands when required, he had his fellow defenders playing their hearts out, each one aware that no-one had given them a chance of winning.

The incessant pressure was bound to tell in the end, however, and after half an hour's play, Koleff and Yanev danced down the left wing with a delightful passing movement that was finished off by Stefanoff from close range.

Great Britain held out for another thirty minutes before their defence was breached again but it was a goal out of tragedy for Bob Hardisty. For sixty minutes he had given a display that had the Bulgarian fans cheering in admiration. They had wondered how this bald man with ageing legs could possibly give such a commanding display with a brand of football without malice. To them, he was a true sportsman, but in one moment he was proven to be human. A long, searching high ball was played in to the Great Britain half, midway between the centre circle and penalty box. Bob had the ball covered and would easily control it—another Bulgarian attack would come to nothing. However, fellow defender, Eric Beardsley, had also moved over to collect the ball and got there before Bob. He had the ball under control and went as if to clear it upfield but changed his mind at the last second. Instead, he played a sideways pass across the goal to Bob who was caught off balance, already anticipating the clearance. The Great Britain captain tried to recover but slipped on the surface and, as he fell to the ground, the grateful Yanev smashed the loose ball past Pinner, in to the roof of the net. Fifty-five thousand Bulgarian voices roared in relief. At 1–0 the visitors had stood a chance of getting back in the game but now that they were two goals down there would be little prospect of a recovery.

Beardsley stood with his head in his hands, instantly acknowledging his error. Bob, seeing his team mate's anguish, walked over to him and patted him on the back, telling him to forget it.

No further goals were added by Bulgaria, thanks to Tommy Farrer and Beardsley, both of whom headed certain goals off the line but, incredibly, it was Great Britain who finished the stronger. Littlejohn, who played his football for Bournemouth, fired a shot that forced Yossiloff to pull off a fine save and in the closing minutes, Bob sent in a sensational stinging drive from thirty yards, that was just turned away by the goalkeeper's outstretched fingers.

There was still time for Great Britain to be awarded a free kick. As Bob strode up to take it, the crowd cheered in unison, honouring this English hero who had done so much for his nation and who had played so well. He placed the ball and sent over a tantalising cross that had the Bulgarian's spinning but Seamus O'Connell's flying header went over the crossbar as the crowd 'Oohed' and 'Ahhed.'

The home side had won but had failed to rattle up a goal tally that could not be overturned. Great Britain had the second leg to look forward to and with a bit of luck could well win the tie—that is provided they could score three times without reply.

The British reporters heaped praise on Great Britain's defensive performance, especially that of Bob Hardisty, and doyen of the press room, Desmond Hackett wrote: 'And of this gallant band, there was none to match team captain Hardisty. Even the Bulgarians had nothing to equal his mastery.'

Norman Creek was quoted as saying that Great Britain had earned a 'moral victory' but having had to defend for almost seventy of the ninety minutes, perhaps that was stretching things a bit far. He had not quite got the 1–2 defeat that he had forecast but for the time being he was satisfied. However, neither he, nor the national press, were really deceived by the score. The Bulgarians had missed a mass of chances and only a magnificent defensive display had curtailed the scoring. To get to Melbourne, Great Britain would have to attack and show a lot more flair than they had in the 'concrete saucer' of the Letvy Stadium.

It would be a long wait for Bob Hardisty and the rest of the Great Britain players until the second leg took place in six months time. 'A lot could happen in six months,' he thought.

It was usual for Derek Lewin to travel by train up to Bishop Auckland from his Lancashire home on a Friday evening. He would check-in at the Castle Hotel where he would be allocated room number eight—his playing number. The hotel was owned and run by Mr A and Mrs L Laverick whose daughter, June, was making a career on stage and television as a singer and dancer. She would become famous by virtue of her appearances on *The Dickie Henderson Show* on London Television. Sometimes, if business commitments at the bacon factory, which he ran with his father, delayed him, Derek would make his way by car to Bishop Auckland but whichever mode of transport he chose, whether it be train or car, he was usually accompanied by that Prince of Clowns, Harry Sharratt.

Bob Hardisty would more often than not meet this duo with a fourth member, Ken Chisholm, who played football for Sunderland and who he had known as a friend a good many years. This manly quartet would spend most of Friday night at the town's snooker hall, in Railway Street, before returning to the Castle for a 'couple of drinks' and perhaps a game of cards—sometimes, June Laverick and visiting friends would join in and form an extended party. In some respects, this arrangement filled a gap in Bob's timetable: Mondays were spent either at home marking school books, attending receptions to which he had been invited, or running training and keep-fit sessions at village halls or clubs; Tuesday evenings were spent training at the football club, as were Thursday evenings, whilst Wednesday evenings were spent marking school books and running training and keep-fit sessions at local clubs. Saturdays, of course, were spent playing football, and Sundays would see him at the Golf or Cricket Club, with or without Betty. All the while, the call for him to attend local clubs and organisations throughout the north-east continued. He was as popular as ever and he never tired of the plea 'Show us your medal, Bob.' It was not only social demands that were made on him; his attendance was also required at meetings of the Education Authority, not all of which took place between the hours of nine and five, and quite often it would be well into the evening that he returned home. Amid all of this, he was expected to attend call-ups by the Football Association for weekend training courses and, of course, present himself for all of the games in which he was chosen to play. With all of this, he also sought to continue his sporting interests by actually playing golf and cricket as well as attending 'the odd day at the races'.

It appears that Betty Hardisty willingly accepted her husband's absences as she was interviewed by a local reporter who wished to present a feature about footballers' wives. Betty said: 'During the football, I count on losing my husband's company for at least three nights every week. Excitement grows high for me as much as anyone. It is my main job to see that Bob gets plenty of good plain food—but none of those fancy, big steaks we hear so much about when athletes are at the peak of their training.'

Just three weeks after receiving plaudits from the press, the other side of the coin had to be encountered by the England amateur footballers when Germany were the visitors to White Hart Lane. On a sultry, Saturday afternoon in mid-November a creditable crowd of over 12,000 turned up to watch twenty-two amateur players, despite a variety of Football League games taking place in the capital, including First Division matches.

The performance by England was not good, even though they went in at half-time with a 2–0 lead through goals from Derek Lewin and Biggs, the Hounslow Town centre-forward. This was, however, misleading as the Germans had overrun the England defenders and only brilliant goalkeeping by Mike Pinner, and a redoubtable display by Bob Hardisty, had prevented them from scoring. In the second half, the English defence capitulated and the visitors scored three times to run out worthy 3–2 winners.

One national newspaper correspondent pulled no punches when it came to gauging England's (that is, Great Britain's), chances of qualifying for Melbourne. In an article berating the technical skills of the modern amateur club player compared to the inter-war period of the 1920s and 1930s, he wrote, after the loss to Germany: '… By comparison, the players of last Saturday, with the single exception of Hardisty, gave no suggestion that they could produce or comprehend the technical standard of football of a Second Division team.'

It was such technical ability that helped Bishop Auckland overcome Durham City in Bishop Auckland's FA Cup First Round match at Kingsway a short time later. Showing the same composure that he had done for the past sixteen years, Bob and his fellow team mates saw off 'The Citizens' to win 3–1, City goalkeeper Lax having a fine game and keeping the score down to a respectable level.

Scunthorpe United of the Third Division (North) were Bishop's opponents in Round Two and the Kingsway crowd of 13,500 saw a thriller, despite the 0–0 score line. From the outset, Bishop put their Football League cousins under pressure, with Derek Lewin causing all sorts of panic in the Scunthorpe defence. His addition to the Bishop Auckland ranks was proving a master stroke. Playing at his normal inside-right position, forward of Bob Hardisty, the pair forged a deadly pairing whilst on the left flank, Seamus O'Connell and Jimmy Nimmins had formed a similar relationship. The action was like watching two pistons in unison as first the right, then the left, created attacking moves, with usually Lewin, O'Connell or their centre-forward, Ray Oliver, climaxing the movement with a goal. Many had already been scored with this brand of football but on this afternoon, no matter how hard they tried, the home side could not break down the massed claret and blue defence.

Spurred on by a partisan crowd, the 'Bishops' tried everything they could but without success. New recruit, Warren Bradley, playing at outside-right, tormented 'The Iron' full-back Brownsword so often that the defender was reduced to cynical fouls to stop the winger's progress. It was much the same on the left-wing where ex-Willington wingman, Stan Rutherford, had the beating of Lamb. Neither player however, could provide the one telling cross that would have given Auckland victory. After the game, Bob told Derek that he could not remember the last time he had played in a game which they had totally dominated, for no reward.

The following Thursday, the replay was held at Scunthorpe's Old Show Ground and, sad to say, nothing went right for Bishop. The half-back line of Hardisty, Cresswell and Nimmins strove hard to repeat the dominance that they had shown over Scunthorpe's forwards five days earlier and to some extent succeeded. However, the link with the forward line was not there and as a result, Lewin, Oliver and O'Connell struggled. Scunthorpe, on the other hand, playing on their own soil, were a different proposition from the first match. They showed a commitment to win every ball and a more positive attacking approach. Harry Sharratt was on top form and it was largely due to his brilliance that the score was restricted to only a 2–0 defeat.

Sadly for Harry, he played a large part in Scunthorpe's second goal. There was not long to go and Scunthorpe were hanging on to their one goal lead. Bob and Jimmy Nimmins had gradually got more and more into the game and were applying pressure to Scunthorpe's defence. Bob sent over a centre intended for Ray Oliver but centre-half Heward intercepted with a lunging tackle and booted the ball out of play on the half way line. In normal circumstances, the throw-in would have been taken by Bob but, trying to save time, Harry ran out of his goal area and took it himself, sending the ball towards Derek Lewin. Unfortunately, the ball came to Derek with a little too much force and he was unable to control it. A Scunthorpe player collected the ball and, left with a clear shot at goal, promptly despatched it into an empty net, from distance.

The youngest member of the Bishop Auckland team for that match was John Barnwell. He had started his football career at Whitley Bay, playing in the Northern Alliance League at the age of fourteen against such clubs as Blyth Spartans and Newcastle United Reserves. His potential had been noticed by many clubs who would have given anything for his signature. His father protected John from making any rash decision about his future and, as a result, clubs like Burnley, Sunderland and Newcastle United were shown the door. Arsenal, however, would show a greater degree of professionalism in their conversations with young John and his father, which would result in him signing amateur forms for 'The Gunners'. For now, he was playing for the 'Bishops' in their cup runs. He remembers the match at Scunthorpe well, in particular a rather comical situation that arose on the journey back to County Durham:

> I had to take time off school. Having drawn at Kingsway we had to travel to Scunthorpe. We stayed overnight in a hotel in Doncaster and that was a major experience for me.
>
> I think we were coming back by train and I remember 'Kit' Rudd sitting there, issuing the players 'expenses'. After a while, he called for me and said, 'Now, young John, how much time have you had off work?'
>
> I just stood there and said, 'But Mr Rudd, I'm still at school.'
>
> 'I'll ask you again, John … how much time have you had off work?'
>
> 'But Mr Rudd, I'm still at school.'
>
> For the third time he asked, 'How much time have you had off work?'
>
> Just then, Bob Hardisty came along, having heard the conversation and said, 'Don't worry, John, I'll handle this.'
>
> A few minutes later I had more money in my pocket than my old fella probably earned in a week.

With the exit from the FA Cup, Bishop Auckland was able to focus its attentions on the main target—holding on to possession of the Amateur Cup, and in the process becoming the first club to record successive Wembley victories in the competition. This is the target that spurred Bob Hardisty and all at the club. There was, however, a major obstacle in the way of repeating last season's success—they were pulled out of the hat to meet arch rivals, Crook Town, at Kingsway.

Crowds started queuing to get in to the ground fully two hours before kick-off for this important game and it was thought at one point that the police would insist on closing the gates early. To the relief of those arriving late, this proved unnecessary, although when the teams took to the field, there were more than 12,000 spectators.

Bishop were in command for the opening ten minutes, a period of play which saw Lewin receive a pass from Bob that led to Frank McKenna, back in the side in place of Warren Bradley, who was unavailable, delivering a thunderbolt of a shot which Jarrie saved, diving to his left. The ball rebounded in the air and Oliver threw himself to connect with a header that struck the prostrate goalkeeper on the legs before the covering Riley was able to clear the danger.

Two minutes later, O'Connell received another arrow-straight pass from Bob and his drive beat Jarrie all ends up, only for the ball to crash against the upright. The ball rebounded to McKenna who provided Oliver with another scoring opportunity which was spurned. Lewin was given another chance to open the scoring but this time Bobby Davison came to Crook's rescue with a lunging tackle to dispossess the inside-forward.

So far it had been one-way traffic and, other than a weak effort from Appleby, the Crook forwards had been very disappointing, with Bob, Corbett Cresswell and Jimmy Nimmins, having a comfortable time. All of that changed after twenty minutes, when Tommy Stewart inexplicably handled the ball in his own penalty area when there was no apparent danger. Crook supporters were delighted. They had seen their club under the cosh throughout this opening spell and now they had been given a life line.

Like two gunfighters, Harry Sharratt and Bobby Davison, stared coolly at each other. Sharratt versus Davison. What a duel: Davison, the arch penalty king against Harry Sharratt, who saved penalties in his sleep. Who would come out on top?

Ignoring the taunting crowd, Davison deliberately placed the ball on the penalty spot and took seven paces back, two more than his usual five, all the while keeping his eyes on the football. On the goal line, Sharratt stood poised, slightly to the right of his goal, offering Davison the chance to place his penalty to the goalkeeper's left. Never for a second did he take his eyes off the football—his dive would be made a fraction of a second before Davison's boot struck the back of it.

Davison stood stock still, all the time focussing his eyes on the football, then took a sharp intake of breath. A quick glance off the ball to take in the picture of Sharratt's stance. He began his run up.

Thwack!

Davison kicked the football as if it were the mother-in-law.

The ball seared up with force and height. Sharratt hurled his body to his left, his arms outstretched.

Loud cheers rent the air as Harry fell to the ground. He lay there for a few moments—watching the Crook players congratulating their penalty marksman.

Bobby Davison's penalty had been despatched into the top corner of the net—an unstoppable shot.

Harry had lost the shoot out.

As a result of the goal, Crook's confidence was raised and they came more into the game, although never threatening to add to their score. The setback of going a goal behind did not deter the home side and they renewed their attacks, unfortunate not to have been awarded a penalty of their own when

Davison—ever the villain—clearly handled the ball inside the area. To the disappointment of the home fans, referee Rhodes gave the infringement outside the area. Bob Hardisty took the free-kick but his effort came to nothing. Further disappointment was heaped on the Bishop supporters when Derek Lewin was injured and had to receive attention to his shoulder.

The second half got under way with Auckland going all out for an equalizer and they were rewarded after only five minutes. Derek Lewin remembers that goal with affection:

> Quite frankly it was the best goal that I ever scored. I had collected the injury when I went for a high ball with Crook defender, May. As we came down, his arm smashed on to my shoulder, quite accidental. I went off for a while but obviously came back on. I had not been on the pitch long when this ball came across from the right and I was loitering with intent, just outside the penalty area, probably twenty or twenty-five yards out. The ball came out to me and I hit it on the volley and it went straight in the goal. That was the equalizer. All the Bishop players came rushing towards me to congratulate me and jump on me and there I am with this, I thought, bloody broken shoulder. I shouted, 'Get off! Get off!' I wasn't able to play in the replay because of the injury.
>
> I went to Blackpool General Hospital and the specialist had a good look at it. He said that the shoulder was not broken although it might have been better if it had. He said that dislocations could take longer than breaks to mend. They could have treated a fracture but with a dislocation all they could recommend was leave it to put itself right.
>
> The following week, a woman Bishop Auckland supporter came up to me and accused me of being a southern namby-pamby for not playing in the replay.

The rest of the game was tedious, rather than exciting, the heavy surface becoming a major factor, with neither team able to take advantage of each other's mistakes, and in the end a 1–1 result was fair enough. Ray Oliver and Bobby Davison had had a battle royal and were spoken to by the referee about their aggressive play—a legacy of the Cup meetings two seasons ago—but had not been booked and there was never any real nastiness in the game. The clubs would have another chance to sort it out in seven days time.

During that week, Bob had as many of his colleagues that could attend, training every night. The standard of play had not been good enough on Saturday and he wanted to see more time spent on ball control and technique. Also, Derek's absence would be a loss to the team but with his place being taken by Warren Bradley, they would still have a side capable of taking on anyone.

There was still snow on the Millfield Ground surface on a murky, misty afternoon when the teams lined up for the replay. Bob had trained his players to the minute and they were ready for the battle.

Disaster struck after only four minutes, when Corbett Cresswell's attempted pass back to Harry Sharratt stuck in the snow and predator, Ken Harrison, waltzed through to give Crook an early lead. The setback stirred the Bishop players and from a Hardisty cross-field pass, O'Connell brought the best out of Jarrie.

It was end to end stuff, with the surface playing a large part in providing the excitement. Last week the game had been played on a heavy surface that took its toll on players' skills; today, the surface was just as heavy but the smattering of snow was causing defenders and forwards to slip and slide.

Dispossessing Harrison, Bob sprayed another cross-field pass, this time to Benny Edwards. The winger served O'Connell whose first-time effort was saved by Jarrie at the expense of a corner. As usual, Bob took up a position beyond the far post for a corner that he was not taking himself, and as McKenna's delivery came over, he braced himself. To his delight, the ball arrived and he was able to divert it into the net as Riley challenged. Bishop Auckland supporters—at least those who could see through the fog—went wild. It was no more than the visitors deserved as, up to this point, they had been the better team.

Better team or not, it was Crook who went into the lead again when they were awarded a free kick, following a foul on McMillan. Bill Jeffs sent a long ball across the Bishop defensive line and Harrison stooped to score with a well placed header. It was a poor goal for Hardisty and company to concede as Harrison had been granted too much room by the Auckland defenders, allowing him to score.

As if still trying to take in the reasons for Harrison's goal, Bishop defenders allowed Crook to score a third. Inside-left, Turney, cheekily out-foxed Hardisty with a clever back-heel and Jimmy McMillan smashed the ball home from twelve yards to put the home side well in front.

Bishop players came back with a vengeance and within two minutes, Frank McKenna combined with Bob Hardisty and Warren Bradley to give himself a scoring chance that he accepted, tucking the ball under the diving Jarrie, with left-half, May, chasing the ball into the net.

Although still a goal behind, it was a confident set of Bishop Auckland players that came out for the second half. It was, however, Crook who should have added to the scoring when McMillan wasted a chance on fifty minutes.

At the other end, Frank McKenna blazed over the bar from only three yards and shortly afterwards, Ray Oliver sent his shot wide of Jarrie's left-hand post. Steadily, Bishop were getting on top as more pressure was applied to the Crook defence in which Davison was as uncompromising as ever. The break came after sixty-two minutes and it was a triumph for the persistence of Ray Oliver, in his duel with Davison. Bob Hardisty had possession of the ball close to the centre circle and feigned to his left, intending to take the ball right. Turney lunged in with a wild tackle that raked the inside of Bob's right ankle and the referee awarded a free-kick, which would normally have been taken by Bob. Bob, however, was still nursing his aching ankle from Turney's challenge and Jimmy Nimmins stepped up to take it. Losing Davison, for once, Ray Oliver rose majestically to receive Jimmy's cross and head the ball home from close range.

Crook were now hanging on and their attacks became fewer and of little danger but defensively they were showing their fighting spirit in holding back the Bishop attack, although some of the tackles could well have been penalised had the referee been stronger. The extra fitness and training sessions that Bob had put his players through were starting to tell as Crook players began to falter. Benny Edwards, though, should have won the game for the visitors when he missed an open goal with only five minutes left and as there was no more scoring, thirty minutes extra time would have to be played on a strength sapping pitch.

Strength was definitely required but it was speed, agility and being light of weight that won the match, in the shape of diminutive Warren Bradley. Warren's light frame meant that he was able to float over the slippery surface and take on the heavy artillery that was the Crook Town defence.

With Bob Hardisty supplying creative passes, despite his painful ankle, the Auckland forwards pressed forward, with Bradley turning defenders one way and then the other. But it was a frustrating first fifteen minutes of extra time for the Bishop Auckland players and their supporters as they failed in their attempts to score the winning goal.

Three minutes into the second period of extra time, the dam burst. Bradley lay claim to the ball and played a telling pass through the middle, for McKenna to run onto. With only Jarrie to beat, McKenna thundered a shot at goal. Jarrie parried the ball but was helpless when McKenna rolled in the rebound.

More in relief, as much as anything, the Bishop players hugged Bradley and McKenna. Crook were not allowed back into the game and a memorable victory was achieved. Bob still had his dream and there would not be any tougher matches than this one to overcome.

Gedling Colliery stood in Bishop Auckland's way for the next round. As a club, Bishop Auckland were satisfied with the game that they had been handed but they were critical of the way the draw had been made. The Football Association had decided, in their infinite wisdom, to adopt a policy of zoning for the Second Round. Not only Bishop Auckland officials but members of all other remaining northern clubs in the competition were furious. The Northern League Management Committee spokesman, Bob Frankland, expressed concern at such an arrangement, arguing that the north only had one major league—the Northern League—with a smattering of smaller clubs covering the rest of the area, whereas the south, and in particular London, had a number of Leagues and, therefore, a greater number of clubs with a better chance of avoiding each other. The FA listened but, as expected, threw out the north's objections.

If the game against Gedling Colliery had made the likes of Bob Hardisty and Jimmy Nimmins wonder just why they were carrying on with their playing careers, one could hardly have blamed them. They could have been at home, sat in front of a nice warm fire, with their feet up instead of taking part in a football match on a frozen pitch somewhere in Nottinghamshire, where they were just as likely to break a leg. The temperature was bitterly cold with sleet swirling into the red faces of supporters who did their best to cover themselves up. A crowd of over 10,000 had been anticipated but because of the freezing conditions, only 2,828 spectators attended. The game was not a classic as conditions were against that but the 4–1 win that the 'Two Blues' recorded could have been closer had Gedling not missed a penalty when trailing 2–1. A goal from McKenna and a hat-trick from Ray Oliver were enough to see the favourites through.

Bishop Auckland were given another local derby for Round Three when they were drawn away to Ferryhill Athletic, a club that held no dangers as far as Auckland supporters were concerned.[†] Notwithstanding the overstated confidence of the Bishop Auckland supporters, in a game devoid of any notable skills, Bishop struggled and were fortunate to come away with a 1–0

---

†   There was no zoning for Round Three, the FA having reverted to an 'all in' policy for the remainder of the competition.

victory thanks to a Seamus O'Connell goal, two minutes from time. The bad news for Bishop was that, during this match, Dave Marshall had suffered a leg injury that would keep him out for six to eight weeks.

It was about this time that the Football Association released the names of nineteen players that they wanted to attend a training session in preparation for the return match with Bulgaria, even though the game was not due to take place for a further three months. To the amazement of everyone, not one Bishop Auckland player was named in the squad. No Hardisty, Cresswell, Nimmins, Sharratt, O'Connell, McKenna, or Lewin was deemed worthy to attend. All nineteen players were from the southern-based clubs, underlining again the magnitude of bias towards them, that the FA favoured. The Bishop Auckland players would have to send their own message to the FA.

The message would be sent via Finchley, who awaited Bishop Auckland in Round Four of the Amateur Cup, as they had done at the same stage twelve months ago. The Bishop players were confident but were fully expecting Finchley to be all out to avenge last year's defeat and as a result Bob had his colleagues put through more gruelling paces with his training sessions. Those that could not attend the evening workouts were ordered to carry out physical exercises on their own or at their nearest club. Thus, Harry Sharratt, a schoolteacher in Leeds, trained at Leeds United's Elland Road and Derek Lewin went to Oldham Athletic or Old Trafford. Nothing was being left to chance.

Things could not have turned out better for the 'Bishops' as Finchley were completely outplayed. Seamus O'Connell was the star of the match, grabbing a hat-trick in a 4–0 win, Benny Edwards claiming the other. Bob gave another outstanding performance at the Summers Lane Ground and was unlucky not to get on the score sheet himself. Only a brilliant save from the agile Taylor, in the Finchley goal, prevented him from opening the scoring, although O'Connell slammed in the rebound to open his account. The Finchley forwards were unable to put any pressure on the Bishop defence as either Hardisty or Nimmins broke up movements with considerable ease and with the game already lost, some home supporters set off for home fully twenty minutes from time. One piece of skill, when Bob dribbled the ball twice past a bemused Cox, had the whole crowd purring and brought a burst of spontaneous applause from all around the ground. As he left the field, at the end of the match, those Finchley supporters who had remained to the bitter end, gave him a standing ovation.

After the game, the Finchley Chairman informed the waiting press that they had gone in to the game with a prepared plan: the forwards were to wear down Bob Hardisty and Jimmy Nimmins with quick passing movements. He was gracious enough to admit that the plan had failed miserably, as both of these players had shown just how skilful they remained and were capable of dealing with the best attacking combinations.

In the crowd, that day, were two of the England selectors, Jack Bowers, Chairman of the England Amateur International Selection Committee, and Norman Creek, Team Manager. They must have been squirming in their seats as the northerners gave their southern hosts a footballing lesson. The press pilloried the selectors and asked how they could have been so blinkered in their selection of the squad for the forthcoming trial. One correspondent took a swipe at them, writing: 'Hardisty had one of his best ever games. He simply toyed with the opposition, weaving and turning so cleverly that often they went the wrong way in bewilderment. Without any doubt, he proved he is still the best amateur right-half in the country.'

The Bishop Auckland players could only leave the arguments and discussions to the newspapers—it was their job. For Bob and his team mates, all that concerned them was playing to the best of their ability and winning the Amateur Cup. Now, only four clubs were left in the competition and they really did not care who they were drawn against. When the draw was made, two days later at FA Headquarters, Dulwich Hamlet and Corinthian Casuals were drawn to meet each other in the other semi-final, to be held at Stamford Bridge, Chelsea. That meant that Bishop's impending semi-final would be against Kingstonian, the team that they had scored twelve against just twelve months earlier. Like Finchley, they would be out for revenge but would Bishop be able to come away victorious again? The game would be played at St James's Park, Newcastle, almost as good as a 'home' game for the Bishop Auckland players and supporters. Everything was looking rosy—what could possibly go wrong?

The banana skin was thrown when Seamus O'Connell was selected by Bishop Auckland and by Chelsea to play on the same day. Seamus had played five games for Middlesbrough during the 1953–54 season, as well as turning out for the 'Bishops' in their Northern League and Amateur Cup fixtures. He had decided to leave Middlesbrough, and signed amateur forms for First Division Chelsea, for whom he had made seventeen appearances during last season, winning a League Championship medal to go with his

Amateur Cup winners' medal achieved with Bishop Auckland. This term, he had made a number of appearances in Chelsea's first team and reserves, and the arrangement appeared to have worked—until now: Seamus was selected to play for Bishop in a Durham Challenge Cup game against Willington but at the same time he was chosen by Chelsea to play in a reserve team game. Seamus chose to play for Chelsea Reserves. When Bishop Auckland Football Club members met on the following Monday evening, to select the team for the semi-final against Kingstonian, it was unanimously agreed that Seamus should be dropped from the team, in view of his decision to play for Chelsea Reserves.

Seamus, unabashed, protested:

> I had an agreement with the 'Bishops' to be free to play for Chelsea when not required for Amateur Cup ties. Last Saturday, I preferred to play for Chelsea Reserves rather than play for Bishop Auckland in a Durham Cup tie. An official of the club told me that if I did not turn out it would affect my selection for the Amateur Cup. I said, it did not matter as I intended to play for Chelsea Reserves.

It is believed that the official of the club who spoke to Seamus was Treasurer, W Cail, who followed up with: 'The 'Bishops' will generally be considered to have weakened their side a little but many of their supporters will, I think, agree that the principle was important'—the principle being that no one man is bigger than the club.

Ray Robertson was a reporter for *The Northern Echo* at the time, writing under the nom-de-plume of 'Ranger', and in the Tuesday morning edition of the newspaper his column broke the news:

> Bishop Auckland FC last night dropped a bombshell. They omitted Seamus O'Connell, the England amateur international inside-forward, and a member of last season's Cup-winning team from the side to play Kingstonian in the FA Cup semi-final at St James's Park, Newcastle, on Saturday.
>
> Since January, O'Connell has played in all of Bishop Auckland's Amateur Cup matches. But he has not played in all of the minor matches and therein lies the reason for his omission from Saturday's big match. His decision to play for Chelsea Reserves last Saturday, instead of assisting the 'Bishops' against Willington in the Durham County Challenge Cup, did not go down at all well with a section of the club's selection committee. Warren Bradley took over at inside-right at Willington, Derek Lewin switching to fill O'Connell's position of inside-left. Bradley turned in a fine performance, scoring two goals and making two others.

Auckland, in making last night's decision, took the view that O'Connell could no longer choose his games in which to play for them. They have made it clear that the team must come first, and for this, I think, they will earn the admiration of all sportsmen.

I know that the inclusion of O'Connell would have had repercussions on the team. A player told me over the weekend that he would refuse to play against Kingstonian, on principle, if Bradley was dropped to make way for O'Connell. The player, who is a valuable member of the side, was strong in his convictions and, I understand, informed the club of them.

Having tracked down Ray, it is unfortunate that, whilst he remembers the affair, the passage of time has erased the would-be informant from his memory, and his identity remains a mystery. In addition, no surviving member of that team remembers any player voicing such an opinion in the open.

If there had been such a threat by one of the players to refuse to play, should Seamus return to the team, the situation could not really have come as a total surprise to the officials of Bishop Auckland Football Club. It was alleged that Frank McKenna had left the club during the previous season because he was dropped from the team to make way for O'Connell's return from duty with Chelsea, despite putting on some good performances. McKenna had taken umbrage and transferred his services to North Shields but had been persuaded to return to the 'Bishops' at the start of the current season.

Derek Lewin remembers speaking to Seamus about this state of affairs:

I usually travelled up to Bishop on a Friday from my Lancashire home for Saturday's game and stayed at the Castle Hotel in Bishop Auckland. It was owned by one of the Committee members whose daughter was the television star, June Laverick. I always stayed in room number eight. More often than not, Bob Hardisty and I would meet up, go for a walk around the town and end up at a Gentleman's Snooker Club, playing until God knows when.

One particular Friday, I decided to go and see Seamus where he was staying in Bishop. Apparently, he had heard it said that someone in our team had commented that he should make up his mind whether to play for Chelsea or to play for us … not just make himself available for us when the Amateur Cup games came around. He was taken aback by the stinging remarks but had decided that it was me who had made them. Why me, I do not know. I went round to where he was staying and tried to have it out with him. He was unbending. No words on my part could persuade him otherwise and for a while we had a fall out. I would like to think that it did not affect the team but it was rather unpleasant for a while between us.

Referring to the article in *The Northern Echo*, Derek questions 'Ranger's' report: 'I very much doubt that any member of that football club would have threatened not to play against Kingstonian. We just weren't like that. I certainly never heard of any suggestion like that from any of the lads in the dressing room.'

It was an unsatisfactory scenario with which to enter a Cup semi-final but there was little else that the players could do, and so it was that a very confident Kingstonian eleven ran on to the St James's Park football pitch. The shenanigans in the Bishop Auckland camp had put them in good heart.

That heart lay broken and bleeding within twenty minutes as the 'Bishops' ripped in to a Kingstonian outfit, reckoned to be the best of the southern teams, that did not know where the next attack was coming from. In those opening twenty minutes, Auckland had found the net four times with a power display few teams could have withstood—and Ray Oliver had scored a hat-trick. Employing the seven-man attack that threw caution to the wind, the forwards, assisted by Bob Hardisty and Jimmy Nimmins, completely overran a bemused Kingstonian rearguard. Derek Lewin scored twice, one from the penalty spot and at half-time the 'Bishops' were leading 5–0.

The 'Two Blues' eased off in the second half and sloppy defending resulted in Bessex grabbing a consolation goal for Kingstonian, much to Harry Sharratt's annoyance.

Bishop Auckland had recorded another 5–1 semi-final win at St James's Park, just as they had done two years ago, when Briggs Sports were the victims. That year, they had gone on to be defeated in the greatest Amateur Cup Final ever, this time they were determined that the same would not happen.

In an interview with newspaper correspondent, Arthur Salter, after the game, Bob commented: 'So, it is Wembley again! It's a fantastic stadium, with wonderful turf. It always brings a lump to my throat. I must pay tribute to Kingstonian, a fine sporting side who, despite a 4–0 deficit in twenty minutes, kept playing football for the full ninety. So, it is Corinthian Casuals. I had boyhood hopes of playing for them. May the better team win.'

There was a happy postscript to the game when Seamus O'Connell entered the 'Bishops' dressing room and announced that his disagreement with the club had been settled and that he was happy to continue playing for the club, provided it was all right with them. There was only one answer—they wanted Seamus playing for them and frightening the life out of opposing defences.

The routine of Cup Final procedures in Wembley's dressing rooms at the end of the stadium's long, dark tunnel was new to Frank McKenna, selected to play at outside-right in place of Warren Bradley, but the other ten players were becoming more used to it and thereby less overawed by the magnitude of the event.

Bob Hardisty was calmer than he had been on previous occasions but that did not mean that he was not nervous. No matter what game it was, for him, Wembley 'made the knees knock' and he had said as much when he had made a guest appearance on the BBC *Sportsweek* television programme, just two days before, when interviewed by Peter Dimmock. Once again, Bishop Auckland had made it to Wembley and were favourites to lift the trophy.

Corinthian Casuals were coached by ex-Fulham goalkeeper, Douglas Flack, in his first season with the club. Their route to Wembley had begun with a 4–1 First Round win over Sheppey United at their Kennington Oval ground. Doughty fighters, Wimbledon, were overcome 3–2 next, once again at home, before they won an away tie by a solitary goal at St Albans in Round Three. Hitchin Town provided stern opposition and after a 3–3 draw at the Oval, 'Cor-Cas' gained an emphatic 5–0 victory to put them in the semi-final, where they beat Dulwich Hamlet 3–1 at Chelsea's Stamford Bridge. This would be the club's first ever appearance in the Amateur Cup Final.

The teams were:

Bishop Auckland (Dark and Light blue halved shirts, White shorts)
Sharratt—Fryer, Stewart—Hardisty, Cresswell, Nimmins—
McKenna, Lewin, Oliver, O'Connell, Edwards

Corinthian Casuals (White shirts, Navy Blue shorts)
Ahm—Alexander, Newton—Shuttleworth, Cowan, Vowels—
Insole, Sanders, Laybourne, Citron, Kerruish

Referee: J H Clough of Bolton

There was a comical incident before the game kicked off when Harry Sharratt and referee, Jack Clough, exchanged words. Harry had brought a tracksuit top out on to the pitch with him, which he intended to wear during the game. Jack took exception to the zip-fastener apparel being worn in such a prestigious game and told Harry to wear the more acceptable traditional jersey. Harry sheepishly relented and changed in to a bright yellow goalkeeping jersey that stood out on a drizzly afternoon.

Ahm was soon in action as Bishop went on the attack from the outset and within the first five minutes was forced into making three good saves. First, he saved a shot from Edwards, then a minute later, he had to dive full length to stop McKenna's drive. Lewin flicked the rebound towards goal but again Ahm saved to tip the ball away for a corner. Thirty seconds later, Oliver's effort went over the bar.

So far, the Casuals attack had not been allowed to come in to the game as Nimmins from the left, and Hardisty from the right, supplied their inside-forwards with incisive passes. In the centre, Cresswell was looking after international centre-forward Jack Laybourne and up to now had him 'in his pocket'.

From one of Bob Hardisty's passes, Lewin was able to get in a shot but his effort went straight to Ahm and then in Bishop's next attack, the same player shot just wide. Jimmy Nimmins slipped a through ball to Oliver who in turn played back to Lewin, whose turn it was this time to send his shot over the bar.

With thirty minutes gone, the majority of play had been in the Casuals half of the field but, despite their superiority, the 'Two Blues' had failed to score and slowly, the Londoners started to get more into the game. Defenders began to win more tackles and forwards were more able to string passes together. They had withstood the tide of Auckland attacks and were now in a position to mount a series of their own, and the 88,000 crowd noticed a shift of balance within the play. If Bob Hardisty and the rest of his team wanted to retain the trophy they would have to improve their shooting.

Forced to defend for the closing minutes of the first half, Bishop were fortunate that a Kerruish header went over the crossbar with Sharratt beaten. Laybourne, for once, got the better of Cresswell but Sharratt palmed the ball away to pull off a superb save and then, with the ball rolling free, was able to pounce on it, just as Insole was running in to score.

The second half began just like the first, with Bishop attacking but every time it seemed as if they must score, there was Ahm to foil their attempts. He was having an inspired game and it was largely down to him that there had been no goals scored.

To the surprise of most observers, Casuals went ahead, after fifty-seven minutes, and it was a goal that illustrated the game so far—scrappy. From a corner, Kerruish and Citron went up together for the ball, as did Cresswell and Sharratt. Citron was adjudged to have headed the ball and as it went goalwards, Bob Hardisty, standing with both feet behind the goal line, breasted the ball down. He had saved a certain goal and then kicked the ball to safety. To his, and the other Auckland players' disappointment, the referee blew his whistle and ordered a goal. Bob could not believe it. In his opinion, the ball had not wholly crossed the plane of the line but the linesman and referee thought different. The favourites were a goal down and had a little over half an hour to get back on terms. Some newspapers gave Kerruish as the scorer but this was later corrected, and the official goalscorer was marked down as Citron.

Going a goal behind gave the 'Bishops' fresh determination and suddenly they found their stride again and their play became more creative. Bob began to construct moves down the right one minute but then would switch play to the left the next. The Casuals tried to force counter attacks but Auckland's defence had everything covered now and were in no mood to concede another goal. Acting as a sixth forward, Bob did everything he could to procure a goal. After seventy minutes, receiving a cross field pass from Tommy Stewart, he collected the ball as Laybourne bustled him with a strong shoulder charge. Bob gave as good as he got and came away with the ball to set up Frank McKenna but the chance went begging.

For all Bishop had done most of the attacking, their football, up to now, had been of a much lesser quality than they had been capable of—that was about to change. Slowly, passing movements were coming off and chances more clear cut and, after eighty minutes, Frank McKenna got the goal that they had for so long threatened. Ray Oliver played a short pass for Derek Lewin to run on to. Bearing down on goal, with only the goalkeeper to beat, Lewin forced Ahm to pull off yet another good save. The ball ran free and McKenna thumped it high into the net. The Bishop Auckland supporters, at last, roared in delight.

For the next ten minutes, Auckland threw everything at the Casuals' defence. Ahm had to save a header from Oliver and a minute later was called to save full-length from a Hardisty drive. Then it was Cresswell's turn to try but again it was Ahm to the rescue as he saved the centre-half's shot at the foot of the post. Without their Danish goalkeeper, the Londoners would have suffered a heavy defeat.

Jack Clough blew his whistle for the end of normal time and for the second time, Bishop Auckland had been forced to play an extra thirty minutes in a Wembley Final.

For all Bishop continued to dominate, they were unable to find the net. McKenna and O'Connell missed what looked like simple chances and to the anguish of players and supporters, Benny Edwards thrashed the ball against the crossbar when he should have scored—Wembley was not his favourite place as far as scoring goals was concerned.

Midway through the second half of extra time, with Bishop attacking, Jimmy Nimmins jumped for a high ball with Casuals' defender Alexander and landed awkwardly on his elbow. Shuttleworth cleared the danger but the ball was immediately returned towards the Casuals' goal whereupon Oliver hurled himself to deliver a flying header. Showing brilliant anticipation, Ahm dived to his left and clawed the ball away. Ahm saved again from Oliver when the Auckland forward tried to take advantage of Newton's error. He had foiled the Auckland attack again and almost single-handedly kept his team in with a chance of hoisting the Cup. Seconds later, the referee blew for the end of the game—a replay at Ayresome Park in seven days time faced the two teams now. The Cup was on hold for another week. They had to do it all over again.

Injured players nursed aggravating wounds in the Bishop Auckland dressing room after the game, the most serious, apparently, that suffered by Jimmy Nimmins who had to be taken to Wembley Hospital—again—with a suspected chipped bone of his right elbow, as a result of his collision in the closing minutes. Ron Fryer had twisted his ankle on Wembley's lush turf and was walking with a definite limp, whilst his fellow full-back, Tommy Stewart, was having a bleeding nose attended to, the result of a challenge by a Casuals' forward. On the positive side, Jimmy and Tommy were expected to be fit, as was Dave Marshall who had been forced to miss the game due to the leg injury received at Ferryhill and had been replaced by, the now injured, Ron Fryer. There was no further news of any other injuries and, as a result, Bishop supporters awaited the replay with their usual anticipation and optimism. No more injury worries—that was good!

Drama and controversy were regular bedfellows at Bishop Auckland Football Club but so far, Bob Hardisty had steered clear of it. Now, all of that was about to change.

The club did their best to keep the press informed of injuries to players but this time they were, to use a modern day expression, 'economical with the truth'. It had been hoped that Jimmy Nimmins would be fit for the replay but, after attending Bishop Auckland General Hospital, x-rays revealed that the bone in his elbow was chipped in four places and that he would not play again that season. Ron Fryer, on the other hand, was standing by, if required, although he expected to be second choice to a fully fit Dave Marshall, now ready to play, on his return from injury.

All of this was not totally unexpected by the Bishop Auckland supporters but on the Wednesday before the game, rumours started going around the town that something was wrong with Bob Hardisty and that he would miss the replay. The attempts of the Committee, to keep Bob's injury a secret, had failed. They admitted that Bob had been injured in Saturday's Wembley Final and that they had preferred news of his injury to have remained secret. Now that the news was out they could do no more than answer press questions.

The news was a bombshell to the club's supporters. To be without Jimmy Nimmins was bad enough, add to that the choice at full-back between the uncertainty of a defender returning from a lay-off or one who had sprained his ankle at Wembley made matters worse but in addition to that, the absence of Bob Hardisty, compounded the difficulty of Bishop Auckland's task of retaining the Amateur Cup.

Bob himself, said that he had felt a sharp pain in his ribs during the Final, possibly a result of Jack Laybourne's, perfectly legitimate, shoulder charge. In the meantime, he had tried doing some exercises but had found that he was having trouble breathing. There was some encouraging news, however, insofar as he had been to the General Hospital and x-rays had shown there to be no broken ribs. Nevertheless, his ribs were extremely painful and although he had tried some training, he had been unable to continue for the full course of the exercises, as he was in too much pain. He went on to say that he was receiving additional treatment from Dr Prescott and he still hoped that he would be in the team for Saturday's game.

As late as Friday, the eve of the tie, the Committee were hoping that Bob's injury would improve but by late afternoon his condition remained much the same. An emergency meeting of the Management Committee was called for that evening and it was decided that John Barnwell, still a schoolboy, would have to take Bob's place.

A message to the appropriate police station resulted in a constable calling on the Barnwell household that evening. The message that he carried was simple: John was required to deputise for the injured Bob Hardisty in tomorrow's Amateur Cup Final replay. He was expected to meet up with the rest of the team at Ayresome Park.

The morning edition of *The Evening Gazette* carried the headline: '17-year-old Barnwell gets 11th hour chance to win soccer fame'. The article explained that Bob Hardisty had not recovered from his injury and that the England Youth international would take his place. With seven internationals, namely, Sharratt, Marshall, Stewart, Lewin, Cresswell, O'Connell and Oliver plus Barnwell, optimism was high and Bishop were expected to win the Cup today. The newspaper stated that one of their reporters had visited the Barnwell home on the previous evening (Friday) and that John had said: 'It is quite a shock. I did not think that I had much chance of playing. I knew there was a slender chance but Bob Hardisty is not one to miss games if he can possibly help it.'

John Barnwell remembers the build up to that weekend and its consequences that rocked the club:

> I always went to the pictures on a Friday night but Mam and Dad always insisted on me being back home by nine o'clock. I was coming up the road and I wondered what all the people were doing outside our house. As I got closer, cameras started flashing and taking my photograph. They were newspaper reporters come to see me. I asked what was going on and one of them said that I had been picked for tomorrow's Final. A fella—from the *Newcastle Chronicle* I think—said that the football club Secretary wanted to speak to me. Well, we didn't have a telephone so this reporter took me to his offices. It was from the *Newcastle Chronicle* offices that I spoke to the Secretary, 'Kit' Rudd, who told me that I was picked for the team and was definitely playing. Whilst he was telling me all the arrangements about getting me to Middlesbrough, all I was thinking about was how I could get tickets for my Mam and Dad. He said not to worry and that everything would be taken care of.
>
> Living opposite us was Newcastle United's chief scout, Temple Lyle, and it was he who took me to Ayresome Park. Mam and Dad would follow along later but because I was down to play I had to be there earlier. I went into the dressing room and someone—I think it was 'Kit' Rudd called me over …

The night before, Bob Middlewood, influential member of Bishop Auckland's Committee, and Chairman in all but name, had visited The Castle Hotel, where he had come across Bob Hardisty, drowning his sorrows at the thought of missing the Cup Final replay. They talked for a while about the player's fitness and after both men had finished their drinks,

Middlewood left, saying that he would see Bob at the Kingsway ground first thing in the morning.

Bob Middlewood was a man who got things done, and upon leaving The Castle, made some phone calls to other Committee members and Dr Prescott. Bob Hardisty was to have a rigorous fitness test in the morning and their presence was required.

Early next morning—the day of the match—in the presence of Dr Prescott and the gathered Committee members, Bob Hardisty was put through a series of extremely testing exercises at Kingsway. He came out of the workout sore but no worse than expected. At the end, the same Committee members were unconvinced and remained unchanged in their views about Bob's inclusion in the team that afternoon. In their opinion, it was too much of a risk to take for such an important game.

'Gentlemen,' said Middlewood, in his persuasive voice, 'this is not some Northern League side that we are playing today, whose players would kick lumps out of you as soon as look at you—this is Corinthian Casuals we are playing. The Corinthians! The Casuals! They are gentlemen! They would not wish to take advantage of Hardisty's injured ribs. They are as likely to pick him up if they were to knock him down. I believe that he should play. It is the very least that we can do for someone who has given so much for this club and town.'

It was the speech to end all speeches. The dissenting members demurred and, although not altogether caving in, accepted Bob Middlewood's wishes and agreed to defer the final team selection until as late as possible—right up until kick-off time if necessary. In the meantime, Dr Prescott would strap up Bob's ribs good and tight but with enough flexibility to allow some body movement—provided there were no repercussions in the next six hours or so, Bob was in with a chance of playing. The strapping may incur some hindrance in body movement but at least it would afford adequate protection.

John Barnwell continues:

'Kit' Rudd pulled me to one side and told me that I would not be playing because Bob Hardisty could play, now that the club doctor had given him some injections and strapped him up. Bob was not one hundred per cent fit but the doctor reckoned that he could see the match through, provided that he did not take a blow to the rib-cage. I cannot remember what my feelings were but, obviously, I was extremely disappointed. I had just returned from playing in the

'Little World Cup' for England Under-17s and everything appeared to be going so well for me.

This was my first distasteful experience in football and it left a scar, which I got over but never forgot. I realized that what really hurt was the manner in how they had told me that I was not playing. It was ruthless. It can be said that the decision was vindicated, because Bishop won, but what they should have done was tell me there was a *possibility* that I would be playing, make sure I was at the ground.

I watched the game from the bench by the touchline but did not enjoy it. The thing that always sticks in my mind is the assertiveness of my father. He was never a loudmouth, never shouted or anything like that, but he entered the dressing room and demanded to know who had been responsible for treating his son in such a shameful manner. He told 'Kit' Rudd that he may be celebrating now but that what had happened was no way to treat a young lad. He told them, in very clear terms, that the way it was handled was an absolute disgrace, and he went on to say: 'You think that you are going to make some money out of this boy but I am telling you now that he is finished with this club.' Then he turned to me and we left the dressing room. A few days later I signed for Arsenal and I have never been back to the club since.

With only forty-five minutes to go until kick-off, it must have been galling for John Barnwell to see his dream of playing in the Amateur Cup Final so cruelly dashed, knowing that the man whose place he would have filled, sat on a bench only three feet away receiving pain-killing injections and with his torso strapped up like an Egyptian mummy. The other players made their views known and it was clear that they wanted Bob to be in the team—he was their talisman and play-maker. John was good but Bob was better.

Ray Oliver remembers the mood in the dressing room that afternoon: 'All of the players wanted Bob to play. We had nothing against young John … he was a brilliant player and was well liked at the club by all of us but we needed Bob for his experience. John might have played and had a blinder but truthfully, the players were more apprehensive about playing the young lad in such an important match.'

Corinthian Casuals were not without problems of their own. Mickey Stewart—a future England cricketer—had been contacted in the West Indies and made himself available for the replay. From the outset, his return journey was beset with problems. The first flight, from Caracas to New York, was delayed due to high winds and Stewart missed his BOAC connection. He decided to fly with KLM to Prestwick instead of London but that flight was delayed and he did not land in Scotland until one-thirty in the afternoon, barely ninety minutes from match kick-off time. A waiting small aircraft flew the final leg to Thornaby Aerodrome from where a desperate car journey ensued and, although the driver did his best, it was 2:57 pm when Stewart was delivered to Ayresome Park's main gate and the teams were already out on the pitch. All that he could do was watch the game from the stands.

The teams were:

Bishop Auckland (Dark and Light blue halved shirts, White shorts)
Sharratt—Marshall, Stewart—Hardisty, Cresswell, O'Connell—
McKenna, Lewin, Oliver, Bradley, Edwards

Corinthian Casuals (White shirts, Navy Blue shorts)
Ahm—Alexander, Newton—Shuttleworth, Cowan, Vowels—
Insole, Sanders, Laybourne, Citron, Kerruish

Referee: J H Clough of Bolton

Thus, Seamus O'Connell was designated to reprise his role in Jimmy Nimmins's position that he had filled in such outstanding fashion two years ago, against Crook Town. Warren Bradley, unfortunate not to have been selected for the first game, was the obvious replacement to fill O'Connell's position at inside-left.

Bishop Auckland supporters cheered to the rafters when it had been announced that Bob Hardisty was playing after all, and when he received the ball to launch Bishop's first attack, the roar was repeated but the raid came to nothing. Bishop were usually good starters and from the outset were the better team but, as so often can happen, they fell behind after being the more dominant of the two teams.

Ray Oliver had seen a shot cleared off the line by Newton and then Ahm watched helplessly as Edwards's effort flew tantalizingly wide but, after thirty-four minutes, Citron ended a Casuals raid by scoring with a fine shot that went in off the post to beat Sharratt (allowed to sport his track suit type top on this occasion).

Bishop came back with more attacks and three minutes later drew level. Bob Hardisty, so prominent already, inspiring the Bishop forward line, played a neat pass forward that McKenna ran on to. From his centre, Oliver forwarded to Lewin, who scored with a rarity for him—a header.

Everything seemed to be coming from Bob Hardisty's midfield position as he directed one pass after another to his wingers and inside-forwards. Lewin was unlucky not to grab a second when his effort went over the bar, before McKenna went wide with another shot with Ahm well beaten.

The score was 1–1 at half-time and as Bob entered the dressing room for a welcome cup of tea, there was Dr Prescott waiting to inspect the strapping on his ribs. Bob had just given a superb display of football and the doctor knew that his patient was going to see out the rest of the game but, not wishing to tempt fate, ordered Bob to have another pain-killing injection.

Starting from where they had left off, Bishop's wing-halves advanced forward and Lewin was unlucky when his shot hit the crossbar, following McKenna's pass. It was a short respite for Ahm and his co-defenders, as five minutes later they fell behind to a stunning Hardisty volley. Ray Oliver looked to have been impeded in the penalty area but as he fell to the ground, the referee merely blew for a corner, which Cowan cleared with a fine header. Positioning himself just outside the Casuals' penalty area, Bob prepared to take aim as he chested the ball from Cowan's clearance. Before it hit the ground, Bob drew back his right foot and thundered the ball into the roof of the net. Ahm made a valiant effort to save but his dive was in vain. The crowd roared again in appreciation of their hero as if they understood the handicap under which he was playing. It was a magnificent goal and it knocked the stuffing out of Casuals.

Derek Lewin remembers that goal vividly and the somewhat predictable, yet comic, response that it drew from one of the Casuals players:

> The ball was swung in from a corner and headed out by a defender. Bob was loitering on the edge of the penalty area and caught the ball on his chest and as it dropped he volleyed into the top corner of the net. It was a tremendous goal. As the teams made their way back for the re-start, Bob met their centre-forward, Jack Laybourne, who was an international, so they knew each other well. Bob said to Jack: 'I think that's it, Jack.'
> 'Fuck off, Hardisty, and get on with the bloody game.'

O'Connell went wide with a header, the type of which he usually scored, but Bishop increased their lead almost immediately when Bradley's shot was parried out by Ahm only for Derek Lewin to be on hand to prod the ball home. At 3–1, and only twenty minutes left, Auckland were coasting and, with the defence under little pressure, Sharratt had an easy time collecting back passes and supplying his half-backs. From one such move, Bob was allowed to take the ball from his own penalty area well into the Casuals half without being tackled. From thirty yards out, he looked up and fired a shot to Ahm's left. It would have been yet another superb goal but, this time, Ahm was able to divert the shot onto a post and the danger was cleared. However, in the final minute, Tommy Stewart was allowed to repeat what Bob had done and ran sixty yards before sending a terrific shot that, this time, Ahm could not stop. Bishop had won the Cup by a comfortable 4–1 score line and the majority of the 35,000 crowd were cheering for all they were worth.

The newspapers made much of Bishop Auckland's achievement in retaining the Amateur Cup and, of course, praised the performance of Bob Hardisty, making numerous references to his strapped ribs. 'Ranger' of *The Northern Echo*, made a pithy observation in his match report when, referring to Bob's injury, he went on to say: '… He used his great knowledge and experience to stay clear of clashes and avoid being bumped. Not once in the game was he hurt, which is also a fine tribute to the clean play of the Casuals.' Bob Middlewood had been proven correct in his assessment of Corinthian Casuals and their sportsmanlike approach to the game of football.

Having obtained another winners' medal, Bob immediately offered it to the unlucky Ron Fryer, who had been forced to miss the game because of his injury. Dave Marshall and Seamus O'Connell made similar gestures but Ron refused, saying that he preferred to wait until he won his medal on the football pitch. He was persuaded to change his mind, however, and it was with gratitude that he accepted Seamus's medal. The camaraderie within the squad was as sound as ever.

Perhaps the final word should be left to Bob Hardisty. Asked after the game to give his views on the events of the last two days, he said this:

> I had a late night appeal on Friday from Vice-chairman Alderman Bob Middlewood to delay my decision until next morning. The club doctor had ruled against my playing but it seemed the club still wanted me around. So I met the full club Committee and players in the dressing room. The team was asked whether they agreed to my turning out. They were unanimous and I understand they thought we would win if I played.
>
> The doctor agreed, provided he was relieved of all responsibility, and gave me three pain-killing injections in the ribs, patched me up like a dummy and warned me that one blow on my side would put me out of the game. The Casuals knew about my condition. They were grand. Not one of their players attempted to charge me.

Having retained the FA Amateur Cup and won the Northern League Championship for the third campaign in a row, the football season was not yet over for Bob Hardisty. He had been selected for the second leg of the Olympic Games Qualifying match at Wembley against Bulgaria—not that the press gave much to the home side's chances. On the eve of the match, one national newspaper labelled the game as the 'Match of Shame', insinuating that the England—(Great Britain)—Football Association would prefer to lose the match in order to save money from the consequential costs in having to attend the Olympic Games in Melbourne. In addition, respected journalists, such as Tony Stevens and Desmond Hackett, berated the football authorities for allowing the Bulgarian squad—who had received training from none other than Ferenc Puskas of Hungary—the 'freedom of Wembley Stadium' for their training sessions, whilst the Great Britain players had to make do with the facilities at Paddington's Recreation Ground. Just what kind of message did that send out to the home squad, the newspapers cried?

As if to send a message of their own to the Football Association, the Great Britain team put up a magnificent effort, in the circumstances. Bob Hardisty, playing at inside-right, surprised the visitors after fifteen minutes with a superb shot to put Great Britain ahead. The joy of the 30,000 spectators was short-lived, however, as the Bulgarians went 2–1 up for half-time. Bob Hardisty scored a second for Great Britain with a clinical header to bring the scores level but at the end, after Jim Lewis had converted a penalty, the best that they could achieve was a 3–3 draw.

Great Britain were out of the Olympic football competition. Bob Hardisty need not learn the words to 'Waltzing Matilda'—he could leave his tucker bag at home.

Chapter Eleven
CRACKS

I t was usual for the players of Bishop Auckland Football Club to go on a mini-tour in the close season. In the past, they had visited numerous London football clubs as well as playing on the continent or the Channel Islands and, of course, in 1953, they had been invited to play in Rhodesia. In 1955 they were invited to participate in The Isle Of Man Football Tournament and a supplementary Five-a-Side competition. They had made a host of new friends and won both competitions; in the Football Tournament they had defeated Cliftonville 2–1 to win the Douglas Trophy, and in the Five-a-Side competition had won the Daily Express Trophy. Alan Ross was the only goalkeeper that Bishop had taken on the tour but he was injured in the first game of the tournament against Bohemians, a game that Auckland won 3–1. Ever versatile, Johnnie Wright, had been forced to play in goal thereafter. For the five-a-side competition Bishop fielded an 'A' and a 'B' team; the 'A' team was successful with Bob Hardisty playing as their goalkeeper—other members of that team were Derek Lewin and Seamus O'Connell (defenders) and Benny Edwards and Ron Fryer (attackers).

This year they had been invited to participate again and players and officials were looking forward to winning at least one, if not both of the trophies on offer. The tournament constituted the best amateur teams, as decided by the Isle of Man authorities, and comprised Bishop Auckland and Leytonstone (England), Bohemians and Cliftonville (Ireland), Newtown (Wales) and Eaglesham (Scotland). The 'Bishops' won through to the Final and defeated

Cliftonville 3–1, the referee for the match being none other than Alf Bond, known to all Bishop Auckland fans as the 'One-armed Bandit', following the 1954 Amateur Cup Final and his part in that marathon outcome.

It was a pleasurable time for the players as, for all it was a competition worth winning, especially with the national newspaper publicity projected through the sponsoring *Daily Express*, it also gave them the opportunity to relax. Such was the reputation of the Bishop Auckland footballers that they were feted wherever they went—Bob and Jimmy, together with Bob Middlewood, were even given the honour of judging The Isle of Man Beauty Contest, much to their delight and envy of the others.

The reputation of footballers as practical jokers and looking out to have a good time is well earned and Bishop Auckland players were no different. Derek Lewin tells the tale of an event that took place one morning:

> The rest of the players flew to the Isle of Man from Newcastle but because I lived in Lytham, I was able to get a flight from my local airport, which got me into Douglas earlier than them. Being the first at the hotel, I had the best pick of rooms, and the landlady or manageress showed me a room on the first floor that had three beds in it. This suited me fine. I always 'roomed' with Seamus and I knew that he would be pleased with the extra space.
>
> The lads arrived later on and everyone settled down for the evening, playing cards or whatever. We had been there about three days when Seamus and I were coming back from breakfast, when we met Bob in the corridor. I think he must have had his breakfast earlier than us and misplaced his room key and was coming along to our room—he was hopping about bursting for a pee. He saw us and, without further ado, rapidly opened the door of the room where we had been staying. Bob entered the room as quick as he could and flopped his todger over the wash-hand basin in the room—completely oblivious of the three Barnsley miners who were sat up in their beds, rather disgustedly staring at him. The landlady had asked Seamus and me if we minded moving to a room with just two beds in order that these three Yorkshiremen could have a room to themselves. Naturally, Seamus and I didn't mind but we had never thought of the need to tell anyone, least of all Bob.

On another occasion, some of the players were in a bar, having played a match that afternoon, and everyone was having a good time. The place was crowded and at one table there was a group of young ladies, sat on their own, and between giggles were giving the good looking Seamus the eye. Exchanging glances with a particularly attractive brunette, Seamus prepared to walk over to them when a slightly older lady walked up to him and presented herself.

Seamus detached himself from the rest of the players and started to weigh up his chances with this very attractive 'socialite'. The lights were dim, the music was loud, the drinks were flowing as the rest of the players sat around the tables chatting away and watching Seamus's 'technique'. To their surprise, after about twenty minutes, the lady rose from her seat and left the room but Seamus did not follow her. He returned and sat down with the rest of the squad who passed him enquiring glances.

'Surprised you didn't get off with that lady, Seamus,' stated Bob.

'No, Bob … she'd had a few too many,' replied Seamus.

'She looked sober to me,' said Dave Marshall.

'I don't mean drink, Dave, I mean birthdays,' exclaimed an unapologetic Seamus.

Ray Oliver asked Seamus, rather enviously, how it was that he was so good at getting off with the opposite sex. He looked at the enquirer and, with a straight face, answered: 'Look, it's like this. When you put your hand on a girl's leg above the knee, you get the inclination to 'start climbing the ladder'. Your hand goes a little further until you come to the giggle line.'

'Giggle line? What the hell is that?' asked Ray.

Seamus, still straight-faced, responded: 'Well, it's called the giggle line because once you're past it, you're laughing.'

Ray Oliver remembers a time when he shared a room with Seamus—before Derek Lewin came to the club—which is, perhaps, worth recording at this point. Bishop were about to play a southern team and had travelled to London. Usually, the players would spend their evenings relaxing in the hotel, with only occasional ventures to other parts of wherever it was they were staying. On this particular evening, Ray, Dave Marshall, Tommy Farrer and Seamus had made their way to a club, just down from their hotel. As ever, Seamus was eyeing up the girls as much as they were looking at him. As the evening wore on, Seamus 'clicked' with one of the young ladies. Ray was not surprised when Seamus did not return to the hotel room—he had obviously made 'other arrangements' with one of the ladies at the bar. Ray takes up the tale, in his Tyneside accent:

> It must have been about fowr in the mornin' when Seamus got in. I heard him knockin' around but I didn't get up. My clock alarm woke me at about seven and I was surprised that Seamus was already up and dressed. I asked him if he had just got in but he said that he had got back about fowr and that he was now going to church.

'Church?' I asked. I didn't knar whether to laugh or cry.

He was a catholic and never missed Sunday mornin' church if he could help it, he told me. Mind you, I never knew if he was praying for a crop failure from the previous night or Deliverance.

During this visit to the Isle of Man, the players attended Douglas's main ballroom one evening where they, and about four hundred others, were entertained by one of Britain's leading big orchestra bands, who had made numerous television and radio appearances. That evening, the music of Benny Goodman and Glen Miller wafted on the cool evening breeze, together with the vocals from the band's resident singers. Later, when the entertainment had died down and everyone had dispersed from the theatre, Bob, Ray, Derek Lewin and Ron Fryer, were sat on a bench along the sea front eating fish and chips, when who should walk past but Seamus, arm in arm with the very attractive lead singer of the band that they had just been listening to all evening. She may have been older than Seamus but clearly, this time, the lady was not considered to have had 'a few too many'.

'Well, I suppose I'm in for another lonely night,' remarked Derek. 'How the hell does he do it? It's a wonder it doesn't drop off,' he added, much to the mirth of the others.

The next day, Bob telephoned Betty to say that he would be arriving back home a day later than the other players. He explained that he had been selected to play in another game, arranged at the last moment, and that he could not really get out of it. Bob arrived home twenty-four hours later than his colleagues and Betty was not best pleased. The newspapers gave no news of the additional match that Bob was supposed to have played in but carried a photograph of him with The Dagenham Girl Pipers, who had been appearing at one of Douglas's theatres, on the boat across the Irish Sea. In the photograph, Bob was showing no signs of being disappointed at his delayed return. The first thin crack had started to appear in the veneer of Bob and Betty's marriage.

Reprieve for the Great Britain football team came when the Olympic Committee announced that a number of countries had withdrawn their teams from the football competition, in protest at Russia's invasion of Hungary. Great Britain's name was drawn by lot, to fill a vacancy and so the Football Association would have to meet the financial demands after all of sending a team to Australia that, in reality, they would have preferred to have avoided, although in public, they presented a united front, stressing that they looked forward to participating in the Games and would give the team all of their support.

In May, Bob Hardisty had seriously considered retiring from football but just as he had done twelve months previously, when contemplating similar action, he decided to play on in the hope of representing Great Britain and playing in his third Olympic Games. He had also decided that he was still able to meet the demands of playing in such an esteemed competition as the Amateur Cup. A few weeks earlier, he had been forced to sit out the four games that had constituted the Football Association tour of Iceland, due to injury. Now, with the Isle of Man Tournament behind him, helping to regenerate his batteries, he looked forward to representing Great Britain in Melbourne, as well as helping his beloved Bishop Auckland win the Amateur Cup for an unprecedented third consecutive time—and he wanted another winners' medal.

Before the new campaign got under way, Bob began to have second thoughts about continuing his playing career. He had achieved everything there was to achieve at amateur level in football—winning an Olympic Gold medal could not reasonably be considered a viable target, due to the interpretation of 'amateur' status adopted by the Eastern Bloc countries, who were better than most professional football teams.

Since gaining his first winners' medal against Hendon, he had been approached by a local newspaper, *The Evening Gazette*, to write a regular football column. The newspaper company had provided a telephone in the Hardisty household, in order that his column could be dictated and recorded more efficiently. Both Bob and Betty were grateful for this added means of keeping in touch. In one full page column, just as the new season was getting under way, Bob voiced some of his concerns and asked 'Are "Bishops" at the Crossroads?' The article gives reasons for his doubting Bishop Auckland being able to continue dominating the amateur football scene and, at the end, it is made clear that Bob expected his Amateur Cup experiences to have already ended with that win in the replay against Corinthian Casuals. Bishop Auckland followers were made abundantly clear that any success in the forthcoming season was not guaranteed. Bob's article is reproduced in full:

So often a really fine side plays together for a few years and sometimes achieves a fair degree of success. Long afterwards, the side is eulogised but I cannot remember a side being admired as great during the playing days of all members of that club.

On the score of age, there are three of us who simply can't go on playing much longer. Jacky Major turned professional with Hull City, Frank McKenna has recently signed professional for Leeds United, Corbett Cresswell has said that he intends to join the professional ranks when he is demobbed (from the RAF) and, through the press, we heard Seamus O'Connell would not be playing at Kingsway again.

Quite an impressive list, and perhaps Bishop Auckland may be about to embark on a period of team building. Well, there will be no panic about that, for the team is lucky, inasmuch as the difference could still be virtually intact. But as a tribute to these boys who have helped to make such a wonderful history in the Amateur Cup, I would just like to give a pen-picture of them for you, with my personal estimate for good measure.

Firstly, HARRY SHARRATT, B Sc and teacher and in my humble opinion one of the best six goalkeepers in the country on his day—that includes professionals.

At Auckland we have always been able to play an attacking game, knowing that if a square ball didn't come off, the defence of Harry, Dave Marshall, Tommy Stewart and Corbett Cresswell could nip any danger in the bud or hedge until Jim Nimmins and/or myself got back.

Next comes DAVE MARSHALL, a teacher who starts at Carnegie in September. The boy who, with a perpetual grin on his face, allowed me to go up with the attack and, more often than I care to remember, tackled my defensive job as well as his own.

TOMMY STEWART is our skipper, and as artistic a left-back as you could wish to see. That drag inside the field and those beautifully driven square balls to his winger would probably have won more praise in professional soccer. An advertising executive with a Newcastle firm, Tommy is, and always has been, a credit to the game.

Then there is CORBETT CRESSWELL, the deceptive, the long-striding centre-half, who looks so slow until you run with him. It is problematical how he will do when he turns professional but he would always be in my side.

Next, my old friend JIMMY NIMMINS, of whom people were saying four years ago: 'Surely he must be finished,' but who is playing as well as ever. The lad who broke his leg at Wembley against Crook and was back there a year later to the day to collect his winners' medal. What a tragedy Jim has been overlooked so far as honours are concerned. Not a solitary cap to crown his great career.

FRANK McKENNA is the ball player, who has to start afresh and make his name in the higher circuit. For my money he will need lots of help up there from wing-half and inside-right. Anyhow, 'Good luck, Frank.'

JACKY MAJOR had a disappointing first season with Hull City but he is not a quitter and will be fighting back this year, although I believe that Hull are five years too late in coming for Jacky.

Our inside-right, DEREK LEWIN, is another ball player who is always trying the unexpected—even trying that dangerous ball behind him without looking. If it comes off he is wonderful; if it doesn't, someone is struggling, but a boy, who, on his game, is really good.

At centre-forward we've had two players, both great-hearted—HARRY McILVENNY (formerly of Bradford) and RAY OLIVER. Harry, the footballing centre-forward, spraying return balls and through flicks for oncoming forwards; Ray, the forager, revelling in going through himself and taking the weight off his inside-forwards.

At inside-left we have had two recently, SEAMUS O'CONNELL and WARREN BRADLEY. Seamus has always been rather difficult to assess. He is strong and packs a good shot in both feet but runs, when he goes for goal, at top speed, in a straight line. How this worked when he was with professional teams I cannot say as I only saw him once play for Middlesbrough. Advice from an 'old codger' would be for him to get some craft and change of pace into his game.

Warren Bradley is a terrier type, never giving in, tackling opposition when it doesn't look as if he has an earthly chance, with an amazing worrying value on the opposition defence.

And last, but by no means least, BENNY EDWARDS, the great little club man, the lad everyone thought was just an average club player until the Amateur Cup replay with Corinthian Casuals at Ayresome Park, last year. Seamus dropped back to left-half that day and literally made Benny have the game of his life.

In Iceland for ten days with four Bishop regulars (Dave Marshall, Ray Oliver, Derek Lewin and myself) has been RONNIE FRYER, the youngest, best club man it has been my privilege to meet. To say his patience and loyalty have been rewarded by two final appearances at Wembley is true and purely poetic justice. At home at full-back or wing-half, his skill and polish would adorn most professional grounds I have played on.

And finally, one quick word on JOHNNIE WRIGHT who, although thirty would take in all his first team appearances, has 'stayed at home' all his playing career. I raise my hat to you, John and thanks for those three nights per week given gladly throughout the 1948 summer to help me get ready for the Olympics.

We have a trainer—JACK SOWERBY. What a character! He is annoying; he is crafty; he shoots home barbs of truth about one's play; he calls a spade a spade—unique person as I have met very few psychology-practicing trainers.

Among that team you have steelworkers, teachers, executives, servicemen and office workers but when the team goes out, the shirt collars come down, the sleeves go up and the 'Bishops' go into action. In ten or twenty years the 1952–56 era will be talked about with a little awe.

In this article I have paid tribute to a few individuals but they are legion; it is the club, the team, that matters. You find a blend, you give it a chance, and results will follow. Durham City and West Auckland are finding this to be true; Crook and Willington have proved it. But the important thing is that amateur football in the North is improving fast, and the monopoly the South held between the wars has gone for good. Teams such as Shildon, Billingham, Crook, Willington and Durham must doubt that this is so and I am with them all the way. How people like Eddie Taylor, Jack Lewthwaite and Jackie Snowdon (remember his game against us at Wembley), Bert Steward, Ron Thompson and Jimmy McMillan have received little or no recognition will forever be a mystery to me.

I would gladly give six caps to Jim Nimmins. It would be pointless (a) he wouldn't accept them and (b) it would have no meaning to him.

May I end with a word for the Auckland committee man—to give his name would be unfair—who, after I'd been declared definitely unfit and out of the side on the Friday evening before the Amateur Cup Final replay with Corinthian Casuals, took a chance and by having called a special meeting one hour before play began, somehow reversed the decision. To you sir, my warmest thanks, for I got the chance to finish my Amateur Cup experience at Ayresome Park where I had been so happy during those war years.

And to JOHN BARNWELL who, as a result of my being declared fit or half-fit to play, did not turn out—my sincere sympathy. This boy will definitely go to the top. Look out for him!

While the inhabitants of Great Britain were going around doing their business in the shivering cold, their athletes were sunning themselves in Australia's wonderful burning sun. Robert Browning may have said, 'Oh, to be in England'; George Bernard Shaw would have retorted, 'Not bloody likely.'

In glorious weather, Bob Hardisty and his companions settled down in their brand spanking new residential quarters at Heidelberg West, Victoria, outside Melbourne. Compared to what the players had been used to in the past, this was luxury. The building complex that housed competitors from a variety of nations may have had its objectors but the financial problems had been resolved, and now it was ready to play its part in housing athletes, swimmers, divers, footballers and all the other sportsmen and women who had journeyed from every continent, in the quest to prove that they were best.

They became known as 'The Friendly Games' and certainly part of that was due in no small way to the friendliness given by the host nation and its inhabitants and contestants. At Heidelberg, countries were not contained in their own private cell, hidden away from other nations; this was a tournament where competitors from different nations were allowed, indeed encouraged, to forge relationships with those from other lands.

Derek Lewin was a member of the football squad and remembers those Games: 'It was a great occasion—just a pity that it ended so soon for us. Everyone joined in helping each other, no matter which country they came from. Some of those Australian lasses were beautiful with their bronzed bodies. They were good fun too—really good fun. God knows what we looked like with our milk white bodies—not that it seemed to matter much!'

The football tournament was an unsatisfactory event as far as the Olympic Games organizers were concerned. Provision had been made for a tournament originally consisting of sixteen nations but five withdrew, for a variety of reasons, and by the time the first ball was kicked, only eleven teams remained to fight for the Olympic Football Gold Medal. The situation would have been even worse had not Great Britain agreed to their reinstatement after being eliminated by Bulgaria, and Germany considered itself honour-bound to compete even though East Germany had withdrawn their co-operation in forming a side to send to Melbourne. Those eleven participating countries were Australia, Bulgaria, Germany, Great Britain, India, Indonesia, Japan, Thailand, United States of America, USSR and Yugoslavia.

Great Britain were drawn to play Thailand in the First Round. The tie held no significant dangers for Great Britain and when Bob Hardisty led his team out he was in confident mood. The Thai's were a team of triers but they proved no match for Great Britain and were swamped 9–0. Bob wore the number six shirt (left-half) but played at inside-right and it is doubtful if he had ever played in such an easy game. He was, however, involved in an unfortunate incident, a complete accident, when he went up for the ball in a heading duel with Thailand's Sophon Hayachanta. The Thai player crumpled to the ground, holding his head, and had to leave the field. It was reported later that he had suffered a fractured skull, much to the distress of Bob and the other players.[†]

Harry Sharratt was selected to appear in goal for this game as Mike Pinner received a hand injury during a pre-tournament practice match against Australia, which the hosts had lost 3–1. George Bromilow had also picked up an injury in the same match, injuring a toe, but it was not serious and

---

[†] The only other time that Bob had been involved with injuring another player had been five years earlier in a Northern League match against Billingham Synthonia. Bob had tackled opposing wing-half, Norman Banbrough, for the ball and the unfortunate Norman came out of it with a broken leg. The incident always remained in Bob's mind, thereafter.

he returned against Thailand, unlike Dexter Adams, who was carried off after only ten minutes with a serious knee injury, caused when he went in hard against an Australian forward. Adams was forced to make an immediate return to England to undergo an emergency cartilage operation.

Sharratt had few worries from the Thailand forwards and watched most of the play from afar as Great Britain's attacking moves brought goals at the opposite end of the pitch. Derek Lewin was not in the playing eleven but was named as the one substitute.

The game had been as one-sided as the score would suggest and had provided Great Britain with little more than a practice session. The 'practice session' was necessary, however—Great Britain's next opponents, just four days later, were their old friends Bulgaria and they would need all the practice they could get if they were to defeat them.

Disappointment struck the Great Britain squad when Bob received a groin injury during a normal practice session, on the eve of their next match, and would be forced to sit the game out. Derek Lewin came off the substitute's bench to play and for forty minutes Bob watched as his colleagues put up a valiant performance. The Bulgarians had opened the scoring as early as the sixth minute through Dimitrov but had failed to add to that due to some sterling defensive work by the Great Britain backs. Jim Lewis dented the Bulgarian's confidence with an equaliser on the half-hour and for a while it looked like Great Britain could be going in at half-time on level terms. The hopes were dashed when Kolev beat Harry Sharratt after forty minutes and on the stroke of half-time, Stoyanov added a third.

It was tough luck on Great Britain to fall two goals behind to one of the competition's favourites but in reality, Bulgaria had deserved to be ahead. Bob did his best and assisted Norman Creek with the half-time pep talk in an effort to encourage the players, but the Bulgarian outfit proved difficult adversaries and scored a further three times, through Kolev and Stoyanov, who completed his hat-trick, to end the game 6–1 to Bulgaria. In truth, Harry Sharratt had not had one of his best games and blamed himself for as many as four of the Bulgarian goals. Only some last ditch tackling from Laurie Topp, Don Stoker and Stan Prince had kept the score down, whilst up front the attack was so ineffective that one national newspaper reporter, Harold Palmer, was moved to say: '… Even a half-pace Bob Hardisty would have been an improvement'—cruel words.

Great Britain were, therefore, eliminated from the tournament. It had been a most disappointing and short-lived one for the football squad and, unlike the previous Olympics, when the players had remained until the events were concluded, this time they would not be staying on. The route back to England was not a direct one, however, as matches had been arranged to be played in the Far East on the team's return back home.

Almost 7,000 spectators turned out to watch Great Britain's players take on Singapore's best and appreciated the football skills that Bob Hardisty and Jim Lewis supplied for their benefit. The home side were losing 2–0 (Hardisty and Lewis the scorers) when they were awarded a penalty that gave them hope. Unfortunately, the penalty was missed and, after further goals from Derek Lewin and another one from Lewis, the Singapore crowd left the stadium disappointed with the 4–0 defeat but grateful that they had seen the legendary Bob Hardisty in his football boots.

Further games took place at Kuala Lumpur and at Rangoon but unfortunately it has not proved possible to obtain any details relating to these two matches. Approaches to the Football Association have proved unproductive as there were no records kept, due to it being an unofficial tour. The game at Rangoon was the last in which Bob Hardisty would be sporting a representative jersey of the home countries.

As Bob Hardisty, Derek Lewin and Harry Sharratt had been representing Great Britain in the Olympic Games they had, naturally, been unavailable for Bishop Auckland's Northern League and FA Cup campaign. Derek Lewin had only played a handful of games due to injury, prior to flying out to Melbourne, and Bob Hardisty too had been suffering irksome knee and thigh strains. The First Round of the FA Cup had provided a shock when the 'Bishops' knocked out Football League Tranmere Rovers 2–0 at Kingsway, thanks to goals from Benny Edwards and Warren Bradley. Round Two had seen Bishop making a rare trip to Wales, where they had to play Rhyl. In a game that was marred by some poor refereeing decisions—at least in the eyes of the many Bishop Auckland supporters, who had travelled to the principality—Rhyl came out of the game the 3–1 winners, Auckland's goal coming from a Bob Thursby penalty.

Bob Thursby was a brilliant right half-back who had been playing his football with another Northern League side, Stanley United. A native of Chester-le-Street, he was destined for England internationals. He had come under the radar of Bishop Auckland with his fine performances on the football pitch and was coveted by a stream of clubs, including those of the Football League such as Wolverhampton Wanderers and Blackpool: his registration for Bishop Auckland was a major coup.

Bob recalls:

> I lived in Chester-le-Street—still do—and Stanley would organize a taxi for me to the ground. It was a bit of a trek but the club was paying the fare. Some time during the close season, I got an invitation to sign for Bishop Auckland. I can't remember who made the call but I was pleased to have the opportunity to join the most famous amateur football club in the world. I did have some doubts, however. I was quite willing to go to Bishop but I asked them how I would get in the team with Bob Hardisty there. I was assured that I would get enough games and that is exactly what happened. Bob was nearing the end of his career anyway, so it was just a matter of time. I was told I could expect £5 a game. I said, 'Hang on … I'm supposed to be joining the best club in amateur football and all that you're offering is £5 a game … I'm on that at Stanley!'
>
> Naturally, I signed for them but I made sure that I got paid the going rate, which was a bit more than the £5 they initially offered. We were amateurs but all the clubs paid the players to turn out for them—'expenses', you see. The southern lads must have been on really good money with the cost of living being so much higher down there … not that anyone openly talked about such a thing as money, mind.
>
> In them days, all that a footballer could look forward to after his career had finished was to look after a pub or something like that. I made up my mind very early on that I would be better than that. Fortunately, I had something between my ears and was able to put my brain to some good use. I studied for university to become a dental student. Not once did I have to apply for a student loan … my football 'expenses' took care of that!
>
> In those early games at Bishop I was used as a stand-in, generally for whenever Bob Hardisty was injured or was on international duty. He was nearing the end of his career when I joined the club but he was still a marvellous player. He had a brilliant footballing brain and his movement was as smooth as silk. Without any shadow of a doubt, he was the greatest. It is ridiculous that I went on to win more caps than him.

The good news was that the Amateur Cup campaign had yet to get under way and the return to the ranks of the 'Olympic Three' was just the tonic that Auckland supporters required. They had seen their team forge to the head of the Northern League table, despite some worrying performances on the field. Not that they had given up hope of the Northern League title. That prize was still a possibility but this season, Billingham, Crook and Shildon, as well as West Auckland, were showing that they too were serious challengers for the Championship and that Bishop Auckland would have a struggle on their hands to retain it. Any cracks in Bishop's shield of invincibility would be exposed and the advantage taken.

Bob Hardisty returned to the side, resuming in his right-half slot but Jimmy Nimmins was not fit and Bob Thursby took over his position when the teams were announced for the First Round Amateur Cup game against Norton Woodseats. The Kingsway supporters expected the 'Two Blues' to win by a much bigger margin than the actual 1–0 result. Indeed, it could have been a lot worse. After ten minutes of unconvincing play, Bishop could have gone a goal down when Woodseats broke away, only for Wain to send in a shot that Sharratt could only palm onto the crossbar. Fortunately for Bishop supporters, Harry was able to regain possession of the ball and complete the clearance. Then, after seventeen minutes, Wain again fired in a strong drive that the Auckland goalkeeper had problems dealing with and, when the centre-forward fired the rebound towards the goal, Bob Hardisty was on hand to save a goal—with his hand. The resultant penalty was weakly taken by inside-left Lamb, and Harry Sharratt was able to notch another saved penalty to his tally, much to the relief of Bishop Auckland players and supporters.

Bishop were invigorated as a result of Sharratt's penalty save and began to create more openings for the forwards. Bob Thursby set up an opportunity for Benny Edwards to run at the Woodseats defence, resulting in Derek Lewin's shot being saved by Newbould. Then, a minute later, Bob Hardisty delivered a telling cross that Seamus O'Connell failed by a whisker to connect with. The deadlock was broken just two minutes before the half-time break when Edwards sent over an inviting cross that Ray Oliver gratefully accepted to nod the ball home. Relief on the 'Bishops' faces was there for all to see.

A rather strange incident took place in the Bishop Auckland dressing room at half-time when one of the Auckland players complained that he was having trouble picking out his colleagues when wanting to pass the ball. Woodseats were playing in their usual colours of pale blue and white stripes, dark blue shorts whereas Bishop were playing in their dark blue and light blue quartered shirts, white shorts. A discussion followed and it was agreed that, for the second half, they would wear the more differentiating second strip of flame shirts with white shorts.

Unfortunately, the change of colours did not produce a change in style, as Bishop continued to show their unusually disappointing brand of football, not that Woodseats could take advantage of the home team's deficiencies.

In the end, Bishop won through but it had been a poor performance and one that would have to be improved upon if they were to advance in the competition.

Bob Hardisty was also harbouring some serious thoughts—he began to wonder if he really was getting too old for this game. Certainly, two months earlier he had been on the international stage and performed admirably but he could not help asking himself if he was doing the right thing in continuing.

A 5–1 win over Gedling Colliery, in Round Two, put Bob in a more positive frame of mind. This was the game that introduced left full-back Bert Childs as a Bishop Auckland player in the Amateur Cup. He had been signed to take over from Tommy Stewart. Derek Lewin was the star man, scoring two and very unlucky not to claim a third, when his blockbuster hit a defender standing on the line. Warren Bradley also scored twice with Seamus O'Connell grabbing the other.

Briggs Sports played hosts to Bishop Auckland for Round Three and a Seamus O'Connell header—that the goalkeeper let slide under his body—after nine minutes, was the only difference between the two sides although the same player, receiving a Dave Robinson cross (standing in for the injured Benny Edwards) once again came close to scoring, but his header thumped against the upright and was cleared to safety, just before half-time.

Midway through the first half, Bob received a nasty gash to his knee following a challenge with Briggs' inside-right, Noble, that considerably slowed him down for the second half. He could have done without that at this stage of his career; the cut required stitches after the match.

The second half was a close fought affair with both teams creating chances on a very difficult surface—continuous rain had made the pitch heavy and in places the surface had churned up to reveal cinder patches. There were quite a few Auckland players sporting injuries after the game and at least seven players had to have bandages applied—not from over zealous Briggs Sports players but as a result of the playing surface. Nevertheless, the injuries were soon forgotten as all that mattered was that they had made it to Round Four—just who would they meet there? The answer came two days later when the name of Bishop Auckland was paired with the one club they would have preferred to have avoided.

Ilford, Wycombe Wanderers, Kingstonian, Corinthian Casuals—all teams that Bishop had defeated in the competition in recent years—Hayes and Tooting and Mitcham United accompanied Bishop Auckland into the draw and all escaped having to meet the Cup favourites. Instead, Bishop were drawn to meet, arguably, their toughest opponents, certainly the toughest that they had met so far in the competition—Crook Town (provided that they overcame Evenwood Town who had held them to a 1–1 draw and now faced a replay). Not only that, they would have to play that match on Crook's Millfield Ground.

A few days prior to the game, in his weekly newspaper column, Bob wrote about how he looked forward to the match and also decided it was time to take a swipe at the administrators of the Amateur Cup competition, who had once again introduced the controversial policy of zoning the draw for the Second Round of the competition, much to the disgust of northern clubs.[†] In his article, he wrote:

> Can Bishop Auckland win the FA Amateur Cup for the third year running, thus setting up an all-time record? Records are made to be broken, and broken again, but if we pull this off it will be a feat that will last throughout my lifetime, and perhaps for the life of everyone connected with the 'Bishops'.
>
> That is why we are all so determined to make an all-out bid for this treble. But first of course, we have to surmount the next hurdle on the road to Wembley—our 'Derby' match against Crook Town or Evenwood Town on Saturday. But more of that later. Before I discuss the prospects, there is something I would like to say about the draw.
>
> This has again favoured the Southern clubs, if only because North-East clubs have to knock each other out for the umpteenth time in this season's competition. I have utmost respect for some of these Southern teams but from what we have seen of the opposition from outside the Northern League, coupled with results and press reports, I feel that such clubs as Billingham, Crook, Evenwood, Willington and ourselves could have accounted for a lot of the Southerners, instead of beheading each other.
>
> On the other hand, of course, the North-East is now assured of having one team in the semi-finals. We in the North have heard so many conflicting reports from the South on their Cup teams that it is difficult to assess from where the chief danger will come to the North's present—dare I say—supremacy? Taking a chance, I would say that Wycombe Wanderers and Corinthian Casuals will probably reach the semi-finals—perhaps easily.
>
> Thinking about our own prospects before yesterday's replay to decide our opponents, I wondered which we would prefer to win—Evenwood with their fast, open play and hard-tackling defence, or Crook, with their polished approach work and hard-hitting forward line. Personally (and I am not speaking

---

[†]   The article was published before the result of the replay game between Evenwood Town and Crook Town was known, which Crook won 2–1.

for either players or committee or supporters) I would always plump for the better ground on which to play—and that means Crook. But on the score of sentiment, my choice would have been Evenwood, the club who have for so many seasons, carried on in the wilderness, their only gleam of encouragement a solitary Championship win seasons ago; and surely it is the ambition of every sportsman in County Durham anyway, to see that glorious day when some such team as West Auckland, Stanley United or Tow Law Town wins the Amateur Cup.

Finally, to our own chances again. So far this season, Bishop's form has been in-and-out but the team has survived a sticky patch and from now on it's sleeves up, collars down and hard into the ball.

Just a few words about Corbett Cresswell, our centre-half. It may seem out of place for me to mention an individual colleague in an article of this kind but his form this year is such that it must be in order to say this: Corbett Cresswell can now stand side by side with such giants of the past as George Atkinson and Norman Christie.

Crook were able to overcome Evenwood Town in their replayed game, winning a close encounter 2–1 and a week later were set to meet the 'Bishops'. The game was played without Bob Hardisty, his leg injury keeping him out of the side. Snow was falling when the players came out to the 11,843 cheering fans, with Bishop having to take up a somewhat strange formation. Bob's injury allowed Bob Thursby to take the right-half position while the left-half slot was recaptured by Jimmy Nimmins, playing in his first Amateur Cup game of the season. Benny Edwards was also carrying an injury and had been deemed unfit to play and in his place, Tommy Stewart was asked to perform at outside-left.

After constant pressure by the Bishop forward line, Crook's defence capitulated in the fourteenth minute. Tommy Stewart collected the ball and ran down his wing; getting close to the bye-line he delivered an inviting cross that Derek Lewin, racing in, finished off with a truly brilliant header, well wide of Fred Jarrie's despairing dive.

From the sublime to the ridiculous. Having opened the scoring with a beautiful goal, Bishop added to their tally with a most fortunate one. Bert Childs collected the ball on the half-way line and launched a long ball into the Crook penalty area. Jarrie, in the Crook goal, made a complete mess of it and misjudged the bounce of the ball which ended up in the back of the net. Bishop supporters were ecstatic—two up against their arch enemies and so far Harry Sharratt had had it easy.

Despite being well on top, Bishop failed to capitalize and after thirty-seven minutes, Crook reduced the deficit when Keith Hopper was allowed time to receive a Bill Jeffs pass and send a shot past Harry Sharratt.

Snow continued to fall during the second half and the slippery surface taxed every player's ability. Crook thrilled their supporters when drawing level after fifty minutes. From a long clearance out of defence, Jimmy McMillan collected the ball and ran towards Sharratt's goal. Without looking up, the winger fired a drive that beat the Bishop goal-minder and, despite a fine attempt by Childs to save the situation, the ball found its way into the net.

Conditions deteriorated but there was no question of play being halted. However, try as they may, neither team could score again and so it was that the game would have to be replayed a week later at Bishop Auckland's Kingsway Ground, and this time Bob Hardisty would be fit to play. That was before a few problems arose.

There was a mini-crisis just before the game started when Dave Marshall arrived nursing a groin injury, sustained that morning in a hockey match of all things, for Bede College, and announced himself unfit to play. Tommy Stewart was the natural replacement but he had failed to make an appearance. To add to Bishop's woes, Warren Bradley was also missing and with less than quarter of an hour to go before the game was due to kick off, the home side were staring defeat in the face without a ball being kicked. Standing in the dressing room was Rance Richardson, a good reserve team member who played at outside-right and who had come to watch the game but who was placed on immediate standby should Warren fail to turn up within the next five minutes. In addition to all of this, Ray Oliver was deemed unfit, as he was carrying a knee injury and it was decided that Bob should play at centre-forward with Bob Thursby fitting in at right-half.

Thankfully, Warren Bradley arrived without a minute to spare and with Marshall being coerced into playing, Bishop were able to provide a battling set of eleven players, without the necessity to include the by-standing Richardson.

The decision to play Bob Hardisty at centre-forward turned out to be a master stroke. For forty minutes the two sets of players gave everything to gain the upper hand; the football was not pretty but it certainly kept the 13,000 crowd—excluding gate-crashers—enthralled. Then, with half-time approaching, Bob accepted a pass on the Crook goal line, close to the corner flag, and headed back into the penalty area. Seamus O'Connell, showing his wonderful anticipation, arrived just at the right time and stretched his neck muscles to meet the ball, sending it flying past Jarrie. It was a brilliantly contrived goal.

Three minutes into the second half, Bob Thursby sent over a high cross and there was Bob meeting it smack in the middle of his forehead to power the ball past Jarrie once more. There was no repeat of the comeback engineered by Crook in the first game this time and had not Gardiner stopped an O'Connell header on the line, Bishop would have inflicted a heavier defeat on their closest rivals. Only Hayes stood in the way of another return visit to the Mecca of football—Wembley.

It would not have been normal for Bishop Auckland to have a Cup run without an element of controversy and this year was to be no different.

Ray Oliver had been with the club for almost four years and had served it well. He had scored well over one hundred and twenty goals for the 'Bishops' and his strike partnership with Seamus O'Connell was awesome. A recurring cartilage injury from the previous season had resulted in him missing a number of games during the current one. Only four weeks earlier, Bishop had acquired the signature of Billy Russell, the Rhyl centre-forward who had given Corbett Cresswell such a hard time only four months ago in the FA Cup. Russell signed for Bishop on February 3rd.

There was a lot of resentment at the time, both from southern clubs as well as those in the north, towards Bishop Auckland's policy of searching for the best players, wherever in the country they may have been situated. They did not like players being drafted in from miles away, claiming that it was not within the amateur ethic and not in keeping with the true spirit of the game. There was even talk that the footballing authorities would introduce a rule that in future, clubs would be unable to field anyone who happened to live beyond a fifty-mile radius of the club's ground. If that had been incorporated into the rules of the Amateur Cup competition, just imagine the huge advantage the southern clubs, particularly those around London, would have had, given the large population that they would have been able to seek players from.

Bishop, however, were unrepentant. The Committee had always made their annual target the winning of the Amateur Cup … the Northern League Championship and everything else were secondary. It was true that players such as Harry Sharratt and Derek Lewin travelled from Lancashire, Seamus

O'Connell from Carlisle and now Billy Russell from Aberystwyth. If these players were prepared to travel and play for Bishop Auckland then that was the club's good fortune. Sentiment played no part in their policy, and if a fine centre-forward like Russell was prepared to commit himself and sign for them, then all the better for the club. Jealousy and sour grapes from other clubs was just ignored.

On the Monday evening, prior to the semi-final, the all-powerful Committee convened to select the team for Saturday's game. According to the press, Ray Oliver had been declared unfit—although the player himself had made it known that, in his view, he would be fit for the match and that his injury was only minor—and was, therefore, not considered for a place in the team. Billy Russell was chosen as Ray's replacement. Only two days before, the twenty-one year-old Aberystwyth University student—surely the only amateur ever to turn out for Bishop Auckland who could speak fluent Russian—had made a brilliant debut in his first senior game for the club in a 5–2 win over Stockton in Round Two of the Durham Challenge Cup, scoring twice and drawing the acclaim of the Kingsway faithful.

On the Tuesday, the morning after the Committee had made their team selections, there was news that Ray Oliver had recovered from his injury, as he had predicted he would, and was now fit. The Committee, showing a complete lack of flexibility, declared that the team had already been chosen, that Oliver would not be required and that Billy Russell was to lead the forward line against Hayes at St James's Park.

A certain degree of farce was to present itself when Wednesday's edition of *The Northern Echo* carried the bombshell news that Billy Russell was under obligation to turn out for the North Wales representative side against a Scottish Junior Eleven at Edinburgh and that the Wales Football Association were not prepared to release him to play for Bishop Auckland. A desperate 'Kit' Rudd implored the Welsh FA to change their mind but they would not budge and reiterated that Billy Russell must play for them in Scotland—he would definitely not be playing in the semi-final of the Amateur Cup.

The Bishop Auckland committee members held an urgent, impromptu meeting at the club and it was decided that 'Kit' Rudd, as Secretary, should inform Ray Oliver that he had now been selected to play in Saturday's match, at centre-forward and his attendance would be required after all.

Ray refused.

Ray Oliver is a very highly principled man and was put on this earth for three things—(a) to have a kind attitude towards his fellow human beings, (b) to save lives at sea and (c) to frighten the hell out of centre-halves. He declined the invitation to play on the basis that he genuinely believed that he should have been selected in the first instance and that the club should not have brought in a complete stranger so late in the season, fine player though Billy Russell was. Ray's record for the club was a magnificent one and he had always given his heart and soul whenever he had turned out for the 'Bishops'. He felt deeply hurt that he had been omitted from the original eleven, especially when his fine goal-scoring feats were taken into consideration and in particular his record of goal-scoring in Amateur Cup semi-finals. The story of his alleged current injury was just that—a story, a complete fabrication—put about to disguise any disharmony within the Bishop Auckland camp. There had been no injury. Ray Oliver had merely refused to play on a matter of principle.

The Northern Echo sports headline for Friday 15th March heralded: 'Ray Oliver "finished" with Bishop Auckland'. The article went on to explain the background of the story and concluded that in the absence of Ray Oliver and Billy Russell, Bob Hardisty, who had not been selected for the original eleven due to the outstanding form of Bob Thursby, would once again fill the centre-forward position. The news was a shock for all Bishop supporters who wondered, once again, what effect these shenanigans would have on the morale at the club.

Bob Hardisty was reported as saying: 'Ray Oliver is one of the best and a grand club man. I wish that I were playing at centre-forward under different circumstances.'

The same team that had defeated Crook in Round Four applied pressure to the Hayes defence from the outset but the 'Two Blues' suffered a setback to their chances when Seamus O'Connell came out of a tackle with a twisted knee and had to leave the field after only three minutes. When he did return, ten minutes later, O'Connell positioned himself on the left-wing rather than his customary inside-left spot.

Being a man down after only three minutes did not alter Auckland's attacking brand of football and the southerners were unable to take advantage with their extra man-power. Bishop created the more clear-cut chances but Lewis, Hayes's goalkeeper, brought off a string of fine saves, none better than when he flung himself full-length to keep out a pile-driver from Bob Hardisty that had 'Goal' written all over it. It was only the actions of their goalkeeper that allowed Hayes to go off at half-time on level terms.

ulgaria v Great Britain, Sofia, 1955. Bob looks on as a Bulgarian attack is brought to an end. Great ritain played well but lost this leg 2–0.

Ferryhill forwards are foiled by Harry Sharratt as Dave Marshall, Tommy Stewart, Bob (number 4) and Corbett Cresswell provide extra cover.

Bishop Auckland v Corinthian Casuals, Amateur Cup Final 1956. Bob is on hand if required but the ball went out for a goal kick.

The ball is about to hit Bob's chest as he stands on the goal line but the referee awarded a controversial goal to Corinthian Casuals.

Bob's thunderbolt from outside the penalty area that helped Bishop Auckland overcome Corinthian Casuals 4–1.

Bob goes through customs on his way to the Melbourne Olympics.

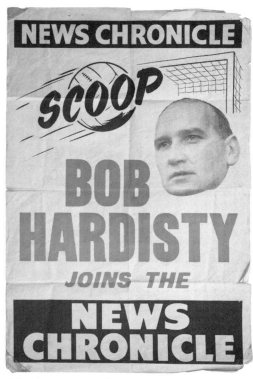

A local newspaper advertisement.

Bob is about to deliver the headed pass that will result in a goal by Seamus O'Connell in this Amateur Cup Fourth Round Replay against Crook Town. Bishop won the match 2–0 to send supporters home happy—now, only Hayes would stand in their way to prevent another return to Wembley.

Bob scores the opener for Bishop Auckland in the Amateur Cup semi-final against Hayes, helping take the 'Two Blues' to Wembley for the fourth consecutive year.

Bishop Auckland v Wycombe Wanderers, Amateur Cup Final, 1957. Bob tries to open the scoring but fails to get his name on the score sheet.

Derek Lewin and Bob are foiled by the Wycombe defenders.

Warren Bradley is out of picture as he puts Bishop Auckland 3–1 up against Wycombe Wanderers in the 1957 Amateur Cup Final.

Bob raises his arms in praise of Bradley's goal.

Bob checks the racing results ... or is he reading his own column?

How THE NORTHERN ECHO caricatured Bob's return to football playing for Manchester United.

Is he asking for the lady's telephone number, or just having his score-card marked?

'I'm getting too old for this game.'

After finishing his playing career, Bob passed on his skills to the youngsters. Here he is at a Durham County Football School, showing the next generation of up and coming football stars just how it is done.

Telephone: 01-727 4113
From: Sir Stanley Rous, C.B.E.

115 Ladbroke Road
London, W11 3PS

18th January 1985

I was shocked to hear of the trouble which has overcome you and send you herewith my very best wishes and thoughts for your welfare.

I am sure your many friends will help to give you support and keep you as cheerful as possible under the circumstances.

This note is merely to tell you of my concern for you and the happy memories of our association over many years.

With all good wishes and thoughts.

Yours ever
Stanley Rous

Bob Hardisty, Esq.,
Ward 9
Bishop Auckland General Hospital

SOUTHAMPTON
FOOTBALL CLUB
LIMITED Founded 1885

Registered office:
The Dell, Milton Road,
Southampton SO9 4XX
telephones:
(0703) 39633/4/5
commercial office:
(0703) 36616

Manager:
Lawrie McMenemy
Commercial Manager:
Malcolm Price
Secretary:
Brian Truscott

LM/VG.

Dear Bob,

4th January, 1985.

I have just heard about your operation. I do hope you are well despite your problems. I am sure that this would knock back many lesser people, but if you apply the same qualities that made you such an outstanding footballer, I am sure you will learn to cope better than anyone.

Please accept my very best wishes. If there is anything I can do, please let me know, and obviously if you could come to see us here at The Dell or anywhere on our travels, you would be very welcome. I do hope that 1985 will be good for you.

Yours sincerely,

L. McMenemy.
Manager.

Directors: A.A. Woodford (Chairman), John Corbett, Sir George Meyrick Bt. MC,
B.G.W. Bowyer TD, JP, F.G.L. Askham FCA, E.T. Bates.

VAT Reg. No: 330 1812 06
Reg No: 53001 England

Two of the many letters received by Bob, following his amputation.

Bob is as genial as ever even though he has had his right leg amputated. He came to terms with his disability and was regularly invited to attend establishments within the community around the north-east, talking with other amputees and the disabled, helping them overcome the trauma of their setback.

Bob's coffin is carried out of St. Andrew's Church by Bob Thursby, Ken Chisholm, Ray Oliver and the hidden Dave Marshall.

Bob Hardisty 1921–1986: Thanks for the memories.

Bishop lined up for the second-half with a slight change of formation, O'Connell taking over at centre-forward and Bob Hardisty moving over to inside-left. The change seemed to confuse the Hayes defenders for a time and their defence began to look vulnerable, trying to adapt to Bishop's more balanced forward line changes. For twenty minutes they continued to hold out but after sixty-five minutes the opening came. Receiving a perfect pass from the still-hobbling O'Connell, Bob had three defenders in front of him. With a sway of the hips he beat one man and then another. His footwork took him past the third and he casually placed the ball to the side of Lewis. It had taken sixty-five minutes and a goal of immense artistry to break down the solid Hayes defence but now the 'Bishops' were ahead and they were not about to give Hayes any chance of pulling back.

Five minutes later, O'Connell sent over a cross that reached the in-rushing Benny Edwards. It may have been a stoop or a dive but whichever it was, his head connected with the ball and, like a rocket, it seared past Lewis into the top corner of his goal. Bishop were 2–0 up and on their way to London.

Hayes tried to raise their game but Bishop had the confidence that a two-goal lead engenders and for the remaining twenty minutes, were able to deflect anything that the southerners could apply.

A welcome visitor to the 'Bishops' dressing room after the victory was Ray Oliver. He had settled his differences with the club, saying that he acted on principle when he objected to the inclusion of Billy Russell, whom he reiterated was a complete stranger to the squad, to lead the attack in such an important game. An approach had been made from the club that he reconsider his threat never to play for them again and he was now quite happy for the incident to be put to bed.

Obviously believing that one controversy was insufficient for Bishop Auckland to deal with, in their quest for another attempt at retaining the Amateur cup, the Gods decided to test the club with another one. This time it was Seamus O'Connell's turn to feel aggrieved. He was still suffering from the injury received in the semi-final match against Hayes but he believed that the knee was getting better and that he would be fit for the Final. The Committee, for some unfathomable reason, continued with their inflexible policy of selecting Saturday's team on the Monday night. They studied a specialist's report and concluded that Seamus would not be fit and, therefore, could not be selected. Billy Russell would play at centre-forward, his first ever Amateur cup game, in place of the injured Ray Oliver, and Bob Hardisty would play at inside-left, the position vacated by O'Connell. Seamus would, however, travel down with the rest of the official party.

On the Friday afternoon, Bishop players went through the routine of their physical exercises, under the guidance and participation of Bob Hardisty, at Chelsea's Stamford Bridge. Seamus stood around but was not allowed to kick a football. There was another drawback. Harry Sharratt, who had decided to drive down to London rather than travel with the official party, had failed to arrive and was missing the practice.

Just as the session was coming to an end, a breathless Harry Sharratt ran on to the pitch and took up his position between the goal posts. He had been driving through London when a tyre developed a puncture, hence his late arrival. Harry's entry onto the pitch, however, coincided with the rest of the squad's departure. To give him some practice, Seamus decided to take his frustration out on the Chelsea footballs that littered Stamford Bridge's playing surface and he rained shots on Harry. Shot after shot, harder and harder, were pounded at England's best goalkeeper and not once did Seamus's knee give way. 'Bugger the Committee,' he thought.

Harry finished the session and, after changing, he and Seamus returned to his car.

'Which one's yours, Harry?' asked Seamus as he inspected a line of parked cars.

'That one there,' said Harry, pointing, 'the one with the flat tyre.'

Next morning, the day of the big match, the players were sat in the lounge about to go in for breakfast when a serious-faced George Waine came up and enquired of Seamus: 'Seamus, I know that you have not been selected to play this afternoon but do you think that is a good reason to take a young lady to your room on the eve of such an important occasion.'

'Wherever did you get that idea from, Mr Waine?' Seamus casually enquired, as if he was asked the same question on a daily basis.

'I have been told but am not prepared to say who by,' asserted George.

'Well, I don't know where you got that from, Mr Waine, but I can categorically state that I did not have a girl in my room last night.'

The Chairman of Bishop Auckland Football Club pondered for a moment before saying, 'All right then, Seamus. I'll accept your word. Consider the matter closed. Thank you for your time.'

George Waine left the players to talk amongst themselves and when he had disappeared into the breakfast room, Bob asked in a quiet tone of Seamus: 'Are you absolutely sure that you didn't have a lady in your room last night, Seamus?' with a wide knowing grin on his face, as the other players looked on in amusement.

'Of course I didn't, Bob. I have a reputation to maintain … There were two of them,' disclosed Seamus with a smile.

For the fourth season in a row, Bishop Auckland had made it to Wembley and Harry Sharratt, Bob Hardisty, Corbett Cresswell and Jimmy Nimmins had been with the 'Bishops' on all four occasions. Bob and Jimmy could also add the losing finals against Crook Town, Pegasus and Willington among their Wembley experiences. Dave Marshall too was a Wembley regular, having only missed last year's Wembley final against Corinthian Casuals owing to injury. Others of the current team, such as Derek Lewin had played in two previous Wembley Finals and Benny Edwards could claim one better as he had played in three. Such was the experience in the Bishop Auckland squad that they could have been excused for thinking of Wembley as their second home.

Jimmy Nimmins had made it known that this would be his last season. Like Bob Hardisty, he had been driven to keep on for one last season by the thought of gaining a third consecutive winners' medal. Now he had made it to Wembley and was to captain the team, this would be his final Final. He had said: 'This will be my last season. I have made up my mind and I will not go back on it. I could continue to play for other clubs but I prefer to finish my career with Bishop. I am thirty-six, three months older than Bob and I'm calling it a day, although I may go on tour in the close season.'

Dave Marshall remembers Jimmy with fondness: 'All of the players would receive a new pair of boots at the beginning of the season from Frank Whitwell's, the leading sports shop in Bishop Auckland. Jimmy would get his a couple of sizes too small. He'd take them home and he would sit with his new boots in a bathtub of cold water. This, apparently, expanded the leather and the boots formed the shape of Jimmy's feet. Nobody else tried doing it.'

Bob Thursby says of Jimmy:

> We didn't do any formal training for Bishop. It wasn't possible for all of the lads to meet at a designated time two or three times a week. Those who lived away

would train wherever and with whoever they could. For instance, Derek Lewin would train with Oldham or Manchester United, Seamus would train with Carlisle and Harry would train with Wigan. One or two might get together on a Tuesday and/or Thursday night down at Bishop but there wouldn't be many.

One day, Jimmy suggested that him and me do some training together up where he lived at Consett. It was bloody freezing so I got well wrapped up in pullovers and two sets of tracksuits as well as a couple of balaclavas. Out comes Jimmy in a bloody tee shirt and shorts.

He was the hardest man that I have ever known. He wasn't particularly tall and was only about 11st 6lbs but by God he was awesome, and not just as a footballer. Because of the amount of body water that he lost in working in the foundry, he would have a pint of beer and a whiskey before a game so that he was not dehydrated. One Saturday, we were in the changing room and I was getting ready next to Jimmy. As he took off his shirt I noticed a great big gash down his left arm, almost to the bone. I asked him what had happened. He told me that that morning he had been putting in a shift at work and he was pouring some molten steel into a tub. Some of the liquid splashed back and spouted onto his arm. The scar looked terrible. I asked him what he did.

He just looked at me calmly and made a nonchalant flicking motion with his right hand across his left arm. 'I just brushed it off like this.' Then I noticed that his right hand was burnt as well, through brushing away the searing liquid. He was the toughest man that I have ever known and an absolute gentleman.

On a lighter note, Ron Fryer recalls: 'Me and another player were studying a photograph of Bob Hardisty and Jimmy together. We decided to have a bit of fun and drew the finest mop of hair on the two bald heads. I was admiring our handiwork when a cuff across the head made me smart. Jimmy had sneaked up behind the pair of us and was not amused with what he saw. The memory of that cuff makes me wince even now, some fifty-odd years later.'

Wycombe Wanderers, in complete contrast to Bishop Auckland, were making their first Wembley appearance, not that this seemed to matter much as some journalists had made them favourites to win the Amateur Cup. Their road to the Final had been a relatively straight-forward one. In Round One they had defeated St Albans away 4–1 and then disposed of Clapton in a home tie 4–2. Round Three saw them vanquishing Hounslow, again at home 3–1 and then they travelled to Ilford to record a 3–3 draw before winning the replay 2–0. They had won their semi-final tie at Highbury by defeating last year's beaten finalists, Corinthian Casuals 4–2.

The teams were:

Bishop Auckland (White shirts, Black shorts)
Sharratt—Marshall, Childs—Thursby, Cresswell, Nimmins—
Bradley, Lewin, Russell, Hardisty, Edwards

Wycombe Wanderers (Red shirts, White shorts)
Syrett—Lawson, Westley—G Truett, Wicks, J Truett—
Worley, Trott, Bates, Tomlin, Smith

Referee: J W Topliss of Grimsby

It was no surprise that Bishop Auckland started in customary high-action fashion; within a minute they were unlucky not to be ahead when Bob Hardisty received the ball and in a moment of exquisite movement brought it under control and fired a rasping shot just wide of Syrett's upright. Two minutes later, the Wycombe defence had a further scare when a promising move down the left wing featuring Bert Childs, Benny Edwards and Bob, broke down when the latter played a misplaced pass that was gobbled up by a grateful defence.

Wycombe responded with a raid of their own down the right but Cresswell broke that up and played a beautiful long ball to Warren Bradley who supplied Billy Russell but the Welshman shot straight at Syrett. That had only been a 'sighter', however, and Bishop's next attacking move brought a goal. Bob collected a weak clearance by Worley, who appeared to stub his toe in the lush turf as he went to kick the ball near the centre circle. With the ball at his feet, Bob moved a couple of paces, arms stretched like Blondin walking on his tight-rope over Niagara Falls, to give him balance, as he turned. On looking up he saw Billy Russell making a run down the inside-right channel. With one slick movement of the hips, he sent an unerring pass that Russell anticipated. He was already running whilst Wicks was still in his blocks. Russell let the ball run for a stride and then sent a low drive past the diving Syrett. The Bishop section of Wembley Stadium erupted. A goal up and Bob Hardisty had constructed it. The 'Bishops' were on the march.

Sixty seconds later, Bishop were awarded a corner on the left. Bob played it short with a pass to Benny Edwards who immediately returned the ball back to Bob. From almost the quadrant by the corner flag, he sent over a lob that entered the net. Two up? No … the referee had blown for offside against Bob. Maddeningly, for Bishop supporters, it was the correct decision.

Harry Sharratt had hardly been forced into any action and when Wycombe did attack, Cresswell was taking charge. Scoring opportunities were presenting themselves at the other end, however, and Russell and Edwards both had shots blocked by fortunate defenders.

Bishop were playing some wonderful football now and the sun came out as if in gratification. Bradley sent a drive skimming past a post and then Russell, making his only error so far, blazed over the bar from Lewin's flick-on when it looked easier to score.

It was fully twenty-five minutes before Sharratt's goal was seriously threatened and it so nearly could have been a goal. Bates was presented with a scoring chance right in front of goal when Bert Childs lost the ball but just as he was about to test Sharratt, Dave Marshall came in with a brilliant tackle.

Wycombe became more confident and, as a result, began to win more balls in the midfield. They had been overrun for much of the game, so far, but were only one goal down. That they managed to find an equalizer was largely due to the promptings of wing-half, Geoff Truett. It was from his long pass that Smith latched onto and sent a stinging shot past the diving Sharratt, as Marshall closed in, too late this time. Marshall and other Bishop defenders protested that Smith had used a hand to control the ball but Jack Topliss would have none of it and the goal stood.

As so often in the past, the goal conceded merely spurred on the Bishop players and three minutes later, they had restored their lead. Warren Bradley, ever tormenting the Wycombe defenders with his mazy runs, played an inside pass to Derek Lewin who was able to beat defenders and goalkeeper to the ball and prod it into the net.

Half-time was blown five minutes later and a pause came to a pulsating game of football. The quality of play had been much better than the last two finals; Bishop were playing with a relaxed authority and passing the ball around with unerring accuracy, whilst Wycombe, after a nervous start, were beginning to come back into it and were only one goal behind. It was anyone's game.

The two teams sparred with each other during the opening spell of the second half and the quality of football dropped slightly but after ten minutes Bob Hardisty ran through to collect a Russell pass and sent in a drive that forced Syrett to pull off a diving save. This was the prelude to further attacks from both teams and the quality of play picked up.

Bradley turned Geoff Truett inside out with a dribble and delivered a pass to Bob. Completely deceiving the two defenders around him, he let the ball pass between his legs to present Benny Edwards with a fine chance. The winger took aim but his shot went wide of the far post.

At the other end, Len Worley teased Dave Marshall and was about to shoot when Sharratt raced out to block his attempt with a brave dive. The Bishop goalkeeper had to make a similar save when Bates burst through, much to the annoyance of Cresswell, who until now, had kept the centre-forward in check. Wycombe were clearly having their best spell of the game and Sharratt had to pull off a superb save when Tomlin connected direct from a corner to send a stunning volley goalwards. Flying to his left, Harry caught the ball as it travelled at speed and clung on to it as if it was a bar of gold.

It was Bishop's turn to go close next when Warren Bradley cut the Wycombe defence to ribbons and sprayed a beautiful pass to Benny Edwards. Alas, with only Syrett to beat, the wingman put the ball wide of goal. Further pressure was applied by the 'Bishops' and Hardisty, Edwards and Lewin all had reasonable opportunities to increase the lead but Syrett saved on all three occasions.

Then, after seventy-two minutes, Bishop got a third goal. Bradley saw a centre from the right cleared upfield but immediately Bob Hardisty returned the ball to him. Taking on his defender, he won a corner which was put behind for a second one. This was better placed and caused a bit of a panic amongst the Wycombe defenders. Lurking on the edge of the penalty area was Jimmy Nimmins and as the ball came out he latched on to it and flicked it to his right for the oncoming Bradley to once again rush past Westley and fire a wicked left-foot shot to Syrett's left. The 'keeper made a valiant effort to save but he had no chance.

That goal knocked the stuffing out of Wycombe and long before the final whistle blew, both sets of supporters knew who would be lifting the Cup in about twenty minutes time. Twice more, Bradley forced Syrett to save whilst at the other end Sharratt had to cope with an effort from Trott but it was Bishop who came closest to scoring again when Derek Lewin's header was cleared off the line by Westley in the dying moments of what had been a thrilling game of football.

A minute later, a delighted squad of Bishop Auckland players congratulated team mates and opponents for such a fine result. Bishop had achieved what they had set out to do and the delayed retirements of Bob and Jimmy had been justified.

It was a very emotional and proud set of players that walked those steps again to receive the Amateur Cup and their individual medals but the two that were proudest of all were the balding phenomena known as Jimmy Nimmins and Bob Hardisty. Jimmy, it was, who received the Cup and was raised shoulder high by his team mates; Bob, it was, who received the loudest cheer from the 100,000 fans who had seen him put on a display of craftsmanship and skill the likes of which would never be seen again, at least certainly within the amateur ranks.

'This should be you up here, Bob,' suggested Jimmy Nimmins, as he was raised onto the shoulders of Corbett Cresswell and Derek Lewin, 'you should be captain.'

'I could never have coped with the responsibility, Jim,' Bob replied, laughingly.

Photographers did their best to, once again, claim the best shots for the Sunday newspapers and some were fortunate not to come a cropper such was the melee in taking the after-match pictures. The usual lap of honour followed as fans cheered their heroes loud and long. They did a complete lap and then returned towards the dressing room where a welcome bath waited.

Reporters followed the players into the dressing room and Jimmy told them: 'Bob and I have played in all six finals together for 'Bishops' at Wembley and this was our easiest game of them all. If we had snapped up our chances we could have scored nine.'

Bob added: 'That idea of wearing them down in the first half and making the ball do the work, certainly paid off.' Before he could say any more, Corbett Cresswell called over to Bob and cadged a cigarette from him. 'It'll be cigars tonight, Corbett,' said Bob.

A beaming Billy Russell proclaimed: 'I was nervous this morning but lost my nerves on the coach journey to the ground. When I scored my goal I could not see the ball for a second because of the goalkeeper. What a thrill when I saw it in the net. Boy, when the ball went into the net, it was my thrill of a life-time.'

In the opposite dressing room, Wycombe Wanderers, the defeated team, were celebrating the occasion as if they had won the cup. All that their players wanted to do was savour these momentous moments. Their captain, Frank Westley, commented: 'Bishop Auckland are a great team … too good for us. Why should we be disappointed? We lost to a far better team and that's all there is to it.'

'Our team went down to a team that played Football League football,' added Wycombe Secretary, Bill Hayter.

An hour later, the Bishop Auckland players came out of their dressing room and readied themselves to get on the waiting coach that would take them back to their hotel. Instead of turning left and getting straight on to the coach, Bob and Jimmy took a slight detour and walked down the tunnel to spend a few minutes of reflection as they gazed out on to Wembley's lush emerald expanse, where they had endured every agony and ecstasy open to a footballer. Sixty minutes ago the stadium was being rocked to the sound of 100,000 football mad supporters, now it was empty and all that could be heard was the sound of ground staff sweeping the terraces.

Taking a long draw on his cigarette, Bob said, 'Well, Jim. That's it. I won't be back here again. I've had some mixed times here. Bad ones—good ones. But I'm pleased that I had the chance to play here. God! I must have been here eight or nine times, including internationals. Some poor sods can play their entire career with a First Division side and never get the chance. So long, Wembley.'

'Aye, so long Wembley. Fucking great place.'

'Then to the spicy nut-brown ale'
L'Allegro (John Milton)

Chapter Twelve
BETRAYAL

I t was time for reflection.

As Bob Hardisty pondered the conversation that had just taken place over the telephone with Jimmy Murphy and the request that he play for Manchester United, he was touched with a sense of pride that he would now be helping his old friend in his hour of need. Murphy had explained that he could not offer Bob a first team place. He wanted him for Manchester United Reserves, the Central League team, to help fulfil their fixtures until the end of the season, totalling about a dozen games or so. They did not have the sufficient number of players available in their squad, following the air crash, and needed as much help as they could get. Despite the outpouring of grief and sympathetic offers of assistance from other Football League clubs, such offers had in fact turned out to be vacuous in the majority of cases. Clubs that had instantly said that Manchester United could have the loan of their players now decided that they wanted to apply terms and conditions to such loans and that certain players could not be included in such a scheme.

Murphy had needed a lot of persuading by his manager to turn to amateur players if professionals were not available, believing that he would not have the same authority of command over them as, by virtue of being amateurs, they would be free to come and go as they pleased. Busby had no such qualms. A compromise, of sorts, was reached when Murphy agreed that he would 'make enquiries' but if he did sign any amateurs then they would only play for the reserves, not the first team. Busby agreed.

A kind of myth has grown up over the years that gives a picture of Matt Busby, from his hospital bed, ordering Jimmy Murphy to contact Bob Hardisty who would help out the club. Such a story is—however fanciful—a little removed from the truth. In reality, Bob was not the immediate person contacted by the club and his playing for Manchester United came via a telephone call from Derek Lewin, who now takes up the tale:

> I used to train with the Manchester United players … Roger Byrne and Geoff Bent were real close friends. When the coffins were flown back to Ringway Airport, Manchester, they were taken to the club premises and laid out in the gymnasium. I called to pay my respects and, believe me, it was an experience I hope no-one has ever to go through. Just seeing those coffins was heartbreaking.
>
> I turned to walk away when Jimmy Murphy beckoned me over and we went into his office … he was pretty much running things. He told me that he had returned from visiting Matt Busby, who was still in the Munich Hospital, and wished to put a proposal to me. Putting it simply, he wanted to know if I would be willing to play for the reserves and could I help get a couple of other players as well, to help fulfil their fixtures, until the end of the season. We might not be needed for every game but if we could help them through these difficult days …
>
> I thought for a minute and suggested Warren Bradley, who came from the area, and Bob Hardisty. It was left to me to telephone them, initially … Jimmy would follow up with a confirmatory telephone call to each of them. Jimmy may have known Bob already as Bob had been to Old Trafford before, training with the Great Britain and England squads, so they would not have exactly been strangers. I am sorry to say it but the story of Matt Busby, minutes away from death, telling Jimmy Murphy to get in touch with Bob Hardisty immediately, is not quite correct but it certainly developed that way.

Busby, still seriously ill, was pleased with the recruitment of Lewin, Bradley and Hardisty by Murphy, and saw the experience of his old friend as the ideal character to help his beleaguered young reserve team through this most difficult period. The players themselves were not really reserves now; the real reserves were being required to appear for the first eleven in the First Division matches. Some of those who would be playing for Manchester United Reserves between now and the end of the season were youth team members.

It has been written in some newspapers and journals over the years, that Harry Sharratt was also approached to join the United Reserves squad but attempts to verify this have failed—certainly, no procurement was made by Derek Lewin. Manchester United were a club in turmoil at the time because of the air disaster and were managing on a day-to-day basis—keeping records was the last thing on anyone's mind at the club. If Harry's name was put forward as a potential player then it would appear that he was not required as the club have no record in their archives of him ever turning out for their Reserves or any other team.

Burnley Reserves provided the opposition for Bob's first fixture in the Central League at Old Trafford. According to reports, he had a very commendable game and certainly played his part in looking after the youngsters.

The Manchester United Reserve team that day was:

> D Gaskell—B Smith, R Holland—R English, Bob Hardisty,
> H Bratt—Warren Bradley, Derek Lewin, R Harrop, J Giles, R Hunter

The following week's Manchester United programme contained this report of the match:

> The new look United Reserve side, confounded the critics in the first minutes against Burnley by displaying real craft with the new amateurs from Bishop Auckland, Bob Hardisty, Derek Lewin and Warren Bradley fitting well into the side. Harrop sent in a fierce drive then English was only inches wide with another brilliant effort. But although the Burnley goal was lucky to remain intact it was the United goal that fell first, Shackleton (of Burnley) scoring from a free kick.
>
> With twenty minutes gone, United got a deserved goal when the United captain, Harrop, forced his way through to head the equalizer.
>
> Hardisty (the Bishop Auckland captain and English international who has come out of retirement especially to help our Central League side) proved a grand stopper and was a dominating figure in the middle and from to time he prompted his wings with clever passes.
>
> United opened the second half strongly and within five minutes were awarded a penalty for a foul on Lewin. Giles took the spot kick but Blacklaw saved. The game swung from end to end with neither side being able to score. The match ended as a draw which well satisfied the large number of spectators.

Two weeks later, Bob played in a fixture against Newcastle United Reserves at Old Trafford and met up with an old friend from the Olympics—Ronnie Simpson, who was recovering back to full fitness after being injured and was keeping goal for the 'Magpies'. It was a game in which defences were definitely not on top as the score was Manchester United Reserves 4 Newcastle United Reserves 7.

It has been mentioned, in a previous paragraph, that because Manchester United were going through the most difficult period of the club's history, certain administrative proceedings, that would normally be taken for granted, had to take a back seat, and that actual records of events as they happened during these dark days, were never properly recorded. Thus, the Minutes of the Book of Directors—the 'Bible'—show incomplete records for the end of the season and, as a result, it has not been possible to ascertain when Bob last played for Manchester United Reserves. It can be confirmed, however, that Warren Bradley was in the eleven that defeated Chesterfield Reserves 3–0 in a home fixture at Old Trafford on Saturday April 12th, a game in which Bob definitely did not take part.[†]

The Wycombe Wanderers Final was not the last game that Bob played for his beloved Bishop Auckland but perhaps he would have been better following the example set by his old colleague, Jimmy Nimmins, in deciding to hang up his boots immediately after that wonderful day in April 1957. He confirmed to the club committee—of which, Jimmy Nimmins was soon to become an elected member—that he would not be available for selection in future—except for, perhaps, an extreme emergency. The door was not quite closed yet.

As predicted by Bob at the beginning of the 1956–57 football season, Bishop had found it difficult to hang on to the Northern League Championship title for a fourth consecutive term. They had become used to coping with fixtures piling up near the end of the season and had been forced to field two teams on the same day, over the years, in order that their fixture programme could be fulfilled. This year had been no different insofar as a hectic end of season campaign followed their Amateur Cup Final success but the end product was disappointing. Unable to produce the brand of football that they had performed on Wembley's big stage, Bishop had finished third, nine points behind new champions, Billingham Synthonia and one point behind runners-up, West Auckland. The times, they were a-changing.

Nor had Bob given up sport altogether. He would continue to 'kick around a football' as well as play golf and tennis whenever the opportunity arose. Spring brought the cricket season to look forward to, turning out for Bishop

---

[†]   A feature of the match programme was that amateur players were accorded the courtesy of including the initial of their Christian name compared with the professionals whose surname only was shown. Attention of the reader is brought to the name of United's inside-left—a young Johnny Giles, who went on to play for Manchester United's first team before being transferred to Leeds United where he gained further success as well as a host of Irish international caps.

Auckland in the North Yorkshire and South Durham League, as he had done for a number of years, as a useful batsman and bowler. In addition, he still took command of Bishop Auckland's training sessions two or three times a week, not forgetting the FA Coaching courses that he ran. And, of course, he had still left that door slightly ajar to allow for any return to playing football. Add to that a regular spot on Tyne Tees Special as a sports correspondent for the television company and one can see that he still had a full sporting timetable.

The Winds of Fate can be very cruel at times and have an unprecedented habit of blowing full force into the faces of even the most famously gifted of humans. To all intents and purposes, Bob was finished playing football, although he continued to sign registration forms for Bishop Auckland, before the new season got under way—just in case. He never thought that he would be required, as Bishop had some good players coming along and, anyway, he was too old now. Amazingly, he was called upon to wear the shirt of the 'Two Blues' again and not just for any old Northern League game—it was for an FA Cup match on November 15th 1958, some nineteen months after the Wycombe Wanderers Amateur Cup Final.

So often over the years, the 'Bishops' had been used to handing out a drubbing to the opposing team but now they were to be on the receiving end. Drawn away to Tranmere Rovers, the Birkenhead team took ample revenge for being knocked out by the 'Bishops' in the same competition two years earlier, winning the tie 8–1. Bob played centre-half that day and did not have the easiest of times, as the scoreline suggests.

John Atkinson was a good friend of Bob's and recollects that day:

> Bob had the coaching job of Bishop Auckland at the time and had decided that he was good enough to play for them in the Cup match—they may have been short of players, I'm not too sure. He had to attend some kind of function on the eve of the match on the Friday night and knowing of this, 'Kit' Rudd asked me to make sure that Bob would be on the nine o'clock train out of Darlington to Liverpool, on the Saturday morning. 'Kit' knew that I was going to the match and elected me to be Bob's escort. I was at Bob's house bright and early and Bob drove us both to Darlington station. We got to Liverpool on time and made our way to the hotel where the official party were staying. We made it just in time, as they were just getting on the team bus and were about to leave. Bob played centre-half but, when they were losing 3–0, he and some other lad switched positions, Bob going to right-half. It didn't make any difference as Tranmere overran Bishop and won 8–1.
>
> Jack Sowerby, Bob and me sat together on the train back to Darlington,

swigging bottles of beer and smoking God knows how many cigarettes. In no time at all Jack and Bob were using the bottles as 'footballers', recreating moves of the game and discussing where things went wrong. By the time they had finished, Bishop had won! God knows how Bob got us home, driving after all that drinking!

The hard lessons learned from the Tranmere game were nothing compared to what lay in store for Bob; he would have been prepared to stay out on Tranmere's Prenton Park pitch until hell had frozen over if he had known what awaited him at home.

It was a stern-faced Betty that confronted him as he entered the home in Princes Street. She held a piece of paper in her hand. Bob had had a long day and was looking forward to a good night's sleep. All that he wanted to do was go to bed. It was obvious that that was not going to happen until he had cleared up whatever it was that had upset his wife so much.

She threw the piece of paper at him in a crumpled ball.

His heart sank. Was it a letter from an 'acquaintance'? How could he have been so careless? Was it from an aggrieved husband? When was the last time? Was it Melbourne or some time after? All kinds of thoughts raced through his befuddled head, not helped by the amount of beer that he had consumed on the train journey from Liverpool.

He bent down and picked up the ball of crumpled paper. Guilt was coursing through his body. He could feel himself turning sick. Unfurling the crumpled letter, Bob read its contents. It was not from a lady friend. It was a letter with an official letterhead. It was from his bookmaker. His blurry eyes scanned the contents, selecting words at random. He read it over and over again. The bottom line was that the bookmaker was bringing it to his attention that a large sum of money was owed (almost £200, equivalent to £5,000 in 2010) as a result of Bob's gambling. No pining lady friend wishing to re-unite their acquaintance. No cuckolded husband ready to cut off his genitals with a bread knife. A bookmaker!

He did not know whether to laugh or cry. Whatever, it did not make any difference. Betty felt cheated and was extremely angry—she had discovered the amount of money that he owed and there could be no denying it—bookmakers did not make mistakes as far as accountancy was concerned. There was only one option open to Bob—he had to confess that he had been stupid and propose that they discuss it at length in the morning—after a good night's sleep!

Sleep? No chance. That crack was beginning to get wider.

Bob continued running the Bishop Auckland training sessions and one day he received a call from a most unlikely source. He was asked to coach the players of local rivals Crook Town. Bob could not believe it. Crook had made it to the Amateur Cup Final and Bob, as well as thousands of Crook and Bishop supporters, wondered why they should ask him to train their players now. They had done very well, thank you very much, without his coaching skills, so far. But the Crook committee men were adamant that Bob was the man that they wanted and were certain that by utilising his knowledge and skills, the Amateur Cup would be returning north to County Durham. It was only going to be a short term appointment but, as far as Crook's members were concerned, it was a necessary one. Naturally, Bob jumped at the chance, with the full blessing of the Bishop Auckland committee, and was buoyed at the prospect of returning to Wembley once more.

Ray Snowball had been on Bishop Auckland's books a few years earlier but the arrival of a certain Harry Sharratt had made him decide that if he wanted first team football, then he would have to move on. Ray was goalkeeper for Crook Town that season:

> I can remember Bob coming to coach us. Some newspaper reports had him down as our Manager but really he was the coach. He had perfect skills in getting players fit and set a good example. None of the lads had any qualms about him coming. True, we had made it without him to the Final but the Crook committee wanted to make sure that we came back from Wembley with the trophy. We all knew Bob, of course, living in the same area and playing against him in the League. Bob put us all—me included—through exercises and tests that we had never attempted before and had us fitter than we had ever been. And he did this in the space of three or four weeks.

It must have been strange for Bob to have gone to Wembley as Manager of Bishop Auckland's fiercest rivals. It must have been even harder for him to watch his players taking on southern club Barnet on the playing surface that he himself had graced so regularly. Sitting on the sideline, in the seated area with all the other Crook members, he saw 'his' team win an entertaining game 3–2. Wembley had held back another winning Final for him.

Bob's short spell at Crook ended soon after the Amateur Cup had been won. His connection now with Bishop Auckland Football Club was not as a player but as a coach/trainer to the reserve team and teaching youngsters to develop their skills and fitness and then elevate them to the first team. The training sessions were tough and Bob tried to train his youngsters to peak fitness, although his resources were limited. That is not to say that there were few opportunities for light hearted banter—sometimes, however, events just turned out to be comical without any effort.

One such event is recounted by Dick Longstaff, a member of the reserve side that Bob was coaching at the time:

> We were due to play Page Bank in an away fixture. We all got on the bus and were cracking tales, when we reached a bridge over the river. There were some works going on and a sign warned us that the bridge had a weight restriction imposed. The driver jammed on the brakes and Bob bellowed that we would all have to get off the bus and walk across the bridge. So we all got off and carried our kit bags and started marching across with the bus following us. On the other side we got back on the bus and I said to Bob—'Bob, if the bus couldn't carry us across with us on it because of the weight, why was it right behind us as we were walking across?' He looked at me for a minute and then, without blinking an eyelid, said 'Carry on, driver!'

Shades of *Dad's Army*.

That same game was prefaced with another funny incident, again remembered by Dick Longstaff:

> We had been trained to the minute by Bob. He was a hard taskmaster and wanted us to be as good as he was—some hope!—and had impressed on us the need to control the ball, look up and then deliver the telling pass. 'Ball to feet'—that was his mantra. He went to great lengths to get us to accept that, with controlled football, composure and ball skills would follow as easily as night follows day. It was, therefore, with some confidence of showing off our capabilities, that we arrived at the Page Bank pitch. We stood there looking at it as Bob took a couple of footballs and rolled them on the grass—or at least, tried to. The grass was about six inches high and the balls only rolled less than two feet. Bob turned round to us and said, 'Aw, just kick the fucking thing.'

In 1960, Bob ended his cricketing days with Bishop Auckland Cricket Club. He had been a member with them for the past twenty years or so and was finding it increasingly difficult to devote the time to attend practice sessions, and wished to make way for younger blood. Naturally, he and Betty would continue to attend matches on sunny Saturday afternoons with young Robert and recent addition 'Beth, now coming up to twelve months old. Nothing could be more natural than a happy family watching leather meet willow, amongst friends and pleasant surroundings.

Bob had proven himself a useful right-hand batsman and could bowl a devious leg-break. He had helped the club win the prestigious Kerridge Cup in consecutive seasons 1953 and 1954. His combined statistics for his cricketing days with BACC were:

Total runs scored	1051
Highest batting score	62
Total wickets taken	9
Best bowling performance	4 wickets for 21 runs
Total catches	27

If giving up his summer sport was intended as an indication that he would be spending more Saturdays and Sundays at home, then that proved not to be the case, as a few months later, Bishop Auckland Football Club asked him to become their Manager, not just coach/trainer. Once again, Bob was honoured, and the newspapers heralded the appointment, some of them proclaiming that this would result in the club recapturing their lost glory—the 'Bishops' had failed to show any significant form in the Amateur Cup competition since the Wycombe Final, their best achievement being two years earlier when they were defeated 3–2 at Barnet in the Fourth Round. Last season they had been knocked out 3–1 in Round Two away to unfancied Loughborough Colleges.

Success, of a kind, came in the Amateur Cup, during Bob's managerial term at the club.

Drawn at home against Whitby in Round One, Wright and evergreen Seamus O'Connell had scored the goals to record a 2–0 victory. Another home tie for Round Two resulted in a comfortable 5–0 win over Lydbrook Athletic which was followed by yet another home draw, which saw the 'Two Blues' pitched against their previous season's conquerors, Loughborough Colleges. Revenge was sweet as the students lost 2–0, thanks to goals from Bob Thursby and Seamus O'Connell.

It was an indication of the wane in interest in the club's football team that the combined attendance for these three home ties amounted to only 7,980 paying spectators. Nearly half of this total had come along for the Loughborough match. The other two ties had clearly failed to capture the public's imagination. Circumstances may have been different if clubs like Walthamstow Avenue, Wycombe Wanderers or Hendon had been the visitors but it certainly appeared that the 'Glory Days' were over as far as the 'Bishops' were concerned. Just six miles up the road, Crook Town were the club in the ascendancy.

Leytonstone were Bishop's opponents for Round Four and it was in the minds of many supporters that under Bob Hardisty's coaching and guidance, perhaps those twin towers of Wembley could be just over the horizon. Bell and O'Connell—inevitably—scored the goals in a fine 2–1 win that put the 'Bishops' into the semi-finals for the first time in five years, where they would face Hounslow.

It has already been recorded within these pages that controversy—no matter how slight—and Bishop Auckland Football Club go hand in hand. Once again, there was to be disagreement before an important football match, and Bob was to come out the loser.

The immovable, unshiftable policy of making the team selection for Saturday's game on a Monday evening, continued within the club. Some flexibility had been introduced where changes could be made 'if deemed necessary for the good of the team/club' but basically the situation was the same. The Committee had not yet delegated sole selection of the team to its Manager, although as holder of that position, Bob sat on the selection committee and made comments, suggestions and proposals as to who should be in the side. It may seem ludicrous today that such a state existed, where a Manager does not have complete autonomy regarding team selections but the Bishop Committee thought differently.

That evening, they listened to what Bob had to say about his players, as he went through them one after the other. When it came to Seamus O'Connell, Bob told the gathered members that the inside-forward was carrying an injury and that he was of the sound opinion that, reluctantly, Seamus should not be selected; Bob was convinced that Seamus could not play flat out for the full ninety minutes.

The committee members listened intently until finally debating the constitution of Saturday's team, deciding that they should accept their Manager's assessment of the O'Connell situation. The Chairman thanked Bob for his candid assessment of each of the players, at which point Bob got up and left the Committee to discuss other matters of business.

His degree of fury can only be guessed at when he learned that the Committee had reneged on his agreed proposal, and that Seamus would be in the team after all. The outcome was that Bob was left to sit and suffer on the touch-line in the Manager's hot seat at Brentford's Griffin Park, watching the semi-final. It was not a good match for the 'Two Blues' and Hounslow won 2–1, thanks partly due to a very questionable refereeing decision which resulted in Hounslow being awarded a penalty—the man in black being sixty yards away from the incident, when he deemed that a foul had taken place within the Bishop Auckland penalty area.

Although Seamus O'Connell scored Bishop's goal, he finished the game hobbling for the last twenty minutes and was no more than a passenger. Bob Hardisty had been proved correct in his assessment and was always of the opinion that, had his team played with eleven fit men for the full ninety minutes, it would have been Bishop Auckland that would have strode out once more on to Wembley's famous turf to meet Crook Town in the Final. It can only be speculated what such a Final that would have thrown up between these two magnificent clubs.

As a result of what Bob saw as the Committee's betrayal, he believed that he had no other option than to resign the post of Manager. His resignation was reluctantly accepted.

Betty had returned to teaching and was working at Woodhouse Lane School, Robert and 'Beth being helped by a family friend who acted as childminder but it had now become obvious that she and Bob could no longer live together, and they decided upon a separation. Disillusionment? Distrust? Betrayal? Arguments? Bickering? Unfaithfulness?—is there ever any one thing that leads to a marriage breaking down? Betty and the children would remain at 'The Laurels' and Bob would move back in with his father, who was now living in a large semi-detached house on Watling Road, on the outskirts of the town. Jack Hardisty had been living on his own in this large 1920s semi-detached house since 1951, following the early death of his wife due to heart failure.

It was a sad and difficult time for all, especially Betty, who had a far more fragile nature than that of her husband. It was she who had the responsibility of looking after the children and trying to make sure that they did not suffer due to their father's absence. She took the separation quite badly at first and, in an attempt to clear her mind, she took herself and the children away from Bishop Auckland to stay with relatives in Cheshire. Those four months did her good, and she returned to 'The Laurels' a brighter and much happier person although, naturally, the emotional scars would remain.

Not that Bob had completely deserted the family home. He occasionally went back to 'The Laurels', although his meetings with Betty did not always run as smoothly as perhaps either of them intended and quite often they were fraught affairs. They still had deep feelings for each other and probably still loved each other but circumstances had reached a point now that it was impossible for them to live together and reconciliation was out of the question. They were like Elizabeth Taylor and Richard Burton, whose sometimes turbulent romance became front page news in the 1960s, with their public quarrels, and just as public, love for each other.

'Beth Hardisty recalls an incident when Bob called on Betty and the children:

> I was in the kitchen cooking, of all things, lobster thermidor. The lobster had been a gift from Ray Oliver. It was my sixteenth birthday and Dad had come around—I only ever saw him once a year. He did not call that often. I came out of the kitchen and could not believe what I saw—Dad was sat on an armchair with mother sat at his feet in total bliss. You would not have thought that this was a couple living apart. Absolutely unreal.

Bob and Betty's marriage came to an official end in October 1972, when the *Decree Absolute* was issued by the courts. Betty continued to live at 'The Laurels' but it became too expensive for her to manage and by 1982 she had moved into a smaller property in Lindsey Street, within the town. The pressure of bringing up two children and separation, followed by divorce from her husband—a husband who was still a local hero in the town's eyes—was probably a major cause for Betty turning to the artificial comfort of the 'gin bottle', during this period of her life. Her excessive drinking was claimed to be a major cause of her early retirement from teaching, a point acknowledged by daughter, 'Beth.

In the other camp, Bob had settled back in with his father, for the time being, and at least had the opportunity of getting out and about by virtue of his employment, and was able to continue with his duties as Area Physical Training Officer for the County Educational Offices. There was no let up with his sports activities either and he did not let the separation from Betty and the children affect his coaching and training schedules at the football club. In fact, one cannot help but feel that Bob accepted the absence from his children with a degree of ambivalence; he was quite happy to see his children just once a year, and usually it was they who made the first call. Son, Robert, and daughter, 'Beth, both confirm that this arrangement seemed to suit their father. In the meantime, Bob continued to receive requests for his attendance at meetings and prize-givings and was regularly asked to play in testimonial football and cricket matches.

In 1966, Newcastle United Football Club held a testimonial evening in honour of their ex-centre-forward, Jackie Milburn, an old acquaintance of Bob, who knew all of the Newcastle players on a personal level. Much to his delight and surprise, Bob received an invitation to play for an Ex-International XI against Jackie Milburn's XI, alongside such players as George Hardwick, Len Shackleton, Stan Mortenson and Tom Finney, in the first game of the evening. A second game would take place between an Ex-Newcastle United XI against an International XI, featuring such players as Nobby Stiles, Paddy Crerand and the Charlton brothers, Bobby and Jack. In addition to playing in the opening game, Bob was also requested to lead a gymnastic display during the interval between the two games. It says a lot for his fitness that, at the age of forty-five, he was able to complete the game of football and the gymnastic display without any undue effects.

During this period of his life, Bob gave up his post as Area Physical Training Officer and took up an appointment at Middleton St George Teacher Training College, a position that carried the benefit of a self-contained apartment on the premises. He was pleased to move out of 'The Garth' and leave his father to get on with his own life but, in 1973, Jack Hardisty died of cancer. Not wishing to keep the large house, Bob sold it and immediately bought a small terraced property in Coundon, a village just outside Bishop Auckland. Bob used this property mainly for storage and after a few months gave it up to move to a similar house in South Church, which he imaginatively named 'Harcrenim', after the Bishop Auckland half-back line of Hardisty, Cresswell and Nimmins.

The Queen was celebrating her Silver Jubilee Year in 1977 and a variety of events and functions were taking place all over the country. When the invitation arrived for Bob Hardisty to attend a Gala Evening on the royal yacht, he could not believe it. He may have been out of the limelight for almost twenty years now but here he was receiving an invitation from the Queen.

'Beth Hardisty tells an amusing anecdote about that event:

> I was nanny to a family in London who were quite well off and obviously thought themselves a bit superior to others. It was the time of the Jubilee Celebrations, in that hot summer of 1977. The lady of the house was issuing me instructions concerning the children, when she proudly boasted that she and her husband would be going aboard the royal yacht the following evening. She was most put

out when she was informed that her 'help's' father would also be in Her Majesty's attendance—and probably sitting on a higher table!

He enjoyed his few years teaching the students but in 1980 he had a serious setback when he suffered a stroke that affected his left side and following this he was made redundant, an experience that left Bob devastated. To add further to his problems, it was during this period that Bob was diagnosed as being diabetic.

It was bad enough that his stroke had resulted in him being forced to give up playing golf, snooker and tennis because of his lack of co-ordination, but what hit home most was the realization that no-one wanted to employ him anymore. He applied for positions all over the country, from Scotland to London but without success. This was, without doubt, the worst time of his life. He did have his loyal circle of friends, however, and it was they who played a major part in keeping his spirits up; Betty was a regular visitor, as was Robert, now married and living in Driffield, but it was probably his ex-team mates—Bob Thursby, Dave Marshall, Ray Oliver and Ken Chisholm in particular—that he looked forward to seeing most, every Wednesday, as they would, more often than not, take Bob to the cricket club where he had played for so many years.

Another close friend was George Romaine. George was a regular figure on Tyne Tees Television in the 1960s and 1970s and probably played a part in getting Bob a television slot as a sports reporter at the company. He had been born George Romaines but, before he became well known in the entertainment industry, had been persuaded to drop the 's' from his surname, his agent believing that it would present a better image, and thereby give him a greater chance of getting on. George agreed and from then on George Romaines became George Romaine.

George recounts one evening that illustrates Bob Hardisty's generosity:

Bob was living at 'The Garth' at the time. One night, we had returned from the television studios in Newcastle, and were having a drink together in Bob's front room when a knock was heard at the door. Bob asked me to answer it and see who it was and when I did, a young boy was standing there, clenching an autograph book. He saw me and timidly asked: 'Are you Mr Hardisty, sir?'

I smiled and informed the youth that I was not Bob Hardisty but that I would take him through to meet him. Upon entering the room, the youth repeated his question and when Bob answered in the affirmative, politely asked for his autograph. Bob immediately signed his name in the treasured book, asking to whom he should dedicate the signature. When he had finished, the lad thanked Bob and gazed admiringly at the signed page. Bob chatted with him for a bit and the lad told us that he was a Bishop supporter, just like his dad. The lad was about to leave, when Bob asked him to wait whilst he went and found something. Bob was gone a few minutes and I heard some drawers and cupboard doors opening and closing in another room as he searched for whatever it was that he was looking for. A few minutes later, Bob came in to the room and handed the lad a small paper bag, saying, 'Give this to your dad'—it was one of his England caps!

Bob did his best to keep the effects of his stroke to a minimum, especially when a trip to the races was concerned. His love of the horses has been alluded to earlier and if watching cricket was now his first love, then a day on the race-course was a close second. He would drive to the local courses, such as Newcastle, Hexham, Sedgefield or Catterick, usually accompanied by a couple of friends but he was never what could be called a successful gambler. However, one of his most financially productive days racing was not at any of the aforementioned courses—not even in this country—but at Longchamp, Paris, in October 1982, when he went with a small party from the cricket club. Bob had been making the annual trip to Longchamp for almost twenty years and nothing would prevent his attending the Prix de L'Arc de Triomphe.

Dave Snowdon, no relation to ex-Willington goalkeeper, Jackie Snowdon, was a member of that coach party and fondly remembers that Parisian Sunday:

I was a regular at the Cricket Club. I didn't play but they had a good social club with a great atmosphere. They would organize trips to all over the place and early in the '80s someone thought that it would be a good idea to arrange a trip to that year's Arc de Triomphe meeting at Longchamp. Bob was one of the party and he was great fun—I think he went every year; he certainly knew his way about. Everybody knew of his ability to pick losers—he was hopeless at backing winners. If Bob fancied a horse, then we knew that it had no chance. Anyway, in spite of the odds being against us, we came away from Paris well in front, thanks to the English raiders.

Bob had told us on the way over how he liked to follow the northern trainer, Steve Norton and his jockey, John Lowe. That jockey/trainer combination had a runner in the first race, the Prix Marcel Boussac, a race for two-year-old fillies. There wasn't much else in the race that we knew about and as we had set off to have a good time and bet on every race, we decided to have a bet on Steve Norton's runner, Goodbye Shelley. It had raced five times already but had only won once, a small event over seven furlongs at Beverley—this one was over a furlong further, a mile.

We tried to pick out the good points about our selection—this is after we had put our money on it, mind—and found that Goodbye Shelley should be suited by the soft going and the extra distance. Convinced that she needed a test of stamina, we were rather hopeful of the outcome on Longchamp's demanding track, even though she was one of the outsiders in a field of eleven runners.

We couldn't believe it when John Lowe had her in the first three early on then took over the lead a long way from home. Bob was shouting with the rest of us like I'd never heard him and all these French men and women were looking round at us. Remarkably, Goodbye Shelley hung on to win by a short-head. There was a Stewards' Enquiry but, thankfully, the result stood, apparently the enquiry had concerned the second and third placed horses. The official odds as given out by the English bookmakers were something like 33/1.

We couldn't have had any more winners as that is all that I remember about the races. It was interesting though, as word went through the crowd, that this bunch of Englishmen, championed by Bob Hardisty, had just won hundreds of pounds. In no time the hundreds became thousands and when we got back to Bishop, everybody thought that we had become overnight millionaires. In fact we had missed out. We had placed our bets on the pari-mutuel and that had only paid odds of about 10/1. Nevertheless, it's pleasing to know that I was one of the party to have been associated with a Bob Hardisty winner—they were rarer than hen's teeth.

Chapter Thirteen
ALLEGORY

The end of the year drew nearer.

The dull, dark days of December seldom bring joy to the hearts, other than those of children, waiting those long anxious hours for Christmas Day, and the religious leaders, also waiting for that day but for more pious reasons.

It was a suchlike dull and dark December day when Bob Hardisty awoke from his morphine injected stupor. The doctors had treated him for the major operation that he had been forced to undergo and he lay in his hospital bed, drowsily trying to make his senses return to reality. His head was still fuzzy and his mouth was as dry as sand. He tried to awaken but immediately slumber took over. On and off for what seemed ages he went in and out of sleep, until eventually his awakening succeeded in the battle.

He tried to put his thoughts in to some kind of perspective order. He could remember what he had come in to Bishop Auckland General Hospital for. Of course, it had been because of his stroke and that confounded diabetes. He had feared the worst ever since it had been discovered that he was diabetic. He had understood the warnings and the magnitude of problems that diabetes and all that was associated with the problem could bring. Now, he remembered, those fears had come to fruition. The doctors had warned him, before putting him under anaesthetic, that he would probably have to attend trauma counselling once the operation was over, even though they had been surprised at their patient's matter of fact attitude towards what was to happen and his considerable good humour, forever laughing and joking.

His eyes scanned the hospital room and he tried to wiggle his toes. So far so good. Now the other foot. Well, no change there, either.

A senior doctor came in to the room, accompanied by two assistants. The doctor in charge explained to Bob that the operation had gone well and that the surgery was perfect in every way. There had been no complications and there was no reason to be pessimistic about the future. He talked Bob through the operation, and looking straight at him, asked Bob if he had any questions.

'Just the one, Doc,' replied Bob. 'It's my right leg. If you've taken it off, how the bloody hell can I still feel it?'

The diabetes and circulatory problems that Bob had endured had resulted in the amputation of his right leg just below the knee. It was a cruel twist that once again the Winds of Fate had thrown at him. The leg that had created passes that penetrated the most stubborn of defences, the leg that had sent thundering shots into opponents nets as if Exocets, the leg that had scored God knows how many goals, the leg that had caressed a football as tenderly as one's first love, lay cremated in a hospital incinerator. O cruel fate.

Bob was not short of well-wishers and visitors; as well as family members, including Betty, he received visits from his work colleagues and, naturally, his old footballing team mates and anyone else that seemed to be 'just passing by'.

Letters arrived from long forgotten quarters when news leaked out about Bob's operation. There were hundreds of cards from ordinary people he had never met, wanting him to know that they wished him well and that they cared. Among the first to write was Walter Winterbottom and another letter was from Alan Wade, chief of the Football Association of Ireland. Others included Bob Paisley, reminding Bob of his time with the club in the 1930s, Lawrie McMenemy, who had managed Bishop Auckland in the mid-1960s before taking up a career as manager in the Football League and who was currently in charge of Southampton, Sir Stanley Rous, now retired from his administrative duties leading the Football Association, the area's Member of Parliament, Ernest Armstrong and of course, Manchester United Football Club.

He was regularly visited by his old football colleagues, almost on a daily basis. Ken Chisholm, Bob Thursby, Ray Oliver and Dave Marshall especially took time to call upon their stricken comrade. Not that the sad circumstances of the situation were allowed to dictate conversation. Dark humour is always bubbling under the surface in the sporting world and footballers in particular show their own brand at the most unlikeliest of times.

One such occasion presented itself when Ken, Bob, Dave and Ray came to see Bob for the first time after his amputation. Gathered around Bob's bedside, inevitably talk began with the operation and how it had gone but quickly turned to football. They had discussed events of the current season and how Sunderland, Newcastle and Middlesbrough were getting on. During a short pause in conversation, Ken said that he had recently been to a European match earlier that season.

'How did it go?' enquired Bob.

'Oh, it was all right but it was a bit like you, Bob.'

'What do you mean, Ken?'

'Well, they lost the first leg,' informed Ken, with a big grin on his face.

'Daft bugger,' retorted Bob, laughing as loud as the others.

These 'four musketeers' continued to call on Bob when he came out of hospital and would take it in turns to wheel him down to the cricket club, where they would spend the afternoon or evening together. Bob tried not to let his disability interfere with his love for life and he would be seen around the town whenever the weather was kind. He had no desire to become a recluse and continued to accept offers to attend fitness groups and clubs, where he would talk about his amputation and reminisce about his football career—there were always ears that wanted to listen and minds to learn, even though he was now spending most of his time in a wheelchair.

He had now moved out of 'Harcrenim' and was living in a Sheltered Housing Scheme at Eden Court, in Bishop Auckland, but for all that the premises offered everything that he could wish for—especially with a new found friend and carer in Ray Humble, who sadly died not long ago—the loneliness and boredom started to take their toll, and Bob started drinking more heavily than he had done previously.

Unfortunately, the illness never totally went away and in October 1986, less than two years after his initial amputation, Bob Hardisty had to lose his left leg. One can only try to imagine what a sickening blow this must have been to Bob, his family and friends.

Just three days after experiencing the ignominy of a second amputation, Bob Hardisty lost his battle with this world. Diabetes, pneumonia, blood circulatory problems all accumulated to attack his weakened body and on October 31st 1986 the end came, with family members gathered around his bedside.

Regrettably, one member of that family was missing. Daughter, 'Beth, states:

> I was working in London at the time and was out of the loop of contact from the hospital ... you know what it was like in those days, with only the family member who was the official next-of-kin being the one to receive information about the patient. There were no such things as mobile phones and it was left to me, mainly, to find out myself what was going on. The seriousness of the situation only became apparent when I was in contact with the hospital and it was obvious that I had to get on the next train to Darlington. The family had tried to protect me from how serious Dad's situation had become, thinking that, because I was pregnant with Gabriel, there may be complications as a result of the stress. Anyway, I was on that train but arrived at the hospital to be told that my father had just died, minutes earlier.

The greatest amateur footballer in the history of the game was no more. His passing was in every national newspaper and tributes poured in from all over the world. But it was in Bishop Auckland, inevitably, where his loss was felt greatest. A pall hung over the town as the name of Bob Hardisty was on everyone's lips. Dads explained to football daft sons just what this man had achieved for the town whilst news desks searched through their archives for footage of those magnificent games, in the 1950s, when Bishop Auckland Football Club and their bald headed talisman almost seemed to be living at a place down south, called Wembley.

St Andrew's Church, where Bob and Betty had been married thirty-eight years earlier, was the scene of John Roderick Elliott Hardisty's funeral. There was not a seat to spare and many of the townsfolk of Bishop Auckland, tearfully listened outside to Reverend John Marshall's words of condolence that ended with: 'Bob was the greatest amateur footballer of our century. Today, we cannot help remembering those old days. It is the kind of material that folk lore is made out of.'

Football stars and personalities of past and present filed out of the church, including Lawrie McMenemy, ex-referee Pat Partridge, Stan Seymour (Chairman of Newcastle United), ex-Middlesbrough stalwart George

Hardwick, Bishop Auckland club doctor Donald Prescott and, of course, all of the squad that remained from those glorious days when Wembley was a second home to the 'Bishops'. To the strains of 'Abide with Me' the coffin was carried from the church by the 'Four Musketeers'—Bob Thursby, Dave Marshall, Ken Chisholm and Ray Oliver—and then onwards to the crematorium, just outside Durham city.

Tributes had poured in following Bob's death, from the famous and the not-so-famous. Stan Blakeburn had played against Bob in the late 1940s for Evenwood Town and West Auckland:

> Bob Hardisty was the best amateur player ever to put on a pair of football boots. Bishop Auckland were the Manchester United of the amateur football world and wherever they went, the opposition always seemed to have a plan to bring about their downfall. West Auckland were no different and one year we were told that Bob Hardisty always tackled with his right foot, never with his left. I was told to attack down our left but instead of going for the bye-line, I was to cut inside and go towards my right, Bob's left, forcing Bob into the tackle. I think the plan must have worked as we only lost fowr nowt. I was so depressed when word reached me of his death.

Sir Bobby Robson had this to say: 'Bob Hardisty helped bring recognition of the north-east to the rest of the world. He was a brilliant footballer and, but for the war, could have been a professional. The likes of him come round once in a blue moon.'

Lawrie McMenemy, who had been recognized as Bishop Auckland's first official Manager—he was allowed to carry sole responsibility for team selection—remembers Bob with affection:

> Bob Hardisty was a brilliant footballer. He had silky smooth skills and had that personal air of authority that all good players possess. It is hard for people these days to understand the level of ability that such amateur players had in them days and Bob in particular. Let's not forget, Bob and the other lads who went to help out Manchester United had to raise their game to a much higher level, and it speaks volumes that they had the ability to do it—especially so for Bob as he was coming out of retirement and must have been about thirty-seven years old at that time.
>
> When I took over as Manager of Bishop Auckland he was one of the first to telephone me and congratulate me on my appointment and gave me his best wishes.
>
> I seem to remember that after the funeral service, the coffin, pallbearers and close family members went to Durham Crematorium for the cremation. The rest

of the congregation went along to the cricket club rooms where the wake was to take place. After about an hour, the pallbearers—Thursby, Chisholm, Marshall and Oliver—arrived back with the Hardisty relatives. I was standing at the back and, being quite tall, was easily spotted by Ken Chisholm. He called across the room to me—'Guess what, Lawrie—ever the old pro, I got to carry the side of the coffin with his leg missing!'

The sobriety of the occasion was lifted with this bit of black humour and a less inhibited atmosphere pervaded after that. No-one took offence at Ken's comical remark and I bet Bob would have laughed at it, too.

'Beth Hardisty scattered her father's ashes over the family grave, where her grandparents, Jack and Mary Hardisty lay buried in Bishop Auckland cemetery, just up from Kingsway. Three years later, a casket, containing the ashes of Betty Hardisty, was placed within the same spot. How allegorical—Bob, scattered around, free to blow in the breeze, whereas Betty remained encompassed in a casket. As in life, so in death.

'Remember me, but ah! Forget my fate'
Dido and Aeneas (Nahum Tate)

Chapter Fourteen
REQUIEM

Bob Hardisty left an estate estimated at between £25,000 and £40,000, and in his will he bequeathed the sum of £500 to Bishop Auckland Football Club, for whom he had served so proudly in the past and there was also at least one pleasantly surprised beneficiary named in that will.

Ray Oliver received a cheque for £200 when details of the will became public—no reason was given for the gift and at first Ray wondered why he should have been left such a sum by his old friend. After some thought, he came to the conclusion that it was all to do with 1956, when Ray had refused, on principle, to play for Bishop Auckland. That had opened the door for Bob Hardisty to make a return to the team and go on to play in that year's Amateur Cup Final. Ray saw Bob's benevolence of the £200 gift as a 'Thank you'—and who would argue?

Many fine words were spoken on Bob Hardisty's departure but all carried the same message—he was the best. There really was no-one better. Corinthians' supporters may talk of the days of C B Fry or G O Smith but that was in the 1880s, a different era, when football had very little competitiveness and trophies could be won by winning just one game—the Cup Final winners were granted free passage to the following year's Final in the early days of the Cup competition. Perhaps the footballer who comes closest to challenging Bob to the title of best—or greatest—amateur footballer would be Edgar Kail, who spent fourteen years with Dulwich Hamlet and played three times for the *full* England team between the wars, scoring twice on his international debut against France. He helped Dulwich win two Amateur Cups in 1919–20 and again in 1931–32 but when one analyses for comparison his career with that of Bob Hardisty, surely it is the latter whose achievements are of greater merit, especially if one accepts that the game had improved and become more skilful since Kail's period.

It is not this author's intention to denigrate, in any way, the achievements of such a fine player as Kail but his Amateur Cup Final appearances were ten years apart and show little consistency in the way of continual dominance when compared with that of Bob's career when he was never far away from winning a major trophy for his team. The awarding of England caps is an irrelevance as England selectors always favoured southern club players and there was a dearth of truly quality footballers with the aftermath of the First World War, that made—in this author's view—international caps, relatively easier to come by.

We shall not see the like of Bob Hardisty ever again. The game has changed and, indeed, is still changing—as these words are being written. Football is a different game now than it was when John Roderick Elliott Hardisty kicked his first football.

Never again will we see amateurs compete in the way that they did for the Amateur Cup, the most prestigious trophy open to all amateur clubs, no matter how great or small they may be. Nor will crowds that flocked to Wembley's giant Empire Stadium to watch those Amateur Cup Finals in the 1950s, gather in such multitudes. The Football Association saw to that when they decided to discontinue the competition, making 1974 the last year for the trophy to be won, when only 30,000 paying spectators bothered to turn up to watch Bishop's Stortford beat Ilford 4–1. The magic had gone, in no small way due to 'shamateurism', for which, sadly, Bishop Auckland were as responsible as any other football club. The payment of 'expenses' had become out of control as far as the Football Association was concerned and they could see no future in continuing with the Amateur Cup competition. Mind, it is worth repeating the words of Gordon Nicholson, member of the Northern League and its Secretary who is quoted in an earlier section as saying: 'What the northern clubs paid in pennies, the southern clubs paid in pounds.'

Bob Hardisty played his football with a ball made of leather and it had a lace in it. The first official laceless football to be used in an Amateur Cup tie is believed to have been the one used in the Bishop Auckland–Willington Final of 1950. Bob played with laceless footballs after that, of course, but even those used in the latter days of his career would seem like a cannon-ball when compared to those used in today's matches. Look at footage of old newsreels and notice the distance—or lack of distance—that goalkeepers achieved when clearing the ball way back then. It was considered a long kick if they could reach the half-way line with a goal kick but now, the balls used are so light that kicks into the opposing half of the playing area are commonplace. In addition, balls swerve in mid-flight and bamboozle goalkeepers so much that often they are made to look stupid. Changes to the spherical properties of the football have been made so that now, footballs have a plastic coating, making it far easier, and safer, to head a ball, again with good distance. The ball has changed so much that it is easier for a player to 'bend' a shot at goal than it is to deliver a straight one. A recent advertisement on television shows an international coach describing the modern day football as being 'rounder'.

Leather boots are now plastic slippers. Just what Bob Hardisty would have made of them is anybody's guess. Certainly, there would be no need for Jimmy Nimmins to spend precious hours in a cold bath wearing them so as to fit his feet comfortably!

The laws of the game have been amended over the past twenty or so years, some for the better, perhaps. 'Thou shalt not put the goalkeeper under pressure under any circumstances', is one that comes instantly to mind. Ray Oliver would be sent off in the first five minutes under today's interpretations as would Bob, who enjoyed the embroilment of battle and took every opportunity to pressurise opposing goalkeepers—within the laws of the game. Such changes were not only frowned upon by outside players—Harry Sharratt was one who voiced his opinion that goalkeepers should not be protected from the shoulder charge but, of course, such calls fell on deaf ears.

Substitutes are taken for granted nowadays; the wonder is that they were never introduced earlier than they were to Football League and FA Cup games. Bob had seen substitutes allowed as far back as the Festival of Britain internationals in 1951, and, of course, they were allowed as routine on the Continent but Bob never played a competitive Northern League or Amateur Cup game where they were allowed. If they had been, perhaps the outcome of the 1954 Final against Crook would have been different, although Crook supporters themselves would justifiably claim that two of their players were injured that day.

Replays have become a thing of the past. Those extra two thrilling games that Crook and Bishop put their fans and the whole country through would not take place today; the penalty shoot out has taken over.

Current recommendations are that two additional assistant referees be employed to monitor 'goal line incidents' in order to ascertain if the football has actually crossed the goal line into the net. The debate rages whether or not this argument could be resolved with the introduction of technological equipment that already exists but FIFA are totally against this, for reasons only known to themselves. Opponents to the use of technology argue that 'something would be lost' if mechanical means were used to decide whether a goal had been scored or not and other opponents point to American Football where delays of up to three minutes or more are quite common, until a decision is reached. But the reference to American Football is a red-herring. That game is played to a programme—moves and counter moves are played as if like a game of chess. The example of Rugby League is a far more appropriate one for football to follow. Anyone who has attended such a match knows that contentious decisions are resolved within a minute and that there are no real delays at all. What is more, the correct decision is—usually—reached.

The Northern League has undergone so many changes that one is left wondering just how many more teams will be admitted to its two divisions. The likes of Ferryhill Athletic, Evenwood Town and Stanley United no longer have football teams, their places having been taken by such names as Jarrow Roofing, Gillford Park and Darlington Railway Athletic. Such past giants as Willington and Crook Town are facing an uphill struggle to survive and it is not conclusive that they will succeed.

Kingsway itself is no more. The scene of so many triumphs—and one or two disasters—has seen its stands and terracing demolished to make way for housing developments and road widening schemes, thereby leaving the ground for the sole use of Bishop Auckland Cricket Club, where Bob continued to spend many pleasant hours, not only in the summer months but the winter ones as well, frequenting the social club there.

Bob himself witnessed the result of some of these changes, and, no doubt, had his own views as to which ones were good and which were bad for the game—he had scathing views about the introduction of coloured cards towards players constantly infringing the rules, an introduction that had him wondering just how far football would go in the number of colours that the game would end up with. It is of little consequence now.

As I pen these words, news reaches me of a proposal that a statue of Bob

Hardisty be commissioned and placed outside the new ground of Bishop Auckland at Tindale Crescent, about two miles from the town centre. Whilst I am all for the erection of such a statue I cannot see why it should be sited at the proposed new ground. Bob Hardisty had no specific connection with Tindale Crescent to my knowledge. I accept that that is where the football club will be playing its football from 2010 (hopefully) but I consider a more appropriate site would be in Bishop Auckland market square. His accomplishments were with the football club but his link is also with the town of Bishop Auckland. At his funeral, Reverend John Marshall had said as much when he told the congregation that: 'People like Bob Hardisty have helped unify the town and brought pride and dignity to the north-east.' Mention Bishop Auckland to anyone in conversation and you will get an instant associated reply of 'Oh yes, Bob Hardisty.' The two go hand in glove. Also, let us not forget that the market square was the scene of such ecstatically wild celebrations when Bob and the rest of the team were applauded long and loud when on the Town Hall balcony, overlooking the market square on those heady April evenings in the 1950s.

Bob Hardisty came into this world to play football and to enjoy himself. He did both of these things but what is more he brought pleasure to thousands of people all over the world and for that we must be grateful. His like will never again grace a football field. Never again.

I met a traveller from an antique land
Who said: Two vast and trunkless legs of stone
Stand in the desert. Near them on the sand,
Half sunk, a shatter'd visage lies, whose frown
And wrinkled lip, and sneer of cold command,
Tell that its sculptor well those passions read
Which yet survive, stamp'd on these lifeless things,
The hand that mock'd them and the heart that fed;
And on the pedestal these words appear:
'My name is Ozymandias, king of kings:
Look on my works, ye Mighty, and despair!'
Nothing beside remains. Round the decay
Of that colossal wreck, boundless and bare,
The lone and level sands stretch far away.

Ozymandias (Percy Bysshe Shelley)

APPENDIX

PERSONAE

John Barnwell: Went on to play for Arsenal and England. After retiring from football, managed a number of clubs including Wolverhampton Wanderers. Was the League Managers Association head man and spokesman for a number of years until giving up the position in 2007. Lives near Retford, Nottinghamshire.

Stan Blakeburn: Lives at Oldham.

Warren Bradley: Signed for Manchester United in 1958. The only player ever to win an Amateur International and Full International cap in the same season. A school teacher and, later, schools inspector. Died 2007.

Corbett Cresswell: Turned professional after win over Wycombe Wanderers in 1957 and transferred to Horden Colliery Welfare. Lives outside Gateshead with wife, Angela.

Bobby Davison: Moved to Alfreton, Derbyshire. Died 2007.

Les Dixon: Played for Stockton after Bishop Auckland. Keen golfer. Lives in Stokesley with wife, Helen.

Benny Edwards: Went to play for Horden Colliery Welfare, then Stockton. Keen golfer. Died 2001 aged 76.

Tommy Farrer: Lives in Maidstone with his wife, Gladys.

Ron Fryer: Lives with wife, Pat, at Birtley, just outside Chester-le-Street.

Betty Hardisty: Died 1989.

'Beth Hardisty: Lives in Leyton, London with Richard. Has a wonderful son, Gabriel.

Bob Hardisty: Died 1986 aged 65.

Jack Hardisty: Died 1973.

Mary Elizabeth Hardisty: Died 1951.

Robert Hardisty: Lives in Cambridge with wife, Jean.

Bill Holmes: Physical training expert. Runs keep-fit classes. Lives in Nottingham.

Derek Lewin: Played on for a few seasons but then concentrated on the family bacon import business. Became a member of the FA Council. Lives in Chorley with wife, Sheila.

Jacky Major: Transferred to Hull City in 1956. Died on his local golf course.

Dave Marshall: Ended his career playing for Bishop Auckland and continued teaching until his retirement. Lives at Low Fell with wife, Jane, close to 'The Angel of the North'.

Jimmy Nimmins: Elected to Bishop Auckland FC Board upon retiring from football but found travelling too much from Consett. Continued at Consett steelworks until closure. Lived with wife, Lillian. Died 1995 aged 74.

Harry McIlvenny: Retired to carry on family woollen business and became a member of Yorkshire County Cricket Club. Lived just outside Ilkley, Yorkshire. Died, July 2009.

Lawrie McMenemy: Had a successful managerial career in professional football including taking Second Division Southampton United to an unexpected FA Cup Final victory over Manchester United. Lives with his wife, Ann, at Braishfield, Hampshire.

Bob Middlewood: Died 1985.

Seamus O'Connell: Signed for Crook Town and won an Amateur Cup winners' medal with them. Returned to play for Bishop Auckland for the 1961–62 season, helping them reach the semi-final stage. Went to live in Spain where he still resides.

Ray Oliver: Continued on the lifeboats and lives at Cullercoats.

Lez Rawe: Lives with wife, Betty, in Bishop Auckland.

George Romaine: Retired from television. Lives at Shildon.

Billy Russell: Signed for Sheffield United after the 1957 Amateur Cup Final, thus only played the one Amateur Cup game for the 'Bishops'.

Harry Sharratt: Continued with Bishop Auckland until 1964. Lived with wife, Diana, at Kirby Lonsdale. Died 2002.

Jackie Snowdon: Kept possession of the ball that was used for the 1950 Amateur Cup Final between Bishop Auckland and Willington. Lives with his wife, Dorothy, at Willington.

Tommy Stewart: Retired from football in 1957. Employment took him to live in Switzerland.

Carl Straughan: Died 1986 (buried same day as Bob Hardisty's funeral).

Bob Thursby: Won 20 England caps. Ran a dental practice with branches throughout County Durham. Lives with wife, Heather. Spends most of his time on Chester-le-Street golf course.

Ken Twigg: Lived near Stockton-on-Tees. Died 2009.

Jack Washington: Died 2002.

Bobby Watson: Lives at Heworth, Gateshead with wife, Heather.

Bill White: Died 2002.

Harry Young: Died 2005.

BOB HARDISTY
ENGLAND INTERNATIONAL CAPS

Date	Opponents	Score	Goals Scored	Venue
24/01/1948	Wales	7–2	0	Bangor
07/02/1948	Ireland	5–0	1	Belfast
06/03/1948	Wales	3–4	0	Shrewsbury
05/04/1948	France	0–2	0	Ilford
1948*	Olympic Games Tournament			
22/01/1949	Wales	4–1	0	Swindon
05/02/1949	Ireland	0–1	0	Norwich
16/04/1949	Scotland	2–3	0	Glasgow
22/05/1949	France	2–1	0	Grenoble
07/04/1951	Scotland	3–2	0	Glasgow
10/05/1951**	Finland	3–2	0	Swindon
15/05/1951**	Norway	2–1	0	Middlesbrough
08/05/1955	France	1–1	0	Brest
17/09/1955	Ireland	4–1	0	Cliftonville
12/11/1955	Germany	2–3	0	Tottenham

* Cap awarded in recognition of Olympic Games Tournament
** Festival of Britain Tournament
(The above information confirmed by David Barber of The Football Association)

GREAT BRITAIN
OLYMPIC FOOTBALL SQUADS

The following list gives the names of squad members, the football club to which they were affiliated and the games in which each competed.

1948 (LONDON)

Player	Club	Country	Netherlands	France	Yugoslavia	Denmark
Manager: Matt Busby						
Goalkeepers: Kevin McAlinden Ronnie Simpson	 Belfast Celtic Queen's Park	 Ireland Scotland	 ✓	 ✓	 ✓	 ✓
Backs: Angus Carmichael Gwyn Manning Jim McColl Jack Neale	 Queen's Park Troedyrhiw Queen's Park Walton and Hersham	 Scotland Wales Scotland England	 ✓ ✓	 ✓ ✓	 ✓ ✓	 ✓
Half-Backs: Eric Fright Bob Hardisty Eric Lee Davie Letham Dougie McBain Julian Smith	 Bromley Bishop Auckland Chester City Queen's Park Queen's Park Barry Town	 England England England Scotland Scotland Wales	 ✓ ✓ ✓ ✓	 ✓ ✓ ✓ ✓	 ✓ ✓ ✓ ✓	 ✓ ✓ ✓

Player	Club	Country	Netherlands	France	Yugoslavia	Denmark
Forwards:						
Andy Aitken	Queen's Park	Scotland				✓
Bill Amor	Reading	England				✓
J A Boyd	Queen's Park	Scotland				✓
Frank Donovan	Pembroke Borough	Wales		✓	✓	
Tommy Hopper	Bromley	England	✓			
Denis Kelleher	Barnet	England	✓	✓	✓	
Peter Kippax	Burnley	England	✓	✓	✓	
Harry McIlvenny	Bradford Park Avenue	England	✓	✓	✓	✓
Ron Phipps	Barnet	England				
Jack Rawlings	Enfield	England				✓

Results

Date	Round	Opponents	Result	Score	Venue
31/07/1948	Round 1	Netherlands	Won	4–3 (aet)	Highbury
05/08/1948	Round 2	France	Won	1–0	Craven Cottage
11/08/1948	Qtr Final	Yugoslavia	Lost	1–3	Wembley
13/08/1948	Bronze Medal	Denmark	Lost	3–5	Wembley

1952 (HELSINKI)

Player	Club	Country	Luxembourg
Manager:			
Walter Winterbottom			
Assistant Manager:			
Bob Hardisty			
Goalkeepers:			
Ted Bennett	Southall	England	✓
Ben Brown	Pegasus	England	
Backs:			
Bombardier Stan Charlton	Bromley	England	
Tommy Stewart	Queen's Park	Scotland	✓
Laurie Stratton	Walthamstow Avenue	England	✓
Ken Yenson	Leyton	England	

Player	Club	Country	Luxembourg
Half-Backs:			
Charlie Fuller	Bromley	England	✓
Bill Hastie	Queen's Park	Scotland	
Idwal Robling	Lovell's Athletic	Wales	
Derek Saunders	Walthamstow Avenue	England	✓
Laurie Topp	Hendon	England	✓
Forwards:			
Derek Grierson	Queen's Park	Scotland	
Bob Hardisty	Bishop Auckland	England	✓
Bill Holmes	Blackburn Rovers	England	
Jim Lewis	Walthamstow Avenue	England	✓
Kevin McGarry	Cliftonville	Ireland	
Alf Noble	Leytonstone	England	✓
Tony Pawson	Pegasus	England	
George Robb	Finchley	England	✓
Bill Slater	Brentford	England	✓

Results

Date	Round	Opponents	Result	Score	Venue
16/07/1952	Preliminary	Luxembourg	Lost	3–5 (aet)	Lahti

1956 (MELBOURNE)

Player	Club	Country	Thailand	Bulgaria
Manager:				
Norman Creek				
Goalkeepers:				
Mike Pinner	Pegasus	England		
Harry Sharratt	Bishop Auckland	England	✓	✓
Backs:				
Dexter Adams	Hendon	England		
Tommy Farrer	Walthamstow Avenue	England	✓	✓
Terry Robinson	Brentford	England		
Half-Backs:				
Henry Dodkins	Ilford	England	✓	✓
Stan Prince	Walthamstow Avenue	England	✓	✓
Don Stoker	Sutton United	England	✓	✓
Laurie Topp	Hendon	England	✓	✓

Player	Club	Country	Thailand	Bulgaria
Forwards:				
George Bromilow	Southport	England	✓	✓
Petty Officer Jimmy Coates	Royal Navy and Kingstonian	England		
Bob Hardisty	Bishop Auckland	England	✓	S
Jack Laybourne	Corinthian Casuals	England	✓	✓
Derek Lewin	Bishop Auckland	England	S	✓
Jim Lewis	Chelsea	England	✓	✓
Charlie Twissell	Plymouth Argyle	England	✓	✓

S = substitute

Results

Date	Round	Opponents	Result	Score	Venue
26/11/1956	Round 1	Thailand	Won	9–0	Melbourne
30/11/1956	Round 2	Bulgaria	Lost	1–6	Melbourne

FOOTBALL LEAGUE AND SCOTTISH LEAGUE APPEARANCES

Bob Hardisty is reputed to have played for a number of Football League and Scottish League Clubs during the war but only the clubs detailed within the following pages have been able to provide documentary evidence that he did in fact turn out for them. During the research for this work I came across many newspaper and football magazines which stated that he played for such clubs as Aberdeen, Rangers, Queen's Park Rangers, Heart of Midlothian and Wolverhampton Wanderers but none of these clubs can provide any evidence to substantiate the claim. Queen's Park Rangers go so far as to state quite categorically that he definitely did not play for them. It is possible that Queen's Park and Rangers somehow became conjoined, thereby giving rise to the error—Bob did in fact play for Queen's Park, the details of which are included within the following pages.

Bob Hardisty's full Football League and Scottish League record is as follows:

Note: In the Opponents column Home games are shown in **bold** type.

Goals column shows the goals that Bob Hardisty scored.

DARLINGTON FOOTBALL CLUB

1946/47: Football League Division Three (North)

Date	Opponents	Result	Score	Position	Goals	Attendance
26/12/1946	**Crewe Alexandra**	Won	4–0	Inside-right	0	–
01/02/1947	Tranmere Rovers	Lost	0–2	Inside-right	0	–
15/02/1947	**Hull City**	Lost	0–2	Inside-right	0	–
13/09/1947	**Mansfield Town**	Lost	1–2	Left-half	0	–
27/09/1947	**Oldham Athletic**	Lost	0–6	Inside-right	0	–
04/09/1948	**New Brighton**	Lost	0–2	Inside-right	0	–

HIBERNIAN FOOTBALL CLUB

No details of individual games are available, however, Bob Hardisty did play at left-half in the team that beat Rangers 8–1, a record defeat for the famous Scottish club.

1941–42: Made 15 Scottish League appearances and 2 Scottish Southern League Cup appearances. He failed to score in any of these games.

1942–43: Made 1 appearance in the Scottish League and failed to score.

MIDDLESBROUGH FOOTBALL CLUB

1940–41: Football League North

Date	Opponents	Result	Score	Position	Goals	Attendance
09/11/1940	Leeds United	Lost	1–2	Right-half	0	1,500
16/11/1940	**York City**	Won	6–4	Right-half	0	1,700
23/11/1940	Bradford City	Lost	2–3	Right-half	0	1,468
07/12/1940	**Doncaster Rovers**	Drew	2–2	Right-half	0	1,000
14/12/1940	**Grimsby Town**	Won	2–1	Right-half	0	700
25/12/1940	Newcastle United	Won	3–1	Right-half	0	4,000
28/12/1940	Doncaster Rovers	Lost	0–5	Right-half	0	3,313
01/02/1941	Newcastle United	Lost	2–6	Right-half	0	4,000
08/02/1940	**Newcastle United**	Won	4–3	Right-half	0	2,000
05/04/1940	Hull City	Won	8–0	Right-half	0	2,000

War Cup

Date	Opponents	Result	Score	Position	Goals	Attendance
01/03/1941	**Huddersfield Town**	Won	4–2	Right-half	0	5,221
08/03/1941	**Leeds United**	Won	2–0	Right-half	0	5,800
22/03/1941	**Newcastle United**	Lost	0–1	Right-half	0	12,799

West Riding Cup

Date	Opponents	Result	Score	Position	Goals	Attendance
11/01/1941	**Bradford City**	Won	8–2	Right-half	0	1,000
18/01/1941	**Bradford Park Avenue**	Won	2–0	Right-half	1	–
17/03/1941	**Leeds United**	Won	3–2	Right-half	0	3,400

1941–42: Football League North (First Championship)

Date	Opponents	Result	Score	Position	Goals	Attendance
25/10/1941	**Bradford Park Avenue**	Lost	0–2	Left-half	0	4,000

League North (Second Championship)

Date	Opponents	Result	Score	Position	Goals	Attendance
18/04/1942	Newcastle United	Lost	1–3	Right-half	0	4,500

1942–43: Football League North (First Championship)

Date	Opponents	Result	Score	Position	Goals	Attendance
29/08/1942	Leeds United	Won	1–0	Right-half	0	3,500
05/09/1942	**Leeds United**	Won	2–0	Right-half	0	3,500
19/09/1942	**Bradford Park Avenue**	Drew	2–2	Right-half	0	4,000
26/09/1942	York City	Drew	2–2	Right-half	0	3,448
03/10/1942	**York City**	Lost	2–3	Right-half	0	3,500
10/10/1942	Bradford City	Lost	2–3	Right-half	0	3,000
07/11/1942	Sunderland	Lost	1–4	Right-half	0	8,500
14/11/1942	**Sunderland**	Lost	3–4	Right-half	0	5,500
21/11/1942	Newcastle United	Lost	0–3	Right-half	0	7,000
28/11/1942	**Newcastle United**	Lost	1–6	Right-half	1	3,500
05/12/1942	Gateshead	Lost	0–5	Left-half	0	2,000
12/12/1942	**Gateshead**	Lost	2–3	Right-half	0	–

1943–44: Football League North (First Championship)

Date	Opponents	Result	Score	Position	Goals	Attendance
25/12/1943	**Sunderland**	Won	4–0	Inside-right	1	9,000

Football League Cup (Qualifying Competition)

Date	Opponents	Result	Score	Position	Goals	Attendance
27/12/1943	**Hartlepool United**	Drew	1–1	Inside-right	0	8,500

Football League North (Second Championship)

Date	Opponents	Result	Score	Position	Goals	Attendance
11/03/1944	**Sunderland**	Lost	2–3	Inside-left	0	3,000

1944–45: Football League North (First Championship)

Date	Opponents	Result	Score	Position	Goals	Attendance
23/12/1944	Darlington	Lost	2–5	Right-half	0	8,097

Football League Cup (Qualifying Competition)

Date	Opponents	Result	Score	Position	Goals	Attendance
30/12/1944	Hartlepool United	Lost	2–5	Inside-right	0	8,097

QUEEN'S PARK FOOTBALL CLUB

1943–44: Scottish Southern League

Date	Opponents	Result	Score	Position	Goals	Attendance
11/09/1943	Third Lanark	Drew	3–3	Right-half	0	—
18/09/1943	Motherwell	Lost	0–6	Right-half	0	—
25/09/1943	**Partick Thistle**	Won	3–1	Right-half	0	—
02/10/1943	Falkirk	Won	3–2	Right-half	0	—
16/10/1943	**Morton**	Won	4–1	Right-half	0	—
30/10/1943	**Albion Rovers**	Won	3–1	Right-half	0	—
13/11/1943	**Rangers**	Lost	1–4	Right-half	0	—

READING FOOTBALL CLUB

1943–44: Football League South

Date	Opponents	Result	Score	Position	Goals	Attendance
27/11/1943	**Brighton & Hove Albion**	Lost	2–3	Right-half	0	3,320
11/12/1943	**Millwall**	Won	3–0	Inside-right	0	3,911
18/12/1943	**Luton Town**	Won	7–2	Inside-right	1	3,020
15/01/1944	Charlton Athletic	A27*	0–2	Inside-right	0	2,300
22/01/1944	Queen's Park Rangers	Lost	0–2	Inside-right	0	7,300
29/01/1944	**Portsmouth**	Lost	1–4	Inside-right	0	4,603
05/02/1944	Tottenham Hotspur	Drew	2–2	Inside-right	0	14,937
12/02/1944	**West Ham United**	Won	3–2	Inside-right	0	5,574
15/04/1944	Brentford	Lost	0–1	Inside-right	0	6,040
22/04/1944	Luton Town	Won	4–2	Inside-right	1	3,299
29/04/1944	**Chelsea****	Lost	1–3	Inside-right	0	3,701
06/05/1944	**Brentford**	Lost	0–3	Inside-right	0	2,424

* Game abandoned after 27 minutes when score was 0–2
** Was an away fixture but game played at Reading

Football League Cup South

Date	Opponents	Result	Score	Position	Goals	Attendance
19/02/1944	**Fulham**	Won	3–0	Right-half	0	4,000
04/03/1944	Arsenal	Won	3–2	Inside-right	0	12,582

1944–45: Football League South

Date	Opponents	Result	Score	Position	Goals	Attendance
26/08/1944	Charlton Athletic	Won	8–2	Outside-left	0	3,781
02/09/1944	**Fulham**	Won	5–4	Inside-left	1	4,399
09/09/1944	**Tottenham Hotspur**	Drew	0–0	Inside-right	0	9,065
30/09/1944	**Queen's Park Rangers**	Drew	1–1	Right-half	0	6,510
21/10/1944	Brighton & Hove Albion	Won	9–3	Right-half	0	3,605
28/10/1944	**Southampton**	Lost	1–5	Inside-left	1	5,929
04/11/1944	**Arsenal**	Won	3–1	Right-half	0	11,959
09/12/1944	Fulham	Won	3–2	Inside-right	0	8,000
16/12/1944	**Tottenham Hotspur**	Lost	2–3	Inside-right	0	9,938
06/01/1945	**Clapton Orient**	Won	3–1	Inside-left	0	3,000
13/01/1945	Queen's Park Rangers	Lost	1–5	Right-half	0	6,272
20/01/1945	**Luton Town**	Lost	0–3	Left-half	0	3,088

MANCHESTER UNITED: MUNICH AIR DISASTER

February 6th 1958

FATALITIES

Players
Geoff Bent
Roger Byrne
Eddie Coleman
Duncan Edwards (died fifteen days after crash)
Mark Jones
David Pegg
Tommy Taylor
Liam 'Bill' Whelan

Manchester United Staff
Walter Crickmere: Secretary
Tom Curry: Trainer
Bert Whalley: Chief Coach

Crew
Captain Kenneth Rayment: Co-Pilot (died three weeks after crash)
Tom Cable: Cabin Steward

Journalists
Alf Clarke: *Manchester Evening Chronicle*
Donny Davies: *Manchester Guardian*
George Fellows: *Daily Herald*
Tom Jackson: *Manchester Evening News*
Archie Ledbrooke: *Daily Mirror*
Henry Rose: *Daily Express*
Frank Swift: *News of the World* (died on way to hospital)

Others
Bela Miklos: Travel Agent
Willie Satinoff: Supporter and friend of Matt Busby

SURVIVORS

Players
Johnny Berry (never played again—died 1994)
Jackie Blanchflower (never played again—died 1998)
Bobby Charlton
Bill Foulkes
Harry Gregg
Kenny Morgans
Albert Scanlon (died 2010)
Dennis Viollet (died 1999)
Ray Wood (died 2002)

Manchester United Staff
Matt Busby: Manager (died 1994)

Crew
Margaret Bellis: Stewardess (died 1998)
Rosemary Cheverton: Stewardess
Bill Rogers: Radio Officer (died 1997)
Captain James Thain: Pilot (died 1975)

Journalists and photographers
Ted Ellyard: *Daily Mail* (died 1964)
Peter Howard: *Daily Mail* (died 1996)
Frank Taylor: *News Chronicle* (died 2002)

Others
Vera Lukic and baby daughter Verona (Saved by Harry Gregg. At time of accident also
    pregnant with son Zola who also survived)
Mrs Eleanor Miklos (Wife of Bela Miklos)
Nebosja Bato Tomasevic (Yugoslavian Diplomat)

BIBLIOGRAPHY

The author acknowledges the following publications in the production of this work and recommends for further reading:

Association Football Volumes 1–4 by A H Fabian and Geoffrey Green
Corinthians and Cricketers by Edward Grayson
Football: The Amateur Game by W T D Reed
History of the FA Amateur Cup by Bob Barton
Hotbed of Soccer by Arthur Appleton
Kings Of Amateur Soccer by Chris Foote Wood
Non-League Football by Bob Barton
Northern Goalfields Revisited by Brian Hunt
Soccer At War 1939–45 by Jack Rollin
The Bishops by W T D Reed
The Far Corner by Harry Pearson

ACKNOWLEDGEMENTS

Dexter Adams (Ex-Hendon FC)
George and Margaret Adamthwaite
Barry and Eileen Adamthwaite
Richard Adamthwaite
Carl Ames (County Hall, Durham)
Mike Amos (*Northern Echo*)
John Atkinson (Ex-Bishop Auckland FC)
John Atkinson (Historian, Shildon FC)
Paul Bailey
J. Balmain (Queen's Park FC)
David Barber (Football Association)
John Barnwell (Ex-Bishop Auckland FC)
Keith Belton and Sheila Middleton (Durham Amateur Football Trust)
Bishop Auckland Football Club
Stan Blakeburn (Ex-Evenwood Town FC and West Auckland FC)
John Briggs
Marjorie Burton
Corbett Cresswell (Ex-Bishop Auckland FC)
Darlington Football Club
Catherine Dawson (Bishop Auckland Town Hall)
David Downs (Historian, Reading FC)
Durham Record Office
Tommy Farrer (Ex-Bishop Auckland FC)
Hugh Forrester (Curator, RUC Museum)
John French (Ex-Middleton St George College of Education)
Ron Fryer (Ex-Bishop Auckland FC)
Joe Gibson
Esme Golightly
Phil Graham
Eileen Hall (Bishop Auckland Town Hall)
'Beth Hardisty
Robert Hardisty
Gabriel Hardisty-Miller

John and Brenda Harper
Jenny Hayball
Hibernian Football Club
Anne Jackson (Durham Records Office)
Terry Jackson (Bishop Auckland FC)
Tony Kemp (Wigton Old Scholars Association)
Derek Lewin (Ex-Bishop Auckland FC)
Dick Longstaff (Ex-Bishop Auckland FC and Durham Amateur Football Trust)
Lawrie McMenemy
Dave and Jane Marshall (Ex-Bishop Auckland FC)
Steve Menary
Mel Metcalf (Bishop Auckland Golf Club)
Dr David Merriott
Middlesbrough Football Club
Gordon Nicholson (Ex-Northern League Secretary)
Ray Oliver (Ex-Bishop Auckland FC)
John and Margaret Peacock
Harry Pearson
John Phelan
Tom Purvis
Queen's Park Football Club
Lez Rawe (Ex-Evenwood Town, Willington and Bishop Auckland FC)
Reading Football Club
Richard Rudnicki
Ray Robertson (Ex-'Ranger', *Northern Echo*)
Sir Bobby Robson
Margaret Robson (Clayport Library, Durham)
Les Rollinson
George Romaine
Diana Sharratt
Malcolm Smith (Chester-le-Street Heritage Group)
Ray Snowball (Ex-Crook Town FC)
Dave Snowdon
Jackie Snowdon (Ex-Willington FC)
Jon Sutton (Manchester United FC)
Amanda Thompson and Chris Reed (BBR)
Bob and Heather Thursby (Ex-Bishop Auckland FC)
Frank Tweddle (Historian, Darlington FC)
Ken Twigg (Ex-Bishop Auckland FC)
Margaret Walker
Thelma Walton (Chester-le-Street Heritage Group)
Bobby Watson (Ex-Bishop Auckland FC)
Christine Watson (*Northern Echo* Archives)
Tom Wright (Historian, Hibernian Football Club)
Mark Wylie (Manchester United FC)
Harry Young (Ex-Bishop Auckland FC)